Performing Arts –
The Economic Dilemma

Performing Arts –
The Economic Dilemma

by WILLIAM J. BAUMOL

and WILLIAM G. BOWEN

A Study of Problems common to

Theater, Opera, Music and Dance

THE TWENTIETH CENTURY FUND

NEW YORK · 1966

FIRST PUBLISHED NOVEMBER 1966
REPRINTED JANUARY 1967
Copyright © 1966 by the Twentieth Century Fund, Inc.
Printed in the United States of America
By Connecticut Printers, Incorporated, Hartford, Connecticut
Library of Congress Catalog Card Number: 66–27618

TO *Lionel and Iris*

*from an old friend
and a new one*

FOREWORD

With more than usual satisfaction I write a brief word of introduction upon publication of one of the Twentieth Century Fund's studies.

The economic condition of the performing arts has been of concern to a growing number of people throughout the country and (if I may add a personal word) has been a preoccupation of mine since President Kennedy asked me to serve as his Special Consultant, to look with a fresh eye at the life of the arts in the United States. The Trustees of the Fund were enthusiastic about the prospect of a study in this field, falling as it did within the broad range of problems which present themselves to an advanced industrial society when the material needs of life seem in a fair way of being met and questions of values and goals begin to appear central.

The analysis which Professors Baumol and Bowen have now completed is somber in its implications. The live performing arts, they show, come within that sector of the economy where productivity cannot be increased at anything like the general rate. Costs, therefore, inevitably mount; revenues do not keep pace. Others have faced the fact that the live performing arts cannot expect to pay for themselves without subsidies, direct or indirect; it was one of the great merits of the Rockefeller Panel Report that it did not evade this issue — a fact the more striking since the panel was composed to so large an extent of businessmen who have traditionally shown little patience with enterprises that could not show a profit. But the present report goes beyond this recognition. Its originality — and its ultimate importance — lie in the way it demonstrates that the gap between income and costs is bound to grow over the years ahead. It is not only that the live performing arts do not pay for themselves, but that, within the developing economic system, they will show deficits of increasing size.

The conclusions, disconcerting as they may at first appear, should not discourage those who are responsible for the expanding cultural institutions of the country. The arts are not alone in being relatively incapable of keeping pace with the rising productivity which is in so many other areas the hallmark of an economic system like our own. One thinks immediately of education. Indeed, one of the authors of this report came to the work directly from a study of the economics of higher education. Though the differences between the two fields are significant, they are alike in being dependent upon toil which is necessarily and inevitably time-consuming. That "art is long" has been generally accepted as a fact of life; and education, in spite of the tendency to speed things up, still moves to the slow and often mysterious measure of the human mind.

A study of higher education twenty years ago would have shown something like the outline of crisis which now confronts the live performing arts. The educational crisis has now largely passed — less because the nature of higher learning has changed than because new resources have been mobilized and have been brought to bear in fresh ways upon a recognized need. Something of the same kind will, we hope, take place in the case of the arts. This study does not go into solutions, excepting insofar as it sketches broadly the alternatives before those responsible for the life of the arts. Yet a number of variables can be noted entering into the authors' rather startling predictions as to the size of the gap between income and revenues which will exist in the future. Any one of these variables may prove more favorable than is anticipated; and beyond such novel but now accepted sources of support as corporations, foundations and government, lies the possibility of elements or combinations not at present foreseen.

A result of this study, it may be hoped, will be a raising of men's sights all along the line. To know the dimensions of a problem is the first step in dealing with it; and one cannot but believe that the American people, with their vast resources and with their readiness to see the arts as crucial to a society worthy of their strength, will assure something more than the precarious and unexamined status that has heretofore been the lot of most artistic institutions. Without wanting to apportion the economic charge, I suggest that the analysis and the figures contained in this report point the way to a considerably larger contribution by government. The National Arts Endowment began with a $10 million annual appropriation. (The amount has subsequently been cut to $8.5 million.) But the experience of the Endowment has already shown that the needs are great, and can be met through a government program that neither limits the freedom of the arts nor diminishes their quality. The sum going to the National Endowment for the Arts seems disproportionately low; it is bound to seem quite hopelessly inadequate if it is not at least doubled within the next five years. To say this is not to belittle in any way the responsibility that falls to other agencies of the national life, both public and private.

It remains to add a word about the genesis of this study. It was conceived as an undertaking parallel to the inquiry of the Rockefeller Brothers panel, the one concentrating on policy recommendations, the other on the economic underpinning. Professors Baumol and Bowen served as consultants to the Rockefeller panel; I was a member of it. Throughout, the Twentieth Century Fund has been shown many courtesies and been given much help by the staff of the Special Studies Project of the Rockefeller Brothers Fund, and by Miss Nancy Hanks, its Executive Secretary, in particular. It is a pleasure to acknowledge this scholarly kinship, even though the work of the two Funds proceeded independently, and though the two studies have been issued with a year and a half between them.

To Professor Baumol and Professor Bowen I extend particular thanks. It was not easy to find economists who would give to the performing arts the prolonged and serious attention which is ordinarily given to more mundane concerns. We were fortunate in our choice of two men who combined high professional skill with a sensitivity to the arts. The following pages will be found, I think, to reveal both these desirable qualities.

AUGUST HECKSCHER, Director
The Twentieth Century Fund

41 East 70 Street, New York City
July 1966

ACKNOWLEDGEMENTS

THIS IS the section of the book in which it is customary for authors to display their clean linen in public. Our difficulty is that on this occasion the size of the wash is truly enormous. More than most economic research, this study, in a field where little statistical information had previously been publicly available, required the cooperation of a vast number of individuals and institutions. A complete list of those who supplied the necessary data and gave generously of their time would resemble a small-town telephone directory. The mountains of information necessary for a study of this kind could not have been accumulated without the patient help and interest of many persons involved in the administration of performing arts* organizations, both small and large. Our debt to them is only dimly reflected by the attributions scattered through this volume. We are indebted also to the team of research assistants who collected information for us throughout the country; the research staff in Princeton who coded the data, prepared punch cards and did a tremendous amount of calculating; the secretaries who typed and retyped, and showed a gratifying interest in the contents of the manuscript; and the several extremely knowledgeable persons who read and commented on our manuscript in moments stolen from their busy lives. We are deeply grateful for the help provided by all these people, and regret that we are precluded by their monumental number from listing them individually.

The study itself occupied a little more than two years. Most of the work was pleasant (though not as glamorous as might be supposed), some of it was very exacting, and all of it required a great deal of hard work. Our location in Princeton proved fortunate in several ways. First, the availability of local professional performing

---

* We want to register our protest against this barbaric expression at the very outset. The arts do *not* perform. Unhappily, usage has left us no serviceable alternative.

organizations enabled us to try out our ideas and techniques among friends, who would overlook the mistakes of novices in their field of activity. Second, we were able to employ a number of intelligent and energetic students, who, because of their natural propensity to remigrate homeward several times a year, were able to administer audience surveys and collect statistics in widely separated geographic areas. We were extremely fortunate also to have available in the community a considerable number of unusually able women who were happy to undertake part-time work for us. And MATHEMATICA, the consulting firm through whose facilities the study was conducted, released us from mundane administrative duties while unsparingly placing its technical resources at our disposal.

Above all, however, we must express our gratitude to the Twentieth Century Fund, not only for having conceived and financed the investigation, but for providing a perfect climate for our research. The Fund's willingness to extend help whenever help was needed, the air of trust that characterized our relationship and its scrupulous avoidance of interference in the details of our investigation made the Fund a model sponsor. We have deeply appreciated the personal interest and encouragement of August Heckscher, Director of the Twentieth Century Fund, Elizabeth Blackert, John E. Booth, Barbara Donald and Ben T. Moore. Working with them has been a great pleasure.

We must point out too the enormous amount of help we received from the Rockefeller Brothers Fund, whose staff gave us their full and unstinting cooperation from the inception of that organization's own study of the performing arts. The availability of working papers prepared for the panel and the ideas gleaned from meetings of the panel were among the many contributions of the Rockefeller Brothers Fund to our study.

Even though we provide no extensive listing of the names of those who helped us, there are a few others whose contribution was such that they simply cannot be omitted: the directors of our English study, Professor Claus Moser and Muriel Nissel; Virginia Gebhardt, who was our chief research associate throughout the investigation; Linda Almgren, Roberta Morse and Taylor Reveley, who saw us through the critical final months, and who, in the process, regularly gave up nights and week ends; Dorothy Fabian, who conducted the cultural center analysis; Professor Stephen Goldfeld, who helped with various statistical problems; Professor Charles Westoff, who served as chief consultant on the development of our audience questionnaire; Robert Bushnell, who more than met our many exacting requirements in the computer programs he designed for us; and Mrs. Katharine A. Beyer, our tactful and resourceful editor, who, together with Mrs. Blackert, battled our pedantic propensities. No brief acknowledgement can capture the perspicacity, care, and good sense which raised Mrs. Blackert's contribution well beyond that of any editor with whom either of us has ever been associated in the past.

We must mention how very important were the contributions of the persons, knowledgeable in the practices and institutions of the performing arts, who so generously gave time to a reading of all or part of an earlier (and less readable) version of this report. They saved us from committing a number of errors of fact or interpretation. We are, therefore, highly indebted for their invaluable comments to F. Emerson Andrews (Foundation Library Center), Isadora Bennett, Ralph Burgard (Arts Councils of America), Irving W. Cheskin (League of New York Theatres), Angus Duncan (Actors' Equity), Lloyd H. Haldeman (Cincinnati Symphony Orchestra), C. Harry Kahn (Rutgers), Herman E. Krawitz (Metropolitan Opera), W. McNeil Lowry (Ford Foundation), Judith Marechal, Thomas G. Moore (Michigan State University), Carlos Moseley (New York Philharmonic), Helen M. Thompson (American Symphony Orchestra League), Albert Webster (New York Philharmonic) and John F. Wharton.

Even more we must thank our wives. Besides displaying incredible patience, such as they have contributed on many similar occasions in the past, both played direct and crucial roles in this project, one as coordinator of the audience data and the other as executive secretary of the entire study.

Two writings which were especially helpful to us deserve more than the usual footnote acknowledgements — an illuminating study of the theater by Thomas G. Moore and an unusually penetrating history of the theater by Emil J. Poggi. Unfortunately, neither of these studies has as yet been published.

Nothing could be more natural than the dedication of this book to Lord and Lady Robbins, whose important role in the arts in Great Britain is well known. Lord Robbins made many important contributions to this volume, both direct and indirect: by discussing with the authors the fundamentals of their approach, by preparing the way for their English study, by having supervised the post-graduate training of one of the authors (and hence having taught the other at second remove). But it is primarily in gratitude for friendship and inspiration that we dedicate this book to them.

Authors traditionally conclude prefaces by accepting full responsibility for whatever errors remain in the book, and we see no alternative but to acquiesce in this tradition, however much we might like to shift whatever onus must be borne. Joint authors sometimes append statements identifying the separate contributions (and therefore responsibilities) of each. This we cannot do, for ours has been a truly common effort and an equal partnership from the beginning, as the alphabetical listing of our names is meant to indicate. Other persons contemplating joint ventures may be encouraged to learn that two good friends, neither of whom is naturally subservient or even reticent, were able to carry out an at times frustrating project of unanticipated scope and complexity, and still speak to each other quite civilly at the end. If anything, the friendship has been strengthened by the bond formed in a shared experience — something like going over Niagara Falls in a barrel together.

W.J.B. and W.G.B.

Princeton, New Jersey
June 1966

CONTENTS

xvi　*Contents*

Performing Arts –
The Economic Dilemma

CHAPTER I

Introduction

In the performing arts, crisis is apparently a way of life. One reads constantly of disappointing seasons, of disastrous rises in cost, of emergency fund drives and desperate pleas to foundations for assistance. While some performing organizations have improved their financial position, there always seem to be others in difficulties. The off-Broadway theater, hailed one year as the repository of vitality for the American stage, is mourned for dead before the next season is half over, and even the venerable Metropolitan Opera has several times threatened to suspend a season. In spite of its artistic success, the Phoenix Theater, one of New York's leading off-Broadway theaters, for a while seemed unable to obtain funds sufficient to prevent a hiatus of at least one year (1965–66) in its operations. Doubtless, some alleged crises represent a tactical stance — cries of woe intended to help in raising funds or in negotiating with unions. But many of the problems are real, as we shall see.

Nor is economic emergency in the performing arts a phenomenon peculiar to the United States. In Great Britain, for example, one finds reports of orchestras in danger, of provincial theaters in difficulty, of staggering rises in costs of operation that severely circumscribe the activities of some of the most firmly established performing organizations.[1] True, in Great Britain as in most of Europe, the arts are supported in part by public funds, which help to cushion such shocks. But even these funds have not sufficed to eliminate the chronic financial problems of the arts. Indeed, the authori-

[1] Arts Council of Great Britain, *Reports.* See, for example, 1952–53, pp. 14, 20; 1956–57, p. 12; 1957–58, p. 5; 1962–63, p. 5.

3

ties who distribute the governmental funds are themselves under recurrent economic pressure. A parliamentary grant which one year seems generous is suddenly rendered inadequate by an unanticipated rise in costs. The Annual Reports of the Arts Council of Great Britain, the administrative arm through which public funds are allocated to all arts organizations, tell of one emergency after another and offer no ground for believing that an end is anywhere in sight. Even in many countries on the European continent, where government assistance to the arts has had a longer tradition and funds have been provided on a far larger scale than in Great Britain, the performing arts sometimes find themselves in financial difficulties.

The central purpose of this study is to explain the financial problems of the performing groups and to explore the implications of these problems for the future of the arts in the United States. It should be pointed out that the authors of this volume are economists who, despite their personal interest in the arts, felt strongly that such an investigation should be conducted as dispassionately as possible, and that it should be carried out much as one would study any industry beset by monetary problems. We did not undertake to discover a panacea which would promise to cure the arts of their financial ills. Rather, we hoped to be able to specify objectively the alternatives facing the arts and to describe their costs and the burdens they require society to shoulder.

Finally, we provide no inspirational message proclaiming the virtues of the live performing arts and their crucial role in the enrichment of human existence. The reader who is not already convinced would surely not be swayed by any report whose focus is the economics of performance.

In order to get at the problem, we naturally undertook, after formulating our basic hypotheses, to assemble the pertinent facts. This turned out to be a task of enormous proportions. Seldom were the pertinent data readily available, and investigation showed that such figures as did exist were often unreliable.[2] We had no choice,

[2] Lest this be considered an exaggeration we offer a not atypical illustration: the often quoted statistics alleging that classical record sales have been growing much faster than sales of popular records. It was found on investi-

therefore, but to seek many of the requisite materials from primary sources wherever these could be found. There ensued months of searching through dusty files in cramped backstage offices, hundreds of hours spent collecting questionnaires from audiences in every part of the country and every type of performance, many interviews with producers, managers and choreographers, and a massive correspondence.

Our data encompass a variety of sub-topics. The main focus of our research was the cost and revenue structure of the performing groups; thus the bulk of our effort was devoted to the accumulation of records of costs, ticket sales, revenues and contributions from other sources. A close second in importance was the information we gathered in trying to determine who constitutes the audience, in terms of education, economic characteristics, geographic distribution, ticket purchasing habits and so on. From these two major efforts we went on to a series of sub-studies: among them studies of performer incomes, of the history and anatomy of cultural centers, of grants and contributions, of the state of the arts in Great Britain (because we expected to find some revealing contrasts there), of particular organizations — case studies conducted in considerable depth.

Our subject matter was defined to include only live professional performance. This territory is at once frighteningly broad and infelicitously narrow. It is, in a sense, too broad because of the vast variety of organizations encompassed, some of which were done an injustice by the inevitable superficiality with which they were studied. One can hardly hope to examine in detail the state of orchestral music, chamber music, opera, ballet, modern dance and the theater, not only the commercial theater on Broadway but regional and off-Broadway theater as well. Yet we have gathered information on each of these and hope we have provided some insights into their problems.

But from another point of view our area is defined far too nar-

gation that the data are in fact unavailable; whatever figures the individual record companies may have on their own sales are a closely guarded secret. Nor is it even clear how one would define the borderline between "popular" and "classical" records. At least some of the published figures had apparently been obtained by lumping all long-playing records in the classical category so that all Beatle albums were presumably grouped along with Buxtehude!

rowly in that it excludes the mass media whose consequences for the state of the living arts have been so profound. One can hardly ignore radio, television and the film in a volume such as this, but these media will not be treated as a matter of independent interest. They will be brought into the discussion only where necessary to help explain the financial state of live performance. Even so, the two forms of performance are in many respects inseparable and, as a result, the mass media will reappear constantly in our discussion.

Another category of artistic activity that was largely excluded from our investigation is amateur performance, which has apparently increased substantially in recent years. It must be admitted that it was not always easy to draw an unambiguous line between professional and amateur activity. In some writings the term "professional" is used to connote high standards of competence; in others it indicates that performers are paid. By and large our emphasis on professional activity meant that we dealt primarily with the major organizations in each field of performance, those which lead the field either in excellence of reputation or financial remuneration and in which the members of the company usually obtain a substantial proportion of their livelihood from performance.

Some of the preceding discussion may appear to suggest that no significant work had been done in this area before the present study. This is, of course, not so. The economic problems of the performing arts have been discussed in a number of recent studies, and we have taken full advantage of the materials they provided. These works, which are listed in our bibliography, are one manifestation of the lively and growing interest in the subject.

Legislators have provided even more dramatic evidence of the growing concern for the financial problems of the arts and have produced a series of bills ranging widely in their provisions. The establishment of arts councils at all levels of government has become extremely fashionable. In a few states they have been given considerable amounts of money and responsibility and charged with a well-specified set of functions. In others, councils seem to have been created as a gesture in support of good works and have been assigned no clearly defined operational purpose. Hearings and legislation have centered on the regulation and the morality of ticket selling practices. Several states and municipalities have undertaken to provide direct or indirect subsidies to the arts, characteristically on a very modest scale, and in 1965 the federal government, through the agency of a national foundation, provided funds to the arts and the humanities, not in order to give work to the unemployed or to exhibit American culture abroad, but, for the first time, simply to help the arts.

Our study would, therefore, appear to be timely. We hope that this book will be of interest to several types of reader. While we expect that our fellow economists will find portions of this study of interest, we have written primarily for the general reader and for those directly concerned with arts organizations.

The sheer mass of our data and the heterogeneity of the audience we would like to reach have dictated the general form of this volume. It would have been all too easy to inundate the reader with statistical detail, but this would almost certainly have obscured the main threads of our argument. Yet it would have been most unfortunate had we suppressed entirely those potentially valuable materials which specialists would want to see. We have, therefore, compromised by keeping the text as straightforward and unencumbered as possible and relegating our more technical materials to footnotes and appendices.

There are three parts to this book. The first is largely descriptive, indicating in some detail the current economic state of the performing arts in the United States. After a brief chapter describing the organizations with which we shall be dealing, the substantive portion of Part I begins with a re-examination of the much-publicized "cultural boom." The discussion then turns to the characteristics of audiences and the financial circumstances of performers, and culminates in an examination of the economic state of the performing organizations.

The second part of the book is more analytic. It discusses the technology of the performing arts and its implications for their financial future. Separate chapters are devoted to trends in total costs, in major cost components, in box office receipts and in other earned income. Special attention is given to ticket pricing policies. The last chapter of this section undertakes to bring these elements together and to depict trends in the over-all financial gap between expenditures and earned income experienced by representative arts organizations.

Part III examines the sources of funds used to cover these deficits: contributions by individuals, firms, foundations and governments. Finally, we discuss the implications of our findings for the future of the arts and for public policy. It should be re-emphasized that in our discussion of policy there will be no attempt to provide detailed proposals or to recommend concrete courses of action. Rather, we shall undertake to examine critically the grounds that have been proposed for public support and to suggest the magnitude of the financial commitment that is involved.

Only three of our conclusions will be indicated at this point, but they will suffice to suggest the general direction of this study.

First, it will be shown that while the phenomenon that has been described as the "cultural boom" is indeed a reality, its scope and magnitude have been exaggerated in many reports on the subject, and its character and significance misunderstood.

Second, despite the allegations of increasing grass roots interest in the arts and the optimistic view that audiences include a wide range of social groups, it will be shown that the typical audience at professional performances is drawn from an extremely narrow segment of the population — a group characterized by unusually high levels of education and income.

Third, we will offer evidence that the economic pressures that beset the performing arts have been growing, and that this is no historical accident, but a consequence of what might be considered the technology of their operations, so that the need of the performing groups for contributed funds is likely to continue to grow ever larger.

Before considering the import of this last conclusion it may be useful to review briefly some of the more direct and simple explanations others have offered for the financial difficulties of live performance and to suggest why they simply will not do.

Perhaps the cause most frequently cited is inflation — the general rise in prices which, as far as we can tell, has affected western society since before the Renaissance. But inflation is not a problem peculiar to the performing arts. Steel price rises and wage increases affect automobile production as well as the theater. Yet the one industry has, by and large, continued to prosper, while the other has been beset by growing deficits. Moreover, as our data will show, costs of performance have risen at a rate significantly faster than that of the general price level. Thus, though since 1957 the over-all rate of price increase in the United States has been negligible, many arts groups have continued to encounter economic troubles. Clearly, inflation is not the basic problem.

Union demands in general and featherbedding in particular have sometimes been nominated as the culprits. Concern with the subject is certainly not unfounded, as is illustrated by the following testimony of a backer of plays:

> A play called "Mr. Roberts," which you have heard mentioned before, the play happened to run in a theater which we were controlling. We were upset to discover we had to have four musicians for the continuance of that season. We thought it would not amount to too much. However, because it was considered a continuing run, for all three or four years that the play ran in the Alvin Theater, four musicians were employed to sit in the cellar and play pinochle. Eventually we had to ask them to play at home, because they were using the services of the ushers to go out and get them cigarettes and beer. It was unfortunate that we did not object to paying $320.00 a week for their not playing, but it was more objectionable to pay them double time for not playing on holidays.[3]

But while other such examples can easily be mustered it does not follow that featherbedding is the heart of the problem.[4] The fact is that in the drama such practices are unimportant except in the commercial theater, and have been of far less significance in musical performance than in the theater. Since it is not Broad-

---

[3] Lefkowitz Hearings, Vol. II, pp. 46–47, from testimony of Mrs. Margaret Cullman.

[4] One reader pointed out that the example cited is somewhat unfair to the musicians' union. Under current arrangements with the union, each theater owner has the right to choose freely whether his theater will be a "contract" house or a "non-contract" house. In the former, musicians are guaranteed employment, but they perform at a lower wage rate than in the latter. Evidently the theater which was chosen for "Mr. Roberts" had elected to be a contract house, a fact which the producer must have known when occupancy was arranged.

way alone that has suffered growing financial pressures, we must look further for our explanations.

Much has been made of dishonest practices in the commercial theater. The Lefkowitz Hearings on the New York theater which were conducted in 1963 brought to light some flagrant cases — members of theater staffs who regularly received bribes in return for the good seats they channeled into the black market, producers who purchased goods and services at inflated prices from companies in which they surreptitiously held an interest, producers who made free use of investors' funds for their private purposes and expended monies before limited partnership arrangements had gone into effect, thereby exposing investors to unlimited liability without their knowledge.[5] But these sensational exposés have little bearing on the basic problem. Every industry doubtless has its share of dishonest individuals. In any event, since lack of integrity of this variety seems to be rather rare among the non-profit organizations that supply the bulk of the nation's live performances, it cannot be regarded as a basic cause of the economic pressures that beset these groups.

One can also produce examples of waste and mismanagement which have clearly aggravated the financial problems of the arts, but they too are not the main culprits — there are too many well-managed organizations that incur substantial deficits for us to credit incompetence as the central cause of the economic problems of the arts.

We believe we shall be able to demonstrate that the basic difficulty arises, not from any of these sources, but from the economic structure of live performance. This conclusion has implications that are rather sobering. It suggests that the economic pressures which beset the arts are not temporary — they are chronic. It suggests that if things are left to themselves deficits are likely to grow. Above all, this view implies that any group which undertakes to support the arts can expect no respite. The demands upon its resources will increase, now and for the foreseeable future. Happily, however, we shall see that contributions have also been growing and that there is some reason to hope that the sources of

[5] Lefkowitz Hearings, Vol. I, pp. 21–35; Vol. II, pp. 41–52.

philanthropy will be able to meet much of the expanding need for funds. Some classes of performing organization — especially the established groups and those with well-organized fund raising machinery — may, therefore, find survival in the future no more difficult than it is today. But for the smaller, more experimental and less well-organized groups, and the organizations which are not operated on a non-profit basis and so do not live by philanthropy, a state of financial crisis may not just be perennial — it may well grow progressively more serious.

PART I

THE CURRENT
STATE OF AFFAIRS

CHAPTER **II**

The Organizations

B EFORE becoming enmeshed in heavily statistical descriptions of the performing arts in America — the size and composition of audiences, levels of expenditures, deficits, salaries of performers and so on — we thought it would be helpful to supply a relatively brief description of the organizations with which we will be concerned and a few comments on their history. It will be seen that the performing arts constitute no homogeneous body about whose components one can always speak simultaneously. They range widely in size of enterprise, artistic and financial objectives, longevity of organization and complexity of managerial structure. The nature and development of the performing organizations could itself contribute the substance of a fascinating study. However, here we wish to provide only the necessary background for the reader unfamiliar with the organization of the arts — to offer him some feeling for the rich and variegated personalities of the groups that have made it possible for the living arts to survive.

The Orchestras

It is not accidental that the orchestras constitute the core of our statistical analysis. They are by far the nation's longest-lived performing organizations, and many of them have kept excellent records.

After a spotty early history of concert life in this country going back at least to 1731, the oldest of the nation's orchestras, the

New York Philharmonic, was founded in 1842.[1] Its origins were rather informal, and for many years (until the regime of Gustav Mahler in 1907) it consisted of a self-governing body of musicians whose democratically elected conductor possessed little more than the power that he could derive by persuasion. For some time New York City had two orchestral groups, the original New York Philharmonic and the New York Symphony. Only under the more autocratic regime of Arturo Toscanini, which began in 1927, and with the final amalgamation of the two groups in 1928, did the Philharmonic attain the form which, in substance, it has today. There are several other venerable orchestras. The Boston and St. Louis Symphonies date from 1881, the Chicago from 1891, the Cincinnati from 1895, and the Philadelphia and Minneapolis Orchestras were established within the first decade of the twentieth century.

A noteworthy characteristic of the early financial history of the orchestras is the extent to which they relied for support on a few very wealthy patrons. Morgan, Carnegie and Pulitzer were among those who supplied the funds needed to induce Mahler to come to the United States as conductor of the New York Philharmonic. A million dollar bequest from the estate of Joseph Pulitzer played a crucial role in the establishment of the New York Philharmonic as a permanent orchestra. Even more remarkable in this respect is the early history of the Boston Symphony, whose sole guarantor for 37 years, from its foundation in 1881 until the end of World War I, was the financier Henry L. Higginson. And as Mueller reports,[2] "Besides Higginson and, later, E. B. Dane of Boston, other financiers who virtually signed a blank check to the credit of the orchestras for a shorter or longer period were: H. H. Flagler (oil) for the New York Symphony, W. A. Clark (mines) of Los Angeles, and Edward Bok (publishing) of Philadelphia. There were others . . . who shared economic responsibility in a more fragmentary but still substantial degree." It should not be concluded, however, that the early history of the orchestras was without its financial tribulations. In general, the contrary was the case, and examples can easily be provided.

[1] Mueller, pp. 19–90, is the source for most of the historical data in this section.

[2] p. 334.

Today the American Symphony Orchestra League classes the nation's orchestras into three main categories on the basis of the size of their annual budgets. The largest group is made up of those it calls "community orchestras," whose annual expenditures do not exceed $100,000. Though some of the community orchestras are professional or quasi-professional in character, many such groups are composed of amateur players with a core of professional "pick-up" musicians who are assembled (with one or two rehearsals) for each performance. On the average, only some 15 per cent of the players in a community orchestra are remunerated for their performance. Well over one thousand community orchestras were in operation in this country in 1965.

The next larger organizations are called the "metropolitan orchestras," and their budgets range from $100,000 to $250,000.[3] Almost all of these are exclusively professional, though a few contain a sprinkling of amateurs. There were 33 orchestras listed in the metropolitan category in 1965, most of them in cities whose population is under half a million, including Honolulu, Oakland, Portland (Oregon), Tulsa, Columbus and Miami. Some of these orchestras are considered to be of extremely fine quality.

Finally, the 25 major orchestras are, in general, the largest, best established and oldest of our musical organizations, though a few of the community groups predate some of the major orchestras and can claim to be equally well established. All of the major orchestras are completely professional; all have annual budgets in excess of a quarter of a million dollars. There is great variation in the magnitude of their operations, and there are corresponding differences in frequency of performance and levels of remuneration. Some of these orchestras have seasons only slightly exceeding 22 weeks, and in 1964–65 the average musician's remuneration in five of these orchestras was under $3,000 per year. The four largest of the orchestras, Boston, Cleveland, New York and Philadelphia, are in a class by themselves with seasons of 52 weeks and budgets on the order of $1½ to $3 million a year. Salary figures for artistic personnel during the winter season alone can be over a million dollars. Yet it should be recognized that in our economy an en-

[3] Some orchestras still listed as "metropolitan" now have annual outlays greater than $250,000. The definitions of this category will be revised in 1967.

terprise of this size must be considered miniscule — even the Metropolitan Opera, with its $9 million annual outlay, is dwarfed by the nation's multi-million dollar industrial corporations.

The largest orchestras may have an administrative staff of some 30 persons. In one of these organizations, for example, there is a managing director who is responsible to the president of the board of directors for the conduct of the entire organization, an assistant manager, a director for fund raising, a press director, a controller who handles all accounting and budgeting, an administrator of the subscription department, an administrative assistant secretary who prepares contracts, schedules rehearsals and handles special projects, and an assistant to the manager who is responsible for the organization of tours, outdoor concerts and the like. Most of these officials have assistants and a secretarial staff.

The conductor has complete and normally undisputed command of the artistic functions of the orchestra — choice of program, hiring of musicians, standards of rehearsal, interpretation of scores, etc. However, in some cases orchestral contracts limit significantly the conductor's authority to hire and fire, and in some cases programing and selection of artists are subject to ratification by the board of trustees. The day-to-day financial operations are normally in the hands of the board of directors, the president and the manager. But the conductor is necessarily also involved in pecuniary matters, in decisions regarding musicians' salaries, in decisions on the amount of rehearsal time budgeted and in acts of public relations where, for example, a prospective donor is to be courted.

The Commercial Theater

The professional theater in the United States has a history far longer if more sporadic than that of the orchestras.[4] As Moore reminds us, "At the first recorded theatrical performance in the American colonies, the performers were arrested." This performance by the citizens of Accomac, Virginia of a play called "Ye Bare and Ye Cubb" occurred in 1665. Apparently the cast was promptly

[4] Most of the materials in this section are drawn from Moore and Bernheim (Chapters II, III and VI).

acquitted. There were early performances in Charleston, New York and Boston (from which, predictably, they were soon banned).

But professional drama arrived only in the middle of the eighteenth century. A number of English actors came to this country in the decades before the Revolution and formed companies that played in Philadelphia, New York, Annapolis and other cities in the colonies. A most remarkable feature of their operation was the apparent frequency with which the theaters burned down and the ease and speed with which they were reconstructed, sometimes even in brick. This suggests that returns on theatrical investments must have been fairly good. The high price of theater tickets in relation to costs confirms this surmise. In New York and some of the other colonies with comparable currencies the cost of admission to a box seems to have ranged from 6 to 10 shillings, and even gallery tickets typically sold at about 3 shillings. This may be compared with the cost of production of a play in New York in 1762 reported by Bernheim.[5] The budget for a double bill including "Othello" and "The Lying Valet" totaled £18 10s. 6d. — an amount that would have been covered by the sale of only 47 box seats (which for this performance were priced at 8 shillings). This budget, however, excludes actors' salaries, which would normally have come from the shared surplus — in this case £114 10s. of the £133 6d. in total receipts.[6]

Colonial ticket prices were also very high in relation to contemporary earning levels. Since a day's pay for a common laborer was almost certainly under five shillings in New York in 1762, the minimum ticket price of three shillings was far higher in terms of workers' earnings than it is today. Curiously, however, it corresponded to the price of some 15 pounds of bread, whose current price, about $3.00, is approximately the same as the price of a balcony ticket at a Broadway matinee.

---

[5] p. 10.

[6] It is very difficult to interpret these figures in contemporary terms, for colonial currency was chaotic. The several colonies issued different currencies having different values; the fact that they were expressed in common nominal units — pounds, shillings and pence — did not render them comparable. Indeed, some colonies seem to have had several currencies — more valuable coin and less valuable paper money — and the meaning of a given price depends on which of these was used in payment.

During the nineteenth century the theater was organized into the stock system: it consisted largely of local resident companies, permanently installed at a particular theater. Beginning about 1820 a succession of British actors and actresses of considerable repute found it profitable to tour the United States and perform with the local companies. The glamorous invasions of Keene, Booth and Kemble were soon emulated by the first American stars, among them Edwin Forrest and James H. Hackett. It was predictable that these skilled performers would soon become dissatisfied with the acting standards of the stock companies. There followed the formation of complete companies which traveled about with the stars to constitute a sort of package presentation, and by 1890 this new structure — the combination system — had largely replaced the resident stock companies.

It was at this stage that the theater became big business and fell under the influence of syndicates which owned chains of theaters and controlled bookings and, through them, fees. There were two outstanding chains — "The Syndicate" (Hayman and Frohman, Nixon and Zimmerman, Klaw and Erlanger), which dominated much of the theater from 1896 until after World War I, and the Shubert chain, which began in the first decade of the twentieth century.

Throughout the nineteenth century the commercial theater grew and flourished, though not without some tribulations. One hears of hard times for the New York theater in 1836 and 1837, and there were complaints of the ruinous salaries demanded by the stars. But by and large the drama continued to thrive throughout the country until the first decade of the twentieth century, and in New York until the middle of the 1920's, when the advent of motion pictures and then the onslaught of the depression seriously curtailed the growing prosperity of the American theater.

An organizational feature of the commercial theater which differentiates it sharply from the orchestra is its impermanence. Each play is a completely new enterprise — as it were, a new business firm organized expressly for the production of that play. Typically, a significant proportion of the openings on Broadway is mounted by new and inexperienced producers. True, there are half a dozen professional producers who earn their living from the theater, but when he has no shows running, even a major producer will pare his staff down to a core of three: a play reader, a production assistant and a general manager. All the other participants in a production — director, actors, designers and the rest — are assembled anew with each new performing enterprise.

One result which significantly affects the character of our statistical materials is an almost complete lack of permanent and directly comparable records for the commercial theaters. One can obtain financial statements for individual plays over a considerable period, but there is no such thing as a continuous series, and it is extremely difficult to determine how the figures for a production in one year should be related to the records of an earlier dramatic undertaking.

A second peculiarity of theatrical organization is, perhaps, a hang-over from the days of the chains. This is the fact that the locus of control of a production is sharply divided between the producer and the owner of the theater in which the play is performed.

While the producer selects his play, controls the artistic standards of the production, raises the funds invested in it, hires the director and the cast, sets wages and decides on outlays on costumes and scenery, there are other matters which he normally does not control completely. A powerful producer can obtain a contract giving him a substantial voice in what may be termed the marketing of a play, but usually this is left largely in the hands of the theater owner, who often supplies, in addition to box office personnel and ushers, several stagehands and, where appropriate, several musicians. He bears part of the cost of advertising, has a voice in the setting of ticket prices and supplies tickets to brokerage agencies. He has complete control of the box office, into which a producer may even be refused admittance. In some cases he may undertake imaginative innovations to encourage the sale of tickets. An example is the establishment, through the cooperation of the Shubert chain, of a set of ticket offices at the R. H. Macy department stores in New York City where the playgoer can obtain tickets to a play at any of the Shubert theaters and a number of other theaters with no surcharge over normal box office prices. At the other extreme there have been allegations of questionable practices — in perhaps isolated cases where, for example, a theater owner was anxious to speed an unsuccessful play out of his theater in order to make room for a more lucrative production. The theater owner normally receives a percentage of the weekly gross of a play so that, aside from the advantages of length of run, it is in his interest to house a successful play. Since the contract usually provides that he can eject a play from his theater when the weekly gross falls below a pre-specified figure, it is alleged that box office personnel have sometimes been instructed to refuse to sell tickets to potential patrons, stating that all the seats were already sold.

The administrative structure of a play is most easily described in terms of a brief history of a production. One of the producer's most difficult tasks is the acquisition of a good script. He obtains candidate scripts from writers' agents, from successful foreign productions and, very rarely, from unsolicited manuscripts. Sometimes, particularly in the case of a musical, the producer develops the idea himself.

The standard Dramatist's Guild contract stipulates that the author receive a non-refundable deposit to be forfeited if the play is not produced within a year or some shorter specified period, plus royalties on a sliding scale ranging from 5 to 10 per cent of the box office gross, and the bulk of receipts from subsidiary rights including films and rights to produce the play abroad. Under the terms of his contract, the writer must be consulted on changes in the script, choice of director, casting and similar matters.

The producer then must find backers for the play. Normally investors enter into a limited partnership, which offers the advantage of limited liability but is not subject to the corporate income tax. The backers are usually guaranteed half of any profits earned by the production. Except for the most successful producers, the raising of these funds frequently requires the exercise of extraordinary powers of persuasion and ingenuity. If the producer is lucky, he will also succeed in dangling before prospective backers a glamorous star who is interested in appearing in the production.

While capital is being raised — indeed, often as a means to obtain investors — the director is chosen. He usually receives a flat fee — an amount that may be quite high if his reputation is considerable. In addition, a well-known director will receive a percentage of the play's earnings. He and an assistant casting director engage the performers, usually through an agency. The director is responsible for rehearsals and interpretation of the play, and is consulted on scenery and costuming. Soon after the play opens, the director's full-time association with the production terminates, but he is committed to return periodically during the run to make certain that standards of performance have been maintained.

The producer must next arrange for a theater. At the height of the season (early fall) theaters are scarce, and the relatively unknown producer will have difficulty in obtaining a house, particularly one that meets his desires as to number of seats, location and musical facilities. Moreover, the terms of his contract with the theater owners will vary with the season of the year and the reputation of the producer. Terms range from 20 to 30 per cent of box office gross.

A press agent is also engaged by the producer. He conducts a major campaign a few weeks before the opening of the play, though he often begins to work several months before that. Designers, lighting directors and choreographers complete the basic cast of characters involved in the staging of a Broadway production.

We have confined the discussion of this section to Broadway because, for all practical purposes, it constitutes the bulk of this country's commercial theater. There does exist a commercial summer theater, whose size, Moore estimates, has more than doubled since 1946, comprising over 160 groups in 1962;[7] and some theaters outside of New York handle commercial productions, particularly pre-Broadway opening tryouts and road company tours of Broadway productions. However, the most vital theatrical contribution outside New York City is currently being made by the resident company, a relatively recent phenomenon that will be described presently.

We close this section with one or two figures that offer some idea of the orders of magnitude involved. During the last few sea-

[7] Moore, Table V, Chapter VII.

sons the number of new productions has ranged from about 50 to the low 60's.[8] This compares with the frequently cited new production figure of 264 plays during the peak year 1927–28. The number of theater buildings declined from 80 in the late 1920's to 36 in 1964. The mid-1960's have witnessed the first new theater construction in New York City since the stock market crash — the building of both a temporary and a permanent theater for the Lincoln Center Company, the New York State Theater also at Lincoln Center, and the reclamation of the old Palace Theater of vaudeville fame from the movie house into which it had been transformed.

The Off-Broadway Theater

In general, off-Broadway theaters represent the more experimental segment of drama in New York City. They are small theaters located in various parts of Manhattan from Greenwich Village to 103rd Street. The off-Broadway enterprises, which are rarely very profitable, have sought to provide outlets for the works of new playwrights, new directors and relatively unknown actors. Almost all the prominent new dramatists of the postwar period have had their works introduced to the New York audience through the agency of the off-Broadway theater.

The scale of operation of an off-Broadway theater is extremely modest. While a non-musical play may cost some $125,000 to mount on Broadway, a comparable off-Broadway enterprise can still be produced at less than $15,000, of which over $5,000 may represent refundable bonds and deposits to the theater and the unions.

While the top ticket price for a drama on Broadway is usually about $7, that for an off-Broadway production is normally less than $5. And while a Broadway theater is likely to hold from 700 to 1500 seats, the typical off-Broadway house has a capacity of 199. The reason for this odd number is that fire laws and union regulations cause a sharp increase in costs with the addition of a 200th

[8] *Variety,* July 22, 1964.

seat; for similar reasons, the larger off-Broadway theaters are usually equipped with less than 300 seats.

Until recently the number of productions offered by this branch of the New York theater (and, by all reports, the professionalism of its operations) has been increasing sharply. From its birth some 15 years ago, off-Broadway advanced to the point where in 1963–64 it offered over 90 productions — over a third more than the Broadway theater. However, its economics have always been extremely precarious. The number of productions declined significantly during the 1964–65 season, and the demise of the off-Broadway movement is now being discussed as actively as was the growth of the movement only a few years ago.

One explanation that has been offered for the decline in off-Broadway activity during 1964–65 is the increase in the Equity minimum which occurred at the start of the season. The minimum rose from $50 per week to $60 per week. This is not the place to evaluate this thesis, but it is worth noting that in the off-Broadway theater the minimum salary is also the typical salary. In a fairly representative production of the 1963–64 season about half of the 15 actors were paid exactly the Equity minimum; three actors in minor roles were not even Equity members and were paid less than the minimum. There were five principals who, at the opening of the production, received between two and three times the Equity minimum. However, when (as typically happens off-Broadway) after a brief period these actors left for more lucrative jobs, their less well known replacements each received perhaps half his predecessor's remuneration.

Actually, the off-Broadway movement is not confined to New York City. In Chicago there has been a development referred to as the off-Loop theater, and some of the so-called regional theaters in the nation's larger cities do much the same sort of thing as does off-Broadway. Nor is the movement as new a phenomenon as is frequently imagined. Poggi identifies it as a continuation of the "little theater" or "art theater" movement, which goes back at least to 1891 with James A. Herne's production of his "Margaret Flemming" in Boston — a play which created a sensation as a result of its naturalistic approach to the subject of illegitimacy and marriage. According to Poggi, several other efforts to establish a non-commercial theater in New York before 1912 were not particularly successful. But by 1915, with the founding of the Provincetown Playhouse, the Washington Square Players (later the Theater Guild) and the Neighborhood Playhouse, something very much like a successful off-Broadway theater made its appearance. Despite all sorts of financial and artistic tribulations, this theatrical movement succeeded in introducing the works of Eugene O'Neill just as, more recently, Edward Albee's early plays were first produced in the off-Broadway theater. The earlier movement also provided a showcase for controversial plays by E. E. Cummings, Paul Claudel, Shaw and others. In sum, it is clear that the post-World War II development by no means represents the first manifestation of the desire for a less commercially inclined theater in which artistic standards and the wish to experiment have priority over earnings.

Nor have these movements been quite as experimental as a hasty glance might suggest. For example, many of the hits of the 1963–64 off-Broadway season were in some sense reruns. They included revivals of Greek drama, O'Neill, and the works of more recent but well-tried foreign playwrights such as Brecht and Pirandello. Yet many of these are not the sort of plays that Broadway would readily undertake.

We should be clear that most of off-Broadway is "commercial" in the sense that the majority of its theaters are legally classed as profit-making institutions, and they do in fact occasionally make a profit. But "profit-making" sometimes means only that the backers report their unreturned investments as business losses instead of listing them in their tax returns as deductible contributions to organizations legally designated as non-profit organizations. The basic fact is that the off-Broadway theater is in practice subsidized by the investors, by the producers and by the performers, whose willingness to work for so little money is as real a financial contribution as the gift of any patron.

The organization of the off-Broadway theater is more variegated and often less formalized than that of the Broadway theater. It consists to a considerable extent of fly-by-night companies and organizations which have never operated before and which, after the current production, will never be assembled again. But, curiously, in a number of cases off-Broadway has nurtured organizations more enduring than those typical of the Broadway theater. The Phoenix Theater has been in operation since 1953. The Circle in the Square and the Living Theater were both founded at about that time; the former is still in existence and the latter collapsed only recently under its tax burdens.

These theaters, together with the productions of Wilder, Barr and Albee, those of Judith Marechal and the plays put on by several other continuing producers, constitute the more enduring off-Broadway enterprises. In each case the organization owes its existence to the continuing efforts of two or three dedicated individuals, some of them making extreme financial sacrifices in the process. In one case the theatrical group has been operated by a business manager and a college professor, in another by two producers and an outstanding playwright, while still another is built on the collaboration of an energetic producer and a fine director. In short, one cannot describe an administrative pattern for the off-Broadway theater. One can only say that the operations are sometimes most informal, that earnings of the administrative personnel are generally very small, that the offices are typically shabby, and that records are usually very poor.

The Regional Theater

A marked increase in the number of resident professional companies of actors outside New York City has occurred recently. Washington, Boston, San Francisco, Cincinnati, Minneapolis, Milwaukee, Houston and Oklahoma City are among the cities that now have theatrical enterprises of considerable repute. More than thirty such troupes were in operation by 1964.[9] The rate of establishment of these theaters has grown continuously. In a sample composed of the leading regional theaters that was investigated in some detail by Sandra Schmidt, the earliest was founded in 1932 (the Barter Theater in Abingdon, Virginia), and not until 1947 did a second one get under way (the Alley Theatre in Houston).

[9] For a listing, see Rockefeller Panel Report, pp. 231–33.

The Arena Stage in Washington, the Actor's Workshop in San Francisco and the American Shakespeare Festival in Stratford, Connecticut followed in 1950, 1952 and 1955. By the end of 1959, eight of these theaters had been founded, and since then one was founded in 1960, one in 1961, two in 1962, three in 1963 and four in 1964.

The historical position of these regional theaters becomes clearer when we recognize that the strongest manifestation of the economic deterioration of the American theater has been the decline of "the road," which is the extension of the Broadway theater outside of New York. By 1910, more than a decade and a half before Broadway's major troubles began, a sharp decline occurred in the operations of the touring companies. From a high of more than 327 companies on tour at the turn of the century the number had fallen to less than 100 by 1915, and since 1932 the number has never risen above 25.[10] Until very recently, except for the vital but temporary activity of the federally financed WPA theater, much of the country had been left without access to living drama. This long, dry spell, together with the demanding artistic goals of many of the regional theaters, explains much of the enthusiasm that has greeted their recent rise and the flow of foundation funds that has helped to finance them.

One characteristic of particular interest for this study is the continuity of the regional theaters' organization. Management and artistic personnel do not change from production to production, or sometimes even from season to season. As a result, and perhaps partly because data are required to support their requests for foundation support, it has in some cases been possible to obtain from these theaters relatively detailed financial figures.

Opera

Opera in the United States has a relatively long history.[11] The first recorded operatic performance on American soil took place in

---

[10] Poggi, Chapter II, Table I.

[11] Some of the European opera houses are, of course, much older than ours, but not all of them have been in continuous operation for as long a period as is commonly believed. While opera has been presented at Covent Garden since 1734, it was only after World War II that it became a full-time, per-

1735 when "Flora, or Hob in the Well" was produced in the court-room at Charleston, South Carolina. The earliest known New York performances presented two works, "The Mock Doctor" and "The Beggar's Opera," both in 1750. Perhaps the first American operatic composition, "Tammany," by James Hewitt, was staged in 1794 under the sponsorship of the Tammany Society. It was nearly a century later (with considerable operatic activity having taken place in the interim) that the Metropolitan Opera was founded in 1883.[12]

Despite this long tradition, professional opera is extremely scarce in the United States. There exist four major companies (the Metropolitan, the New York City Opera, the Chicago Lyric Opera and the San Francisco Opera) and an even smaller number of rather specialized and younger operatic groups — the Santa Fé and Central City Summer Operas and the Goldovsky Touring Theater.[13] In addition, there are less than 40 professional opera producing groups that generally offer fewer than 25 performances a year, some of which (the Boston Opera for one) provide some of the country's more interesting operatic experiments.

The outstanding economic characteristic of grand opera is the extreme complexity of its operation and the costliness of its performances. In effect, this art form combines all the economic burdens that beset the other varieties of performance, for a grand opera brings to its audience a full cast of singers, a complete orchestra and a ballet company. Traditionally, its scenery, costuming and lighting are the most elaborate that can be provided. The magnitude of the operation is suggested by the size of its cast. An opera can easily require 4 leading singers, 10 supporting singers, 75–100 members of the chorus, 20–40 members of the ballet

manent institution—the Royal Opera of today. For a few years before the war Sir Thomas Beecham had presented annual operatic seasons of about six weeks each. During the war the building served as a Palais de Danse, a public dance hall. It reopened after the war under the management of Boosey and Hawkes, the music publishers. The present arrangement was not inaugurated until 1949, and most of the records that we have had available to us therefore date only from 1950.

[12] *Encyclopedia of American History,* Harper & Bros., New York, 1953, pp. 612–14, 620.

[13] Rockefeller Panel Report, p. 28.

troupe, 80–120 in its orchestra and 10–150 extras, a total of 200 to 300 performers. With the seating capacity of most opera houses less than four thousand persons, this provides a maximal audience of 20 persons per performer. It is as though a two person cast in a Broadway play were to try to run night after night before an audience of forty! But the problem is even worse than this would suggest. Because different operas with different casts are performed from evening to evening, rehearsal costs are proportionally far higher than those of a theatrical production with a moderately long run. Add to this the very high fees demanded by the most glamorous operatic stars (whose presence is usually demanded by the opera audience), and the picture of grand opera's extreme financial burden is complete. Thus the $1½ million deficit of the Metropolitan Opera in 1964–65 is hardly surprising.

Here again the complexity of operations dictates the size of administrative machinery. Thus, the Metropolitan Opera has an administrative staff even larger than those of the major orchestras or the larger theaters. The Met's bookkeeping is also elaborate and detailed. But because there are so few other major companies, and because of their great diversity, it is impossible to make many illuminating comparisons among the operatic enterprises. As a result, in our study opera is never discussed as a unified entity which can be subjected to a single encompassing analysis.

The Dance

The number of highly professional organizations involved in the dance is almost as small as the number involved in opera. There are three renowned companies that specialize in the classical ballet — the New York City Ballet, the San Francisco Ballet and the American Ballet Theatre. In addition, there are about half a dozen leading modern dance groups, notably those of Martha Graham, Alvin Ailey, Merce Cunningham, José Limón and Paul Taylor. During 1964 four new professional companies were formed.

The largest and best established of the dance organizations is the New York City Ballet, which has recently become associated with Lincoln Center. Its annual budget runs to $1½ million, and it maintains close to 70 dancers in its troupe. Despite the high quality of its administration, its world reputation, various forms of indirect governmental subsidy, its Ford Foundation grant and the extremely generous support of a single individual who is its chief patron, the New York City Ballet has not had an easy time financially.

But its problems are minor in comparison with those of the American Ballet Theatre, a group that has produced a more diversified set of works than any other American company. For 25 years the company has survived through the generosity of a single patron — Lucia Chase. Yet, despite its important contribution to the revival of American ballet, this organization had, until recently, not received foundation support and reported that, after a successful season at Lincoln Center in the spring of 1965, it was on the verge of collapse.

Most modern dance companies have led an incredibly precarious existence. The case of Martha Graham has recently been an exception. The continuing support she has received for part of her career from the B. de Rothschild Foundation has guaranteed her against bankruptcy. Yet even she has been unable to afford New York seasons totaling more than three weeks in a year despite her large audiences. Modern dance is the only performing art form other than jazz which is an American creation and in which Americans are clearly pre-eminent. It is curious, therefore, that despite the international acclaim it has received, it is the most impoverished of our art forms.

Typically, a modern dance organization is administered in all its aspects by a single person — the choreographer. He either serves as his own secretary, accountant and business manager or entrusts these tasks to his wife or a friend. Except when the State Department finances a trip abroad, his company usually gives only sporadic and isolated performances, frequently requiring travel for a single performance to some distant campus (the colleges being for him a prime source of audiences). He will typically operate a dance school or serve as a visiting faculty member at a college as a means of livelihood, and a desk, telephone and typewriter just outside his dance area may serve as his office. The studio — equipped at the choreographer's expense with a special floor — may be on the top story of a slum walk-up, because the rent is low and dancers have more endurance than cash. When an engagement is arranged, the choreographer must interrupt his teaching program and reassemble his troupe, whose members arrange leaves from the large variety of jobs at which they earn their living.

But from the point of view of audience size, none of the organizations discussed constitutes the heart of dance in the United States. Rather, the audiences flock to the glamorous foreign troupes — the Bolshoi, the Royal Ballet, the Royal Danish Ballet and the other visiting troupes. The fact that these fine groups are seen by so many Americans is, of course, no ground for complaint. But it is curious that among our native dance groups, many of which are hailed abroad as the peers of any dance company in the world, only the New York City Ballet's audiences even begin to approach those of the visitors.

Geographic Dispersion

A significant characteristic of the organization of the performing arts in the United States is the geographic dispersion of performing groups. The accompanying map (Figure II-1) shows the location of some of the organizations to which we have already referred — the major and metropolitan orchestras, the regional theaters, the major opera companies. Since it is impossible to show all the Broadway and off-Broadway theaters, the map seriously understates the degree of concentration of performing activity in New York City. Nevertheless, it is true that the arts are more widely distributed throughout the United States than is often supposed.

We have seen that the organizations which provide artistic performance in the United States are remarkably diverse in size, in complexity of operation, in number of companies involved in a particular art form and in almost any other respect one can imagine. In no case is the number of professional organizations very large; they range (in 1965) from about 60 metropolitan and major orchestras and 40 to 50 permanent theatrical groups to perhaps 7 opera companies and a slightly larger number of dance groups. In number of performers they vary from a dance company of 6 to an

FIGURE II-1
LOCATION OF PRINCIPAL PERFORMING ARTS ORGANIZATIONS

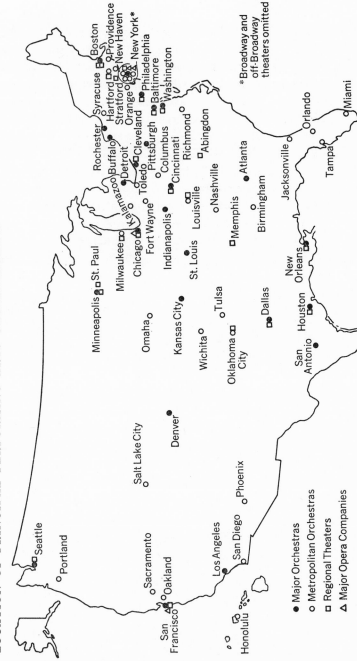

*Broadway and
off-Broadway
theaters omitted

- ● Major Orchestras
- ○ Metropolitan Orchestras
- □ Regional Theaters
- △ Major Opera Companies

Data for this map are from 1964-65 American Symphony Orchestra League listings, Sandra Schmidt's listing of regional
theaters, and the Rockefeller Panel Report discussion of major operas.

orchestra with over 100 musicians and grand opera with a cast of over 200. The managerial arrangements vary from the sophisticated and complex organizations of the leading orchestras and the Metropolitan Opera to the office which is, in effect, maintained in the hat of the choreographer-manager of a modern dance company. The degree of continuity of the organizations is equally diverse; some have survived various metamorphoses for over three quarters of a century, while others are dissolved after each production.

One result of these dissimilarities is that statistical analysis of aggregated financial data for the performing arts as a whole is largely ruled out, and that direct comparisons of the statistics pertaining to the various art forms reveal only one common economic characteristic — the financial pressures to which they are subject. Yet we shall attempt to show that despite all their variety the financial problems of these organizations can be ascribed to a common set of sources.

CHAPTER III

The Cultural Boom:
A New Look at the Evidence

THE "cultural boom" is perhaps the best publicized art phenomenon of the decade. Newspapers and magazines have heralded its advent, it has been discussed on radio and television, and recently a book has been devoted to the subject. Yet there have been a few discordant voices — skeptical commentators who have suggested that the highly touted resurgence of interest in the arts is little more than self-deception. A close examination of the literature shows that the evidence produced to support either argument is meager, and that the data cited are often undocumented or suffer from a variety of more serious shortcomings. This chapter describes the available evidence on the current levels of performing arts activities and their trends. In the first half of the chapter we describe total consumer spending on the performing arts and try to place recent developments in their historical perspective. We also examine the geographic distribution of artistic activity. In the second half of the chapter we disaggregate our results and report on levels of activity (numbers of performances and attendance) in major metropolitan orchestras, Broadway, off-Broadway, the regional theater, dance groups and operas. The rates of growth in these various compartments of the arts world have been significantly different, and the danger of treating the "cultural boom" as one large, undifferentiated mass is evident in the results of this part of our analysis. This section of our work is concerned only with quantitative measures of activity, since any indication of quality must elude the numerical data with which we have to work.

What emerges from this investigation, as the reader will see, is evidence of a modest expansion in performing arts activity, one which, though by no means negligible, is far from universal and can hardly be called a cultural explosion. It should be pointed out, however, that we are not interested in the "cultural boom" because it provides a good subject for debunking. Rather, the purpose of this chapter is to present a clear picture of the degree of public interest in the performing arts in the United States, so far as interest can be gauged by the number of enterprises and performances, their rates of growth, and the relationship between expenditures for admissions and other consumer outlays. This chapter, therefore, provides a backdrop for the rest of our study.

Literature of the "Boom"

Alvin Toffler's volume, *The Culture Consumers,* is perhaps the most enthusiastic and most recent addition to the literature of the "cultural boom." An extract should convey the flavor of his viewpoint:

> Americans spent or donated, all together, a rock-bottom minimum of $3 billion for culture last year [1960], a figure that excludes public funds and business gifts. The significant point is that this sum is 70 per cent more than the comparable estimate for ten years ago. . . . This rate of growth was nearly four times greater than the rate of population growth during the decade.
>
> Americans have been delighting their ears as well as nourishing their minds. According to the American Symphony Orchestra League, the increase in symphony attendance in recent years has been nothing short of "phenomenal," with the League now receiving more reports of sold-out concert halls than at any time since it began keeping records. . . .
>
> At the same time, culture consumers were thronging record stores, taking home with them each year about 17.5 million discs of what not long ago was derisively termed "long hair stuff." Housewives have been buying classical LP's along with their frozen vegetables at the nearby supermarket.
>
> . . . until the current breakthrough began, [the professional theater lay] within a tiny area in mid-Manhattan. Today, despite the mournful cries issuing from the offices of Broadway producers, the theater in America is bubbling with vitality. Not since the death

of vaudeville has the average American had more opportunity to enjoy live drama. While audiences for high-cost Broadway productions dwindled during the 'fifties, a new theater has sprung up right next door. . . . This is, of course, the off-Broadway theater which has grown from a handful of houses in 1950 into thirty-two playhouses in 1964 and which, according to Paul Liben of the League of Off-Broadway Theaters and Producers, annually takes in an estimated $3 million from nearly one million theater-goers. . . .

For the arts have been liberated from their prison cell and brought into the sunlight. In the process, they have lost some of their charisma. They appear now to be less mystifying, less "special," less exalted than in the past. There they are, as it were, on the supermarket shelf, and what could be more natural?[1]

Toffler's study is not the first to express such views. One of the standard sources for almost all discussions of the "cultural boom" is a study conducted by the Stanford Research Institute in 1962. This study reports:

. . . consumer spending on the arts rose in the seven years shown [1953–1960] by about 130%, or considerably more than twice as fast as spending on all recreation, and better than six times as fast as outlays for spectator sports or admission to movies.

It adds that there are —

* more piano players than fishermen (or, at least, that pay for fishing licenses)
* as many painters as hunters
* twice as many who attend concerts and recitals as who see major league ball games
* and more theater goers than boaters, skiers, golfers, and skindivers combined.[2]

These propositions have since been widely accepted; explicitly or implicitly they appear in an article in the *New York Times'* National Economic Review for 1964,[3] in Toffler's book and in other writings. Similar pictures of growth in the level of cultural activity have been drawn elsewhere, including a publication of the Federal Reserve Bank.[4]

[1] Toffler, pp. 16, 18, 20, 21, 23.

[2] Mitchell, pp. 7, 9 and 11.

[3] Milton Esterow, "Plato to Puccini: A $7 Billion Future," *New York Times*, Jan. 11, 1965, p. 125.

[4] Murdock.

But even as these enthusiastic reports were appearing, expressions of doubt were also voiced. As early as 1961, Representative Dave Martin of Nebraska observed in the course of a notable set of hearings on the economic conditions in the performing arts, "I attended the symphony concert last night, a very fine performance, but I was quite surprised, in view of all this testimony that we have had as to the great interest in the arts, that the opera house was not sold out by quite a number of seats."[5] And about two months later, at the same set of hearings, Representative Roman C. Pucinski of Illinois recalled, "We have performances here at the Library of Congress, no admission charge, or at least a very small, slight service charge, and great artists performing over there, and we do not have a great frequency of attendance . . . you almost have to give the tickets away to attract a decent crowd for these people."[6]

Since then, Harold C. Schonberg, music critic for the *New York Times,* has undertaken the role of leading protagonist of the skeptics' position. In a number of articles beginning early in 1962, he questioned in turn each basic premise of the literature of the cultural explosion. Using the term "phony" to characterize the boom, he cast doubt on the statistics of cultural center construction, suggesting that many of the building complexes classed under this heading have little dealing with artistic activity. He went on to say:

> We do have some of the best opera singers in the world — but they are not in America. Most of them are solidly entrenched in European opera houses. Naturally. Where else can they go? The sad fact is that America has only one major opera house — the Metropolitan. And there is only one ballet company in America with any sort of international standing.
>
> Since the end of World War II this country has produced a dazzling crop of instrumentalists, especially pianists. But, cultural explosion notwithstanding, young pianists today are a drug on the market. Of some 50 unusual talents, perhaps six can make a living giving concerts.[7]

Schonberg has also questioned the allegations on audience growth, and has maintained that in recent years music in New

[5] House Hearings, II, p. 363.　　[6] *Ibid.,* p. 592.

[7] Harold C. Schonberg, "The National 'Culture Explosion' Is Phony," *Saturday Evening Post,* July 13–20, 1963.

York City has not fared very well. In an article headed "Vanishing Audience,"[8] he argued that while more music may be available than ever before, audiences do not seem particularly interested. He reported that some managers believe the recital business is all but dead.

A more balanced view is provided in the Rockefeller Panel Report, which points out that "A tremendous expansion has taken place in the arts in this country in the past two decades." But after a brief recital of "cultural boom" statistics of the usual variety, the Rockefeller Panel Report remarks:

> Next to this glowing picture must be placed another, more sobering one: *Almost all this expansion is amateur.* . . . comparatively few are ever exposed to any *live professional* presentations. . . .
> Broadway . . . has reduced its output from an average of 142 productions per year during the thirties to 63 in 1963–64, and its playhouses have diminished in number from 54 to 36 in the same span of years.
> The number of commercial theaters in the country has dropped from 590 in 1927 to barely 200.
> Of 1,401 symphony orchestras, only 54 are composed predominantly of professional musicians.
> . . . there are only five or six dance companies that meet high professional standards and possess any real degree of institutional stability; only one approaches giving year-round performances.
> Of the 754 opera-producing groups, only 35 to 40 are fully professional, and not more than 10 of these provide performances more than fifteen days in the year.[9]

Amidst such diversity of viewpoints, a new look at the available evidence seems very much in order.

AGGREGATE DEVELOPMENTS

The Cultural Centers

If there is any one manifestation of the "cultural boom" which might indeed constitute a significant development, it is the growth of cultural centers, the magnificent new building complexes designed to house the living arts. Lincoln Center in New York, the

[8] *New York Times*, Oct. 25, 1964, Section 2, p. 11.

[9] Rockefeller Panel Report, pp. 13–14.

Los Angeles Music Center of the Performing Arts and the John F. Kennedy Center currently under construction in the nation's capital have all been highly publicized, and scores of others exist or are going up around us. The fashion extends beyond the United States: several centers are on their way in Great Britain, including one very ambitious group of buildings in London on the south bank of the Thames, part of which is already in operation.

In trying to determine just how many such centers there are in the United States and to find out something about their mode of operation, we encountered contradictory reports, mostly undocumented, some hailing the cultural center as a prime instrument of the expansion of artistic performance, and others implying that many of these centers are little more than a sham — designed more often than not for conventions, sports activities, meetings, dances and trade shows. We felt, therefore, that only a direct investigation could produce the pertinent facts. (The questionnaire used in our cultural center survey is reproduced in Appendix III–1.) Inquiries were sent to 194 municipalities — those with the largest populations in each state and those known or believed to be engaged in some interesting cultural activities — and 148 responses were received.

More than half (82) of the 148 cities from which we had replies claimed to have or to be planning cultural centers as of December 1964. In all, 93 centers were reported by 91 cities, 54 in operation and one of these plus 39 others in various stages of completion, ranging from "we hope to have" all the way to "buildings going up." By any strict definition, the number of cultural centers given by our survey is probably on the high side, since borderline organizations are doubtless tempted to class themselves as cultural centers now that the concept has become fashionable.

The dates of construction vary surprisingly. A few date from early in this century. Of the 54 operating centers, 24 were built prior to World War II and 26 were opened since 1950. Few of the older centers are leaders in the nation's cultural life; there is reason to believe that many of them devote themselves largely to local activities. That the pace of building has accelerated during the last few years is evident; when one adds to this the observation that 40 of our 148 cities expected to complete centers between 1965 and about 1970, it does seem that a "boom" in the construction of cultural centers is in progress.

The number of auditoriums where performance is possible in existing and planned cultural centers ranged from one to nine. On the basis of specific listings of the types of equipment and facilities they had available, we inferred that most of them are fairly well equipped — that their facilities usually permit some flexibility in staging, that dressing rooms are not too much like telephone booths, that there are at least 1,000 square feet of space for storage of scenery, and that some provision has been made for subtleties of lighting. The responses suggest that some thought had usually been given to these matters when the auditoriums were designed. However, performers who have used these facilities are not always unqualified in their enthusiasm about convenience and design. In a few interviews even some of the most elaborate centers were criticized by artists who had appeared in them.

Perhaps the most important question to be raised about cultural centers is whether as much thought has been given to the nature of their presentations as to the design of the buildings. One suspects that the planners of some of the centers have not really considered in any detail what should be done with the buildings once they were completed, but have proceeded on the assumption that quality of performance would somehow take care of itself. Our questionnaire, though it could not deal with this matter directly, provided some indication that the planners have treated it rather casually. Of the 54 operating centers, only 18 claimed to have professional performing arts groups in residence, though nearly twice this number reported such arrangements with semi-professional or amateur groups. Eight centers had no resident groups; and of the centers that were not yet completed, at least 25 had not made plans for any resident groups.

It appears, then, that while cultural centers are not as new an institution as one might have thought, and while not all of them have systematic programs to ally themselves with performing organizations, the number of centers has increased substantially in recent years. If their rate of growth is not startling, at least it does not conflict with the view that there has been an upsurge in cultural activity in the United States.

Relative Expenditures on the Arts

The basic piece of evidence that has been used to document the magnitude of the cultural boom is the fact, first publicized by the Stanford Research Institute, that consumer expenditures on the arts increased by 130 per cent during the seven years 1953–1960. The datum is derived from statistics provided by the U. S. Department of Commerce in its *Survey of Current Business*. This figure, and other similar magnitudes, are correct as given, but their interpretation has been seriously misleading.

The raw statistics are described in the *Survey of Current Business* as "Admissions to Legitimate Theater and Opera and Entertainments of Non-profit Institutions (except athletics)."[10] Thus the figures are in fact the total expenditure figures in which we are interested: they represent the total outlays by audiences on all forms of the live performing arts, and are available in a series going all the way back to 1929. We will refer to these figures as "total arts admissions expenditures" instead of repeating their rather overwhelming appellation.

According to these statistics, in 1963 some $433 million was spent on such admissions. This was less than 1 per cent of the nation's total output of goods and services — its Gross National Product or G.N.P. It amounted to $3.23 per capita if we consider only persons 13 years old and over. (Here, as throughout this study, in our per capita figures we disregard younger children and infants, who can hardly be expected to attend professional performances on any regular basis.) In one sense this per capita expenditure of $3.23 on live performance is surprisingly high, for it is over one third the amount spent in 1963 on movies ($9.31), and significantly higher than the expenditure on spectator sports ($2.25). Yet it is well below the amount spent in that year on books and maps ($13.00), or on television receivers, records and musical instruments ($9.51). This is a mixed bag from which one cannot select just the comparison with movies and sports for particular notice.

But at least as illuminating as the absolute expenditure figures are their rates of growth, which alone can indicate whether ex-

[10] See Appendix Table III–A for the exact source of all expenditure figures reported in this section.

penditures on the arts have, in fact, been increasing at a significant rate.

If we trace expenditures over a fairly long period, say the 31
years from 1932 to 1963, and then in more recent periods, say
1947–1963 and 1961–1963, we begin to get to the heart of the matter. We find, for one thing, that over the long stretch total arts
admissions expenditures rose at a higher average annual rate (8.2
per cent per year) than during the two more recent periods (6.5
per cent and 4.0 per cent per year, respectively). As we shall see,
this observation must be interpreted with some care. But, even so,
it seems rather strange behavior for an activity which is said to be
booming. And when we compare this category of consumer expenditures with others or with indicators of the general performance of the economy (see Appendix Table III–B), we again find it
faring less well than the "cultural boom" hypothesis would suggest. Whereas, for example, the annual growth rate of total arts
admissions expenditures over the entire period 1932–1963 slightly
exceeded that of expenditures on all services, during 1947–1963
outlays on services grew more rapidly, and during 1961–1963 this
difference increased further. Even the frequently cited comparison between recent growth rates in expenditures on the arts and
expenditures on spectator sports has created a false impression.
Sports have simply been growing very slowly all along; they have
in fact been falling behind the G.N.P., which over the entire period
grew 8.2 per cent per year as compared with a 6.0 per cent annual
rate of increase for spectator sports. Therefore, the statement that
outlays on the arts have been advancing more rapidly than those
on sports does not say very much.

Finally, we note that over the 31 year period expenditures on
the arts just about held their own with the G.N.P.: their rate of
increase of 8.2 per cent per year was just exactly "average" for
all goods and services. But during 1961–1963 there was a drop
that reduced the growth rate for arts expenditures below the average annual increase in the G.N.P.

Correction for Price Level, Population and Income Growth

If read by themselves, the dollar figures given by the *Survey of
Current Business* do suggest that the rate of expansion of total arts

admissions expenditures has been very substantial. The series begins in 1929 — which was probably a peak year of the pre-war era — and is summarized in Appendix Tables III–A and III–C for anyone who wants the year by year figures. The amount spent on admissions increased from $127 million in 1929 to an impressive $433 million in 1963. If one wanted to make the rise look even more sensational, it could be measured from the $41 million spent in 1933. But whatever the starting point, these figures are subject to a number of systematic distortions, each of which has magnified the real rise. Let us examine each of these distorting influences in turn, removing them one at a time like a set of veils, to reveal ultimately the basic facts that are concealed beneath.

One of the most obvious adjustments that must be made in the raw dollar figures is to correct for changes in the price level during the period. With all the talk one hears of fifty cent dollars, it is curious indeed that so few discussants of the "cultural boom" have felt it necessary to correct for this misleading influence. Clearly, if expenditures on the arts had quadrupled over the period but the dollar had decreased to exactly one fourth its initial purchasing power, there would have been no change in the real consumer outlay on the performing arts. The amount of purchasing power devoted to admissions would have remained exactly the same.

In fact, the appropriate price level correction is not quite so drastic. If expenditures in each year are translated into dollars of equal purchasing power, there still remains a significant rise in admissions expenditures between 1929 and 1963. But now that we have converted our original figures into dollars of constant ("real") value, the rise in expenditures is seen to be much smaller than the original data suggested. Instead of an increase of 240 per cent from 1929 to 1963 (from $127 million to $433 million), the rate of increase in real dollars is found to be no more than 65 per cent.

But the price level correction has only removed the first veil. While real expenditures have been increasing, population, too, has been rising. If population and real expenditure on the arts were both to rise by 50 per cent, this would not constitute a significant increase in demand. If ticket prices and the price level had risen at roughly similar rates (which, in many cases, is not too far from the truth, as we shall see later), it would mean only that admissions had just about managed to keep up with the number of the nation's inhabitants, and that attendance habits had remained the same. Therefore, to see whether our 65 per cent increase in real expenditure actually signifies a rise in the amount a typical American has spent on the arts we must adjust our figures to take account of population growth. The relevant figure now becomes real expenditure per capita — the amount spent, in real terms, divided by the number of persons 13 years of age and older in the country.

The effect of this second adjustment is considerable. Real per capita expenditures on admissions increased hardly at all over the period: they rose from $2.51 to $2.72 — an increase no greater than 8 per cent. It is also interesting that, after falling sharply during the great depression, real expenditures per capita did not regain their 1929 level until 1960.

But this is still not the end of the story. One more adjustment must be made before the significance of our total admissions data is fully revealed. During the 34 years in question, Americans have grown wealthier. If it were to transpire that they have been spending a smaller and smaller proportion of their incomes on the arts, then it would follow that expenditures on live performance have become a less important part of the consumer's budget. Surely "cultural boom" — the allegation of a rising interest in the arts — implies the reverse: that consumers are now willing to devote larger shares of their incomes to the arts than they were heretofore. To test whether this is the case we recalculated our figures once again, this time expressing expenditures on arts admissions as a percentage of the consumer's average income. (The measure used for this purpose was disposable personal income, or income after taxes.)

Expressed in these terms, the amount spent on the arts has actually fallen by about one fourth since 1929. Total arts admissions expenditures, we find, have decreased from 15 cents of each $100 of disposable personal income in 1929 to only 11 cents of each $100 in 1963. Thus the adjustments necessary to divest the total admissions figures of the spurious elements that concealed their underlying significance have deflated the alleged 240 per cent increase to what now appears to be a 25 per cent decline.

The effects of this series of adjustments are perhaps seen more

FIGURE III-1

INDEXES OF EXPENDITURES ON ADMISSIONS,
1929-1963

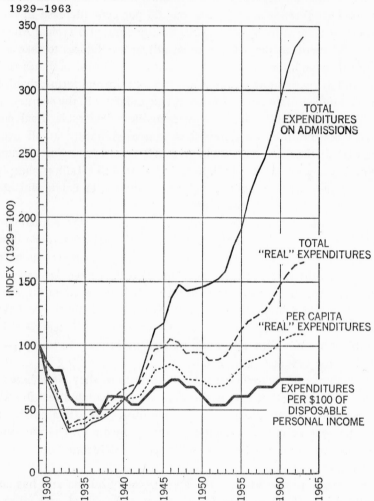

To permit comparisons among statistics as heterogeneous as total expenditures and per capita expenditures, the data are all expressed in terms of the corresponding 1929 figure, which is taken as 100. For example, the total expenditure on admissions in 1939, $64 million, is approximately 50 per cent of the 1929 figure, so that the 1939 index number is 50, and that is the admissions figure plotted for 1939 in the graph. All of the lines start off from exactly the same level (100) because the 1929 figure is, by definition, always equal to 100 per cent of itself. For the basic data see Appendix Table III-C.

clearly with the aid of Figure III–1.[11] This graph portrays for each of the 34 years (1929–1963) for which the data are available the history of the various measures of consumer expenditure on the arts, each expressed as a percentage of the corresponding 1929 figure. Looking at the right-hand end of the graph we see that the upper curve represents, as an index number, the total dollar outlay for admissions from which this discussion began, and that by 1964 this total had risen dramatically from its 1929 level. When we correct for changes in the price level, the graph (again referring to the right-hand end) drops to the second line from the top. Another drop, not as sharp, follows when correction for the increase in population is made. Finally, the heavy curve at the bottom of the chart gives an undistorted picture of the state of demand for the arts.

Since expenditure data are not available prior to 1929, there is no way of judging, on the basis of the *Survey of Current Business* data, whether admissions as a percentage of disposable income had been rising or falling in preceding years. However, we do have figures for the number of new Broadway productions as far back as 1899 (see Figure III–4 below), and the late 1920's were definitely a peak period for this series. Hence it seems reasonable to assume that 1929, or some date close to it, was also a peak year for admissions.

Examining Figure III-1 over the entire period 1929–1963, we see that arts admissions expenditures per dollar of disposable personal income have been roughly constant — there has been neither a catastrophic decline nor an explosive rise. By and large, the performing arts have just about held their own in the competition for the consumer's dollar. In recent years there has been a slight and fairly steady rise, outlays having gone up from a low of 0.08 per cent of disposable income in 1951–1953 to about 0.11 per cent in 1960–1963 — a real but not terribly spectacular increase,[12] which leveled off during the last four years.

[11] Specialists who wish to see all the data will find them in Appendix Table III–C.

[12] This observation brings out another source of distortion in the often reiterated statement that consumer spending on the arts rose 130 per cent in the period 1953–1960. This happens to have been an atypical period characterized by an unusually rapid rate of increase in admissions (8.9 per cent per year as compared with the 6.5 per cent figure for the whole period 1947–1963 and 4.0

Before leaving the graph, two of its more interesting general features should be noted. One obvious observation is that all four curves reached their lowest point during the great depression, a fact which suggests that economic prosperity is especially conducive to consumer expenditure on the arts. But one should not leap to this conclusion, for it was just at this period that the talking picture was introduced, and its influence on paid admissions to live performances was probably substantial.

It is also worth observing that there have been three distinct peaks in audience expenditures as a percentage of disposable income. The first occurred in 1929 (or began at some earlier date for which we have no statistical information). The second peak occurred in 1946–47, and the advent of television can perhaps be blamed for the subsequent decline. The third peak was reached in 1960; it was followed by at least three plateau-like years in which expenditures on arts admissions per dollar of disposable personal income were remarkably constant.[13]

If consumer expenditures on the arts as a percentage of disposable income have not risen spectacularly since 1929, neither have the shares of disposable income devoted to most other related services. Even outlays on "radios, television receivers, records and musical instruments" have never reattained their 1929 level, despite the success of television after the war. There is only one noteworthy exception to the general pattern of decline: consumer expenditures at institutions of private education and research (Figure III–2 and Appendix Table III–D). Since World War II this item in the consumer's budget has been growing rapidly and quite steadily at an average compound annual rate of 9 per cent. The 1963 ratio is more than 75 per cent higher than the 1929 level of 0.8 per cent of disposable income, and indeed the present figure (1.41) is nearly 40 per cent higher than any corresponding per-

per cent for 1961–1963). However, the Stanford Research Institute, which first publicized the 130 per cent growth figure, should not be criticized for choosing 1960 as the terminal date for its calculation, since it was then the latest figure available.

[13] We have tried to determine whether experience abroad has been similar to ours. Unfortunately, the necessary figures do not seem to have been published for any of the European countries.

FIGURE III–2

SELECTED CONSUMER EXPENDITURES PER $100 OF
DISPOSABLE PERSONAL INCOME, 1929–1963

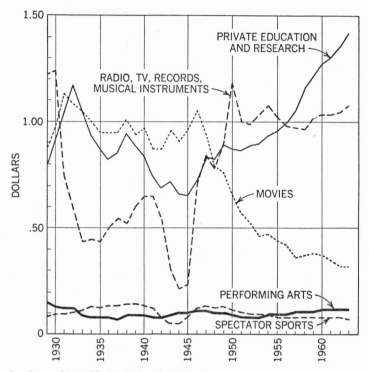

See Appendix Table III–D for the basic data.

centage figure before the recent upsurge which dates from about
1954. It should be noted that these figures relate only to *private*
educational and research institutions; if consumer expenditures
at state and municipal institutions were included in the total, the
rise would almost certainly be even more impressive.

When we compare these trends with the record of expenditures
on the performing arts (lowest line in Figure III–2), two things
stand out: how small, comparatively, are expenditures on the arts,
and how relatively steady they seem to have been since 1929. If
the postwar years have exhibited a cultural explosion, it appears to

have been an educational boom much more than an expansion in relative demand for the performing arts.

DEVELOPMENTS BY ART FORM AND REGION

The history of what has been happening to the measurable aspects of activity in the various art forms can be told most succinctly by means of graphs, and the remainder of this chapter abounds in them. They will display a very mixed picture — some art forms have prospered, some have declined and the growth of some others has been more apparent than real.

Opera and Dance

Let us begin with those art forms about which we have the least information: the opera and the dance. As we noted in Chapter II, this country has four major opera companies which operate on a long season basis, and somewhat less than 40 professional and semi-professional groups which perform for shorter seasons. That there is, in addition, a good deal of amateur activity is indicated by the 754 opera companies of all kinds reported in 1963–64 and the 3,877 performances recorded for that year (see Appendix Table III–E).

Estimating attendance for any part of this varied assemblage of opera companies must be regarded as something of a black art, but an order-of-magnitude estimate for the roughly 40 professional companies is possible, and our figure is somewhat under 2 million admissions in 1963–64. This is based on attendance figures of various degrees of reliability for the main companies and what are little more than guesses for the others. The Metropolitan Opera is, of course, the giant of the group, having performed for about three quarters of a million people a year even before it added an extensive series of summer operas in Lewisohn Stadium. It now has added a national company which will tour various major cities.

There has been a marked upward trend in total operatic activity over the entire postwar period, as Figure III–3 indicates, though

FIGURE III-3

TRENDS IN DANCE AND OPERATIC ACTIVITY,
1952–1965

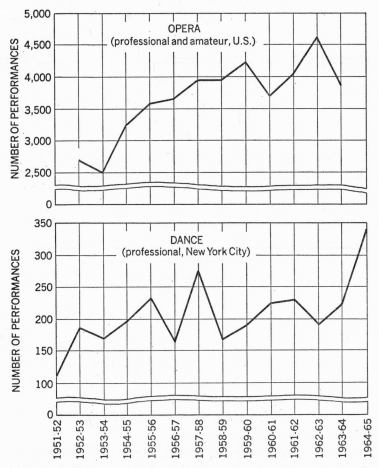

The basic data on operatic performances appear in Appendix Table
III–E; on dance performances, in Appendix Table III–G.

in the last five years the figures are highly erratic, with marked declines between the 1959–60 and 1960–61 seasons and again between 1962–63 and 1963–64. In the 1963–64 season the total
number of performances was below the 1957–58 level. Neverthe-

less, the over-all growth rate in number of performances from 1952–53 to 1963–64 was 4.2 per cent per year. When corrected for the growth in population, this amounts to a 2.7 per cent rate of increase in performances per capita. Since Figure III–3, like most other graphs in this part of the chapter, has *not* been adjusted to a per capita basis, it tends to overstate the "true" rate of expansion, "true" meaning the rate of expansion over and above that which was necessary simply to keep up with increases in the general population.

Moreover, the bulk of the growth we have just described is apparently amateur. Professional performance by major companies has grown much more slowly. The number of performances by the Metropolitan Opera, for example, increased only from 216 to 244 between 1947–48 and 1963–64. But the number of tours required to fill out the season has dropped substantially since the war; the Metropolitan's New York audience has grown sufficiently to permit it to spend the bulk of the season in the city. Its New York performances rose from 131 in 1947–48 to 190 regular and 16 World's Fair performances in 1963–64. The national company was formed to take over much of the resident company's road schedule. In this respect the increase in the total number of performances, cited above, significantly understates the growth in the audience of the Metropolitan Opera. In per capita terms one may surmise conservatively that the number of professional performances by major opera companies has remained just about constant.

It is hard to estimate total attendance at the dance, but the figure of "under 1 million" used by the Rockefeller Brothers Report seems plausible if we exclude the glamorous foreign troupes, such as the Bolshoi and the Royal Ballet.[14]

Using *Dance Magazine* as a source, it is possible to compile statistics on recent trends in the number of dance companies. The figures show a steady growth in the number of groups of each type — American professional, foreign or ethnic professional, semi-

[14] This figure, given on page 44 of the Rockefeller Report, is in line with known attendance data for the companies with the longest seasons. In Chapter IV of the present study, where we need a number in order to weigh audience survey results for different art forms, we use 750,000.

professional and amateur (Appendix Table III–F). However, the data are not clear-cut, because "professional dancing" is a difficult category to define. Very few dancers, no matter how serious and competent they may be, support themselves solely by dancing. This *Dance Magazine* listing is comparatively new, and long-established companies in the no man's land between professional and non-professional status may well have been including themselves in the listing only as they first became aware of the possibility of doing so.

More dependable is our information on professional dance activity in New York City from 1951–52 through 1964–65 (Appendix Table III–G). The figures were assembled laboriously from the *Dance Magazine* calendar of events and its other notices, and are described graphically in Figure III–3. The statistics show a pronounced, though highly erratic, growth rate. The irregularity of the growth path is largely a result of the small number of major groups in operation — a change in the number of performances by the New York City Ballet Company has a sizable impact on the total number of New York performances. The importance of foreign touring groups, most of which visit New York sporadically, also contributes to the variability of the year-to-year changes in total performances. This should not, however, be allowed to obscure the main point — that there has been an unmistakable trend toward more dance activity in New York City. In this period of 13 years the number of performances increased at an average rate of 4.2 per cent a year, or about 2.7 per cent a year per capita.

Even more impressive has been the growth in touring activity (see Appendix Table III–H). Between 1952 and 1964 the number of dance performances on tour and the total number of towns and villages visited have each quadrupled, and if we take the relatively poor 1964 showing to have been an aberration, this figure becomes significantly larger. Thus, with the development of the college and university circuit, the dance really seems to have expanded its audience in this country, and the number of areas outside our major cities in which dance performances are available has increased correspondingly. Here is a performing art in which there really seems to be a substantial rate of expansion.

Activity in the Theater: Broadway

As before, we will subdivide theatrical activity into three categories: Broadway, off-Broadway and the regional theater. Two important segments of the theater, both of which contribute immensely to total theater activity, will be omitted from the discussion: summer stock and "the road" (the commercial touring companies that emanate from Broadway).[15]

In the Broadway theater in 1963–64, 82 different productions were presented, of which 63 were newly mounted. There were 7,975 performances (Appendix Table III–I), and we estimate that attendance totaled 7 million.[16] Figures published in *Variety* show that the number of new productions was up slightly in the 1964–65 season (to 67), and that the total dollar gross was up substantially — about 29 per cent above the $39 million grossed in 1963–64.[17] It is impossible to judge whether this represents the beginning of a period of resurgence or is merely a temporary upswing, perhaps

[15] Moore (Chapter IX) gives some information on the first, and Poggi on the second. Poggi's comments on "the road" were summarized in Chapter II, above; Moore's estimates of audience size will be found at the end of this chapter.

[16] Attendance was estimated by dividing separate estimates of dollar grosses for straight shows and musicals by indexes of average ticket prices. More specifically: (1) An estimate of the total Broadway gross for the 1963–64 season of $39 million was taken from *Variety* (July 22, 1964). (2) Moore has estimated that for February of 1963 the gross for straight shows was 39 per cent of the total gross. (See his Appendix Table A–4.) Applying this ratio to the *Variety* estimate of total gross, we obtain an estimate of separate grosses for straight shows and musicals of $15.2 million and $23.8 million, respectively. (3) We obtained estimates of average ticket prices in 1963–64 of $4.89 for straight plays and $6.11 for musicals. This was done by calculating the average price of a seat at each show playing during the week ending February 5, 1964, on the basis of the data on capacity gross and number of seats published in *Variety* (February 5, 1964, p. 57), and then calculating over-all averages for straight shows and musicals. (4) We divided the estimated grosses by the estimated ticket prices to obtain estimated attendance figures of 3.1 million for straight shows and 3.9 million for musicals. (5) Summing these two figures, we obtained a total estimated attendance of 7 million.

[17] *Variety*, June 2, 1965, p. 62. The increase in total dollar gross is presumably the product of price changes and attendance increases. As we do not have a measure of average ticket price in 1964–65 which would be comparable with figures for earlier years, we are unable to prorate this increase between the price change and the attendance change in any precise way. However, if as a rule of thumb we assume that 5 per cent of the increase in grosses was attributable to ticket price increases, we can adjust our attendance estimate of about 7 million for 1963–64 upward by 24 per cent to arrive at a figure of approximately 8.7 million for 1964–65.

related to the presence of the New York World's Fair during 1964 and 1965.

Comments bemoaning the demise of the Broadway theater usually rely for their evidence on a misleading comparison between the present situation and that of the late 1920's, an extraordinary peak period beside which almost anything would compare unfavorably. For those interested in the precise dating of the peak, Chapter III of Poggi's study is required reading. Poggi points out that if one measures activity by number of playing weeks ("theater weeks" in his terminology) rather than by numbers of productions — and the number of playing weeks is certainly a more indicative measure, since the number of productions can be high if there were many failures that had to be replaced — the peak season turns out not to have been 1927 (as we would conclude from the number of productions) nor 1928–29 (as is implied by those who blame the "talkies" and the stock market for the decline), but *1925–1926*, a period far earlier than one would expect on the basis of other discussions. What seems to have happened is this: though the number of productions in theaters remained near the peak till the end of the decade, there was a definite decrease in total activity after 1925–26, meaning that plays must have tended to close more quickly. The steady fall of the new productions curve in Figure III–4 suggests that the notorious decline of the New York theater began as long ago as 1926, and that one must look earlier than 1928 or 1929 to find the reasons for its decline.

Nevertheless, the number of new productions has declined *over the postwar period* as well as since the late 1920's. Between 1947 and 1964 the average rate of decrease was 1.9 per cent per year, or about 3.15 per cent per year per capita — hardly a negligible rate of decline. On the other hand, it may surprise some readers that while average weekly attendance and total performances fluctuated considerably, they have not exhibited any real trend over the postwar period as a whole. Between 1947 and 1964 the average annual growth rate for number of performances was almost exactly zero, and attendance actually increased at an average rate of 0.8 per cent per year (compare Figure III–4). In these respects, then, the recent "decline" of the commercial theater seems less pronounced than is generally supposed. Moore, who seems to have

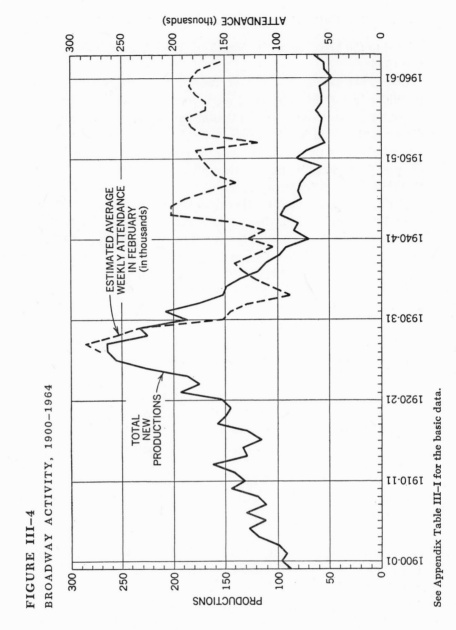

FIGURE III-4

BROADWAY ACTIVITY, 1900–1964

See Appendix Table III–I for the basic data.

56

been the first person to call attention to these contrasting patterns, has also pointed out the implication — that in recent years productions have typically run for longer periods.

Unfortunately, one cannot derive much comfort from these last observations. In per capita terms even attendance and number of performances have fallen over the postwar period (at rates of 0.4 per cent and 1.9 per cent a year). Moreover, both fell sharply between the 1960–61 season and 1963–64. Over this three year period the number of performances declined at an average annual rate of 5 per cent (or a per capita rate of 6.5 per cent). The decline in non-musical productions has been even more pronounced than the over-all decrease, and the plight of the drama in recent years seems to have become quite serious. In an article by Sam Zolotow in the *New York Times* of June 21, 1965 (some of whose figures have subsequently been questioned) it was reported that the dozen dramas produced during the 1964–65 season were all financial failures. During a year's run, "The Subject Was Roses," winner of the Drama Critics Award, the Pulitzer Prize and the Tony, never earned as much as $31,000 in any week in a house capable of grossing over $44,000 a week at capacity.

It is clear that there has been no boom on Broadway. On the contrary, since World War II Broadway has barely held its own in terms of attendance, despite rising population and incomes. And the number of new Broadway productions has been declining in absolute number, let alone relative to population growth, for a considerable period of time, though in this respect there has been a gradual but steady improvement since 1960–61.

Off-Broadway

Despite its recent difficulties, the off-Broadway theater has been a very important phenomenon, not only in terms of its artistic contribution but also in the magnitude of its activity.

In the last few years more new productions have been presented off-Broadway than on. In 1963–64, there were 86 new off-Broadway productions (excluding works in repertory), as compared with 63 on Broadway. There were over 9,000 off-Broadway performances, compared with 8,000 on Broadway. Of course, the typical off-Broadway theater is almost always far smaller than a Broadway house, and total attendance was therefore correspondingly lower. We estimate very roughly that total off-Broadway attendance during 1963–64 was somewhat under a million,[18] compared with 7 million for Broadway, so that even in this respect off-Broadway, though relatively small, is by no means negligible.

The sharp and, until the last few years, steady increase in off-Broadway activity since its inception at the end of the 1940's is quite remarkable. The growth in the number of productions from 1953–54 through 1964–65, plotted in Figure III–5 in aggregate terms, proceeded at an average per capita rate of 13 per cent per year, and the corresponding figure for performances is 18 per cent. There certainly has been a "boom" here, by anyone's definition.

It is equally clear, however, that there has been a decline in activity in recent years. The number of new productions reached its peak in the 1961–62 season, and attendance was at a maximum in 1963–64. Though the initial numerical drop was not as catastrophic as some of the newspaper stories implied,[19] the decline has continued, and its consequences may be more serious than the figures suggest. Several of the most experienced producers reduced their off-Broadway activity, and very few works by new playwrights were produced except for the notable season of new plays presented under the sponsorship of Barr, Wilder and Albee and those presented at the Theatre de Lys. Furthermore, one of the important off-Broadway theater owners has decided to convert his theatrical properties to other uses. At this point, then, the future of the off-

[18] Based on a producer's estimates of typical weekly attendance per show, divided by eight shows per week, and then multiplied by number of performances. It is encouraging to note that our estimate of off-Broadway attendance is very similar to one made by Moore (Chapter IX) using a totally different procedure. For the 1962–63 season he estimates off-Broadway attendance as 0.7 to 1.1 million on the basis of deflated dollar gross estimates.

[19] Several columnists in the *New York Times*, for instance, appear to have presented an unduly grim account of the decline. Lewis Funke mentioned what he termed "figures of production," which differed substantially from those given in the *Times'* "statistical reviews" for the same seasons. Funke listed 90 productions for 1961–62, 102 for 1962–63, and 80 for 1963–64, while the "statistical reviews" for the respective seasons gave the figures of 104, 87, and 100. (See *New York Times*, June 24, 1962, II, p. 2; June 30, 1963, II, p. 3; October 17, 1964, p. 18; December 20, 1964, II, p. 1; and June 28, 1964, p. 3.)

FIGURE III–5

OFF-BROADWAY ACTIVITY, 1954–1965

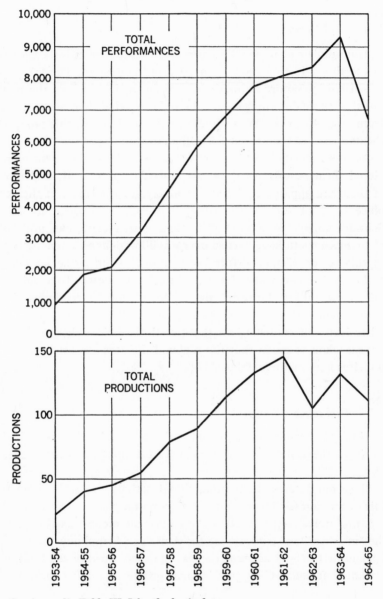

See Appendix Table III–J for the basic data.

Broadway theater is very much in question despite the protracted and dazzling rise which came to a halt so recently.

Regional Theaters

The number of regional theaters varies with the criteria used to define them. Listings run from 20 to 40 and more. The 20 theaters listed by Sandra Schmidt in a recent article include the most noted of these enterprises, and she indicates that their seasons run from 20 to 45 weeks. We estimate total attendance at this group of theaters to have been about 1.5 million in 1963–64.[20]

As was indicated in Chapter II, the rate of establishment of regional theaters rose continuously since World War II, and most of them are apparently doing reasonably good business at the box office — 14 of the 18 for which figures are provided by Miss Schmidt grossed over $90,000 in their most recent year, and one of them seems to have earned over a million dollars. Thus, activity in this sector of the performing arts does seem to be booming, and there is no evidence of any impending slowdown. To avoid any misunderstanding, however, the reader should be reminded that many regional theaters depend heavily on foundation grants and other forms of contribution; the growth in their audience should not be taken to mean that the regional theaters are profitable enterprises with no financial problems.

The Orchestras

Finally we come to that sector of the performing arts for which we have the fullest and most reliable information — the orchestras.

Since our interest is in professional activity, we will ignore in this discussion the large number of community orchestras and college and university orchestras. And since the orchestras classed in the "metropolitan" category by the American Symphony Orchestra League in 1963–64 account for less than one third of the total attendance at concerts by professional groups, we will concentrate

---

[20] This estimate was obtained by dividing box office income data by estimated ticket prices for the theaters in Miss Schmidt's sample, and then making an upward adjustment to allow for important theaters not included in her study.

FIGURE III-6

TRENDS IN ACTIVITY FOR THE "AVERAGE" MAJOR
ORCHESTRA, 1937–1964

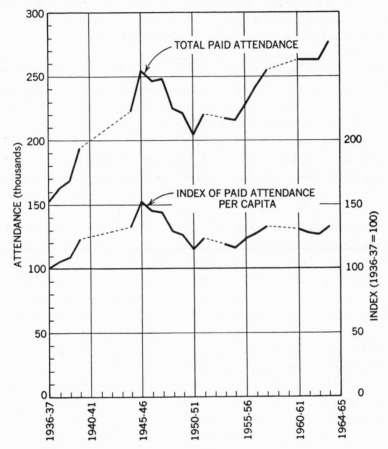

See Appendix Table III–K for the basic data.

on major orchestras. During the 1963–64 season the 25 majors
played to a total estimated audience of 6.6 million, in contrast
with an audience of perhaps 2 million attracted by the 29 metropolitan orchestras.[21]

The upper graph in Figure III–6 depicts the trends in paid at-

[21] The attendance figure for the majors is the League's estimate, taken from
the major orchestra compiled reports. Our estimate of 2 million for the metropolitans is based on the League's figure of total attendance of 1,630,314 for 22

tendance for an "average" major orchestra during the past quarter of a century. It shows that attendance has gone up over the period as a whole, and that the rise was especially sharp in the last two years. Data on number of concerts and length of season (Appendix Table III–K) exhibit very similar trends. Thus, it is not surprising that orchestra activities have often been cited as important evidence of the "cultural boom."

The general growth in orchestral activity has not extended to touring — the average number of tour concerts has been remarkably constant over the entire postwar period (Appendix Table III–K). Youth concerts (tabulated in the same appendix) provide a sharp contrast. From 7 in the late 1930's, the average number of youth concerts increased to 12 to 14 per season over the ten years 1945–1955, and then to 34 in the 1963–64 season —a record which indicates clearly the increased commitment of the major orchestras to education and audience building.

Paid attendance for the typical major orchestra increased 1.1 per cent per year on the average over the entire postwar period, 1947–1964 (Appendix Table III–L).[22] As the ups and downs in Figure III–6 testify, this average result encompasses years of slow growth, and even decline, as well as the much faster growth in more recent years. We do not know whether the history of the metropolitan and community orchestras has been similar, but the graph certainly shows that the growth of the major orchestras has not been uniform. A more general conclusion is that this over-all increase of 1.1 per cent per year again illustrates the danger of using raw figures that have not been appropriately adjusted. In fact, the increase in attendance has been slightly slower than the increase in population — the result being that during the postwar period paid attendance per capita has at best remained constant. The lower graph in Figure III–6, which represents paid orchestral attendance adjusted for the growth in population, shows this clearly

such orchestras reporting in 1963–64, adjusted to account for the other 7 metropolitans on the assumption that their admissions were slightly lower than the average for the 22 that reported.

[22] In this discussion annual rates are derived for our "basic" set of eleven major orchestras and are weighted by orchestra size in order to reveal industry trends. See Appendix III–2 for a more detailed description of our "basic" orchestras.

and indicates that there is no obvious upward trend despite the increase in attendance per capita since 1961 (a rise of about 2 per cent per year). Thus, if there is a boom in orchestral attendance it is a recent phenomenon, and it remains to be seen whether it is a temporary aberration or the beginning of a period of significant growth in public interest.

Geographic Patterns of Activity

For anyone trying to determine how performing arts activity is spread through the country, and whether or not it is becoming less concentrated in particular areas, the *Census of Business* is probably the best source of information. In this census, which is usually taken at four or five year intervals, data are collected for each establishment, an establishment being a single physical location at which business is conducted and therefore being not altogether synonymous with "company."

Not surprisingly, the *Census of Business* reveals an extreme concentration of performing arts establishments on the two coasts and, particulary, in the Middle Atlantic region. Of all such establishments that reported a payroll in 1963 — a measure which excludes most but not all amateur activity — between 22 and 46 per cent, depending on the particular art form examined, were in the Middle Atlantic region (comprising the states of New York, New Jersey and Pennsylvania). The proportion in the Pacific region (California, Oregon and Washington) ranged from 19 to 22 per cent of the total. These two populous regions together included about half the classical music establishments and well over half the theatrical enterprises in the United States (Appendix Table III–M).

Of course, the major geographic divisions differ widely in density of population. The Mountain region, for instance, is so thinly settled that it would naturally have fewer establishments of almost any kind than most other regions of the country. When numbers of performing arts establishments are reallocated on a per capita basis (Appendix Table III–N), inter-regional differences are considerably reduced, but they do not disappear by any means. While the Middle Atlantic and Pacific areas together then account for only about one third of the nation's musical establishments, they still provide the home for half the nation's theatrical groups. It turns out that the Pacific region has considerably more orchestral establishments per capita than does the Middle Atlantic, and the Mountain region runs the Middle Atlantic very close competition. But no region comes anywhere close in theatrical groups to the 32 per cent that are found in the Middle Atlantic area, even after recalculation on a per capita basis.

A count of enterprises, however, could give a distorted impression of the spread of artistic activity throughout the country if the enterprises in some areas were typically very small or performed very infrequently. A better measure is, therefore, total receipts. Although a region-by-region distribution of receipts is unavailable, we do have receipts figures for the New York metropolitan area which can be related to those for the country as a whole. In 1963 this area accounted for the following percentages of the United States total:[23]

	Classical Music Establishments	Theatrical Establishments
Total Receipts (excluding income from investments, gifts, grants, etc.)	39	56
Number of establishments with payroll	16	29

Thus New York *alone* accounted for nearly 40 per cent of all receipts from performances of classical music in the United States and for over half of all theatrical receipts — about twice the degree of concentration the distribution of enterprises suggests. New York still dominates the nation in receipts after these are put on a per capita basis. Per head of total population including all age groups, New York theatergoers spent $1.42 on concert tickets and $17.94 on theatrical admissions in 1963, compared with national

[23] The data are for the New York Standard Metropolitan Statistical Area, and are from the *Census of Business, 1963, Selected Services*, United States Summary, Table 2. We have included receipts for establishments with no paid employees as well as for those with some employees and a payroll because we wanted to approach the *Survey of Current Business* coverage as closely as possible. Actually, there is very little difference (well under 5 per cent) between the combined receipts figure and receipts for the latter group alone.

average expenditures of 29 cents for music and $1.88 for theater.[24]

No matter how one looks at it, centralization of performance along the two coasts seems to be an inescapable fact, despite a slight trend toward decentralization that has manifested itself between 1958 and 1963. Performing arts establishments were, in general, more widely dispersed at the end of the period than at the beginning, with the Mountain states the most persistent gainers on a per capita basis (Appendix Table III–N). The proportion of U. S. orchestral establishments in the Middle Atlantic region fell from 16 to 13 per cent in per capita terms. But, all told, there is surprisingly little difference between the regional distribution of establishments in 1958 and in 1963.[25]

The shaded portion of the accompanying map (Figure III–7) shows those states in which we know there was a decline in number of performing establishments between 1958 and 1963 — the only years for which the *Census of Business* provides comparable data. The map almost certainly understates the extent of the reduction because information is not available for a number of the states. There were some substantial percentage rises, but not all of

[24] Population figures are for total number of people (no age breakdown was available for New York) as of July 1, 1963, and are taken from U. S. Department of Commerce, *Current Population Reports*, Series P–25, New York from No. 298, U. S. from No. 297. Expenditure figures are from the 1963 *Census of Business* and are for establishments with payroll. Theater expenditures are for the category "Theatrical Presentations, Services" (no finer breakdown was available for New York). Music expenditures are for the category "Classical Music Groups" in the New York volume, and the sum of two categories, "Symphonies . . ." and "Other Classical Groups," for the United States.

[25] A rigorous test of the proposition that performing arts activities became more widely dispersed geographically between 1958 and 1963 confirmed that while there was some increase in the dispersion of performing activity, the movement was weak and not very significant. We ranked states according to their performing arts receipts in 1958 (separate rankings were made for classical music and theater presentations) and according to the percentage change in their receipts between 1958 and 1963, and then calculated Spearman rank correlation coefficients. We found a rank correlation of −.40 for the classical music group rankings and a correlation of −.28 for the theater rankings. This negative correlation means that performing arts activity did tend to grow most in states where the level of activity was initially small. The correlation coefficients are fairly low, however, and because of the smaller number of observations for the music group, we can be less confident that the −.40 coefficient really means something (it is not significantly different from zero at the 95 per cent confidence level) than that the −.28 coefficient is significant (it is significantly different from zero at the 95 per cent confidence level).

FIGURE III–7

GEOGRAPHIC DIVISIONS AND STATES WITH DECREASED NUMBER OF PERFORMING ESTABLISHMENTS, 1958–1963

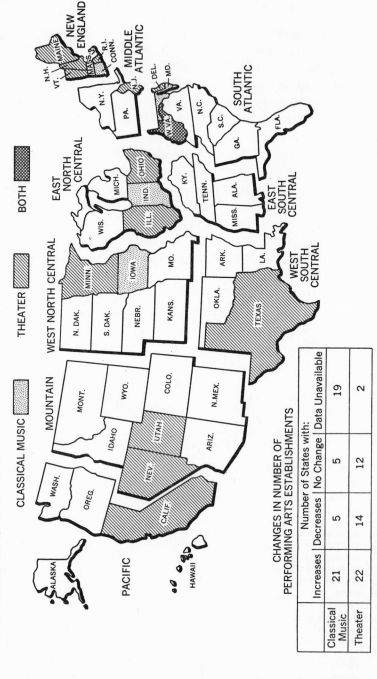

CLASSICAL MUSIC ▦   THEATER ▨   BOTH ▦

CHANGES IN NUMBER OF
PERFORMING ARTS ESTABLISHMENTS

	Number of States with:			
	Increases	Decreases	No Change	Data Unavailable
Classical Music	21	5	5	19
Theater	22	14	12	2

The data for this map are from *Census of Business, 1958 and 1963, Selected Services*, state volumes.

TABLE III–1

Estimated Attendance at Live Professional[a] Performances, 1963–64

Orchestras	
Major	6,600,000
Metropolitan	2,000,000
Theaters	
Broadway	7,000,000
Off-Broadway	900,000
Regional	1,500,000
Opera	1,700,000
Dance	750,000
Total	20,450,000

SOURCE: Attendance records of the main companies, estimates for others.

[a] "Professional" means that the performers are paid and are working at their vocation. The term is not meant to imply any standard of performance.

these represent very large absolute increases, since in several cases the initial number of establishments was small. The two business censuses also permit comparison of total receipts, but these data are more spotty and we have not reproduced them. Their story is similar: 4 of the 12 states for which there are musical receipts figures and 7 of the 38 states with theatrical receipts data showed a decline in receipts, and some of these declines exceeded 40 per cent. Again, as the map emphasizes, the "cultural boom" is shown to be an extremely spotty affair, with some levels of activity increasing, some declining, and the over-all result amounting at best to a small and patchy pattern of growth.

Table III–1 summarizes our attendance estimates for 1963–64 by art form. Attendance at all of the forms of live professional performance represented in this table totals about 20 million, or roughly one evening during the year at a live performance of some sort for every 10 persons in the United States. The total attendance figure increases to well above 35 million if we add to this Moore's estimates of 7.8 million attendance for "the road" and about 9–10 million for summer stock.[26] Note that "the road" and summer stock are estimated each to have an audience at least as large as that of the New York commercial theater, and together to have almost as large an audience as that for *all* other live professional performance.

Dividing total arts admissions expenditures ($433 million in 1963) by a wild guess as to average ticket price ($3.00), we get a crude estimate of total number of attendances of about 133 million, which is vastly larger than our 35–37 million total attendance estimate. The difference between the two figures is in large part a measure of the tremendous attendance at semi-professional and amateur performances.

The central question this chapter sought to answer was whether these total figures were growing, and if so, whether they were growing as impressively as the people who talk cultural explosion would have us believe. We have seen that the answers are mixed. Over-all real per capita expenditures on the performing arts have risen only very slightly, and when taken as a proportion of disposable consumer income, these expenditures have remained virtually constant.

Among art forms and by geographic region, the picture is again mixed. There has been real growth in the activity of the dance, the regional theater and the off-Broadway theater, though the expansion of the latter may have come to an abrupt end. The major orchestras and the operas have held their own and the commercial theater in New York has been declining, though not as rapidly as is sometimes alleged.

In sum, this analysis of the record entitles us to conclude neither that the nation has entered a great cultural renaissance nor that it is lost in an artistic wilderness. Rather, as is often the case, one is forced to a comparatively colorless in-between position — that over the course of the last decade and a half, the over-all progress of professional activity in the living arts has amounted to

[26] Moore's figures, presented in his Chapter IX, Table IX–1, are not strictly comparable with ours since his "road" figure is for 1962–63 and his figure for summer stock pertains to the summer of 1962. In that year Moore estimates total Broadway attendance to have been 7.6 million, as compared to our estimate of 7 million for 1963–64.

little more than a continuation of past trends. Yet, in some particular fields of activity, there is no doubt that an air of excitement and growth has manifested itself in the last few years and has given rise to a degree of enthusiasm that may presage much more for the future. Perhaps, then, interest in the living arts may be much greater tomorrow, but there is little in the trends that are so far apparent to suggest that a universal increase in attendance can be expected to occur spontaneously, with no great expenditure of effort by those who are now concerned with the arts.

CHAPTER IV

The Audience

THE relevance of an analysis of audience characteristics to a study of the economics of the performing arts may not be immediately apparent. After all, one might argue that, from a purely pecuniary point of view, the only pertinent factor is box office receipts, and not the identity of the individual who buys the tickets. If the box office does a sufficiently brisk business, a performing company's finances will be in satisfactory condition, no matter who purchases its tickets. Why, then, do we care about the makeup of the audience?

In fact, there are many reasons for our concern. First and perhaps most important, though not from an economic point of view, we care who attends because we believe participation in an audience contributes to the welfare of the individual. If the arts are a "good thing," we must concern ourselves with those who are deprived of the experience.

Second, we must know the characteristics of the audience if we are to evaluate ticket pricing and distribution policies. The complaints one hears about high ticket prices discouraging certain groups of people from attending can be evaluated ultimately only in terms of audience composition.

A third reason for concern with the nature of the audience is associated with the issue of government support. Both the desirability and the political feasibility of government support may depend, at least in part, on the composition of the audience.

Fourth, even if we consider the performing arts dispassionately as a product and nothing more, effective marketing policy requires that we know something about those who demand the commodity, just as an automobile manufacturer needs to know who buys his cars. This information helps the manufacturer to merchandise his product and to plan his physical facilities: by giving him a better idea of his future market potential, it enables him to reach more rational decisions on investment policy and on the size and direction of his future activities.

Audience data are necessary, too, for a variety of analytical purposes which arise out of the questions with which we shall deal in later chapters. We have already mentioned one such fundamental question, the effect of ticket prices on audience composition. Equally significant is the relationship between the make-up of the audience and the extent of the contributions which the performing organization can hope to receive. However, the present chapter is primarily descriptive; it is essentially a report on who attends performances today, not an examination of the influences which determine attendance or a discussion of the possible effects of policy changes on the nature of the audience.

Survey Methods

Most of this discussion is based on our own data — on figures compiled from direct questioning of a sizable sample of audiences throughout the country — because, by and large, detailed statistics on the audience for the performing arts throughout the country are unavailable. There do exist a number of earlier studies treating particular sectors of the arts, especially the theater. We shall refer to some of these later, but their structure and specialized character restrict the extent to which they can be related to our findings.[1]

Some explanation of the nature of our survey and the procedures used in conducting it is necessary.[2] Our general procedure involved

[1] For a few other audience survey results see: Moore; survey of the Tyrone Guthrie Theatre audience (Minneapolis); survey of the Charles Playhouse audience (Boston); *Playbill* surveys; survey of the Sadler's Wells audience (London); survey of the UCLA Theater Group audience (Los Angeles); survey of Baltimore Symphony subscribers; survey of the national FM radio audience by *Broadcasting* magazine and two Carnegie Hall surveys. Full references to all of these will be found in the Bibliography.

[2] Appendix IV–I gives a detailed description of our survey methods, including copies of the questionnaires, a list of organizations surveyed and a tabular summary of response rates.

the use of questionnaires which were distributed to a predetermined sample of the audience (usually 50 per cent) at performances of various kinds, by inserting copies into the programs. Recipients were requested to complete the forms and return them to us before they left the hall. The respondent was asked about his age, education, occupation, income, distance traveled to the performance, the amount he spent on tickets, transportation, restaurant and other expenses associated with his attendance, his frequency of attendance at other types of live performance, his inclination to contribute, and so on. Critical to the success of our survey was the truly extraordinary cooperation we received from the organizations involved. A request for permission to conduct a survey was rarely refused, and once it was granted we were usually offered all possible assistance.

The surveys were conducted from September of 1963 through March of 1965. In order to determine who should be surveyed, we first compiled a roster of professional organizations for each of the art forms, and then developed a sample which, though not random in a technical sense, gave us wide coverage in terms of art form, region and night of the week. In all, we surveyed 153 performances (88 theatrical, 30 orchestral, 8 operatic, 9 dance, 5 chamber music and 13 free open-air performances) and obtained 29,413 usable replies. The distribution of usable responses by art form corresponded closely to the distribution of estimated audience sizes (see Appendix Table IV–A). Only the Broadway audience was relatively under-represented by our survey, and this was deliberate, for we already had a great deal of information about the New York City audience from other sources.

As a direct consequence of the geographic distribution of the nation's professional performing organizations, most of our surveys took place in cities of substantial size. The geographic scope of our investigation is best indicated by the list in Appendix Table IV–B of cities in which surveys were conducted. The list includes Los Angeles, San Francisco, Portland (Oregon), Seattle, Oklahoma City, Dallas, Houston, Chicago, Ann Arbor, Minneapolis, Cleveland, Cincinnati, Pittsburgh, Atlanta, Abingdon (Virginia), Washington, Baltimore, Philadelphia, Brooklyn and Boston.

On the average, our response rate — the proportion of persons who returned the questionnaires they had been given — was almost exactly 50 per cent. This rate is high for a survey requesting information about income and other personal matters. Broadway and opera audiences produced the lowest rate of response — about 25 per cent in each case. While the low rate of return on Broadway is fairly easily accounted for by the special nature of its audience, which will be described later, our results for opera are less easily explained. The response rate is important not just because it affects the number of usable questionnaires, but also because it may have significant implications for the degree of bias in our results. For example, if bachelors were more willing than married men to provide the information requested, the tabulated results of the survey would report a proportion of married people in the audience much smaller than the true figure.

In order to determine whether, in fact, our results were seriously biased, we undertook several tests. In general, the results are reassuring. There were no marked differences in rates of return from various classes of seats; that is, holders of expensive tickets did not reply at a significantly different rate from holders of less expensive tickets. There was a very slight relationship between response rate and median income, with a small increase in rate of response associated with increases in the median income of audiences; and there was also a slight relationship between response rate and proportion of males in professional occupations — the higher the number of professionals, the higher the number of returns. However, most of these relations were very weak and, in technical terms, did not satisfy the requirements of "statistical significance" (see Appendix Table IV–C). From a more general point of view, what is most comforting is the great consistency of our results. The fact that they show the same pattern at performances differing widely in type and geographic location suggests very strongly that they are not the consequence of accidental biases imparted by the nature of particular audiences.

Characteristics of the Audience: Age

Before presenting the results of our survey we shall comment briefly on one important audience characteristic which, for a variety of reasons, we did not investigate directly — ethnic composition. Several persons experienced in the management of performing organizations emphasized that this is a crucial characteristic. As one commented, musical performances are often in trouble in a city without a large German, Italian or Jewish population. A Jewish holiday can decimate the audience even in a Midwestern city. Several managers noted that Negroes, on the other hand, attend infrequently, even where there is no overt discrimination, except perhaps when Negro themes and performers are presented. Of course, these are only casual observations, and we have no way of substantiating them — let alone any way of separating out the effect on attendance of ethnic characteristics *per se* from the effect of income.

What does our survey tell us about differences between the typical audience and the population as a whole? A succinct summary of our principal findings is given in Table IV–1, where we present a composite profile of the audiences at the various art forms, each weighted by estimated attendance in 1963–64, and a corresponding profile for the urban population of the United States as of 1960.

TABLE IV–1

Profile of the U. S. Performing Arts Audience, Compared with the Total Urban Population

	Performing Arts Audience[a]	Urban Population[b] (1960)
SEX		
Male	52.8%	48.4%
AGE		
Under 20	6.9%	37.1%
Over 60	9.0	13.1
Median Age	38 yrs.	30.3 yrs.
OCCUPATIONAL CATEGORY		
Males:		
Employed Persons:[c]		
Professional	63.0%	12.7%
Teachers	10.3	1.1

(*Continued on following page*)

TABLE IV–1 (continued)

	Performing Arts Audience[a]	Urban Population[b] (1960)
Managerial	21.4	12.6
Clerical and Sales	13.0	17.2
Blue Collar	2.6	57.5
Students[d]	13.9	
Females:		
Employed Persons:[e]		
Professional	63.2%	14.0%
Teachers	25.4	5.6
Managerial	7.2	3.9
Clerical	24.9	34.3
Sales	2.8	8.5
Blue Collar	1.9	39.3
Students[d]	15.1	
Housewives[d]	35.2	
EDUCATION		
Males (age 25 and over):		
Grade School and Less Than		
4 Yrs. High School	2.2%	56.6%
4 Yrs. High School	6.5	22.1
1–3 Yrs. College	12.8	9.8
4 Yrs. College	23.1	6.2
Graduate School	55.4	5.3
Median Category	Grad. work	2 yrs. h.s.
Females (age 25 and over):		
Grade School and Less Than		
4 Yrs. High School	2.8%	55.1%
4 Yrs. High School	15.3	28.9
1–3 Yrs. College	23.6	9.5
4 Yrs. College	26.7	4.5
Graduate School	31.6	2.0
Median Category	4 yrs. college	3 yrs. h.s.
INCOME		
Over $5,000	91.3%	64.8%
Over $15,000	39.5	5.4
Over $25,000	17.4	1.5
Median Income	$12,804	$6,166

TABLE IV–1 (continued)

	Performing Arts Audience[a]	Urban Population[b] (1960)
FREQUENCY OF ATTENDANCE Average Number of Performances Attended in Last 12 Months:	Number	
Theater	8.4	
Symphony	5.1	
Opera	1.7	
Dance	1.2	
Other Serious Music	2.2	

[a] Based on Twentieth Century Fund audience survey; 24,425 respondents. The figures given here are weighted averages of the results for individual art forms. The weights are based on estimated attendance in 1963–64 and are as follows (on a 100 point scale): Broadway = 38, off-Broadway = 5, regional repertory theater = 9, major orchestras = 38, opera = 6, dance = 4. See Appendix Tables IV–A and IV–J for the derivation of these weights and a comparison of this profile with the profile which uses numbers of questionnaires completed as implicit weights.

[b] Data from *U. S. Census of Population, 1960: Detailed Characteristics, U. S. Summary*, Tables 158, 173, 185, 194, 203, 224. A composite profile could have been built for just those cities where we conducted surveys, but some experimentation indicated that this refinement would have made little difference.

[c] The number of employed persons is the base for the following percentages. The percentage of teachers is a component of the "Professional" category.

[d] The base for these percentages is the total number of respondents.

The first thing these data suggest is that the performing arts audience, contrary to what many people believe, seems to be somewhat more heavily male than the population as a whole. Nearly 53 per cent of our respondents were male, whereas only a little more than 48 per cent of the urban population is male. However, this probably should not be taken too seriously. It may simply reflect a male prerogative: if a husband and wife were present and the questionnaire was contained in the wife's program, it is very possible that the husband would have filled it out.

Though the median age for the U.S. population is 8 years below that of the arts audience, this indicates simply that children do not often attend the theater although they are included in the Census. The rest of the data on age indicate that the audience is relatively

FIGURE IV–1

AGE DISTRIBUTION OF THE U. S. PERFORMING ARTS AUDIENCE AND OF THE TOTAL URBAN POPULATION

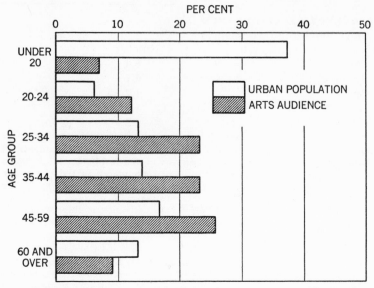

See Table IV–1 for the data on which this graph and others in this chapter are based.

young. This is shown most easily with the aid of Figure IV–1. In that graph, the dark bars represent the proportion of the audience in different age groups and the light bars the proportion of the urban population as a whole in these age groups. We see that relative to total population the arts audience is greatest in the interval 20 to 24 years of age. Twice as high a percentage of the arts audience (12.2 per cent) lies in that age interval as is the case for the total urban population (6.1 per cent). This ratio of 2.00 is what we call the *relative frequency;* it is equal to the proportion of the audience within a given category divided by the proportion of the total urban population in that same category. Calculation of such figures for each of our other age group categories (Appendix Table IV–D) shows very clearly that relative frequency declines steadily with age once we get beyond the interval under 20 years of age. These figures tell us that the audience at a typical performance is far younger than the urban population as a whole, and that the older the age group, the smaller is its relative representation in a typical audience. Consequently, older people (those over 60) are the scarcest members of the audience in relation to their numbers in the urban population of the United States. In a word, audiences are young. With the proportion of the nation's population in the younger age brackets growing rather rapidly, this fact may be quite significant.

Two alternative hypotheses can explain the relative youthfulness of the arts audience. If the same age patterns have always characterized the audience, it means that people attend performances when they are young and then gradually drop out of the audience as they grow older. They may become less interested, or attendance may become more difficult for them, or other interests and responsibilities may keep them from the theater. The second hypothesis is more sanguine. It may be that the performing arts are now attracting a younger audience than ever before. If young people did not attend very frequently in the past, this would account for the smaller number of older patrons today, the absentees never having developed an interest in live performance. If this is so and younger Americans are attending in far higher relative numbers than they did in the past, then we may be building a base for a great future expansion.

Unfortunately, because there is so little in the way of comparable survey results for earlier years, we cannot be sure which of these alternatives applies. The only source of historical data known to us is a series of *Playbill* surveys of the Broadway theater audience going back to 1955–56. These data (Appendix Table IV–E) show almost no change in the age composition of the audience and thus support the view that the audience is *not* growing younger.

Occupation, Education and Income

Turning next to the distribution of audiences by occupation, we see that roughly 15 per cent of all our respondents were students, and that among *employed males* only 2 to 3 per cent of the total audience included in the survey was composed of blue collar workers, as compared to a figure of nearly 60 per cent for the urban population as a whole. We conclude that the audience for the arts is made up preponderantly — indeed, almost entirely — of people from the white collar occupations. In the typical arts audience all of the white collar groups are over-represented (in comparison with the urban population), with two exceptions, clerical and sales persons. The degree of over-representation is by no means the same, however. Among males there are roughly nine times as many teachers in the audience as in the urban population of the United States, and nearly five times as many professionals of all sorts (see Figure IV–2 and Appendix Table IV–D). The arts' share of professionals is also much greater than their share of managerial personnel. In general, the very high proportion of members of the professions in the arts audience is characteristic of both sexes. However, the proportion of teachers in the audience is much higher for men than for women. As a possible explanation one might surmise that a high rate of theatergoing is characteristic of teachers at more advanced professional levels, and that female teachers are more heavily distributed in the lower grades of the schools.

Two numbers not shown on the table or the chart are of interest. Three per cent of our employed male respondents were themselves performing artists or performers and 5 per cent of the females were in this category. These proportions are surely significantly higher than those for the population as a whole, but the unavailability of related Census data prevents a direct comparison.

Next we turn to the educational attainment level of the audiences, reported in Table IV–1 and shown graphically in Figure IV–3. All of these results refer only to persons 25 years of age and over, in order to avoid the biases introduced by including persons who are still in school. We conclude that the audience is composed of *exceedingly* well-educated persons. Less than 3 per cent of the males and females did not graduate from high school, as compared to the more than 50 per cent of the U.S. urban population 25 years and over who did not do so. At the other end of the spectrum, over 55 per cent of the males attending performances did some work beyond college — an educational level attained by only 5 per cent of the urban population. Almost one third of the women in the audience did some graduate work, as compared with 2 per cent of the female urban population who did so. In Figure

FIGURE IV-2

OCCUPATIONAL DISTRIBUTION OF THE U. S.
PERFORMING ARTS AUDIENCE AND OF THE
TOTAL URBAN POPULATION

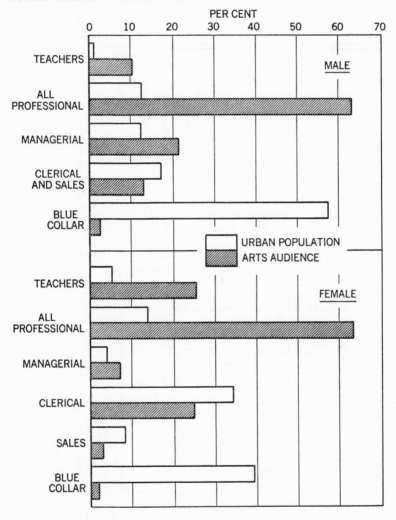

IV–3 the sharp decline in the length of the light bars as we move
from top to bottom means that the proportion of the urban population at each educational level falls very rapidly as the level of

FIGURE IV-3

EDUCATIONAL ATTAINMENT OF THE U. S.
PERFORMING ARTS AUDIENCE AND OF THE
TOTAL URBAN POPULATION

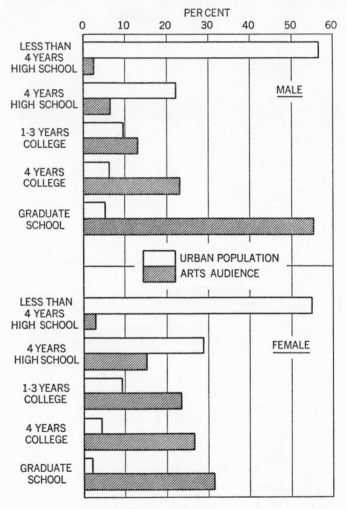

educational attainment increases; the reverse is true of the arts audience.[3]

[3] The only serious disagreement between the results of other surveys and our own relates to the quantitative effect of level of education. While other

FIGURE IV-4

INCOME DISTRIBUTION OF THE U. S.
PERFORMING ARTS AUDIENCE AND OF THE
TOTAL URBAN POPULATION

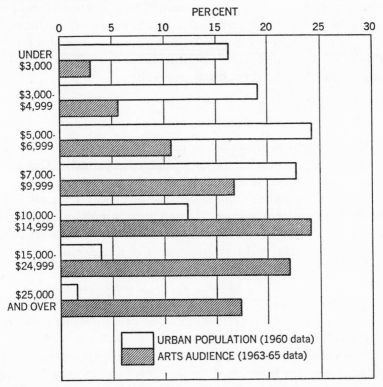

The last socio-economic characteristic reported in Table IV–1, audience income, is described in more detail in Figure IV–4. Once

investigations also report that the audience is very highly educated, their conclusions are not quite as extreme as ours. In general they show a plurality of persons with college degrees rather than a plurality of persons who have attended graduate school. Examples are the Baltimore Symphony audience survey: college graduate 41 per cent, graduate school 21 per cent; the UCLA Theater Group audience survey: college 55 per cent, post-graduate 13 per cent; the 1964 *Playbill* survey (males): college 50.3 per cent, graduate school 28 per cent; the Guthrie Theater audience survey (males): college graduate 25.4 per cent, post-graduate 45 per cent. These figures suggest that our questionnaires, perhaps because of their length, were answered more readily by highly educated persons. But, despite some disagreement on the magnitudes involved, all of these results confirm fully our qualitative conclusion: that the audience for the arts is *very* highly educated.

more the results are clear-cut and extreme. They show that the median family income among a typical arts audience is roughly *twice* as high as that for the total urban population. Forty per cent of our arts audience had incomes of $15,000 or more, and 17 per cent had incomes of $25,000 or more. The proportion of the arts audience in the category $15,000 to $24,999 is nearly six times as high as that of the urban population as a whole; and about 11½ times as large a proportion of the audience earned over $25,000 as is true of the urban population generally.[4]

Differences in Profiles among Art Forms

What variations in audience characteristics can be observed when the several art forms are examined separately? Our findings are summarized in Appendix Table IV–F.

The most remarkable finding is that audiences from art form to art form are *very* similar. They all show a median age in the middle 30's; over 60 per cent of the audience for each art form consists of people in the professions (and this finding holds for both sexes); all exhibit an extremely high level of education, with 50 per cent of the males having gone to graduate school and 50 per cent of the females having at least completed college; and there is a consistently high level of income, in no case involving a median under $11,000.

Some moderate differences by type of performance are worth pointing out. For instance, there are differences in attendance by sex among art forms. Women tend to predominate in the audiences of symphonies and the dance, whereas men constitute the majority attending the theater, opera and programs of chamber music. There is also a slight difference in age among the various audiences, with symphonies having a higher percentage of persons over 60. However, we must point out that symphonies, per-

[4] Since the income figures for the urban population of the United States are based on the 1960 Census, and income in 1963–1965, when our survey results were obtained, was undoubtedly somewhat higher, the true differential between the income of the audience and that of the general public is a bit smaller than our results suggest. Nevertheless, the differential is so substantial that a correction for this discrepancy would alter our numerical comparisons only slightly.

haps more than other art forms, frequently have special young people's concerts, none of which were surveyed by us. The existence of these concerts must surely bias our estimate of the age distribution of symphony audiences, because many of the young people who attend such special concerts might otherwise have been found in audiences attending other performances.

As to occupations, we find that a relatively small number of students attend ballet, opera and the theater, but that chamber music audiences are heavily peopled by students, teachers and professionals in general. While the number of blue collar workers is low for all art forms, the highest proportion is found at the opera. This finding could reflect the effect of the culture of Europe, where opera is a popular art form, and may, therefore, report what is primarily an immigrant group. On the other hand, because of the small number of operatic organizations surveyed, it may simply represent the influence of the New York City Opera with its low admission prices.

The number of blue collar workers remained consistently low throughout the survey. Their share of the total male audience reached 6 per cent in only 5 of our 35 theaters, never reached 5 per cent in any of the 12 major orchestras surveyed, constituted 5 per cent of the audience at the Brooklyn Opera, and 7 to 9 per cent of the audience for non-contemporary opera at the New York City Center. In dance, the proportion of blue collar workers was 7 per cent of the total at a performance of the Alvin Ailey Dance Theatre (a Negro company with a considerable Negro following), while in three of the other audiences surveyed there were no blue collar workers. In chamber music audiences the number of blue collar workers never reached 2 per cent.

Educational level was the most consistent element of all, with chamber music drawing the most highly educated audience — over 75 per cent of the males and 52 per cent of the females having attended graduate school.

Incomes also were consistently high, though theater patrons had an income about $1,500 higher, on the average, than members of the audiences of other art forms. In only 2 of the 35 theaters surveyed did median audience income fall below $10,000. The highest median income was not found on Broadway, but at a West

Coast theater, where it was over $18,000. A Broadway theater did, however, come in a close second. In 29 of our 35 theater audiences, median income was between $11,000 and $15,000. The top figure for any *single* performance was almost certainly higher, because these figures represent the average of all the surveys taken at each organization (there was more than one in almost every case). All 12 major orchestras surveyed showed median audience incomes above $10,000, the highest being $15,000. Again, the results varied little; 8 of the 12 exhibited median incomes between $11,000 and $13,000. Audience incomes at dance and chamber orchestra performances were slightly lower than those of audiences in general. Two of our five dance surveys reported median incomes under $10,000. Three of the five chamber group audiences were in this category, but one of the string quartet audiences had a median income over $16,500.

A distinct pattern emerges from the responses to questions about frequency of attendance. Theater is shown to be the most popular art form. With one exception, the patrons at *all* types of performance — members of dance, opera or chamber music audiences — indicated that the theater was the art form which they attended most frequently. Even in the exceptional case, the symphony, theater came in a very close second in frequency of attendance; that is to say, members of the symphony audience indicated that they attended theaters almost as frequently as they went to orchestral concerts.

The New York Audience

We also investigated the audience in New York City by itself. This enabled us to deal with a constant basic population, one drawn primarily from a single region. It also permitted us to make a direct comparison between off-Broadway and Broadway audiences, casting some light on differences between audiences for more and for less experimental theater groups. The detailed data for the New York audience are given in Appendix Table IV–G.

In general, the off-Broadway audience resembles more closely that of the other art forms than it does the audience of the Broadway theater. On Broadway the age distribution is concentrated in the middle range — comparatively few persons under 20 and over 60 attend. Similarly, the Broadway theater audience includes fewer members of the professions than does any of the other art forms in New York, both among males and females. But even there, professionals constitute more than 50 per cent of the audience. Broadway seems to draw a larger proportion of its audience from among the managerial group than do the other art forms. More housewives are represented in the Broadway surveys and, incidentally, in the orchestral audiences, than at other art forms. The educational level is slightly lower on Broadway, though even there it is remarkably high, with nearly 50 per cent of the men having done some post-graduate work. While income levels are highest in the orchestral audiences, they are not very much higher than median incomes of attendees on *and* off Broadway, and the off-Broadway incomes are surprisingly close to the incomes of the Broadway audience. In terms of socio-economic characteristics there is no evidence to support the notion that off-Broadway attracts a clientele significantly different from that of any other art form.

The only reasonably comparable series of historical data on audiences which we have been able to find applies to the New York theater. The *Playbill* survey of the audience for the commercial theater on Broadway has been conducted for more than a decade, though at some point there was a change in procedure so that the data are not strictly comparable.[5] What is most noteworthy in the figures for the six years that are usable (summarized in Appendix Table IV–E) is how little change in audience composition has occurred during the decade. One can only say that today's audience is about the same as that of a decade earlier except that it earns more money now than it did then. Even this is a misleading observation, for incomes per capita in the United States have also been rising.

[5] Unfortunately, we have been unable to locate a complete set of survey reports either from *Playbill* or any of the library theater collections. In fact, we have not seen the original report on the 1955–56 survey; our data for that year had to be reconstructed from figures quoted in an article by Max Frankel in the *New York Times* (May 20, 1956, Theater Section, p. 1).

Indeed, the figures suggest that in this respect, too, the theater audience has remained about the same in relation to the rest of the population.[6] Thus, if there was a "cultural boom" — a movement toward "mass culture" — there is little sign of it in the composition of the audience of the commercial theater.

Audiences Outside New York

Since our investigation of the audience outside New York City showed the same patterns reported for the New York audience, a few brief comments on the subject will suffice. Three differences stand out (see Appendix Table IV–H). We found a relatively high proportion of students in the theater audience outside New York, a group which was comparatively poorly represented on Broadway. About 21 per cent of the theater audience was composed of students, as compared with figures of 8 per cent for Broadway and 11 per cent for off-Broadway. The same general pattern was evident in the orchestral and operatic audiences. Members of the professions made up a slightly larger proportion of the audiences outside New York City, and, if anything, the educational level was higher in other parts of the country. Income, however, was slightly higher in New York, though the median outside New York City was over $11,000. Frequency of attendance was somewhat greater inside the city, but not nearly as much greater as one might have expected, given the availability of performance in New York. Indeed, attendance at chamber music concerts was, if anything, somewhat higher outside the city.

The main point, then, is that the general features of our over-all

[6] This can be seen as follows. The median income of the audience in 1959–60, the first year for which this statistic was calculated, was $9,650, whereas the figure for 1963 was $11,011. (As already indicated, the 1964 jump to $16,700 should probably be ascribed to the influx of World's Fair visitors and so is irrelevant for a calculation of the basic trend.) This represents a rise of a little over 14 per cent during the three year period. Now, according to the U. S. Census, median family income in the United States rose about 9.5 per cent over the same time interval. (*U. S. Census of Population, 1960: Occupational Characteristics,* Final Report PC[2]–7A.) Since incomes of people in the professions have recently been rising more rapidly than those of the population as a whole, one suspects that the incomes of members of the audience of the commercial theater were perhaps just about keeping up with the incomes of others in the same socio-economic classes.

audience profile are by no means due solely to the characteristics of New York audiences — as a matter of fact many of its most noteworthy elements are even more apparent outside New York City.

The British Audience

Because our results for the United States suggest that the audience of the performing arts comes from such a very limited segment of our population, it is important to ask whether this reflects a peculiarity of the American culture — whether in other countries, with other traditions and other educational systems, the audience represents a broader spectrum of the general public. For this reason (though we did not know our American results at the time) we decided that a few audience surveys should be undertaken in Great Britain, along with other kinds of research to be described later.

When we discussed our plans with British colleagues, they offered two general predictions: first, that our response rate would be lower in Great Britain than in the United States because the Englishman is particularly sensitive to any invasion of privacy; second, that the British audience would indeed be drawn from a wider group because British education places greater emphasis on the humanities and less on the sciences than does education in the United States. Both conjectures proved to be wrong.

We received a total of 2,295 usable responses at seven surveys conducted in the spring of 1965, two at the National Theatre (formerly the Old Vic), one at the Ballet Rambert, one at a performance of the New Philharmonia Orchestra, one at the London Philharmonic Orchestra, one at the London Symphony Orchestra, and one at an operatic performance at Sadler's Wells, all of them in London. Our over-all response rate was 50.3 per cent, almost exactly the same as the rate for the United States.

The similarity of the British and American results is remarkable. Table IV–2 provides data for Great Britain analogous to the figures given in Table IV–1 for the United States. The precise figures for British audiences should not be taken at face value. They are almost certainly distorted by the unrepresentative weighting of different art forms, a source of error for which we could not correct because of the small number of surveys conducted. Nevertheless, the results once again are very consistent from survey to survey and from art form to art form, and the orders of magnitude of the figures can, therefore, be accepted with considerable confidence. (The only noteworthy difference among British audiences by art form is that the British theater seems to draw its audience from a particularly exclusive group. In our sample the members of theater audiences have higher educational levels and higher incomes and are more frequently in the professional classification than the members of other audiences. The theater also has the highest frequency of attendance, with orchestral performances second.)

TABLE IV–2

Profile of the British Performing Arts Audience, Compared with the British Population

	Performing Arts Audience[a]	Population[b]
SEX		
Male	54.3%	47.6%
AGE		
Under 20	12.0%	30.8%
Over 60	5.5	16.6
Median Age	31 yrs.	. . .
OCCUPATIONAL CATEGORY		
Males:		
Employed Persons:[c]		
Professional	60.5%	7.5%
Teachers	11.7	
Managerial	19.1	10.9
Clerical and Sales	15.9	12.7
Blue Collar	4.6	68.9
Students[d]	17.8	
Females:		
Employed Persons:[c]		
Professional	54.8%	9.7%
Teachers	22.8	
Managerial	5.3	4.2
Clerical	35.0	25.9
Sales	1.9	11.4

TABLE IV–2 (continued)

	Performing Arts Audience[a]	Population[b]
Blue Collar	3.0	48.4
Students[d]	20.1	
Housewives[d]	16.2	
EDUCATION (school-leaving age)		
Males:		
14 or Under	7.1%	57.9%
15	6.9	20.2
16	13.5	9.3
17, 18, 19	24.0	5.9
20 and Over	48.5	3.7
Median Category	age 17–19	14 or under
Females:		
14 or Under	3.8%	59.7%
15	5.9	19.2
16	16.0	9.2
17, 18, 19	32.0	6.8
20 and Over	42.3	2.7
Median Category	age 17–19	14 or under
INCOME		
Over £499	96.1%	78%
Over £1,749	47.3	14.5
Over £2,500	29.2	5
Median Income	£1,676	£990 (est.)
FREQUENCY OF ATTENDANCE		
Average Number of Performances		
Attended in Last 12 Months:	Number	
Theater	10.2	
Symphony	7.9	
Opera	4.6	
Dance	1.7	
Other Serious Music	2.9	

[a] Based on Twentieth Century Fund audience survey; 2,295 responses. Implicit questionnaire weights. No attempt has been made to weight according to attendance at different art forms.

[b] Figures obtained from preliminary tables to be included in the 1961 Census volumes, from special tabulations made for us by the Central Statistical Office, and from the *Demographic Yearbook* of the United Nations.

[e] and [d] See notes to Table IV–1.

All of the special features which characterize the American audience are apparent in the data for Great Britain in Table IV–2. The same high proportion of professionals was found: among male members of the audience, 60.5 per cent were in the professional classification in Great Britain and 63 per cent in the United States; for females the figures are 55 per cent in Great Britain and 63 per cent in the United States. There was a somewhat larger representation of blue collar workers (4.6 per cent in Great Britain and 2.6 per cent in the United States), but this group still constituted an insignificant part of the total audience; and, as in the United States, the operatic audience contained an unusually high proportion of blue collar workers — nearly 8.5 per cent of the males were in that category. The educational level of the British audience was extraordinarily high, just as was true of the American audience. Since there is not so well organized a system of post-graduate education in Britain, a direct comparison with the American results is not possible, but the similarly high level of educational attainment is shown by the fact that nearly 50 per cent of the males in the British audience left school at age 20 or over, while this level of education is reached by only 3.7 per cent of the entire British male population. The British audience, like ours, seems also to be very well off financially. Its median income of nearly £1,700 is a little less than twice that of the general public. Incidentally, frequencies of attendance were slightly higher than those in the United States, but their ordering by art form was the same, with theater attended most frequently in both countries, orchestral performances second, opera third and dance last.

Some noteworthy differences were found between British and American audiences. While the American audience was young, the British audience was even younger. The proportion of the American audience aged 20–24 was twice as high as that in the general population, but the British audience proportion was about 3½ times as large (Appendix Table IV–D). And while the proportion of the American audience aged 60 and over was only 0.69 per cent of that in the general population, the comparable British audience ratio was less than half as large. Thus Englishmen are even more likely than Americans to attend when they are young, and even less likely to attend when they are older. An even higher proportion of British professionals seems to attend the arts than is true in the United States. In Great Britain the proportion of male professionals in the audience was over eight times that in the British population, whereas the corresponding American ratio was about five. There was also a somewhat higher proportion of clerical-sales occupations represented in the British audience.

The relation between income and attendance differs somewhat for the British and American audiences. Low income groups are about equally represented in the audiences of both countries. However, the British lower middle income groups are a little more heavily represented, while in our country it is the upper income groups who are relatively more frequent in their attendance. This, then, is about all that can be said in support of the view that the British audience represents a broader segment of the population than does that in the United States. Even here, however, the differences are small.[7]

The Frequent and Infrequent Attenders

It should be clear by now that "the common man" is fairly uncommon among those who attend live professional performances. But one may well ask whether he is much better represented among those who go only very occasionally. To some extent this turns out to be the case. A breakdown of our data by frequency of attendance shows that people who are well educated, well-to-do, and who are engaged in professional occupations constitute a particularly large proportion of those who attend performances frequently. Conversely, those who attend only rarely have lower incomes, are a bit more frequently blue collar workers and have a slightly lower level of educational attainment. This relationship, the fact that the infrequent attenders more closely approximate "average citizens," was first observed by Moore among the members of the Broadway audience.[8]

---

[7] The differences between the income distribution relationships in the two countries are shown more clearly in a fairly technical diagram (Appendix Figure IV–A). All of the relative frequency ratios for both countries are summarized in Appendix Table IV–D.

[8] See Moore, Chapter IV.

Our regional theater surveys show that among males who attended only once during the year of our survey 59 per cent were professionals, 8 per cent were blue collar workers, the median educational level was four years of college, and the audience's median family income was $9,500. But for those who attended at least 10 other performances that year the corresponding figures were 67 per cent professional, 3 per cent blue collar, the median educational level was graduate school and the median annual income was $14,500. Appendix Table IV–I, which presents these data in detail, shows that similar differences between frequent and infrequent attenders hold (but to a smaller degree) for the major orchestras and (much more markedly) for the Broadway theater. Moreover, with few exceptions, the relationship between these variables and frequency of attendance is perfectly regular. For example, among the audiences of the major orchestras one observes the following pattern:

Number of Performances Attended Per Year	1	2–5	6–10	over 10
Family Income	$9,500	$10,500	$12,500	$13,000

Curiously, students are generally better represented among the infrequent attenders, perhaps because their studies or their social activities keep them too busy or because they cannot afford to attend very often, though the availability of reduced rate student tickets may cast doubt on the latter explanation.

On the whole it appears that the group that attends performances very rarely is more similar to the general population in its composition than is the audience as a whole. Yet even the infrequent attender is no "common man." His (median) family income is over $9,500, his (median) educational level is at least four years of college, and, if he is an adult, there is a better than even chance that he is engaged in a professional occupation. This is still a highly select group.

The Size of the Arts Audience

The data we have just discussed permit us to estimate the size of the audience for the live performing arts. We saw in Chapter III that in 1963–64 approximately 20 million tickets were sold by

TABLE IV–3

Average Estimated Attendance, by Art Form

	Average Estimated Attendance[a]	Average Number of Times Attended in Last 12 Months[b]	Number of Individuals Attending (col. 1 ÷ col. 2)
	(1)	(2)	(3)
Broadway	7,000,000	4.5	1,555,556
Off-Broadway	900,000	6.5	138,462
Regional Theaters	1,500,000	4.5	333,333
Major Orchestras	6,600,000	4.8	1,375,000
Opera	1,700,000	2.6	653,846
Dance	750,000	2.3	326,087

[a] Taken from Table III–1.

[b] An average weighted inversely by frequency of attendance to correct for over-representation of frequent attenders in our sample (if individual A attends twice as often as B, he is twice as likely as B to be included in our sample). Specifically, let i represent any one of our frequency of attendance categories (once, 2–5, 6–10, over 10), let f_i be the average frequency of attendance for the given art form and category, and let N_i be the number of individuals in the category. Then our weighted average figure in column 2 is obtained from the expression $\Sigma f_i (N_i/f_i)/\Sigma (N_i/f_i)$ or, more simply, $\Sigma N_i/\Sigma (N_i/f_i)$.

Broadway, off-Broadway and regional theaters, major and metropolitan orchestras, opera groups and (American) professional dance companies. But since most of the individuals who purchased these tickets attended more than one performance, we can be sure that the number of different persons purchasing tickets was considerably under 20 million. Table IV–3 summarizes our estimates of the number of different individuals who attended each of these art forms.

How large, then, is the number of Americans attending some type of live performance? That number must be considerably smaller than the total of the corresponding figures for the individual art forms because of the overlap in the audiences for different types of performance. If 50 persons attend only theater, 50 attend only opera and 50 attend both, then the theater and opera will each have 100 patrons even though, in all, only 150 individuals are involved. An intense examination of our data has led us to estimate that (excluding "the road" and summer stock) the audience of the live professional performing arts in the United States totaled 2½ to 3 million persons in 1963–64. We suspect that this figure and the estimates for the individual art forms in Table IV–3 are a little low since, as any student of survey techniques would affirm, respondents tend, perhaps unconsciously, to exaggerate the frequency with which they attend performances. In addition, the frequency figures are inflated by our inability to remove from them attendance at non-professional performances. If average frequency of attendance is lower than our figures indicate, then the 20 million tickets sold in 1963–64 must have been distributed among a correspondingly larger group of people. Nevertheless, it seems to us quite unlikely that the audience comprises more than 5 million individuals, a figure which would be 4 per cent of all residents of this country 18 years of age and older.

In this chapter we have tried to provide an extensive profile of the audience of the live professional performing arts in the United States. Two of its features are especially significant.

The first is the remarkable consistency of the composition of audiences from art form to art form, from city to city and from one performance to another.

Second, the audience is drawn from an extremely narrow segment of the American population. In the main, it consists of persons who are extraordinarily well educated, whose incomes are very high, who are predominantly in the professions, and who are in their late youth or early middle age. This finding has important implications for the nature of whatever growth has occurred in audience demand for the arts. Even if there has been a significant rise in the size of audiences in recent years, it has certainly not yet encompassed the general public. If the sociological base of the audience has in fact expanded, it must surely have been incredibly narrow before the boom got under way. This result indicates also, in a larger sense, that attempts to reach a wider and more representative audience, to interest the less educated or the less affluent, have so far had limited effects.

Yet there is also evidence that something can be done to broaden the audience base. As will be shown later, when professional performances are given free of charge or with carefully set low prices, the audience is drawn from a consistently wider cross section of the population. But even here there are no easy and overwhelming victories — in these audiences the number of blue collar workers is almost always under 10 per cent and the number of professionals is always well over 50 per cent; over 50 per cent of the males have completed college; and median incomes are almost always well over $9,000. Obviously, much still remains to be done before the professional performing arts can truly be said to belong to the people.

CHAPTER V

The Performer, the Composer,
the Playwright
and the Choreographer

*The personal satisfaction of a job well done is the highest
reward in a profession which offers little financially.
I enjoy being a musician — I wouldn't discourage my
children from becoming musicians — but I wouldn't
want my daughter to marry one.*
—COMMENT BY AN ORCHESTRAL MUSICIAN

THE POVERTY of the artist is so much a commonplace that it
has become difficult to impart substance to it. The most anguished
protests, the most appalling facts seem only to elicit apathy from
a public whose responses have been dulled by the stereotyped and
somewhat romantic notion of the engarreted and starving artist.

We shall see in this chapter that there is little romance in the
economic circumstances of the performer. He is not quite as poor
as might have been imagined, but he is likely to be harried by constant economic pressures and by the need for incessant work, often
in occupations far removed from his profession, in order to eke out
a living for himself and his family.

Voices of Protest

In recent years a rising chorus has responded to inquiries by the
unions, independent investigators and Congressional hearings to

99

the effect that the circumstances of the individual who seeks to earn a livelihood in any of the performing arts are deplorable. Apparently the performer, who traditionally is supposed to live from hand to mouth, no longer is content to do so — today he wants to live "like everybody else" and hopes to be paid accordingly. The most comprehensive source of commentary is the set of hearings conducted late in 1961 and early in 1962 by a subcommittee of Congress under the chairmanship of Representative Frank Thompson, Jr., of New Jersey. The report of these hearings, upon which we shall rely heavily as the chapter proceeds, provides many striking and sometimes moving pieces of testimony which summarize the mounting protests against the unhappy state of the performer in America. We begin with only one quotation from this source, in which Mr. Paul Hume, music critic for the *Washington Post,* advises young people considering their future vocation, "Do not go into music as a career unless you are prepared to sacrifice any thought you may have of making a decent living at it. . . . unless you are ready and able to take on two, three, or four jobs in order to earn a living sufficient to let you marry and raise a family . . ."[1] Even the Department of Labor's conservative career guidance publication warns, "Many performers . . . supplement their incomes by teaching, and thousands of others have to work much of the time in other occupations. . . . the difficulty of earning a living as a performer is one of the facts young people should bear in mind in considering an artistic career."[2]

A 1961 survey of musicians in the 26 major orchestras elicited comments such as the following:

> Playing as much as I can I play about 26 weeks a year and counting odd jobs too, I make about $2,500 per annum in music. In eight years of playing I've hardly recovered the cost of my education and instrument.
>
> . . . music and house painting — quite a combination for a God given gift of music talent. But believe me, if it wasn't for painting I, my wife and child, could not make it.
>
> Full time work (by which I mean morning, noon and night) in symphony playing, jobbing, and teaching every afternoon and all day Saturday nets me per year less than $3,000!

[1] House Hearings, II, p. 473.

[2] "Employment Outlook in the Performing Arts," p. 214.

My pay from the symphony orchestra is that of a first chair artist and yet with the season only 24 weeks I still earn only about $3,000 a year. By holding down a second full time job at Sears, Roebuck and Company I find my schedule as high as 60 and 65 hours a week. This is too much for me to keep up many years. I must commend Sears, Roebuck and Company at this point. . . . They have put up with absences of mine due to performances of the orchestra many times. Even when it worked a hardship on my fellow salesmen (extra hours, etc.).[3]

The status of the actor is even more precarious. Joseph Papp, producer of New York's Shakespeare Festival, characterized it by commenting that "Banks and landlords consider him a credit risk without visible means of support."[4] And, as already noted, the actors themselves are by no means content with their lot. The slightest expression of interest elicits a flood of feeling which is well illustrated by this comment we received from an off-Broadway actor: "One works about 18 hours a day at one's work or simply at getting work. One conceals from most people that one is an actor because most people . . . want to shun you, to exploit you . . . or to romanticize about your heavenly existence."

Broad Occupational Comparisons

The United States Census is the most comprehensive source of broad occupational comparisons. The 1960 Census has provided a report on a large number of "professional-technical" occupations, giving for each the level of income received *from all sources*. From these figures we can learn whether the typical actor, dancer or composer is poor or well off, but not whether his earnings *as an artist* are high or low.

In Table V–1 the 49 professional-technical occupations included in the Census report are arranged in decreasing order of median[5]

[3] American Federation of Musicians, "The Symphony Musician Speaks Out."

[4] House Hearings, II, p. 111.

[5] A median is a measure which serves as a substitute for an ordinary arithmetic average. Given a series of numbers, arranged in order of size, the median is that number which divides the series in half: 50 per cent of the numbers are above the median and 50 per cent below it. Statisticians usually consider the median to be a more representative figure than the arithmetic average, because the latter is heavily influenced by a few far out numbers. For example, the arithmetic average of the five numbers 1, 2, 3, 4 and 90 is 20, but the median is 3.

TABLE V–1

Professional-Technical Occupations Ranked According to Median Income in 1959

	Males	
Rank	Occupational Group	Median Income (from all sources)
1	Physicians and Surgeons	$15,013
2	Dentists	12,392
3	Lawyers and Judges	11,261
4	Airplane Pilots and Navigators	10,514
5	Osteopaths	10,279
6	Veterinarians	9,178
7	Aeronautical Engineers	9,127
8	Chemical Engineers	8,948
9	Architects	8,868
10	Optometrists	8,772
11	Electrical Engineers	8,710
12	Metallurgical Engineers	8,639
13	Miscellaneous Engineers (excl. mining)	8,522
14	Mechanical Engineers	8,494
15	Natural Scientists (n.e.c.)	7,965
16	Social Scientists	7,868
17	Industrial Engineers	7,790
18	Civil Engineers	7,773
19	Personnel & Labor Relations Workers	7,669
20	College Presidents, Professors & Instructors	7,510
21	Pharmacists	7,385
22	Chemists	7,245
23	Managers, Officials, Proprietors (except farm)	6,838
	(All Men in Professional Occupations)	(6,778)
24	Accountants and Auditors	6,758
25	AUTHORS	6,745
26	Chiropractors	6,463
27	ARTISTS & ART TEACHERS	6,333
28	Farm and Home Management Advisers	6,159
29	Radio Operators	5,975
30	Funeral Directors & Embalmers	5,967
31	Draftsmen	5,794
32	Teachers (elementary & high school)	5,709
33	Photographers	5,692
34	ACTORS	5,640

TABLE V–1 (continued)

	Males	
Rank	Occupational Group	Median Income (from all sources)
35	Therapists & Healers (n.e.c.)	5,591
36	Sports Instructors & Officials	5,519
37	Social & Welfare Workers (excl. group)	5,481
38	Athletes	5,394
	(Craftsmen, Foremen & Kindred Workers)	(5,318)
	(Sales Workers)	(5,119)
	(Service Workers (excl. private household))	(5,023)
	(Clerical & Kindred Workers)	(4,916)
39	Foresters & Conservationists	4,873
40	MUSICIANS & MUSIC TEACHERS	4,757
	(All Males 14 Years of Age and Over in Experienced Civilian Labor Force)	(4,720)
41	Technicians, Medical & Dental	4,614
42	Librarians	4,592
43	Surveyors	4,486
44	Nurses, Professional	4,400
45	Recreation and Group Workers	4,395
	(Operatives & Kindred Workers)	(4,373)
46	Clergymen	4,151
47	Entertainers	3,674
48	DANCERS & DANCING TEACHERS	3,483
49	Religious Workers	3,241
	(Labor, excl. farm & mine)	(3,036)
	(Farmers & Farm Managers)	(2,302)
	(Private Household Workers)	(1,293)
	(Farm Laborers & Foremen)	(1,181)

	Females	
Rank	Occupational Group	Median Income (from all sources)
1	Physicians & Surgeons	$5,989
2	Chemists	5,045
3	Lawyers & Judges	5,024
4	College Presidents, Professors & Instructors	5,013
5	Natural Scientists (n.e.c.)	4,919
6	Farm & Home Management Advisers	4,907
7	Personnel & Labor Relations Workers	4,574

(*Continued on following page*)

TABLE V–1 (continued)

	Females	
Rank	Occupational Group	Median Income (from all sources)
8	Social Scientists	4,541
9	Social & Welfare Workers (except group)	4,444
10	Draftsmen	4,307
11	Sports Instructors & Officials	4,244
12	Accountants & Auditors	4,242
13	Teachers (elementary & high school)	4,095
14	Pharmacists	4,086
15	Therapists & Healers (n.e.c.)	3,955
16	Librarians	3,864
17	ARTISTS & ART TEACHERS	3,743
	(All Women in Professional Occupations)	(3,711)
18	ACTRESSES	*3,464*
	(Managers, Officials, Proprietors (excl. farm))	(3,435)
19	Technicians, Medical & Dental	3,258
20	Nurses, Professional	3,239
21	AUTHORS	*3,189*
	(Clerical & Kindred Workers)	(3,064)
22	Dieticians & Nutritionists	3,022
	(Craftsmen, Foremen & Kindred Workers)	(2,961)
23	Entertainers	2,666
24	Photographers	2,628
	(Operative & Kindred Workers)	(2,384)
	(All Females 14 Years of Age and Over in Experienced Civilian Labor Force)	(2,333)
25	Recreation & Group Workers	2,320
	(Labor (excl. farm & mine))	(1,969)
26	Clergymen	1,927
27	Religious Workers	1,700
28	DANCERS & DANCING TEACHERS	*1,680*
	(Sales Workers)	(1,619)
29	MUSICIANS & MUSIC TEACHERS	*1,566*
	(Service Workers (excl. private household))	(1,487)
	(Private Household Workers)	(758)

SOURCE: *U. S. Census of Population, 1960: Subject Reports, Occupational Characteristics,* Final Report PC (2)–7A, Table 25. Ranked occupations are all from the broad professional-technical category. The medians for the main occupational categories are included in parentheses, but have not been assigned rank numbers.

n.e.c.: not elsewhere classified.

income in 1959. The table is divided into two parts, the first pertaining to males and the second to females; for reference purposes it also includes the earnings of a number of non-professional occupations. To simplify the discussion, most of the comments which follow refer to the male section of the table, but in general they apply with equal force to the earnings of women in the arts.

There are five occupations in the table which directly include *any* of the arts: authors, artists and art teachers, actors, musicians and music teachers, and dancers and dancing teachers. None of these deals precisely with a category of individuals with whom this study is concerned. The figures on musicians, for instance, also include music teachers' incomes and are, in any event, not confined to performers of classical music. Yet these figures are of interest, and they are the most relevant data provided by governmental sources. It will be noted that all five of the arts occupations appear in the lower half of the list of 49 professional-technical occupations when these are ranked according to income. Moreover, all three classes of performer — actors, musicians (and music teachers), dancers (and dancing teachers) — fall well within the lowest third of the professions. In this listing of 49 professions, authors are twenty-fifth, artists and art teachers twenty-seventh, actors thirty-fourth, musicians and music teachers fortieth, and dancers and dancing teachers forty-eighth. The only profession more poorly remunerated than the dance is that of religious worker, whose median annual income was some $240 below the $3,483 received in 1959 by dancers and dancing teachers.

Comparing performers' incomes with those of non-professional workers, we see that only actors did better than craftsmen or clerical and sales workers, that musicians received just about the median income for all workers in the experienced labor force, and that dancers did only a few hundred dollars better than unskilled non-farm laborers.

The circumstances of women are very similar. Among the 29 professional-technical occupations for females, all of the arts occupations are again in the bottom half of the income list. Dancers and musicians, respectively, occupy the last two places on the list. They receive significantly less than female laborers and barely more than female service workers.

In every arts occupation, the proportion of persons receiving less than $3,000 in 1959 was larger than that for all persons in professional-technical occupations. (See Appendix Table V–A.) While only 11 per cent of all males in the professions received less than $3,000, 23 per cent of all male actors, 30 per cent of all male musicians and 40 per cent of all male dancers had an income lower than this amount. The relative figures for females (whose absolute incomes are generally lower) follow the same pattern.

While all arts professions include large proportions of persons whose earnings are relatively low, they also include a perhaps surprisingly substantial segment of well-paid individuals. For males, 9 per cent of *all* persons in professional-technical occupations had an income of $15,000 or more in 1959. But 10 per cent of all actors, 8 per cent of all authors and 6 per cent of all artists and art teachers also did this well. Among women this pattern is even more striking. While a negligible proportion (nearly zero per cent!) of all professional women received at least $15,000, this income level was attained by 9 per cent of all actresses, 6 per cent of all authors and 1 per cent of artists and art teachers. Clearly, while acting pays many actors very badly, some of them are also very well remunerated.

Thus, there is another side to the coin: not all performers are terribly poor. True, the typical performer earns far less than most individuals with other types of professional training and experience — a point which will become clearer when we discuss the cost of performer education later in this chapter. Nevertheless, it is also true that his income is sometimes as high as that of many Americans. The median income of an actor, though lower than a school teacher's, is higher than that of a sports instructor or a social worker. At the median a musician receives more than the typical adult male in the labor force, and more than a librarian, a surveyor or a nurse. A woman artist or art teacher receives more than the median for all professional women, and a representative actress receives very nearly this amount.[6] And, as we shall see, at least in

[6] The use of the present tense in this paragraph assumes that the general tenor of the 1959 figures (which are the most recent available) still holds today. Except for some of the most affluent orchestras, the Metropolitan Opera and a few other particularly fortunate organizations, we have no reason to question this assumption.

recent years there has developed a relatively comfortable upper echelon of performers — the actors in successful Broadway plays, the musicians in the large-budget major orchestras and leading singers at the Metropolitan Opera. Except for the stars, the incomes of this small but significant segment of the profession are by no means enormous, but they do represent respectable middle class achievement. The improvement has also filtered down to orchestral musicians in general, but as late as the 1964–65 season the average salary of performers in the 25 major orchestras was reported to have gone up to only $5,267 for a season of 30.4 weeks. This represents a 20 per cent rise from their earnings two years earlier.[7]

Before turning to a more detailed examination of the circumstances of the performer, let us consider briefly the economic position of those who do the basic creative work — the composers, the authors and the choreographers.

The Composer

There is only one real source of data on the state of composers' earnings — a survey conducted in the spring of 1961 by the American Music Center (an organization devoted to the welfare of American composers), and reported by its general manager, Lester Trimble.[8] A questionnaire was sent by this organization to 1,171 composers (it is not clear how the sample was selected), of whom 430 replied. The composers were asked about the income they received during the preceding twelve months for original works from music publishers, in commissions for concert, ballet or opera, and from performing rights. They were also asked about other sources of income. Since, as the results confirmed, it is often difficult to define and identify a *professional* composer, one may raise questions about the sample, but the results are suggestive in any event.

The basic conclusion to be drawn from the findings of the survey is that one cannot expect to earn a living by composing serious music and doing nothing else. Of the 430 respondents, only 16 earned $5,000 or more during the year from serious composition.

[7] See Ford Foundation press release, Oct. 22, 1965.

[8] House Hearings, II, pp. 106–9.

Half the composers earned an annual total of less than $99, and 145 reported no income at all from this source. This does not mean, of course, that most composers starve. Rather, it implies that they must combine composing with other occupations. Of the respondents to the survey, 343 listed teaching as the mainstay of their income, while 92 reported that a substantial proportion of their income was derived from performance. Indeed, at a meeting of a small number of composers which was attended by the authors of this book, it was asserted that a very large proportion of reputable composers (90 to 95 per cent) teach at universities, and that their incomes are now moderately respectable, certainly far more so than in earlier decades.

Some composers seem to feel that the need to work at other occupations imposes on them a serious and stultifying burden. Though some of them enjoy teaching and consider it a desirable way to achieve true artistic freedom, others regard it as a distraction from their primary activity. They may be right, but it should be pointed out that in this respect their circumstances differ, if at all, only in degree from the situation of the nation's leading scientists and scholars, most of whom also teach in colleges and universities; they are as much "part-time researchers" as the writers of music are "part-time composers." The circumstances of the two groups are comparable in yet another respect. If one were to ask college teachers in general to report on the income they receive from their scholarly writings, there is no doubt that they would show earnings quite similar to those derived from serious musical composition.

If many composers are college professors and their incomes are no worse than those of many of their academic colleagues, can we conclude that the economic position of the composer is in general quite satisfactory? This is, in fact, not so. The composer still encounters financial problems of another sort which seriously inhibit his work. First, he is plagued by heavy occupational expenses — notably the cost of copying scores (which can be considerable for an orchestral work) and of travel to sometimes distant places where the composer's works are given what may be their only performance.

Unless he has the opportunity to hear his work played, it is difficult for the composer to improve it and to profit from his experience when he writes a future piece. But performance is extremely expensive. The American Music Center survey, which included a question on this topic, reported that 97 of the 421 respondents to this question at some point had had to make a contribution to performers for the rehearsal or performance of their works. We shall see later in this book that performing organizations find it very expensive to play contemporary works. In part this is because their relative unpopularity cuts down on box office receipts, but it is also a consequence of the higher rehearsal overhead cost which is apparently incurred in preparing adequately a modern work that may be performed only a few times. Items of the standard repertoire, which orchestras know well, need not always be rehearsed with the thoroughness necessary for an unfamiliar piece of an unfamiliar genre. In recent years there has been a marked increase in the performance of contemporary works despite the expense; even the more conservative organizations play some of the "safer" modern pieces, and more experimental works are often performed with foundation support. However, because union regulations prohibit the non-commercial recording of a live presentation, the composer is prevented from making a record of what may well be the only performance of his composition.[9]

For the same reason that he cannot easily get to hear his own work, the composer has difficulty in finding out what many of his contemporaries are writing. The publication of music is expensive and there exists no journal that makes widely available a variety of current works. Financial problems, therefore, tend to isolate the composer from his colleagues and severely limit his opportunities to hear what he has written. Thus, even if poverty is not the composer's most pressing problem, the economic circumstances under which he writes are by no means easy and often impose serious handicaps on his work.

The Playwright

The economic circumstances of the playwright are very similar to those of the composer. We have three sources of information about the playwright — financial reports for a sample of dramatic

---

[9] This may seem a harsh measure, but the union can point to cases where copies of a composer's pressing somehow appeared on the counters of record shops with no arrangements having been made to remunerate the performers.

productions assembled by the League of New York Theatres (un-published), a survey conducted by Thomas B. Moore and one by William J. Lord, who produced a very thorough study of the sub-ject with the assistance of the Author's League of America.

The League of New York Theatres obtained summary financial statements for 30 straight plays produced between 1961 and 1965. We have no way of evaluating the representativeness of this study, but its implications about playwrights' earnings are interesting. The statements show that typically the author of a drama earns more than the producer or the investors. Frequently the author's royalties were more than ten times the producer's reported income. More-over, even when new plays lost money, some authors did well. While 8 of the authors whose plays were financial failures received less than $6,000 for their efforts, 16 of them received $20,000 or more, at least some of this from movie rights.

Moore surveyed the 47 authors who had at least two presentations produced on Broadway between 1959 and 1963; 33 responded. His survey, therefore, describes a small, unusually successful group of the nation's playwrights. According to Moore, the minimum Broad-way contract specifies that a dramatist be paid 5 per cent of the first $5,000 in box office receipts for a straight play, 7½ per cent of the next $2,000 and 10 per cent of everything above that. The minimum for musicals is slightly higher, and some successful playwrights simply receive a flat 10 per cent of the gross. For an "average play" produced on Broadway, Moore calculates that the author's direct compensation might be about $30,000. In addition, subsidiary income such as movie rights would average more than $15,000, and there would very likely be some income from tours. Since the average playwrights in Moore's very restricted group had a play produced every 2½ years, this corresponds to an annual income of about $20,000 for this top group in the profession. Never-theless, Moore tells us that in his sample of "active dramatists" only about one fourth received as much as 90 per cent of their income from playwriting, and another 25 per cent received less than half their income from this source.[10]

Lord's survey covered a much broader group of writers. He

[10] Moore, Chapter II.

mailed 2,250 questionnaires to all 1,719 active members of the Author's League and to a little more than half (531) of its inactive membership. His usable response rate was 18 per cent. We shall report only his data on the earnings of the playwright, defined as "a writer earning any income from his plays between 1953–1957" (the period of the survey).

Lord found a fairly steady rise in the median personal income of his sample of playwrights, from $6,800 in 1953 to $7,500 in 1954, $8,000 in 1955, $8,550 in 1956 and $10,440 in 1957. This does not necessarily mean that the circmstances of the profession as a whole have been improving, for these individuals were five years older at the end of the period than at the beginning. Therefore, the rise may reflect, at least in part, the normal increase in income that can be expected to accompany added experience and growing reputation. The fact that American incomes in general increased about 25 per cent over this period also warns us against too sanguine an interpretation. Lord's data show further that playwrights, while not wealthy, are moderately comfortable in terms of family income. In 1957, 30 per cent of the sample received more than $5,000 but less than $15,000, and of the remaining 40 per cent who received at least $15,000, more than half (20 per cent of the total) had incomes of $25,000 and over.[11] Only a very small proportion of this income was derived from stage plays. Indeed, even though 70 per cent of the playwrights responding reported some income from stage plays during the five year period, the average playwright received only about 6 per cent of his income from this source. (See Table V–2.) Some 60 per cent of the earnings from stage plays came from the original play, the remainder from subsidiary rights, including over 20 per cent from motion picture rights but less than 4 per cent from television — presumably because a drama written for the stage is more readily adaptable to the screen than to the medium of television. Writing for films and television provided a far higher return than writing for the stage, but the largest single component of the playwright's income was made up of earnings

[11] Lord, p. 194. In interpreting these statistics it should be remembered that they pertain to 1957 and are, therefore, six or seven years earlier than most of the figures in this chapter. Incomes in general have, of course, risen since then, and the corresponding current figures should be quite a bit higher.

TABLE V–2

Median Income of Playwrights, by Source, 1953–1957

Source of Income	5 Year Median	Per Cent Receiving Income in Category
Plays	$ 684	70
Other Free-Lance Writing	957	49.2
Movie and Television Rights	2,700	55.7
Magazines, Ghost Writing, etc.	1,329	14
Non-writing Sources	3,149	40
Total Personal Income	7,873	
Spouse's Income	1,800	30
Family Income	10,795	

SOURCE: Lord, pp. 163, 177, 179, 181, 185, 196.

from non-writing sources. Many of the playwrights in Lord's sample who earned non-writing income stayed close to their own field: 24 per cent worked as actors, 10 per cent as producers or directors, 10 per cent taught, 20 per cent worked in editing and research, and the rest took jobs in miscellaneous fields, including public relations, real estate and typing.

Like the composer, the playwright has difficulty in getting his works produced. Performance of plays is difficult to arrange because of the very substantial cost of a new production in the commercial theater. It can be argued that in this respect the novelist is in a far better position — it is much less expensive to publish a book than to produce a play, and many more books than plays make their appearance each year. Lord's figures on the returns to the two types of writer seem to agree with this view. In his sample, only 31.5 per cent of playwrights obtained a yearly income from their writing, while 58.9 per cent of the authors of books met this test. The book writers' median income from books over the period 1953–1957 was $1,600, more than twice as much as the dramatists' median income ($684) from plays.

It is true that the commercial theater is constantly searching for promising new scripts — indeed, producers on Broadway complain that good new plays are their greatest shortage. Yet, typically, what they are seeking is a manuscript which seems a reasonably safe financial investment. Consequently, the efforts of several off-Broadway producers to make possible low-cost production of the works of new playwrights are of obvious significance. Such programs have been undertaken by various groups, notably the American Place Theater and the Playwrights Unit of the Actor's Studio, with some assistance from the Ford Foundation, the Rockefeller Foundation and the New York State Council on the Arts. These undertakings are designed to attack what may be one of the most important needs of the innovating playwright — a forum for the product of his creative efforts.

The Choreographer

There seems to be no systematic information available about the earnings of the choreographer, but it is clear that characteristically his circumstances are much worse than those of the playwright or the composer. The seriousness of the situation will become clear when we discuss the dancer, for usually the choreographer is also a member of a dance company — often his own — and shares the dancers' tribulations. However, a brief excerpt from the testimony of Agnes De Mille may be illuminating. In reading this it should be remembered that Miss De Mille is one of the nation's best-known choreographers, whose contribution to "Oklahoma!" is credited with revolutionizing the American musical comedy.

> Quite a few years ago I produced a ballet called "Rodeo." I was not too young a woman at the time. . . . I wanted to dance in it myself, so I worked five months for the Monte Carlo Ballet in that production and got $3 a day for my expenses while traveling, $500 for "Rodeo," and that is what I lived on. . . .
> When I did "Oklahoma" . . . I signed away the ownership rights of my dances to the producers. I was granted a royalty of $50 a week for a limited space of time and then nothing.[12]

Salary Scales of the Performer

All the information we have been able to accumulate about performers' salaries is summarized in Table V–3. We are painfully

---

[12] House Hearings, II, pp. 172, 177. Miss De Mille also complained about union restrictions which prevent the filming of a choreographer's work — a limitation which has the same hampering effect as the injunction against the recording of his piece by the composer. The Directors and Choreographers Guild has been organized since that time, and hopes to negotiate improved conditions for its members.

TABLE V–3

Salaries and Estimated Earnings of Performers,
Live Performances, Recent Years

	Season (1)	Min- imum Per Week (2)	Notes to Column 2 (3)
ACTORS			
Broadway	1964–65	$125	Equity minimum. *Source:* "Equit Rules Governing Employment o Broadway," June 1964.
Off-Broadway	1964–65	60	Equity minimum; raised in 1965 66 to $65 per week. *Source:* Sam as above.
"Regional"	ca. 1964–65	50–125 (av. 80)	Estimated on the basis of a surve of regional repertory theaters cor ducted by Sandra Schmidt ("Re gional Theaters: Some Statistics") supplemented by information ob tained from the managements o 16 leading regional theaters. Th mean of the minimums paid b these 16 was $80.31; the media fell between $75 and $90.
All Equity Actors	Spring of 1965	N.A.	
MUSICIANS			
Major Orchestras	1963–64	90–205 (av. 150)	Arithmetic average for 24 orches tras in the regular season weighte by the number of performers i each. If the Boston, Chicago, Nev

(*Table continued on pages 116–119*)

Season's Earnings from Primary Employer (4)	Notes to Column 4 (5)	Annual Earnings from Live Performances (6)	Notes to Column 6 (7)
$2,335	Estimated median earnings during 1964 for members of Actors' Equity who performed solely on Broadway. The estimate is based on a detailed distribution of earnings kindly provided by Martin E. Segal Company. The arithmetic mean of these earnings data is $4,569, and the mean number of weeks worked is 16.3. Earnings over $1,500 per week are excluded.	$ 6,900	Median, hit Broadway musical cast.*
N.A.		N.A.	
3,200 (32 wks.)	Estimated average weekly earnings of $100 times median number of weeks (32). Since the average minimum was $80, this estimate cannot be far off, especially in view of the Equity data which show relatively small gains over the seasons immediately preceding 1957–58.	5,000	Median, Repertory Company A.*
N.A.		2,164	Median, survey of unemployed actors.*
4,945 (29 wks.)	Arithmetic average, derived in the same way as the minimum per week. If the 3 orchestras named are omitted,	$10,400	Minimum for New York Philharmonic. Based on provisions of agreement between the New York

Particular groups which responded to a special survey conducted in the spring of 1965. ee Appendix Table V–B for more detail.

TABLE V–3 (continued)

Season	Min-imum Per Week	Notes to Column 2
(1)	(2)	(3)
		York and Philadelphia Orchestra are excluded, the average minimum per week is $135 and th average per week is $149.
Metropolitan Orchestras 1963–64	N.A.	
On Broadway ca. 1964–65	$135–223	Minimum scales for members of Local 802 of the AFM in New Yor City in 1964–65 were as follows dramatic productions, contracte houses, $135; dramatic produc tions, non-contracted houses, $175 musicals, contracted houses, $186

Season's Earnings from Primary Employer	Notes to Column 4	Annual Earnings from Live Perform-ances	Notes to Column 6
(4)	(5)	(6)	(7)
	this average drops to $4,052. Both weekly and season data were calculated from the American Symphony Orchestra League's "Compilation of Operational and Financial Data for the 1963–64 Season as Reported by Twenty-seven Major Symphony Orchestras."		Philharmonic Society and Local 802 of the AFM for the 1964–65 season. All musicians are guaranteed 52 weeks of pay at a minimum of $200 per week. Average annual income is higher than $10,400 for several reasons: some musicians are paid more than the minimum per week; there are overtime and "extra" earnings from the Philharmonic; some musicians have performing income from sources other than the New York Philharmonic.
$894	Mean salary paid by 18 orchestras for the 1963–64 season, weighted by each orchestra's number of performances. Calculated from the American Symphony Orchestra League's "Compilation of Operational and Financial Data for the 1963–64 Season as Reported by Twenty-five Metropolitan Orchestras."		
N.A.		$10,000	Median, hit Broadway musical orchestra.*

TABLE V–3 (continued)

	Season	Min-imum Per Week	Notes to Column 2
	(1)	(2)	(3)
			musicals, non-contracted house $223. *Source:* League of New Yo Theaters.
Opera Orchestra	1964–65	195	Average, Metropolitan Opera.
Ballet Orchestra	Spring 1965	N.A.	
Chamber Group	Spring 1965	N.A.	
SINGERS			
Opera Chorus	1963–64 and 1964–65	65–160	Based on information supplied four opera companies.
DANCERS			
Dance Companies	1963–64	40–150	Based on the minimum salarie paid by 3 dance organizations.
Opera	1964–65	50–177 (av. 144)	Metropolitan Opera.

Season's Earnings from Primary Employer (4)	Notes to Column 4 (5)	Annual Earnings from Live Performances (6)	Notes to Column 6 (7)
8,900 (35 wks.)	Metropolitan Opera. *Source: New York Times,* Oct. 9, 1964, p. 31.	5,170	Median, an opera orchestra.*
N.A.		7,000	Median, a ballet orchestra.*
N.A.		5,000	Median, a chamber orchestra.*
8,776 (42 wks.)	Metropolitan Opera, 1964–65; singers with 10 years seniority. Salaries for a full-year chorister for 1964–65 and 1965–66 (projected) are: 1964–65 1965–66 Highest $9,748 $11,337 Medium 8,776 10,043 Lowest 6,953 8,003 For 1964–65 there is a 42 week guarantee, and for 1965–66 a 49 week guarantee.	3,821	Opera chorus.
3,728–7,018 (40 wks.)	New York City Ballet. AGMA's records for 1961 indicate that the yearly salary for the New York City Ballet performers ranged from a top level of $7,718 through a medium of $5,046 to a low of $3,728 (House Hearings, II, p. 29).	3,781	Median, a ballet company.*
6,046 (42 wks.)	Metropolitan Opera; dancers with 5 years seniority. *Source:* Metropolitan Opera Association.	N.A.	

aware that, though the figures have been assembled most laboriously, the data are extremely spotty, and more space is devoted to notes than to numbers. But the notes are important, and ignoring them may lead one to read more into the figures than one should. For example, not all the data refer to the same year; some are rough estimates, while others are very reliable figures; the definitions vary in terms of the categories of earnings included — some are medians, others arithmetic averages. In short, the table has been a nightmare to construct and, we must warn the reader, is a nightmare to interpret even with the aid of the notes.

Nevertheless, several important findings do stand out. The minimum weekly salary scales revealed by this table are low indeed — $60 off-Broadway ($65 in 1965–66), $50 at some regional theaters, $65 in some opera choruses, and $40 in some dance groups. Some organizations do not have a minimum at all. Even among major orchestras some of the minimums are very low; though over $200 per week in some, in others (at least in the 1963–64 season) they were as low as $75.

The minimum figures, which are undoubtedly the most reliable data in the table, are highly significant because large numbers of performers are at or very near the minimum. For example, as we saw in Chapter II, the wages of substantially more than half and probably considerably more than three-quarters of off-Broadway performers are at the Equity minimum. The situation in the major orchestras is obviously very similar, since average earnings in these orchestras were only $16 above the minimum. Thus the fact that the minimums are often very low indicates that, in practice, a considerable number of performers must be receiving very low incomes from their professional activities. Indeed, this is confirmed by some of our other information. We know that many musicians in major orchestras still received from their orchestras well under $4,000 per year in 1963–64. The average earnings of all actors on Broadway came to $4,600 per year, while 50 per cent of these actors received less than $2,500 during 1964 from their Broadway performances.

Data on earnings from live performance in Great Britain during the 1964–65 season, obtained directly from the organizations involved, can be translated into units comparable with the American statistics by relating the weekly earnings per performance in each country to average weekly income of its labor force. In this way we can estimate how high performers in these countries stand on their society's income scale. We present such data only for orchestral musicians, for whom we can say with some degree of confidence that the analogy between the two nations' organizations is beyond reasonable doubt.

For major orchestras in the United States, excluding the top five, the minimum weekly wage is 1.11 times the average weekly income of the U. S. labor force.

For Great Britain's provincial orchestras the minimum weekly wage is 1.09 times the average weekly income of the British labor force.

For the Metropolitan Opera Orchestra the ratio to the labor force average is 1.41.

For the Covent Garden Orchestra the ratio is 1.37.

From these few figures it would appear that, despite government subsidy, British musicians are no higher on the British income scale than American instrumentalists are on ours. This seems to be one more indication that there are no major structural differences in the arts between the two countries.

Wage Settlements as Part of a "Package": The Full-Year Season

Aside from the psychic income — the sheer satisfaction in playing an instrument or acting or singing before an audience — performers' willingness to continue to accept a given wage level may be explained by the other things that go along with the job. In recent years the "settlement package" which is commonly arrived at between the performers' unions and the performing organizations has begun to include fringe benefits such as pensions and medical insurance. In a number of cases, as we shall see, performers have apparently been induced to forego increases in weekly wages by contracts offering them longer seasons, sometimes extending over most of the year. One reason actors are willing to work for $65 a week off-Broadway is that the off-Broadway (stock) Equity contract also offers the performer an unusual amount of freedom of movement; under the contract terms the performer may resign from the cast with very little notice (normally two weeks) if a more desirable job opportunity presents itself. As a result, the off-Broadway theater has been plagued by frequent changes in cast. On Broadway, where the "run of the play" contract is standard, this difficulty does not normally arise, but the actor must then be compensated for his longer term commitment.

The short period of time during the year that the performer can count on regular earnings is one of his more serious difficulties, and is a problem which besets most orchestras, the regional theater, and all but a few major opera and dance companies. Despite this, some performers manage to obtain comfortable levels of remuneration. Some productions in the commercial theater have very long runs and so provide high annual earnings to their casts: about 10 per cent of Broadway actors earned over $10,000 and 3 per cent over $25,000 from their Broadway appearances in 1964. Other relatively comfortable groups are those employed by organizations which have gone into year-round operation — the musicians who play for at least eight of the more affluent of the major orchestras, and the Metropolitan Opera performers. Their seasons now extend from 48 weeks upward, and their minimum annual pay has also gone up considerably, ranging from close to $10,000 in one orchestra to a minimum of $12,500 in another (where these figures include receipts from television and recordings). All of these exceptional groups are small and select, however, comprised of performers who have reached the very top of their profession.

Needless to say, this hardly makes the short season a dead issue for other performers. The average length of season in 1963–64 was 29 weeks in the major orchestras, and this yielded an average income per musician of less than $5,000 for the season; in the metropolitan orchestras the corresponding seasonal income figure was less than $900 in 1963–64. Thus, more than one instrumentalist has complained that "it just isn't possible to support a family on a yearly basis on the income received from a 22 week playing position" or that "It is not the salary as much as the number of weeks of work available. The plight lies in an average of only half a year's employment in the field."[13]

It is interesting that there has been some dissatisfaction in or-

[13] American Federation of Musicians, "The Symphony Musician Speaks Out," pp. 2 and 8.

chestras which have gone over to a full-year season. In at least one case participation in a chamber orchestra which had been made up of members of a major orchestra was prohibited outright, producing complaints and even defection[14] among the highly sought after first-chair string players. These artists, often soloists in their own right, feel that playing only in a large orchestra is limiting, both because of the predominantly conventional repertoire and the necessity of subjugating one's own musical ideas to those of the conductor — playing in a team, as it were. Solo and small group performance allows musicians to play as independent artists and, in addition, can bring in considerable extra income. For this reason it is somewhat paradoxical that the full-year season has come only to those orchestras which can afford to employ players able to do very well on their own, rather than to those in which most of the players would welcome a 52 week season enthusiastically. It is also interesting to note that there seems to have been little objection to full-year seasons from non-string players (winds, brass, etc.), whose opportunities to perform serious music are comparatively limited.

When viewed as part of a package settlement, the adoption of the full-year season has significant implications for the future course of musicians' earnings. It has been alleged that while the length of the season is being extended, the rate of increase in weekly earnings has slowed, and that in at least one case a cut in weekly earnings had been proposed by management.[15] The other side of this coin is that once full-year seasons are firmly established, a faster rate of increase in weekly earnings will perhaps be resumed.

Short seasons also obviously affect total incomes in the regional theaters, where a reported 32 week period of operation provides an average income of $3,200. Similarly, the San Francisco Ballet offers its dancers a 26 week season and a compensation level of $2,200.

[14] *New York Times,* Dec. 29, 1964, p. 23.

[15] In an attempt to test this allegation, we correlated the average increase in weekly salaries with changes in length of season for the major orchestras. When an orchestra's financial resources increase, both of these might be expected to grow, and over the period 1947–1964 they did in fact vary together: we obtained a low but positive correlation (a coefficient of rank correlation of +.10). For the 1961–1964 period, when the year-round contract began to be instituted, we obtained another weak correlation, but this time it was negative (−.22).

Income from Live Performance

The last column of Table V–3 provides estimates of total annual earnings from live performance, including free-lance work and other moonlighting activities. This information was derived from a survey of our own, whose details will be discussed presently. Though the data may look fairly complete, their appearance is deceptive. They are based on a simple questionnaire that we devised and distributed (it is reproduced in Appendix V–I). The survey was in no sense "scientific." A sample of organizations was selected which seemed to us to be representative of different types of performers. We obtained usable information from 110 performers in 11 performing groups, our returns representing a 23 per cent response to the questionnaires sent out. We have no way of knowing what distortions were introduced by the (expectedly) small response rates — whether, in any group, the poorer or the more affluent performer was likelier to answer our questions. Still, we did receive a reasonably large number of responses from certain groups represented in the table. Moreover, the results at least have the advantage of plausibility, and where the figures are comparable there is a very high degree of concurrence with Census data.

Since our sample includes a hit Broadway musical, one of the most solidly based off-Broadway companies, and what are undoubtedly the best financed of American ballet and modern dance companies, it may well over-represent the upper echelon of performers. Even so, the results show annual incomes clustering within the $3,500–$7,000 range. Only musicians in *some* of the major orchestras have been doing better than this. Such incomes clearly do not represent generous remuneration levels for demanding and highly skilled professions.[16]

[16] Unfortunately, despite several attempts, we were unable to obtain information on the earnings of orchestra musicians from *all* professional sources. What we do have is information on earnings from the primary orchestral employer. In 1963–64 the average season income for musicians in all 25 major orchestras in the United States was $4,945; but when the four highest paying orchestras are excluded, the average falls to $4,050. If we assume that the *typical* musician earns 20 per cent of his total income from other professional activities (probably a very liberal assumption), the average annual professional income of all major orchestra members would have been $6,250, and the comparable figure that excludes the four highest paying orchestras would be $5,000.

These observations can be substantiated by many case histories. For example, we talked with an actor whose face would be familiar to New York theatergoers of the last ten years and to the audiences of some celebrated regional theaters. His career is a patchwork of successful professional activity, grueling weeks on tour and periods of frustrating inactivity.

> My first New York appearance was in the spring of 1957 in an off-Broadway show. Take home pay was $30 — less than unemployment insurance. . . . How do you live on $30 a week? . . . You live in a rooming house and you eat Dennison's chili con carne. . . . I saved money. . . .
>
> That summer I toured at $125 per week. It sounded like a lot, but touring is very expensive. You have to live in hotels and eat in restaurants. . . . Even so, I managed to save some, which was fortunate because when I got back I was unemployed until October. . . . then I played Caesar for 6 weeks at $40 per week. . . .
>
> . . . 7 weeks summer stock. . . . and then I was unemployed through December. This was from choice, as I was keeping myself available for a role I desperately wanted to play. It closed after 13 performances. I was out of unemployment insurance and out of savings. . . .
>
> . . . September 1960 I did my first show on Broadway. The pay was $160, and I got my first apartment. You don't know what that means after living in rooming houses. . . .
>
> . . . I earned over $7,000 last year and have my own apartment. I sometimes wonder what I would have done if I had had a family . . .

Yet when compared with dancers, actors are relatively well off. The dancer's earnings are generally the lowest, the span of years during which he can find employment is typically the shortest and his employment generally the most uncertain, his working conditions are often the worst among the performing arts. Among the best remunerated dancers are those in Broadway musicals (as of the end of 1966 they receive a minimum of $127.50 per week) and the members of the Metropolitan Opera ballet (in 1964–65 those with at least five years' seniority received an average of $144 a week). One manager observed that dancers are paid very little in part because they are usually so much younger than other performers — at 30 a dancer is old, and by 40 (unless he is a top star) he is superannuated. But it must be remembered that in other occupations where the span of one's professional life is short, earnings tend to be high, perhaps to compensate for the brevity of the individual's career. With only three American professional ballet companies having regular seasons in their own communities, the dancer usually performs during tours made up of one night stands. As one Congressional witness commented, it is no accident that the Broadway vernacular for a dancer is "gypsy."

We know of the workings of one of our leading modern dance companies which has received international acclaim. The choreographer himself periodically acts as teacher-dancer in residence at a few of the nation's colleges and universities. He does this whenever the company is in desperate financial straits, and he uses his earnings to meet its deficits. He also earns something from a dance studio in which two members of his company also teach, if there are enough pupils. The other members of his company earn a living by teaching, making dummies for book publishers, selling books and postcards in a museum and waiting on tables — jobs they can keep in spite of periodically having to go off on tour on short notice. The company meets three times a week for unpaid rehearsal.

A "tour" itself consists of an engagement of two or three performances, sometimes in fairly well separated locations. The fee is about $1,000 (of which 20 per cent goes to the agent when she arranges it), but about half the time the company receives considerably less. The company travels in a small, crowded bus, which carries costumes, props and scenery, dancers, musicians and a stage manager. The choreographer pays the expenses of food and lodging (about $13 per day per person), each member of the company receives between $25 and $50 per performance (recall that the entire "tour" may consist of a single performance with perhaps four days of travel), and the choreographer may have a little left over if the performance is close to New York. If the trip takes the company as far as Chicago, he calculates that he just about breaks even.

In addition to fairly low income, the performer suffers from extraordinarily disadvantageous arrangements in many of his working conditions and in the fringe benefits that are provided to him. To illustrate these problems we will discuss in turn the uncertainty of his employment, his hours of work, his required professional expenses, and his pension, vacation, and other fringe benefit arrangements.

Unemployment of Performers

Unemployment is one of the most serious and persistent problems of the professional performer. This arises from two main sources: the short seasons of many performing groups and the free-lance nature of many of their working arrangements. We have already discussed the seasonal unemployment problem of many orchestral musicians, actors in regional theaters and some opera and dance companies, where regular employment amounting to little more than *half the year* is not atypical. Moreover, even when the performing group has a short season it is usually very difficult for the performer to find other professional jobs during the remainder of the year, because each company naturally chooses its weeks of activity during the height of the artistic season and releases the artist precisely during that period when very little performing activity is going on elsewhere.

Many performers have no long-term professional commitments of any sort. Many dance and chamber groups perform only when their services happen to be requested by someone, and then, for all practical purposes, they disband (except for unpaid rehearsals) until the next performance or set of performances can be arranged. And in the commercial and off-Broadway theaters, since (with one or two exceptions) there is no such thing as a permanent company, the actor is unemployed as soon as a show closes. As a result, unemployment rates among performers are extremely high.

According to the 1960 Census, 4.6 per cent of musicians, 7.6 per cent of male dancers and 26.1 per cent of actors were officially unemployed during the census week: they had no paid employment of any kind, *in or out of their chosen field,* and were seeking work. Among all males in the professional occupations, the unemployment rate was only 1.4 per cent. (See Appendix Table V–C.) Actors' Equity has estimated that in an average week about 75–80 per cent of all its members have no work in the theater, that 55 per cent of its members acted less than 10 weeks in 1957–58.[17] Undoubtedly this figure is inflated by the perhaps sizable number of persons without commitment, training or ability who describe themselves

[17] House Hearings, II, p. 193.

as actors and take out union membership. But even after discounting for this source of exaggeration, professional unemployment among actors is no doubt very high.

The findings of the 1960 Census on number of weeks worked per year (also summarized in Appendix V–C) show that, whereas among all males in the professional-technical occupations 77.5 per cent worked between 50 and 52 weeks, only 28.3 per cent of all actors, 37.9 per cent of all dancers and 42.6 per cent of all musicians were able to obtain this much employment at all types of work combined. The same general pattern holds among females.

Small wonder, then, that unemployment compensation plays an important role in the compensation of the performer. Throughout the Congressional hearings on economic conditions in the performing arts the subject of unemployment compensation recurred. Actors and musicians listed it as a part of their income. The chairman of the orchestra committee of a major symphony reported that his group had worked it out so that the musicians were covered by state unemployment compensation in the summer.[18] While the importance of unemployment compensation is a constantly recurring theme in any set of statements by performers, attitudes toward this source of income vary considerably — some feel strongly that reliance on such payments is degrading. One can well sympathize with the musician who wrote, "After the end of the season my wife has to go to work; I am ashamed to collect unemployment benefits."[19]

Fringe Benefits and Working Conditions

A performer's working hours, while not always terribly long, are unlike those of the rest of the community. Under the rules of his union, the actor is usually asked to participate in 8 performances a week, with not more than 12 hours of rehearsal per week. Prior to opening he may rehearse 8½ to 12 hours per day, with suitable breaks. The Rulebooks of Actors' Equity also note his obligations to be prompt and neat — and "at the written request of the Manager, to change the color of his hair." Happily, the management

[18] House Hearings, II, p. 313.

[19] American Federation of Musicians, "The Symphony Musician Speaks Out," p. 5.

absorbs the cost of the change as well as "restoration to the original color at the close of the engagement."

The usual orchestral musicians' contract does not specify a fixed number of working hours; rather, it commits the performer to a certain number of "services" per week — usually 8 to 9. A service generally consists of a rehearsal or a performance and normally occupies about 2½ hours. This would appear to require only a 20 hour working week, but that is highly deceptive. In an American orchestra (in contrast with the practice in at least some European groups) the musician is expected to rehearse his part very thoroughly by himself on his own time so that official rehearsals can be devoted exclusively to coordination of the performance. Hence the actual number of hours expected of the performer is much greater than his nominal commitment, especially when he goes on tour — a subject which will be considered presently. Add to this the extremely demanding nature of the occupation — the heavy expenditure of nervous energy incurred by orchestral performance — and a musician's working week no longer seems so short.[20]

The working week of the performer involves other peculiarities, among them the fact that he must usually work late at night, something which makes normal family life rather difficult. As rehearsal scheduling goes, there is nothing extraordinarily atypical in a working day of a member of the Metropolitan Opera chorus: 11 a.m. to 11 p.m., with a few hours off in the late afternoon.

Tours may separate the performer from his family for weeks, or even months, at a time. The many hours of travel time in buses, automobiles, and even less comfortable conveyances (one dance group traveled about for a considerable period in an antiquated hearse!) are not normally compensated or taken into account in estimates of working time. Tours of individual performers and small ensembles, incidentally, often seem badly planned from the point of view of total distance traveled. Agents arrange dates as they come, and apparently make little effort to schedule them so as to avoid unnecessary travel. At concerts in Princeton we are not surprised when we find that a visiting string quartet has performed the night before in the deep South and has an engagement in the

[20] House Hearings, II, statement by Carlos Moseley, Manager, New York Philharmonic, pp. 66–67.

South on the following night — the entire trip negotiated by automobile, with the members of the ensemble taking turns driving.

The professional expenses of the performer are relatively high. These include both costs comparable to what in industry would be called capital outlays — the performer's training costs — and the annual outlays necessary for the pursuit of his occupation. It is very difficult to calculate costs of training, but testimony at Congressional hearings suggests that for a number of art forms 10 years of preparation and total training outlays in excess of $5,000 are extremely conservative figures.[21] Annual expenses as estimated from our own survey amounted on the average to about $1,200 for musicians and actors, $1,350 for singers and $950 for dancers. The most consistently recurring expense item is union dues. In addition, actors, singers and dancers reported substantial expenditures for make-up, costumes, photographs and publicity, telephone, travel expenses and coaching. The musicians' major item of expense was repair and upkeep of instruments (median $420), professional clothing, music, promotion, travel and studio rent. When annual earnings in the performing arts typically range between perhaps $3,500 and $7,000, annual expenses of $1,000 or more are not easy to manage.

However, one of the clearest financial disadvantages to which the performer is subjected is the relatively small range of fringe benefits he receives. The following is a brief summary of the main types of fringe benefit provided to various groups of performers:[22]

Major Orchestra Musicians (1963–64 season)
1. Paid vacations — provided by 8 of the 22 major orchestras for which data were available, ranging from 6 to 14 days.
2. Pensions — provided by 14 of 22 orchestras.
3. Hospital insurance — provided by 9 of 22 orchestras, but performers pay most of the cost in 6 of the 9 cases.
4. Sick leave — provided by 19 of the 22 orchestras, ranging from 6 to 14 days.

Broadway Actors (1964)
1. Paid vacations — 1 week after 1 year with a single production, rising thereafter.

[21] See House Hearings, II, pp. 25, 40, 49, 59, 71, 172, 231, 383, 488, 578.

[22] This information has been culled from the applicable contracts and rule books. Detailed provisions are often so complicated that we can do no more here than try to indicate in general terms what types of benefits are available.

2. Pensions, health, and group life insurance ($3,000) paid by management to Pension and Welfare Trust Fund. Coverage increases with length of employment.
3. Insurance to cover loss or damage of personal property up to $1,000; insurance (if obtainable) to compensate injury in the course of employment.
4. Sick leave — 1 day per month of performance.

Off-Broadway Actors (1964)

1. Pensions and 3 months welfare coverage paid by management to Pension and Welfare Trust Fund.
2. Insurance — management must have liability insurance covering all auditions.
3. Sick leave — 1 day per month of performance.

Actors' Equity Stock Contract (1963)

1. Pensions — managements contribute to Pension Fund.
2. Insurance (if obtainable) to compensate for injury in the course of employment; insurance to cover loss or damage to personal property.

AGMA (Associated Guild of Musical Artists)

Has been unable to negotiate fringe benefits, but maintains $1,000 life insurance for each of its members.

Choreographers and Directors

None.

American Federation of Musicians, Local 802 (1963)

1. Payments are made by management into the union's Pension, Welfare and Vacation funds.
2. Sick leave is provided.

Metropolitan Opera (1964)

1. Paid vacations — 1 week for 40 weeks work, increasing with length of service.
2. Retirement plan for eligible employees.
3. Hospitalization and major medical insurance — after 3 to 4 years service.
4. Sick leave — 2 weeks after 1 to 3 years of service, increasing to 52 weeks after 19 or more years of service.
5. Stagehands have their own pension fund, to which the management makes contributions, and they also have somewhat more generous vacation provisions.

The summary speaks for itself. Fringe benefits are obviously much more substantial in some of the major orchestras and at the Metropolitan Opera than in most other performing arts organizations. The actor used to be very badly off indeed in terms of fringe benefits, but since 1960 his situation has improved markedly, especially if he is fortunate enough to work at his profession a large part of the year. In the commercial theater, when the 5 per cent admissions tax was revoked, it was decided, after a curious set of negotiations, to retain the 5 per cent of ticket receipts to finance a pension and welfare fund administered jointly by Actors' Equity and the League of New York Theatres. But while this is a great step ahead for those employed in New York City and on stock contracts in the rest of the country, it does not apply to actors in resident stock, dramatic stock and summer stock companies. They have no fringe benefits other than group medical plans. Their existence is further complicated by the requirement in the unemployment insurance regulations of a number of states that the individual be resident in that state and employed for at least a certain number of weeks before benefits are available to him. The nature of the industry sometimes makes it impossible for the actor to meet these requirements.

The Performer's Total Family Income

There remains one important question: Is the performer really poor? So far we have discussed primarily his professional earnings, but he frequently supplements these by performance in the mass media, by teaching, by work unrelated to his profession and through the earnings of his spouse.

How the performer supplements his primary source of income is one of the subjects examined by our survey described earlier in this chapter. The results of the survey are summarized in Table V–4, and in much greater detail in Appendix Table V–B. As might have been suspected, most performers have some supplementary sources of income. In most groups, earnings from live performance constituted some 70 to 80 per cent of total income. There were three exceptional groups: the unemployed actors included in the survey, the members of a modern dance company, and a chamber orchestra which happens to include a substantial number of married women (as a result, over half of these performers reported significant contributions to family income by a spouse). As noted earlier, dancers constitute a rather distinct economic problem. In the case of the unemployed actors, the large proportion of earnings from other sources is hardly surprising. What is interesting is that these out-of-work actors were able to claim total incomes whose median was

TABLE V–4

Income of a Sample of Performers, During 1964

		For Performers Having Any:	
Source of Income	Per Cent Having Any	Median	Interquartile Range (range of middle 50%)
Professional Sources:			
Live Performances	99	$4,877	$3,100–$ 7,586
Television and Related Sources	49	250	150– 1,000
Teaching and Coaching	34	1,000	300– 2,000
Total from Professional Sources	100	5,771	3,395– 8,700
Unrelated Sources	20	813	327– 1,476
Spouse	22	4,300	2,000– 8,900
Other Income	40	450	300– 1,000
Total Income	100	7,275	4,128– 10,500

SOURCE: Questionnaire survey conducted for this study. More detail is provided in Appendix Table V–B.

just about the same as that for the members of a comparatively well established regional theater company. Perhaps the implication is that actors are unemployed so frequently that almost any one of them is likely to be jobless at a particular moment, and that, therefore, a sample of those unemployed at a particular moment of time may not be unrepresentative of the entire profession.

A high proportion of performers (49 per cent of our 108 respondents) had some earnings from television and other related opportunities, but the amounts tended to be small. Except for the members of two companies and the unemployed actors, the medians[23] from this source for each group were $300 or less. Teaching and coaching was a somewhat less common activity (34 per cent of our respondents reported income from this source). However, the amounts derived from this source were often more substantial, particularly among musicians and members of the modern dance

[23] This is the median for those who reported such earnings; those who obtained nothing from television or related opportunities were excluded from the calculation.

group, where the median of these earnings ranged from $1,000 to $1,750 per year and constituted roughly 20 per cent of the family income of the performers having any income from this source. A particularly interesting result was that, in general, only a fairly small proportion of our sample of performers earned money from sources unrelated to their profession. In most cases no more than 25 per cent of a company, and often a substantially smaller percentage, had income from miscellaneous types of work. For those who did, the list of occupations is extremely varied and includes waiting on tables, office work, house painting, work as make-up artists, scenery painters, department store salesclerks, Santa Claus, and one night club bouncer. The only two groups in which a large proportion of performers undertook non-professional jobs were, once again, the unemployed actors and the modern dancers.

Performers' spouses frequently contributed a rather large share of total family income — a finding which perhaps gives substance to the view that the arts are, in effect, subsidized by persons who are married to the performers.

What over-all impression does all of this convey? It shows a skilled performer who has a median family income of $7,275. Our typical performer earned 67 per cent of his family income from live performance — a median amount of only $4,877.

In many ways, then, the working conditions of the performer fall below what might be considered reasonable standards. His exhausting tours, high professional expenses, frequent unemployment with its accompanying uncertainty, the rarity of paid vacations and the frequent lack of provision for retirement, all add up to what most of us would consider a nightmare world were we suddenly plunged into it. This applies with special force to those associated with the dance, where earnings are lower and economic insecurity far greater than in the other performing arts.

Most performing artists are unlikely to starve, but society has not been overly generous in the compensation it has provided the artist in exchange for his contribution to the living arts. We have relied heavily on the willingness of the performer to perform, no matter what it costs him.

Hopefully, however, the happier situation provided by the leading major orchestras and the Metropolitan Opera, where year-round employment and more reasonable income levels promise to restore the performer to the status of a respectable member of the community, will serve as a precedent for other groups. But to make any real progress in this direction it is necessary to come to grips with the vexing financial problems of the performing organizations themselves, the central topic of this book to which we turn in the next chapter.

CHAPTER VI

The Financial State
of the Organizations

THIS CHAPTER is the culmination of our report on the present economic condition of the performing arts. It summarizes the financial operations of the performing organizations as a group and completes the background of facts required for our analytical investigations in Part II of the book. In this chapter, as in most of Part I, we shall concentrate on a description of the current state of affairs rather than on trends.

The significance of the materials here presented need hardly be emphasized. The economic stability of the live performing arts rests ultimately on the finances of the performing organizations, and we shall find in this chapter that, as a group, the performing arts do not pay their own way. As William Schuman has aptly said, they are "in the business of losing money wisely."[1]

Total Expenditures

The first question one might well ask about the finances of any organization is How much money is involved?

Table VI–1 summarizes the available data on the size of budgets for the several art forms in recent years. The categories have been kept as homogeneous as possible in an attempt to arrive at representative values for each of the groups listed. We have not, for

[1] *Business Week*, August 3, 1963, p. 43.

137

TABLE VI–1

Median Expenditure Per Year, Per Performance and Per Seat, by Art Form

	Season or Year	Annual Expenditure	Expenditure Per Performance	Expenditure Per Seat
Orchestras:				
Major Orchestras:				
Five Largest[a]	1963–64	$1,873,174	$12,841	$5.33
All Twenty-five[b]	1963–64	715,051	6,647	1.91
Twenty-five Metropolitan Orchestras[c]	1963–64	181,730	4,716	1.99[d]
Opera Companies:				
Metropolitan Opera	1963–64	8,748,219	35,853	9.85
Ten Other Operas[e]	1963	182,244	12,808	5.21
Dance Companies:				
New York City Ballet	1964–65	2,289,418	10,266	3.87
Two Civic Ballets	1963	13,390	893	.51
		20,355	925	1.32
Two Modern Dance Groups	1963	9,181	1,147	1.17
		37,857	2,295	3.83
Theater:				
Broadway:				
Musicals[f]	1964–65		6,509	4.90[g]
Plays[f]	1964–65		3,077	2.83[g]
Off-Broadway Plays[h]	1964–65		758	3.81[i]
Thirteen Regional Companies[j]	1964–65	250,000	720	1.98

[a] The Boston Symphony, Chicago Symphony, Cleveland, New York Philharmonic and Philadelphia Orchestras.

[b] Includes the 23 major orchestras listed in Appendix III–2 and also the Denver and Seattle Symphonies, which are classified as majors by the American Symphony Orchestra League. Financial data from the ASOL's 1963–64 Major Orchestra Report.

[c] Financial data from the ASOL's 1963–64 Metropolitan Orchestra Report.

[d] Based on only 22 orchestras because the New Jersey Symphony plays in various halls and because no seating capacity was reported for the Omaha Symphony.

[e] The Boston Opera Group, Opera Society of Washington, Civic Opera Association of St. Louis, St. Louis Festival Society, Brooklyn Opera, Chicago Lyric, Cincinnati Summer, Houston Grand, Kansas City Lyric, and New York City Operas. Expenditure figures obtained from questionnaires submitted to these organizations or from their annual reports.

[f] Weekly operating costs for Broadway musicals were estimated at $40,000 on the basis of detailed information for two 1964–65 musicals; similarly, weekly operating costs for straight plays on Broadway were estimated at $17,000 on the basis of detailed informa-

example, simply combined the Metropolitan Opera with an agglomeration of smaller opera groups to come up with some sort of "average" company, which could not represent either the one or the other. Similarly, data for the five largest orchestras are presented separately from the figures for all major orchestras. Data on expenditures for dance and chamber groups are both diverse and spotty, and the table, therefore, offers estimates for individual dance companies instead of attempting to provide representative values; it omits chamber groups altogether.

The Metropolitan Opera, with a budget in 1963–64 of $9 million,

Notes to Table VI–1 continued

tion for two 1964–65 productions. Each estimate was divided by 8, the average number of performances per week, to determine expenditures per performance. Production expenditures were calculated by determining the median capitalization figures for 31 plays ($100,000) and 13 musicals ($400,000) reporting to the New York Attorney General for the period June 1, 1964 through May 31, 1965, and then subtracting from these figures, respectively, $20,000 and $50,000, the average amounts of overcall and returnable bonds estimated on the basis of the relation between capitalization and actual production costs of the two plays and two musicals mentioned previously as the sources for weekly expenditures. The estimated total production costs were then prorated over the median number of performances (84 and 232) for the 43 plays and 23 musicals listed in the *New York Times'* statistical summary for the 1964–65 season (issue of June 27, 1965, Section 2, p. 3). Finally, the total expenditures per performance were determined by adding estimated operating and production costs.

ᵍ Obtained by dividing estimated expenditure per performance by average number of seats (1,328 for musicals and 1,089 for straight plays); these latter figures were calculated from *Stubs*.

ʰ Running costs per performance were calculated by dividing 8, the average number of performances per week, into $3,272, a figure agreed upon by six of the most experienced off-Broadway producers as the amount of gross income needed to balance weekly operating expenses. (Data from *New York Times*, September 6, 1964.) Capitalization costs, prorated on a weekly basis, were determined by finding the median original capitalization figure ($20,000) from among those filed by 22 off-Broadway productions with the New York Attorney General for the period June 1, 1964 through May 31, 1965, subtracting from this figure the estimated average amount of returnable bonds and deposits included in production costs, and dividing the resulting $15,000 by 43, the estimated median length of run of off-Broadway productions in 1963–64 (calculated from length-of-run information given in the *New York Herald Tribune*). The expenditure per performance is the sum of the estimated running and production costs.

ⁱ Calculated by dividing the estimated expenditure per performance by the average capacity of off-Broadway theaters, 199 seats.

ʲ The Actor's Workshop, Alley, Arena Stage, Barter, Center Stage, Charles Playhouse, Cleveland Play House, Cincinnati Playhouse, Dallas, Front Street, Guthrie, Hartford Stage, and Seattle Repertory Theaters. The expenditure figures are estimates compiled by Sandra Schmidt.

is the giant of the live performing arts. Nevertheless, by American business standards, the Metropolitan is a tiny operation. It is dwarfed by the smallest of the 500 largest corporations in the United States.

The other performing groups operate at a level of expenditure considerably lower than the Metropolitan Opera's. The median budget of the five largest orchestras is slightly under $2 million (two orchestras have larger budgets than this and two have smaller budgets, since the median is the figure which divides the cases in half). On the next rung down the economic ladder are the 25 major orchestras, whose median annual expenditure is about three quarters of a million dollars. Orchestras in the next size class, the metropolitan orchestras, spend about $200,000 annually.

Opera companies other than the Metropolitan Opera are about on a par with the metropolitan orchestras. However, these opera companies are such a diverse group (excluding extreme cases, their budgets range from $63,282 to $271,611) that no single figure can properly characterize them.

Regional theaters, with a median expenditure of one quarter of a million dollars per year, are slightly more costly operations than the smaller orchestras and opera companies in the table. We provide no annual expenditure figures for the Broadway or the off-Broadway theaters, since they plan only in terms of single productions. As explained in the notes to Table VI-1, however, we estimate median capitalization costs to be $20,000 for an off-Broadway production, $100,000 for a straight show on Broadway and $400,000 for a Broadway musical.

Expenditure Per Performance and Per Seat

A large budget need not indicate that a particular organization or art form is very expensive. It may mean merely that the typical company in that area of endeavor is active for a large number of weeks during the year. Because of differences in length of season, a better way to determine whether it is inherently more costly to supply one type of artistic activity than another is to compare costs *per performance*.

These costs amount to about $36,000 at the Metropolitan Opera. All other opera companies spend a median amount of about $13,000 per performance, which is approximately the same as the cost per performance of the five largest orchestras. Thus, a performance by one of the smaller opera companies is about as expensive an operation as a concert by one of the most costly orchestras, even though the opera's annual budget is much smaller.

For all major orchestras as a group the cost per performance drops to less than $7,000. The operations of the metropolitans turn out to be more expensive than one might have guessed — nearly $5,000 per performance. Regional theaters and off-Broadway companies have median costs of only about $750 per performance. Costs on Broadway are, of course, higher; they amount to $3,100 per performance of a straight show and $6,500 for a musical.

Finally, it is of interest to examine the costs per potential member of the audience. After all, the unit of "final product" of the performing arts is not the single performance but the seat at a performance (where an empty seat can perhaps be considered an unsold product). The last column in Table VI–1, therefore, reports cost per seat.

When the Metropolitan Opera's 1963–64 budget is divided by the number of performances given and then by the number of seats in the opera house, the cost per seat amounts to about $10. The other operas and the five top orchestras — on the basis of the seating capacity of their home auditoriums — operate at a cost of about $5 per seat, and this figure drops to about $2 for the major orchestras as a group.[2]

In this calculation the relative costs of the off-Broadway and regional theaters no longer appear so low. At regional theaters the cost per seat is about $2, and so is almost the same as that of the major orchestras as a group. And because the off-Broadway houses are small (typically having 199 or 299 seats), their costs per seat

[2] Because an undetermined amount is expended in making recordings, the actual performing cost per seat is undoubtedly somewhat lower than the figures indicate. Also, to the extent that the auditoriums in which the orchestras perform while on tour are larger than the halls in which they regularly play, the true cost per seat of an orchestral performance will be lower than our $2 figure.

are high, averaging approximately $3.80, which is about as high as the cost per seat at any type of performance except the opera, the 5 largest orchestras and Broadway musicals. We can now see more clearly one of the major sources of off-Broadway's financial woes.

In general, the real costs of performance in Great Britain are of the same order of magnitude as those in the United States. This is true of regional theaters and top orchestras. It is also the case when the expenditures of Covent Garden, which includes an independently functioning dance organization, are compared with the combined expenditures of the Metropolitan Opera and the New York City Ballet. To make these international comparisons, our figures were translated into a common unit — the amount of labor which the money expenditures could buy in the respective countries; details are reported in Appendix Table VI–A.

The similarity between the two countries in cost per performance is again remarkable. We found, for example, that the cost of a performance by the New York City Ballet would just about suffice to cover one and one half year's average income of a member of the U. S. labor force, and a performance by the Metropolitan Opera costs the equivalent of five and seven tenths man-years of labor. Fortuitously, performances at Covent Garden are distributed between opera and ballet in just about the same proportions as are performances by these two American organizations. We, therefore, averaged our index of the cost per performance of the New York City Ballet (1.6 man-years of labor) with the figure for the Metropolitan Opera (5.7 man-years) and obtained a figure of about 3.7 man-years, which is extremely close to the Covent Garden figure of 3.8 man-years. A performance of American regional theater companies was found to cost the equivalent of 0.16 man-years of labor as against 0.15 for British regional groups. Real costs per performance for top orchestras are 2.4 man-years of labor in both countries.

The Composition of Expenditures

The next logical question, once total outlays have been discussed, is: For what is the money spent?

Answers in broad terms are given in the "pie" charts of Figure

VI–1. The main thing to be observed from these diagrams is that the salaries of artistic personnel account for an overwhelming proportion of total costs — an observation that holds true not only for the three art forms whose expenditures are plotted but for others as well. However, there are differences. In plays on Broadway, salaries of artistic personnel constitute only one third of total cost; for operas the figure is two fifths; and in the major orchestras the artistic personnel salary component reaches its peak, at two thirds of total expenditure.

One of the main reasons for the difference between the theaters and the operas is the variation between them in the relative importance of such items as costuming and staging. Much of the category "other" in these diagrams is composed of this sort of outlay. In terms of proportion of expenditure on artistic personnel, as might be expected, opera lies between orchestra and theater, since the former includes elements of both of these other art forms. Two other differences are interesting both economically and artistically. The first is the large expenditure on advertising by Broadway theaters and the small share of the budgets of operas and orchestras used for this purpose, a finding which demonstrates a difference in the mode of operation of commercial and non-profit organizations. The second dissimilarity is Broadway's substantial expenditure on authors' fees (at least when musical productions are omitted), an expense which is proportionately much smaller in opera and orchestra budgets. Underlying this contrast is the fact that most of what is done on Broadway is newly written, whereas the large musical organizations tend to specialize in a more standard repertoire. If a work is old enough, there is no need to pay authors' fees. Yet major orchestras do commission a number of new works every year, at widely varying rates of remuneration to the composer, and also make payments for the performance of contemporary pieces to the American Society of Composers, Authors and Publishers and to Broadcast Music Inc. — the composers' guilds — which, in turn, provide royalties to their members.

The variations among art forms in the share of expenditure allocated to artistic personnel carry over almost exactly to Great Britain. This suggests strongly that the variations reflect fundamental differences in the technology of these arts, and not just fortuitous

FIGURE VI-1

DISTRIBUTION OF THE EXPENDITURE DOLLAR,
BY ART FORM

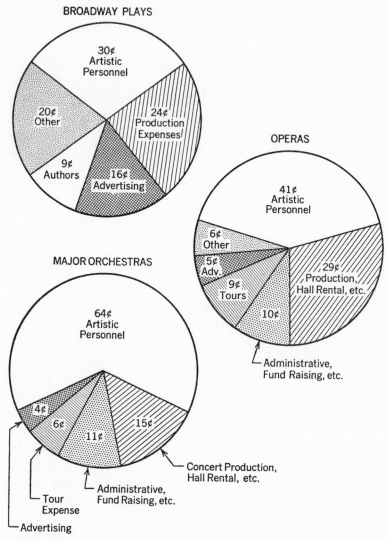

Broadway Plays: The distribution is derived from 1960–61 figures in a table
supplied by Moore entitled "Total Earnings and Expenditures for Life of Play,
Various Factors." "Artistic Personnel" includes cast salaries only. "Production

(*Notes continued on opposite page*)

historical developments. The share of salaries of artistic personnel in total expenditures was:[3]

> 64% for major U. S. orchestras
> 72% for the London Symphony Orchestra
> 67% for the Bournemouth Orchestra
> 41% for the Metropolitan and City Center Ballet combined
> 41% for Covent Garden
> 44% for Sadler's Wells
> 30% on Broadway (excluding musicals)
> 25–35% in U. S. regional theaters
> 26% in the Royal Shakespeare Company

Greater regularity would probably be hard to find among economic phenomena.

Sources of Earned Income

Let us now shift our attention from the cost to the income side of organizational finance. It will be no surprise that the vast bulk of the earned income of performing arts organizations — their in-

---

[3] Data calculated from sources listed in Appendix Tables VI–A and VI–B.

Notes to Figure VI–1 continued

Expenses" includes crew and stagehands, directors, scenic designers, managers, scenery, props, costumes, electrical and sound costs.

Operas: The distribution is based on a simple average of the percentage distribution of expenditures of the Metropolitan Opera (1963–64) and the New York City Opera (1962–63). The percentage distributions by broad categories were remarkably similar for these two very different organizations. ("Artistic Personnel" includes salaries of singers, dancers and musicians.)

Major Orchestras: The breakdown of spending was constructed after finding the average figure for each category of expenditure reported by the 25 major orchestras in the 1963–64 Major Orchestra Report of the American Symphony Orchestra League. A more detailed summary of the expenditures of these organizations is as follows:

Artistic Personnel (musicians, conductors, soloists)	$ .64
Music Rental, etc.	.01
Hall Rental	.05
Program Expense	.02
Advertising and Promotion	.04
Concert Production and Stage Expenses	.05
Summer Concerts	.02
Tour Expenses (excluding salaries)	.06
Fund Raising Expense	.01
General and Administrative	.10
	$1.00

come from sources other than gifts and grants — comes from the box office. Except for some plays and a few major orchestras, the other sources of earned income are items such as parking lot fees, program advertising and refreshment stands. But these are never very important.

All except a few organizations, which we will discuss next, derive over 90 per cent of their earned income from the sale of admissions, as is illustrated by the following figures for the 25 major orchestras.[4]

Source of Income	Per Cent of Total Income
Subscription Series Ticket Sales	47
Other Home Concerts	23
Tour Concert Receipts	15
Grants for Which Concerts Were Required	6
Subtotal: All Concert Income	92
Program Advertising	2
Broadcasting and Recording (net)	5
Total	100

While all major orchestras obtain income from the first two items in the table — subscription series ticket sales and other home concerts — and while 23 of the 25 reported some *net* income from touring, only 14 reported any *net* income from broadcasting and recording, and the bulk of the income in this category was earned by 5 or 6 orchestras. Thus, for most of the major orchestras, recording and broadcasting is a negligible source of income, even more so than the preceding table suggests. Nevertheless, earnings from sources other than admissions account for a substantial part of the incomes of some of the largest orchestras. In one not atypical case, *net* earnings from record royalties, broadcasting, television,

[4] Mean percentages are listed, based on data from American Symphony Orchestra League Compiled Annual Reports for 1963–64. Because of rounding, the figures do not add precisely to the totals shown.

Lest anyone compare the 15 per cent tour receipt statistic and our tour expense figure of 6 per cent and conclude that touring is necessarily profitable, the reader is reminded that the two percentages are not comparable. The touring cost item does not include salaries of performers, and the bases on which the two percentages are calculated also differ significantly.

and so on constituted 15 per cent of total (gross) earned income, and (though we do not have the figure) the gross earnings from these sources were surely considerably higher.

For some Broadway theatrical productions, income from the sale of movie rights can be very important. These sources sometimes provide amounts comparable with or even exceeding the total box-office returns. A notable example is "My Fair Lady." The total gross from its Broadway run was $9.6 million, while the movie rights were sold for $5.5 million. The report of the League of New York Theatres for 1962–63 indicated that the producers of 25 shows received an aggregate income of over $500,000 from motion picture royalties, but that one half of this went to just two productions (only one of which was a musical). Yet many a Broadway play is produced with an eye to potential sale of movie rights. Despite the narrowness of its distribution, this type of income undoubtedly plays an important motivating role for the commercial theater, and its prospect sometimes makes all the difference in raising funds for a new production.

Authors, producers and investors also derive some income from amateur, stock company and foreign performances; however, the average play receives little from these sources, which often serve primarily as an additional bonanza for the big hits. Even so, a number of producers have been tided over periods of financial stringency by this type of return on plays they had put on in the past.

The Income Gap

We arrive now at the critical financial item — the gap between expenditures and earned income. Heretofore we have referred to this as the "operating deficit" — a fairly standard term, but not a felicitous one when applied to a non-profit organization. To say there is a "deficit" implies that something has gone wrong, that costs must be cut or earnings increased so that the (reprehensible) deficit may be eliminated. But surely the fact that earnings fall short of costs raises questions which ought not to be prejudged in the case of the arts. For just this reason, in educational institutions, where expenditures characteristically exceed tuition receipts, people do not speak of an "operating deficit," nor do they think in such terms. The phrase "income gap" seems to come closer to what we mean. It emphasizes that the corresponding magnitude represents a lacuna in the organization's finances which needs somehow to be filled.

We turn now to the facts as summarized in Table VI–2. The total gross earned income — concert receipts, recording and broadcasting fees and services — of the median major orchestra in 1963–64 was $415,000. On the average, earned income was just about equal to the amount needed to pay the salaries of artistic personnel. In effect, all other expenses had to be paid out of contributed income. The income gap for the typical major orchestra was $327,000, a sum amounting to 46 per cent of the total budget of such an organization.

The main point to be derived from Table VI–2 is the near universality of the gap. Such gaps occur in the finances of the major orchestras, the Metropolitan Opera, the regional and off-Broadway theaters and most dance groups, though the gaps vary both in absolute amount and in relation to the size of budgets.

The median gaps are almost all very large. They amount to 32 per cent of total expenditures for the five largest orchestras, to perhaps 50 per cent for many dance groups, to nearly 50 per cent for major and metropolitan orchestras, to 45 per cent for operas other than the Metropolitan, to 21 per cent for the Metropolitan Opera and to 15 per cent for the regional theaters.

The theater, and particularly the commercial theater, comes closest to avoiding a gap between earned income and expenditures. Indeed, while much is made of the losses sustained by individual Broadway productions, it appears that Broadway as a whole continues to show a profit.[5] But in the regional theaters an income gap is now almost universal.[6] Even the Arena Stage in Washington,

---

[5] We must say "appears" because the data required to calculate an accurate rate-of-return figure for the total Broadway investment in recent years are not available. Watts calculated a rate of return for a sample of Broadway plays produced between 1948 and 1958; his annual rate of return figure of 19.5 per cent seems rather high.

[6] Schmidt, p. 50.

TABLE VI–2

Median Earned Income, Median Expenditure and Median Income Gap, by Art Form

	Season or Year (1)	Earned Income (thousands) (2)	Expenditure (thousands) (3)	Net Gap* (thousands) (4)	Gap as Per Cent of Expenditure (5)
Orchestras:					
Major Orchestras:					
Five Largest	1963–64	$1,539	$1,873	$ (750)	32
All Twenty-five	1963–64	415	715	(327)	46
Metropolitan Orchestras	1963–64	88	182	(83)	48
Opera Companies:					
Metropolitan Opera Association	1963–64	6,871	8,748	(1,877)	21
Ten Other Operas	1963	65	182	(82)	45
Dance Companies:					
New York City Ballet	1964–65	1,744	2,289	(545)	24
Two Civic Ballets	1963	6–8	9	(14)–(6)	70–40
Theater: Fourteen Regional Companies	1964–65	157	250	(40)	15

See notes to Table VI–1.

* Col. 4 need not equal col. 3 minus col. 2 because medians cannot be subtracted from one another.

which has escaped the problem until now, believes it will not be able to hold out much longer.[7]

The same phenomenon — the wide presence of an income gap — is found in Great Britain. (See Appendix Table VI–B.) The most striking piece of information on this subject is the magnitude of Covent Garden's gap between earned income and expenditures. At 44 per cent of the total budget, it easily overshoots that of the Metropolitan Opera. Perhaps this large figure can be ascribed in part to the help provided by the Arts Council — which might reduce pressures to undertake economies considered to be undesirable on artistic grounds. However, a number of British organizations have gaps smaller in relation to total budgets than our own. For example, the two London orchestras included in Appendix Table VI–B have income gaps ranging from about 12 to 18 per cent of expenditures, as compared with 46 per cent for major orchestras in the United States.

We conclude that a gap is certainly present — indeed, except for the commercial theater, it is nearly omnipresent. And it amounts to a sum that is by no means negligible. For a substantial proportion of professional performing organizations in the United States it amounts to more than 40 per cent of their expenditures.

The Total Gap

The size of the total income gap is a crucial figure. This is the amount which, at the present time, society must be prepared to

[7] Chamber music is not included in this discussion. Because chamber music is performed by very small groups, this field usually lacks the formal operations and the budgeting procedures that would permit us to investigate its income gap. It is not even easy to distinguish between performer and organization. However, two illustrative cases may be illuminating. One not atypical chamber music group of which we know succeeded in covering its expenses only twice in seventeen years; both occasions were years in which the State Department sent the group on concert tours abroad. In 1962, the group's best year, its fees for concert performances in the United States and abroad were $42,300. After expenses this left an adjusted gross income of about $6,500 per man.

The other (very famous) group is one whose fee per concert is about $1,000, from which the usual 20 per cent is deducted by the group's agent. Recordings bring very little direct financial return (less than $500 per year per per-

contribute, by some means, if the nation's existing performing arts organizations are to be kept solvent.

In making our estimate we include neither amateur nor strictly commercial organizations. The Broadway theater is omitted because at least a considerable part of its activity is avowedly commercial, and society is not asked to take direct financial responsibility for its survival. Much off-Broadway activity does not qualify legally as "non-profit," but we include all of it in our estimate because, whatever the intention of the producers, off-Broadway theaters are rarely profit-making institutions. Groups operated by colleges and universities are excluded because their function is often as much teaching as it is performance, and their financing may be considered only an indirect social responsibility. The figure we want to arrive at is the gap between expenditures and receipts from admissions and other payments for services rendered. This gap is by no means equivalent to a final deficit. Some of the gap is currently being met out of other sources of funds — committed contributions, income from endowment funds, and the like. In effect, then, the gap figure is an estimate of the deficit which is funded out of voluntary contributions.

Table VI–3 shows our calculation of the total income gap. In this table items based on firm data are separated from those derived from estimates or guesswork. Where an estimate was necessary the table provides, in effect, a plausible range rather than a single figure. Each guess is based on some information as to scale of activity and was made, wherever possible, after consultation with knowledgeable persons in the field.

Our estimate of the total gap ranges from about $20 to $23 million per year. Since about three quarters of this total is based on firm figures, and since the organizations carrying out the most costly activities all have given us their figures, the order of magnitude of our estimate can probably be accepted with a considerable

former), but serve as a valuable vehicle of publicity. After decades of unremitting labor with no vacations, each member of the group now earns an average of $16,000 annually, before taxes, from all sources of income — including teaching, recording, concerts and occasional individual free-lance work. The members of the group have never supported themselves entirely through concerts, nor do they ever expect to do so.

TABLE VI–3

Calculation of Total Income Gap: Non-profit, Professional
Performing Organizations, about 1964 (thousands)

KNOWN FIGURES		
Twenty-five Major Orchestras (1963–64)	$ 9,400	
Twenty-four Metropolitan Orchestras (1963–64)	2,210	
Metropolitan Opera (1963–1964)	1,877	
Ten Other Operas (1963)	1,116	
New York City Ballet (1964–1965)	545	
One Modern Dance Company (1963)	5	
Fourteen Regional Theaters (1964–65)	980	
Total Known Gap	$16,133	

ESTIMATED PORTION OF GAP	Conservative Estimate	Liberal Estimate
Other Metropolitan Orchestras[a]	$ 300	$ 400
Other Operas[b]	400	1,000
Other Ballet Companies[c]	500	1,200
Other Modern Dance Groups[d]	50	100
Other Regional Theaters[e]	800	1,250
Off-Broadway[f]	800	1,400
Miscellaneous[g]	500	1,000
Total of Estimated Figures	$3,350	$6,350
Estimated Total Gap (rounded)	$19,500–$22,500	

[a] Based on the assumption that metropolitan orchestras not reporting data operate on the same or a slightly smaller (¾) scale than the average for the metropolitan orchestras reporting.

[b] Based on the assumption that the 25–30 or so other operas offer on the average about 5 performances per year and have a gap of $5,000 per performance.

[c] Based on the assumption that the other half dozen or so professional ballet companies have gaps totaling at least as much as the New York City Ballet's ($545,000).

[d] Based on the assumption that the other 7 or 8 more or less permanent modern dance companies have gaps about the same as or larger than the one for which we have data ($5,000).

[e] Based on the assumption that the other regional theaters (approximately 25) have total gaps slightly larger than total for the 14 for which we have data ($980,000).

[f] Assumes an average capitalization of $15,000–$20,000 per show, and assumes that about 60 of the new productions and half of about 20 holdovers will have losses amounting to between ¾ and all of their capitalization.

[g] Based on information on the income gap of a chamber orchestra. Assumes the existence of 10–20 miscellaneous organizations of this magnitude.

degree of confidence, even if some of the individual components may be wide of the mark.

It is very important to recognize that a total income gap of less than $25 million for all the professional performing arts in the United States is an extremely small figure, given the scale of our economy. Twenty-five million dollars will not begin to pay for 25 miles of superhighway in a moderately populous area (in urban areas the cost approaches $100 million per mile). Nearly twice $25 million is spent on advertising *every day* of the year, and the advertising budgets of some companies are as high as $100 million per year. The federal government spends more than $25 million every two hours of the day and night, including Sundays and holidays. The total income gap is the price of perhaps three transatlantic jet-liners. A substantial number of universities *each* receive more than $25 million annually from the federal government; a few receive $100 million or more per year in federal funds.[8]

We do not mean to imply that the guaranteed provision of $20–$25 million would solve all the financial problems of the performing organizations. The very nature of their economic problem, and the psychological disposition of the artist, preclude a "this much and no more" type of settlement. Moreover, our figures deal only with operating costs; they make no provision for construction of theaters and other capital costs, which, as the experiences of cultural centers have shown, can be very substantial indeed. To us, the noteworthy implication of our total income gap figure is the small scale of professional independent non-profit performing activity in the giant American economy, and the miniscule fraction of the nation's wealth that is required to finance its continued operation.

Filling the Gap: Contributions and Net Deficits

Contributions of various kinds have enabled most performing groups to fill the gap between their earned income and their expenditures. This chapter will not analyze the sources and forms of these contributions — that is a subject for the last part of this book. But

[8] *Industrial Research,* April 1965, pp. 46–49.

it is worth noting that, in addition to the usual sorts of direct monetary contributions by individuals, business firms and government agencies, the organizations have benefited substantially from what might be considered contributions "in kind" — typically, the rent-free use of auditoriums. Statistics on this sort of contribution are difficult to obtain, for it cannot easily be assigned a pecuniary value and is seldom mentioned in an organization's accounting records. As a result, our estimates of the financial gaps often understate their true magnitude, and our data on contributions are correspondingly incomplete.

The data on contributions and net deficits (the difference between the income gap and contributions) are reported in Table VI–4. It will be observed that in a number of cases the amount of contributed income comes very close to meeting the gap in the years covered by the table. For example, the five largest orchestras are left with a median deficit of only $4,000 per year — two tenths of one per cent of their expenditures. The median deficit for the major orchestras is less than $4,000, for the metropolitan orchestras it is only $90 (!), and for no group of organizations have we found a median deficit in excess of $5,300 for the year. While it is true that some organizations end some years with staggering deficits, on looking over the budgets for individual organizations one is struck by the frequency with which contributions are almost precisely equal to the financial gap. In fact, one often encounters cases in which the net deficit is reported to be zero: contributions match the gap to the penny.

There are several reasons for this. One important explanation is the residual contribution. For example, the members of a board of directors, either individually or collectively, may be prepared to make up a reasonable deficit, and therefore will match their year-end donations to the amount of expenditure that has not yet been covered. In part, too, the degree of correspondence between total receipts and expenditure reflects good budgeting and careful management which prevent the organization from spending more than it has received or is likely to receive. Sometimes an accounting adjustment eliminates the *appearance* of a deficit, making it harder to interpret the net deficit figures and reducing their usefulness.

TABLE VI–4

Median Income Gap, Median Contributed Income and Median
Surplus or Deficit, by Art Form (thousands)

	Season or Year	Income Gap	Contributed Income	Net Surplus* or (Deficit)
	(1)	(2)	(3)	(4)
Orchestras:				
Major Orchestras:				
Five Largest	1963–64	$ (750)	$ 703	$ (4)
All Twenty-five	1963–64	(327)	294	(4)
Twenty-five Metropolitan				
Orchestras	1963–64	(83)	86	0
Opera Companies:				
Metropolitan Opera	1963–64	(1,877)	1,638	(240)
Ten Other Operas	1963	(82)	93†	(3)†
Dance Companies:				
New York City Ballet	1964–65	(545)	477	(68)
Two Civic Ballets	1963	(14)–(6)	11–6	0–(3)

See notes to Table VI–1.

* Col. 4 need not equal col. 3 minus col. 2 because medians cannot be subtracted from one another.

† New York City Opera omitted for lack of information.

This adjustment may draw on endowment funds, and relabel them "income on contributions." Conversely, if a surplus appears to be in the offing, a non-profit organization may quickly appropriate funds for "special projects," since a surplus can be embarrassing to such an organization, both in its future fund raising efforts and in its relations with the tax authorities.

Despite the generally low median deficit figure, there are organizations with serious financial troubles. For example, it was reported that in 1965 the Chicago Symphony faced a million dollar deficit.[9] And, in a special release, the National Repertory Theater indicated that during a recent three year period the group accumulated a deficit of $300,000, 83 per cent of which was in the form of a bank

[9] *Chicago Tribune and Sun-Times*, June 17, 1965.

loan.[10] According to news stories, the Royal Shakespeare Theatre in England was in serious financial difficulty in 1965. Despite a state subsidy of £40,000, it had apparently been losing money at a rate of £40,000 to £50,000 per year, and its funds were nearly exhausted. Other examples of such crises can easily be found in the records of the recent past.

What happens in such cases? There have been organizations that simply died — the Civic Repertory Theater in New York and the Ballet Russe de Monte Carlo. More frequently, the organization manages to hang on by borrowing money, sometimes from a bank, sometimes from individuals. Organizations sometimes live indirectly on the succeeding year's subscription income, and thereby postpone a financial crisis from year to year. Indeed, a person quite familiar with finances of symphony orchestras commented that no board of directors wants to stop operations when there is a deficit, for the members of the board might then feel morally obligated to dig into their own pockets in order to pay off creditors. They find it easier to pay off obligations from endowment funds or from advance ticket sales for the following season.[11] By such means it is possible, with the aid of an occasional emergency fund drive, to stay alive indefinitely. This staving-off procedure is particularly well suited to orchestras, which characteristically sell tickets by advance subscription, and it no doubt accounts, at least in part, for the amazing survival record of the major orchestras.

However, manipulation of funds is not the whole of the story. It is hard to believe that when an organization is in financial difficulties the quality and scale of its operations can long remain unaffected. Eventually it must begin to cut corners, and that cannot fail to change the product in ways which are not desired either by the organization itself or by the audience.

The total income gap of the nation's independent professional non-profit performing organizations is small by current economic

[10] National Repertory Theater, *Crossroads*, 1964, p. 3.

[11] A board of directors may well reason that it is better to employ the available funds than to pay 6 per cent on a loan. Strictly speaking, it is illegal to use future subscription money in the current season. Some organizations put such money in a savings account, to accumulate interest, and take out a bank loan to cover current deficits, thereby paying only a small differential interest rate.

standards. But for the individual performing group an income gap can mean the difference between life and death or, at the very least, between satisfactory and unacceptable standards of performance.

Here, then, is the financial problem of the performing organizations: the pressure that is imposed by the nearly universal financial gap, and the threat to quality which hangs over a group that incurs a significant and protracted deficit. In Part II we will undertake an analysis of the sources of these financial problems. The following chapter provides the analytic apparatus which will be utilized for this purpose.

PART **II**

THE TRENDS
AND THEIR ANALYSIS

CHAPTER VII

Anatomy of the Income Gap

In March 1720, Vanbrugh estimated that the [Royal Academy of Music subsidy] fund stood at £20,000, a sum sufficient, he thought, to maintain opera "till Musick takes such Root, as to Subsist with less aid." Instead of less support, however, it constantly needed more . . .[1]

IT SHOULD now be clear, if it was not before, that performing organizations typically operate under constant financial strain — that their costs almost always exceed their earned income. This chapter undertakes to analyze the reasons for this income gap and to determine, on the basis of this analysis, whether the gap is likely to be a chronic phenomenon of the future as it has been of the past.

Anyone familiar with the financial history of the performing organizations knows that the gap between costs and box office receipts characteristically has increased from year to year.[2] Sheer extrapolation would lead us to suspect that these pecuniary problems will continue to worsen. This chapter points to a far less qualified conclusion: because of the economic structure of the performing arts, these financial pressures are here to stay, and there are fundamental reasons for expecting the income gap to widen steadily with the passage of time. An understanding of the basic eco-

---

[1] Avery, p. lxi, citing Sir John Vanbrugh, Works, IV, 125–26.

[2] Trends in costs, earned income, contributions and deficits are examined in detail in the chapters that follow.

nomics of the live performing arts makes it clear that any other course of events is unlikely.

To explain why this is so, we shall first have to discuss the technology of the performing arts and show in what essential respects it differs from that of many other sectors of the economy. Here it is helpful to treat the arts, not as an intangible manifestation of the human spirit, but as a productive activity which provides services to the community; one which, in this respect, does not differ from the manufacture of electricity or the supply of transportation or house-cleaning services. In each case labor and equipment are utilized to make available goods or services which may be purchased by the general public. In each case there is a technology whereby these inputs are transformed into a finished product.

When the performing arts are viewed in this matter-of-fact manner, it will be seen that the tendency for costs to rise and for prices to lag behind is neither a matter of bad luck nor mismanagement. Rather, it is an inescapable result of the technology of live performance, which will continue to contribute to the widening of the income gaps of the performing organizations.

Productivity Gains and the Technology of Live Performance

The record of productivity gains in the United States is truly remarkable. For most of the twentieth century, output per man-hour (the amount of goods and services yielded by one hour of labor) has gone up at a steady rate of about 2½ per cent per year compounded.[3] This rate of increase means that output per man-hour has doubled approximately every 29 years. What is important about this observation is not the precise pace of advance but the fact that increasing efficiency in our economy has been continuous and cumulative. The factors responsible for productivity gains — new technology, an increasing capital stock, a better-educated labor

[3] The steadiness of the growth in output per man-hour is shown vividly in Figure VII-1 at the end of this chapter.

Output per man-hour is the simplest and best-known measure of productivity, but it is subject to some well-known limitations. For a discussion of more sophisticated measures, which allow for changes in the quality of labor and in the quantity and quality of the capital stock, see John W. Kendrick, *Productivity Trends in the United States*, National Bureau of Economic Research, Princeton University Press, Princeton, N.J., 1961.

force, economies of large-scale production — have combined to produce a dramatically steady record of compounded increases in output per man-hour.

The live performing arts have not shared fully in this growth in productivity. Though new means of presenting performances to the public have been developed, performing groups dependent on personal contact with the audience have been affected by them to only a very limited degree.

The development of motion pictures and phonograph records, radio and television has made possible a revolutionary change in the mechanics of presentation whose proportions it is difficult to exaggerate. This in turn has meant that the cost of providing a given hour of entertainment to each member of the audience has dropped precipitously. The change is probably far more radical than that experienced in any other economic sector where vigorous technological progress has been observed. For example, an orchestral performance on television, which, we are told by the professionals, takes less than twice the man-hours of a live performance, can reach an audience of 20 million instead of the 2,500 persons who occupy a concert hall, thus yielding an increase in productivity of four hundred thousand per cent![4]

But these developments have not helped the live performing arts directly. In fact, the competition of the mass media for both the audience and personnel of the living arts has sometimes had serious adverse consequences for the performing organizations.

To be sure, organizations providing live performance have benefited from some technological innovations. Air conditioning has made year-round operation possible for many groups that formerly had an enforced summer hiatus, and the jet airplane has speeded tours and decreased the cost of travel. Administrative operations in the larger organizations have benefited materially from the availability of new types of office equipment. But these developments have been sporadic and have had little effect on the technology of performance. They have done little to increase the hourly

---

[4] It is true that a great deal of labor has gone into the development and manufacture of the television sets required to provide this performance. But live performance also requires a great deal of auxiliary equipment per member of the audience — the hall itself and the costly transportation equipment used to get the audience there.

output yield of the performer himself, and, as we have seen, it is the salaries of performers which constitute the bulk of the outlays of the performing organization.

Though there have been improvements in lighting facilities, in the methods used to shift scenery and in a few other peripheral areas, the basic character of performance itself has stayed much the same. The playing of an instrument or the acting of a role remains today largely what it has been for centuries. From an engineering point of view, live performance is technologically stagnant.

The characteristic of live performance which precludes substantial changes in its mode of operation is that the work of the performer is an end in itself, not a means for the production of some good. When a customer purchases a typewriter, he usually neither knows nor cares how many man-hours of what kind of labor went into its manufacture. Any innovation which reduces the number of man-hours embodied in one such machine makes absolutely no difference to its buyer — except, of course, insofar as this affects its price. But in live performance matters are quite different. The performers' labors themselves constitute the end product which the audience purchases. Any change in the training and skill of the performer or the amount of time he spends before the audience affects the nature of the service he supplies. For, unlike workers in manufacturing, performers are not intermediaries between raw material and the completed commodity — their activities are themselves the consumers' good.

The immediate result of this technological difference between live performance and the typical manufacturing industry is that while productivity is very much subject to change in the latter, it is relatively immutable in the former. Whereas the amount of labor necessary to produce a typical manufactured product has constantly declined since the beginning of the industrial revolution, it requires about as many minutes for Richard II to tell his "sad stories of the death of kings" as it did on the stage of the Globe Theatre. Human ingenuity has devised ways to reduce the labor necessary to produce an automobile, but no one has yet succeeded in decreasing the human effort expended at a live performance of a 45 minute Schubert quartet much below a total of three man-hours.

In the live performing arts there is as little room for productivity increases through the accumulation of capital as there is for new technology. In manufacturing, capital accumulation, the provision of more and increasingly powerful machines and equipment which do not represent new inventions, has undoubtedly made an important contribution to the average product of a unit of labor. As business prosperity has enabled firms to devote more money to equipment, output per man-hour has risen correspondingly. Analogously, in the living arts the availability of more rehearsal rooms can save some performer time, and larger theaters can enable them to serve larger audiences with a given expenditure of effort. But where does one go from there? More expensive costumes for the acting group? More and larger drums for the orchestra? It is clear that since capital equipment plays so small a role in the productivity of live performance, accumulation offers little promise of enhancing output per man.

This is not meant to imply that increased efficiency or innovation is totally impossible for the arts or that increases in productivity per man-hour are completely precluded. We shall see, for example, that economies of larger-scale operations can increase productivity through the agency of longer seasons. Yet the arts cannot hope to match the remarkable record of productivity growth achieved by the economy as a whole.

Moreover, the performing arts find themselves in this position largely as a result of their inherent technology — something which is out of the hands of their managements and beyond the reach of the efficiency expert.[5]

[5] A colleague who took exception to some of these arguments brought to our attention the following statement, which we reprint from the *Bulletin* of the American Association of University Professors, Autumn 1955. The first few paragraphs appeared previously in *Harper's Magazine* for June 1955, as an "anonymous memorandum circulating in London, 1955." Apparently the statement had been published before that in the *O & M Bulletin*, the house organ of His Majesty's Treasury of the Courts, by permission of the *Ministry of Transport Bulletin*.

HOW TO BE EFFICIENT WITH FEWER VIOLINS

The following is the report of a Work Study Engineer after a visit to a symphony concert at the Royal Festival Hall in London:

For considerable periods the four oboe players had nothing to do. The number should be reduced and the work spread more evenly over the whole of the concert, thus eliminating peaks of activity.

All the twelve violins were playing identical notes; this seems unnecessary

At this point it would be useful to present statistics on productivity trends in the arts. We could then put to a direct test our hypothesis that productivity increases in this sector have been negligible — certainly smaller than productivity gains in the economy as a whole. Unfortunately this is impossible, in part because the outputs and inputs of the arts are difficult to measure or even to define satisfactorily, and in part because no major effort has as yet been made to overcome these difficulties. We can, however, report some of the preliminary results of a study of productivity trends in the entire service sector of the economy, much of which suffers from productivity limitations similar to those besetting the performing arts.

In spite of the fact that the service sector includes many industries which have recently benefited from important technological changes (insurance and finance, for example, now make extensive use of electronic data processing equipment), output per man-hour has gone up much less rapidly in this sector than in the goods sector. Over the entire period 1929–1961, output per man-hour increased 2.5 per cent per year in the goods sector and only 1.6 per

duplication. The staff of this section should be drastically cut. If a larger volume of sound is required, it could be obtained by means of electronic apparatus.

Much effort was absorbed in the playing of demi-semi-quavers; this seems to be an unnecessary refinement. It is recommended that all notes should be rounded up to the nearest semi-quaver. If this were done it would be possible to use trainees and lower-grade operatives more extensively.

There seems to be too much repetition of some musical passages. Scores should be drastically pruned. No useful purpose is served by repeating on the horns a passage which has already been handled by the strings. It is estimated that if all redundant passages were eliminated the whole concert time of 2 hours could be reduced to 20 minutes and there would be no need for an interval.

. . . it was noted that the pianist was not only carrying out most of his work by two-handed operation, but was also using both feet for pedal operations. Nevertheless, there were excessive reaches for some notes on the piano and it is possible that re-design of the keyboard to bring all notes within the normal working area would be of advantage to this operator. In many cases the operators were using one hand for holding the instrument, whereas the use of a fixture would have rendered the idle hand available for other work.

Obsolescence of equipment is another matter into which it is suggested further investigation could be made, as it was reputed in the program that the leading violinist's instrument was already several hundred years old. If normal depreciation schedules had been applied, the value of this instrument should have been reduced to zero and it is possible that purchase of more modern equipment could have been considered.

cent per year in the service sector. In the postwar period the difference has been even more pronounced: output per man-hour in the goods sector has increased at a compound rate of 3.1 per cent per year as compared with 1.7 per cent per year for services. The magnitude of this difference can be illustrated by noting that a quantity growing at a rate of 3.1 per cent per year doubles in less than 25 years, whereas a quantity growing at a rate of 1.7 per cent per year requires more than 40 years to double.[6]

On Productivity and Cost

It is clear that the limits to technological improvement which characterize the live performing arts must affect their costs of operation. On first consideration it might be thought that these handicaps would only prevent costs from going down; it is by no means obvious that they can impose rising expenditures on performing organizations.

Rising costs could be avoided if the arts were to exist in isolation. But, in fact, they must operate within a complex economy. And the interrelationships of the various sectors of the economy, together with the inability of the arts to achieve a sustained increase in productivity, make ever-higher costs an inevitable characteristic of live performance.

To understand these cost relationships it is necessary to consider in general terms what differential rates of growth in productivity within the economy imply for the relative costs of its various outputs.[7]

Let us imagine an economy divided into two sectors, one in which productivity is rising and another in which it is constant,

[6] The source of these data and some alternative calculations are presented in Appendix Table VII-A.

[7] There is nothing new in these observations on the effects of differential rates of productivity change on costs and prices. See, for example, Tibor and Ann Scitovsky, "What Price Economic Progress?," *Yale Review*, Autumn 1959. Only the application of these to the state of the arts is relatively new. Some of the general ideas are suggested in Poggi, in some of the annual reports of the Royal Opera, and in Toffler, Chapter XI, esp. p. 163 ff. See also Jean Fourastié's interesting comparisons of productivity rates, by century and nation, in his *The Causes of Wealth*, The Free Press, Glencoe, Illinois, 1960, Chapter IV.

the first producing automobiles, and the second, performances of Haydn trios. Let us suppose that in automobile production, where technological improvements are possible, output per man-hour is increasing at an annual rate of 4 per cent, while the productivity of trio players remains unchanged year after year. Imagine now that the workers in the automobile industry recognize the changes which are taking place and persuade management to agree to a matching rise in wages. The effect on the auto industry is easy to trace. Each year the average worker's wage goes up by 4 per cent, but his labor output increases by exactly the same percentage. As a consequence, labor cost per unit (the ratio between total labor cost and total output) remains absolutely unchanged. This process can continue indefinitely in our imaginary world, with auto workers earning more and more each year, with costs per car remaining stationary, and with no rise in automotive prices necessary to maintain company profits. If the number of hours worked by auto workers does not decline, the total output of the economy must increase, for more and more vehicles will come off the assembly lines every year.

But what of the other industry in our little economy? How is trio performance faring in this society of growing abundance? Here we must consider several alternatives. At one extreme is the case of a typical performer whose wage remains constant year after year, so that none of the economy's prosperity rubs off on him. His ability to buy goods and services does not increase at all. This implies more than is obvious at first, for it means that the musician must become increasingly impoverished. If an auto worker's wages go up every year at a compound rate of 4 per cent, before very long an instrumentalist, with his fixed remuneration, will come to be considered very poor, both by himself and by others. This in turn will presumably discourage some people from becoming musicians and will encourage movement into the automobile industry.

Consider now a second alternative for the music sector of our economy. Suppose that the trio players somehow succeed in getting their wages raised, and that their standard of living keeps up with that of the auto workers. What does this situation imply for the costs of trio performance? If the earnings of string players increase by 4 per cent per year while their productivity remains unchanged, it follows that the direct labor cost per unit of their output must also rise at 4 per cent, since cost per unit is equal to total cost divided by the number of units of output. If in a forty hour week the string player provides just as many performances as he did the previous year, but his wage is 4 per cent higher, the cost per performance must have risen correspondingly. *Moreover, there is nothing in the nature of this situation to prevent the cost of performance from rising indefinitely at a compound rate.* So long as the musicians are successful in resisting erosion of their relative incomes, the cost per performance must continue to increase along with the performer's income. Rising costs will beset the performing arts with absolute inevitability.

There is a third alternative, which, in fact, comes closest to what we find in practice. Wages of performers do rise, but they do not always manage to keep up with wages in the rest of the economy. Because performers frequently are dedicated individuals who are willing to work under economic conditions which would be considered appalling in other activities, the performing arts are relatively insensitive to general wage trends, especially in the short run. Even in the long run, earnings in the performing arts may lag behind wages in occupations which provide less in the way of psychic income. Whereas most unskilled workers, for example, are likely to regard the hourly wage as their primary reward for working, the typical performer presumably receives, in addition, considerable pleasure and personal satisfaction from his work. The important point is that, as the general level of real income increases over time, people may well feel that they are better able to afford to pursue careers which offer relatively lower money incomes but larger psychic incomes.

It is largely for these reasons that performing arts organizations in financial difficulty have often managed to shift part of their financial burden back to the performers and to the managements, who also are often very poorly paid by commercial standards. The levels of income in this broad field must be considered remarkably low by any standards, and particularly so in light of the heavy investment often made by the artists in their education, training and equipment.

However, all of this makes no essential difference to the logic of our analysis. With productivity per man-hour roughly constant, *any increase in wage rates, however modest, must lead to a corresponding increase in costs.* If wages go up 6 per cent elsewhere in the economy, but performer incomes rise by only 2 per cent, the direct labor cost of each performance must also increase by 2 per cent unless there is an offsetting reduction in the number of labor hours per performance.

It is important to recognize that price inflation plays no role in the logic of our analysis either. That is, so long as the wages of musicians in this two sector economy increase at all, the cost of a live performance will rise relative to the cost of an automobile, *whether or not the price level is changing;* the extent of the increase in the relative cost of the performance will depend *directly* on the rate of growth of productivity in the automobile industry.[8]

[8] In our illustrative case the change in relative costs was associated with some over-all inflation. While the cost and the price of an automobile remained constant, the cost and, presumably, the price of a live performance went up, causing an increase in the economy-wide average price level. However, this inflationary effect is a consequence of the assumption that auto workers' wages and musicians' wages both rose as fast as productivity in the automobile industry. This need not happen. Suppose wages of both auto workers and musicians were to rise at a rate of 2 per cent per year rather than 4 per cent per year. In this case automobile costs would decline by about 2 per cent per year, while costs per performance would increase by 2 per cent. If the industries each accounted for half of the economy's sales (and thus received equal weights in the consumer price index), there would then be no increase in the general price level — but there would be the same increase in the *relative* costs of a live performance as in the previous, inflationary case. While inflation *per se* may have various effects on the performing arts (and we shall return to this subject later), it is the relative change in the costs of a live performance which is of paramount importance, and therefore the accompanying degree of inflation need not concern us here.

It should be noted in passing that the President's Council of Economic Advisers has attempted to see that wages in each industry go up no faster than the *average* increase in productivity for the economy as a whole (2 per cent in our example), even though productivity in any one industry may be increasing more rapidly than in others. This policy is based explicitly on the proposition just spelled out — that this kind of wage behavior can produce shifts in relative costs without leading to inflation. (See *Economic Report of the President,* January 1962, and succeeding *Reports.*) It is also interesting that some well-known models of the inflationary process are based on the premise that the Council's admonitions will not be heeded, that in fact workers in a technologically progressive industry, such as automobile production, will receive wage increases in excess of the economy-wide average rate of increase of productivity, and that these "excessive" wage increases will be emulated by service industries (like the performing arts) which experience little if any gain

It will be evident that the foregoing analysis is applicable to many services other than the performing arts.[9] It accounts for the rising cost of fine foods, whose preparation still requires as much personal attention as the legendary Escoffier lavished on his product many decades ago. It helps to explain the financial problems of higher education, which have received even more publicity than those of the arts. Education, like the arts, affords little opportunity for systematic and cumulative increases in productivity. The most direct way to increase output per hour of teaching — an increase in the size of classes — usually results directly in a deterioration of the product which is unacceptable to much of the community. Thus, the financial problems which beset education are, at least in part, another manifestation of the fundamental relationship between productivity and costs which is so critical for the living arts.

The central point of the argument is that for an activity such as the live performing arts where productivity is stationary, every increase in money wages will be translated automatically into an equivalent increase in unit labor costs — there is no offsetting increase in output per man-hour as there is in a rising productivity industry. This leads to an important corollary: the extent of the increase in relative costs in these activities where productivity is stationary will vary directly with the economy-wide rate of increase in output per man-hour. The faster the general pace of technological advance, the greater will be the increase in the over-all wage level, and the greater will be the upward pressure on costs in any industry which does not enjoy increased productivity. Faster technological progress is no blessing for the laggards, at least as far as their costs are concerned. And in this connection it is relevant to

in productivity. Thus, our first model, positing a 4 per cent increase in wages and productivity in the auto industry, will have a familiar ring to many economists. (The best-known discussion of this model of the inflationary process is by Charles L. Schultze, in *Recent Inflation in the United States*, 86th Cong., 1st sess., Joint Committee Print, Study Paper No. 1, Government Printing Office, Washington, 1959.)

[9] See the Note at the end of this chapter for a discussion of statistical evidence on the general relationship between productivity and costs — evidence that strongly supports our analysis.

note that output per man-hour in the private sector of the economy has been increasing slightly more rapidly in the postwar years than in the earliest part of the century.

On the Economics of Ticket Pricing

We turn now to the other side of the income gap relationship — to the subject of earned income and, more particularly, to the principles of pricing as they apply to the performing arts.

In any industry we expect prices to bear a reasonably close relation to costs, especially in the long run. Therefore, if cost per performance increases steadily, it seems only natural to expect ticket prices to increase at about the same rate. Of course, if this were to happen (and it seems to be the general impression that it is just what has happened), then, assuming that attendance was unaffected, operating deficits would increase exactly in step with costs and prices, all going up at a rate of, say, 4 per cent per year. So long as revenues kept up with costs, the income gap would increase in absolute amount, but it would not increase *relative* to total expenditures. However, as will be shown in Chapter XI, ticket prices have in general lagged behind costs of performance.

How does one account for the lag in the rate of increase in prices? In offering our explanation we emphasize that this situation, too, contains elements which can be considered structural, and consequently the problems cannot be expected to disappear by themselves or through any dosage of "sound management" — that mysterious solvent so often proposed as the answer to any pecuniary problem.

Three basic influences can be expected to restrict severely the rate of increase in ticket prices:

(1) the disinclination of individual arts organizations to raise their prices, on moral grounds;
(2) the place of the arts in the ticket purchaser's hierarchy of necessities; and
(3) the forces of competition.

The first reason for expecting some lag in ticket prices lies in the doctrine of "just price," which colors the attitudes of those who supply performance as well as those who attend it. Since a performing organization is generally a dedicated group, firmly convinced of the value of its product to society, it is natural that it should seek to distribute its services as widely and as equitably as possible. The group is usually determined to prevent income and wealth alone from deciding who is to attend its performances. It wishes to offer its product to all who care to avail themselves of it — to students, to the impecunious, to those who are not yet devotees but who might learn to appreciate it, and to a variety of others whom high prices might deter from attending.[10]

It is easy to visualize what might happen to the performing arts if their prime objective were profit maximization. One can envision the nation's performing arts reduced to a vestigial state, with a very small number of theaters and orchestras catering to an exclusive group of persons who could afford to pay the very high and ever-rising prices necessary to keep them going.[11]

There are clear-cut cases where management continues to resist price increases even though there is an excess demand for the organization's services. The Metropolitan Opera is a case in point. Despite the fact that tickets must be rationed and most of the performances are typically sold out, the Metropolitan has not raised prices to the levels the traffic will bear. It is presumably not morally acceptable to turn the Metropolitan Opera House into an institution analogous to an exclusive restaurant in terms of the magni-

[10] The manager of one well-known non-profit organization assured us repeatedly that moral principles have nothing to do with the pricing decisions of his organization. Prices are kept low and deficits are maintained, he insisted, simply because this is the most effective way to raise money. While there is no doubt an element of truth in this statement, it is surely something of an exaggeration, even in his own case. More generally, we are convinced that most officials of performing arts organizations are completely sincere in asserting that low prices, in and of themselves, are one of their important policy objectives.

[11] The Broadway theater world comes closer to conforming to the profit maximization model than any other segment of the performing arts. Most investors on Broadway, notably the corporations which have been backing a number of musicals in recent years, doubtless go into the theater for the money they hope to make. The fact that the annual number of new productions on Broadway, especially the number of serious plays, has declined significantly (see Chapter III) is certainly in line with what one might expect to follow from a profit maximization goal. Nevertheless, even the Broadway theater is not a case of pure pursuit of profits. At least a few "angels" apparently invest more because of a commitment to the theater and a sense of psychic pleasure in participation than out of a calculated assessment of profit possibilities.

tude of its prices and the economic class of its clientele — and such a policy might also hurt fund raising.[12]

It is noteworthy, however, that higher education has instituted rather substantial price increases in recent years despite the fact that educators share the performing groups' reluctance to raise their fees. True, the colleges and universities have tried to soften the effect of tuition increases on less affluent students by increasing scholarships and making loans more easily available, but tuition levels have gone up by significant amounts nonetheless.

This brings us to the second influence that has held back ticket prices and kept them from rising as rapidly as tuitions. The explanation may lie, at least in part, in the difference in the intensity of demand for the services of the arts organizations and the colleges. Higher education has come to be regarded as a career requisite by a substantial segment of the population, who are willing to pay whatever price is demanded of them. But few people class the arts along with food, shelter, clothing, medical care — and now education — as items which must be purchased and paid for no matter what their cost. If performance becomes too expensive, most people can manage to get along without it. It is not easy to document this assertion, but there is much impressionistic evidence that it is valid. In any event, even if those who set ticket prices merely believe this to be true, their assumption will inhibit plans for raising admission costs.

The third reason for expecting ticket prices to be relatively stable lies in competition from the mass media. Ticket prices are held down by the very fact that there exist close and low-priced substitutes for live performance. As dramatic productions can be seen in the movies or on television and not only on the stage, and music can be heard on records and on radio, the price of live performance cannot be allowed to get too far out of line.

We see then that technological development, which places live performance at such a cost disadvantage, entraps it at both ends, as it were. The pattern of technological change causes costs of live

---

[12] The effect on fund raising is debatable. The same manager who argued that principles have nothing to do with ticket pricing maintained that contributions to his organization continued to rise even in years when it raised its ticket price scale.

performance to rise progressively, while at the same time it limits prices through the competition of the mass media.

Some Ameliorative Measures

Under the stress of the mounting operating deficits which plague the performing arts, all sorts of schemes have been suggested and all sorts of experiments are being undertaken. A variety of cost saving methods have been proposed and tried out. Thus, a number of Broadway producers have recently dispensed with out-of-town, pre-opening tryouts, and several cities seeking to provide music to the public have turned from the full-scale symphony to smaller, less expensive chamber orchestras. The spate of two and three character plays on Broadway during the 1964–65 season has also been interpreted as an economy measure undertaken in response to financial pressures.[13]

Performing arts organizations can also reduce the rate of increase in their unit costs by permitting the quality of their product to deteriorate, through fewer rehearsals, the use of less well trained performers, shoddy costumes and scenery, and so on. But such a course is never popular with organizations dedicated to quality, and, furthermore, it can lead to a loss of audience and community support. Nevertheless, it is not an uncommon "temporary" expedient, imposed by the realization that the cutting of corners may be the only alternative to abandonment of the enterprise.

There have also been experiments with ticket pricing which seek to disguise price rises or to attract larger audiences. For example, in many cases price scales have ostensibly remained unchanged, but

[13] See *New York Times*, January 24, 1965, Section II, p. 1. However, by the middle of the following season, no new small-cast productions had been mounted and, as a matter of fact, several very large-cast dramas were opened. Our own data (see Appendix Table VII–B) going back to 1895 show no evidence of any over-all trend toward smaller casts, though this may be accounted for, at least in part, by the rising number of musicals. There has, in contrast, been a decrease in the number of productions of intermediate cast size. What the experiences of the two or three character productions did show was that such a play can have a rather long and fairly profitable run even though the house is far from being filled to capacity. In this respect these plays were able to achieve a return to the theater economics of perhaps four decades ago.

a number of formerly inexpensive seats have been transferred to higher price brackets. Some producers have experimented with variations in scales of ticket prices over the course of the week, trying out higher prices for days in the latter part of the week, when audiences are larger and presumably willing to pay higher admission fees.

However, if this chapter's analysis is valid, all measures such as these are in the nature of palliatives. Once-and-for-all reductions in cost cannot indefinitely offset the cumulative pressures which technological advance in the rest of the economy will continue to impose on the arts.

This chapter has proposed a set of analytical hypotheses which can explain the observed difficulties of the performing arts and can, therefore, serve as a guide to policy. We have offered various pieces of evidence as partial tests of the hypotheses, but have only speculated on the course of costs and receipts in the various performing arts. The next chapters will report on the relevant historical trends and will thereby permit us to test further the model described.

A Note on Semi-logarithmic Graphs

Both parts of the accompanying graph (Figure VII–1) use exactly the same data to show the record of productivity change in the American economy since 1909, but the data are plotted on an ordinary graph scale in part A and on a semi-logarithmic scale in part B. Since semi-logarithmic graphs will be used many times in subsequent chapters, a brief explanation of their properties is in order for the benefit of readers who are unacquainted with this device.

The basic advantage of a semi-logarithmic graph is that it shows more clearly than an ordinary graph whether the percentage rate of growth has increased or decreased from one year to another.

Suppose an initial $200 grows at an unchanging rate of 100 per cent per year over a number of years. This means it rises to $400 during the first year; to $800 during the second year; to $1,600 the third year and so on. Although the percentage rate of growth is constant, the absolute change increases in each year because of compounding: previous accumulations grow from year to year along with the initial amount. An ordinary graph of these figures (like A in Figure VII–1) would curl upward more and more steeply as one moves from left to right, but this curvature would conceal the fact that the *percentage* rate of growth has been constant.

A semi-logarithmic scale (like that used in part B of Figure VII–1) is designed to correct for this compounding phenomenon. It *un*compounds a cumulative growth history and, if the percentage rate of growth has been constant, it transforms the graph that curls upward into one that is relatively straight. It does this by the simple device of compressing the vertical scale more sharply the higher one goes in the graph. On a conventional graph equal numbers are evenly spaced — the first inch above the origin represents, say, $100, the second inch $200, the third inch $300, etc. In the corresponding semi-logarithmic graph the higher one goes the more closely the numbers are spaced. If the distance between the $100 and the $200 level is still one inch, the second inch mark represents $400 rather than $300, a third inch would bring us up to $800, and so on. In other words, on a semi-logarithmic graph the vertical scale is compressed just enough to undo the compounding effects.

The "semi" in the appellation "semi-logarithmic" indicates that only one of the two axis scales has been distorted in the manner indicated. The word "logarithmic" appears because the uncompounding effects obtained by compressing the vertical scale are the same as those which one would obtain by plotting logarithms of the dollar figures on ordinary graph paper.

Thus, the first of the two diagrams in Figure VII–1 represents productivity data with all of their compounding included, while the second gives the same information after the compounding has been removed. The fact that in diagram A the quantity on which successive percentages are calculated keeps changing tends to obscure the actual percentage change; in the years since about 1935, for example, the rate of increase seems to be rising steeply. But if one were to place a ruler along the points in diagram B for the years since about 1935, he would notice that they form an almost

FIGURE VII–1

INDEX OF OUTPUT PER MAN-HOUR,

UNITED STATES, 1909–1964 (private sector)

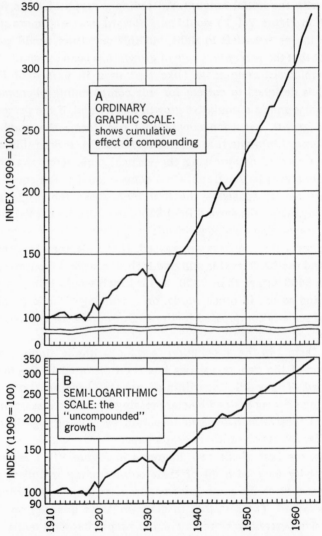

The data were calculated from indexes of output per man-hour, 1957–1958 = 100, 1954 dollars, *Economic Report of the President,* January 1965, p. 227. Figures for 1909–1946 were obtained by multiplying output per man-hour on a 1947–1949 base (from Bureau of Labor Statistics Bulletin 1249) by .7325, which is the approximate ratio between the two series for 1947–1949.

perfectly straight line. The linearity of the relationship means that the annual percentage rate of growth of productivity has in fact been almost constant.

A more rigorous way of estimating the steadiness of the rate of growth employs a measure called the "coefficient of determination" (R^2) of the regression used to calculate the average annual rate of increase. This measure tells us how closely the dots cluster about a straight line. If the dots fit very closely, R^2 is approximately unity; if the dots do not form a linear pattern, R^2 is approximately zero. For the period 1947–1964 in the present instance, the R^2 has the very high value of .99, meaning that 99 per cent of the variation in the output per man-hour figures is accounted for simply by the linear trend.

A Note on the Statistics on Productivity and Costs

The central proposition of this chapter, that the cost of a live performance can be expected to rise relative to costs in general, is investigated specifically in the next chapter, where we present the results of our studies of cost trends in the performing arts. Before ending this more general discussion, however, we shall cite some of the work being done in related fields in support of the fundamental analytical point we have been making — that differential rates of increase in productivity among industries lead to predictable differences in rates of increase in costs.

Kendrick's monumental study of productivity trends in the United States is the source of one relevant piece of evidence.[14] In this study Kendrick correlated changes in total factor productivity among industries with changes in "unit value added" (a measure of the amount spent by buyers, after the cost of raw materials is deducted, on each unit of a commodity) for the whole period between 1899 and 1953 and for various sub-periods. The results were fully consistent with our theoretical expectations: unit value added (net prices to consumers) tended to increase most in industries where productivity increased least, and vice versa.[15]

[14] Kendrick, Chapter 7, especially pp. 200–1.

[15] Kendrick ran his correlations for a set of 33 major industries and a set of 80 manufacturing industries, in six sub-periods. The correlations were neg-

As indicated earlier, we have evidence that productivity has increased less rapidly in the service sector than in the goods sector, and so a direct comparison of the movement of relative prices in these two sectors is also very much to the point. The most appropriate price measures — the G.N.P. implicit price deflators, by major type of product — show that prices rose 11 per cent in the service sector and only 4 per cent in the goods sector between 1958 and 1962.[16]

Comparison of the more widely known service price index with the wholesale price index also yields clear-cut results. During the postwar period 1947–1964, the service price index went up at an average rate of 3.3 per cent per year, whereas the wholesale price index rose only 1.5 per cent per year. During the last three of these years, when productivity seems to have risen unusually fast, the wholesale price index rose imperceptibly (.03 per cent per year), while the service price index went up 1.89 per cent per year.[17]

In short, the available data are entirely consistent with the predictions generated by the simple theoretical model described earlier in this chapter.

ative for both sets of data in each sub-period. Over the long period (1899–1953), the correlation was −0.74 for the 33 industries group and −0.57 for the 80 manufacturing industries group; both coefficients were easily significant at the 99 per cent confidence level. The strength of the negative correlations becomes particularly impressive when we recognize that total costs are also affected by movements in raw material costs, changes in the relative importance of raw material costs and other elements which have no clear relation to productivity.

[16] See "G.N.P. by Major Industries, Revised and Updated," *Survey of Current Business*, September 1963.

[17] The average annual rates of increase given in this paragraph were calculated by fitting a trend line to annual observations. The basic data came from the *Economic Report of the President*, January 1965.

CHAPTER VIII

Trends in Over-all
Cost of Performance

I N THIS chapter we discuss trends for the first time. Here we are primarily concerned with rates of change in the costs of a performance and their relationship to trends in the general price level. The behavior of these variables constitutes a direct test of our central analytic hypothesis, for, if it is valid, we would expect costs per performance to rise more rapidly than the over-all price level.

A tremendous data problem besets this sort of inquiry. If the data do not span a very considerable number of years, we run the risk of being misled by temporary aberrations that have little or no relation to the underlying trends. But statistical series which are continuous over a considerable time interval are difficult to find. Few organizations have long, continuous histories, and fewer still have preserved their early records. Fortunately, however, we have been able to obtain some remarkable sets of records spanning very long periods. These case histories enable us to form a clear picture of long-term trends and cyclical patterns in costs and prices for two major orchestras. The data are sufficient to enable us to report on a wide range of art forms.

Our investigation of costs has also permitted us to undertake a somewhat more ambitious analysis. We have sufficient information on the major orchestras to investigate how costs per unit (costs per concert) vary with the scale of activity. Knowledge of this relationship enables us to determine the extent to which performing organizations have available to them the economies of large-scale production: whether it is true for them, as it is for many

181

industries, that an increase in output can yield a reduction in cost per unit of output.

This chapter shows very clearly that costs per performance have risen more rapidly than costs of other activities in the economy as a whole. This finding is documented in terms of several long-period case histories, in terms of the different stages of the business cycle, and for all organizations for which we have been able to assemble postwar data. The detailed discussion in the chapter will be of interest primarily to those readers who are especially concerned with historical relationships and wish to know precisely what the record shows.

Some Evidence on Cost in the British Theater

There is still extant a set of 21 account books for the Drury Lane and Covent Garden Theatres in London which span the period 1740–1775.[1] These are the earliest usable data found, and they permit a crude comparison between costs for that period and current costs on the London stage. In interpreting our results it should be recognized that such comparisons involve two difficulties. First, the scale of activity has changed: length of season today is not the same as it was in the 1700's. This source of error can be corrected, at least to some extent, by dealing with cost per performance instead of cost per year or season. Second, there have probably been changes in the elaborateness and quality of production which also influence costs. Unfortunately, as we have no way to measure these changes, we can do little to allow for them. Historical records may shed some light on qualitative changes, but this is a problem which will plague us throughout the chapter.

To determine cost trends for the London theater, we calculated the average cost per performance in the Drury Lane over the five year period 1771–72 through 1775–76 and the 1963–64 cost per performance of the present Royal Shakespeare Theatre. The earlier figure came to £157 and the more recent figure was £2,139.[2] Comparing them, we conclude that costs per performance have risen

---

[1] These records are tabulated in Stone, pp. ccxxxiv–ccxxxv.

[2] Calculated by taking ⅛ of the total weekly expenditure at the Royal Shakespeare, there being 8 performances per week.

some 13.6 times over this period, which is the same as saying that there has been an average annual rate of increase of 1.4 per cent compounded.

The key issue, of course, is whether this rate of increase in costs is greater or less than the rate of increase of prices in general. Thanks to the efforts of two British economists, there is available a price index which can be used to answer this question.[3] Over the period 1773–1964 we find that the price level rose to about 6.2 times its initial level; that is, prices grew at a compound rate of about 0.9 per cent per year. Thus, the average annual rate of increase in costs per performance was nearly 60 per cent greater than that in prices, and the cost per performance over the period as a whole went up more than twice as much as the price level.

One may ask whether qualitative changes in the theater between the two periods can account for this difference — whether theatrical costs might have risen much more slowly if the two companies had been more similar in their operations. An examination of the facts suggests the contrary. During the earlier period, although contemporary dress was frequently worn, costumes and scenery were quite expensive and elaborate.[4] More telling is the fact that at the Drury Lane Theatre at that time some 51 different full-length plays and 25 different "afterpieces" seem to have been performed each season, and many of these were new productions.[5] It is hard to believe that any contemporary theater could operate on this scale without a substantial rise in its costs.

[3] For our price index we use the index of a "composite unit of consumables" constructed by E. H. Phelps Brown and Sheila V. Hopkins for the years 1260 to 1954. (See their "Seven Centuries of the Prices of Consumables, Compared with Builders' Wage-Rates," in *Essays in Economic History*, Vol. II, edited by E. M. Carus-Wilson, Edward Arnold Ltd., London, 1962, pp. 179–96.) Their index is based on 1451–1475 = 100, and for the years between 1771 and 1776 its median value is 835. In the last year of their index, 1954, the value is 3,825. We projected this value forward to 1964 by assuming that it increased at the same rate over this recent period as the official retail price index, which rose from 125 in 1954 (1950 = 100) to 169 in 1964. (See United Kingdom, Ministry of Labor, *Statistics on Incomes, Prices, Employment, and Production*, No. 13, June 1965.) This gives us a projected value for the Phelps Brown-Hopkins index of 5,174 for 1964.

[4] Stone, p. clx ff.

[5] Stone, p. clxii ff.

Continuous Histories:
The New York Philharmonic and Cincinnati Orchestras

So far we have compared costs at two distinct points in time and for two different organizations whose similarity is not entirely clear. Analysis of year-to-year changes in a single organization's costs over a long period of time is a much more satisfactory procedure, and, through the cooperation of the managements of the New York Philharmonic and Cincinnati Symphony Orchestras, this is possible.

The New York Philharmonic was founded in 1842 and is the oldest orchestra in this country. From its extraordinary collection of historical materials we were able to compile financial data for 100 of the 122 years of its existence. The gaps in our data correspond to the periods 1876–1883, 1909–1914 and 1920–1927, at least two of which were somewhat troubled periods in the history of the orchestra.

Our other long series describes the Cincinnati Orchestra from 1920 through 1964. Though the Cincinnati data do not go back as far as those for the New York Philharmonic, they are continuous over the period of the 1920's when there is a serious gap in the Philharmonic records. The existence of this second, very detailed case history lessens the danger of our being misled by some quirk in the history of the New York Philharmonic.

The expenditures of the New York Philharmonic amounted to less than $3,000 in 1850 as compared with its total outlay of roughly $3 million in 1965–66. It was then composed of 64 musicians — about three fifths of its current membership — and was organized as a cooperative.[6] Figure VIII–1 summarizes graphically the total expenditures of the orchestra over the entire period, and shows that its growth was very steady despite some relatively brief but violent fluctuations.[7] This graph, like most in this chapter, is drawn on a semi-logarithmic scale. It will be recalled from the discussion of this device in the preceding chapter that

---

[6] Some of the flavor of the early operations of the orchestra is conveyed by the financial statement for the year 1850, reprinted in Appendix Table VIII–A.

[7] There are a number of accounts of the history of the New York Philharmonic: Krehbiel, Erskine, and Mueller (pp. 37–69). On the history of the Cincinnati Orchestra see Mueller, pp. 113–22.

FIGURE VIII–1

NEW YORK PHILHARMONIC: TOTAL EXPENDITURES, 1843–1964

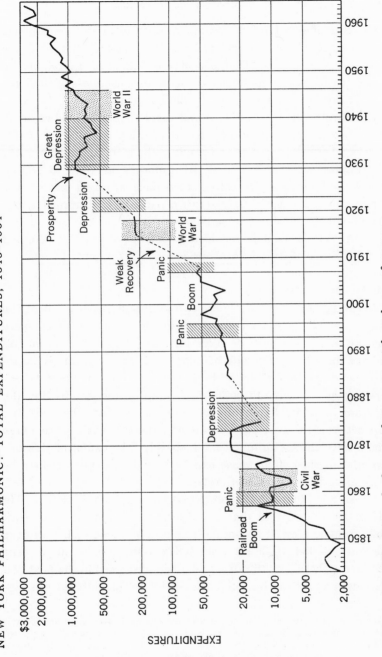

In this and the following graphs the years shown represent the end years of seasons; 1954, for example, refers to the season 1953–54.

on a scale of this kind a *constant* compound rate of growth will yield a graph which is a straight line. Thus, the fact that the graph in Figure VIII–1 is a fairly good approximation of a straight line (short-period variations aside) attests to the steadiness of the long-term growth in expenditures of the Philharmonic.

Specifically, between the terminal years 1843 and 1964 expenditures rose at a compound annual rate of 6.1 per cent. Part of this very rapid growth in outlay is a result of the increase in the number of concerts per year (from 4 performances in 1843 to 183 in 1964), and we must, therefore, turn once again to expenditure per performance to obtain a series capable of indicating the rise in cost of a given amount of activity.

Figure VIII–2 depicts the history of expenditures per concert and the course of the wholesale price index.[8] (Cincinnati Orchestra expenditures per concert are also shown on this graph, but they will be ignored for the moment.)

It will be noted that while the two graphs start out at about the same level, the cost per concert graph slopes upward much more sharply than the wholesale price line. In interpreting the magnitude of this differential rate of increase, it must constantly be remembered that a semi-logarithmic scale compresses absolute differences as we move to points higher up on the graph. Had the diagram been drawn on an ordinary graph scale, the widening gap between the cost per concert and the wholesale price index would have shown up much more sharply. The extent of this differential in rates of increase can be brought out most clearly by calculating numerical growth rates.

Considering first the longest period for which data are available (1843–1964), we find that costs per concert for the New York Philharmonic grew at an annual rate of 2.5 per cent per year over the entire period, while the price index went up only 1.0 per cent per year. (These growth rates, and others discussed in the next two sections, are summarized in Table VIII–1.) This difference is sig-

---

[8] For our purpose the wholesale price index seemed more appropriate than the consumer price index. The reasons for this, the consequences if we had used a consumer price index in our calculations and some possible sources of bias in our calculations are discussed in Appendix VIII–1.

nificant. Over 121 years, the length of our period, an amount increasing at 2.5 per cent is multiplied twentyfold by compounding, whereas an amount increasing at a 1 per cent growth rate merely quadruples. In other words, over our 121 year period the cost of a New York Philharmonic concert rose five times as much as the wholesale price index.

Between 1890 and 1964 cost per concert grew at a remarkably steady rate of 2.5 per cent per year, while the wholesale price index, after a long period of decline (1865–1887) rose at a rate of 1.6 per cent.

If we start our long-term comparison from 1920 we are also able to include the Cincinnati figures.[9] Again the disparity between the rate of increase of orchestral costs and wholesale prices is clear and considerable. The annual growth rate for the Philharmonic was 3.9 per cent; for Cincinnati, 2.2 per cent; and for wholesale prices, only 0.4 per cent.

In appraising these growth rates it would be misleading to ignore changes in the quality of the New York Philharmonic, to which some of the rapid rise in its cost per concert must undoubtedly be ascribed. Probably throughout its early history and certainly at the turn of the century, because of its continued adherence to what Mueller describes as "the obsolete system of cooperative organization,"[10] it was a thoroughly second-rate enterprise. Some of the performers were poorly qualified, and all were inadequately disciplined and rehearsed. As late as World War I, "The Philharmonic could not escape odious comparison with its sister orchestras."[11] It must have been expensive to turn a mediocre orchestra into the outstanding organization it subsequently became. As a result, for our purposes, we must discount some of the high rate of increase in cost per concert shown in our graphs, treating it not as a manifestation of the technology of performing organizations in

[9] We use 1920 only because that is when our Cincinnati figures began. It is not a good base year, since it came just at the end of a period of sharp wartime inflation, which affected wholesale prices more than orchestral costs.

[10] It is noteworthy that the four London orchestras are all currently operating as cooperatives.

[11] Mueller, p. 54. On problems of quality in the Philharmonic at the turn of the century see Mueller, pp. 46–51.

FIGURE VIII-2

NEW YORK PHILHARMONIC AND CINCINNATI ORCHESTRAS: EXPENDITURES PER CONCERT AND THE WHOLESALE PRICE INDEX, 1843–1964

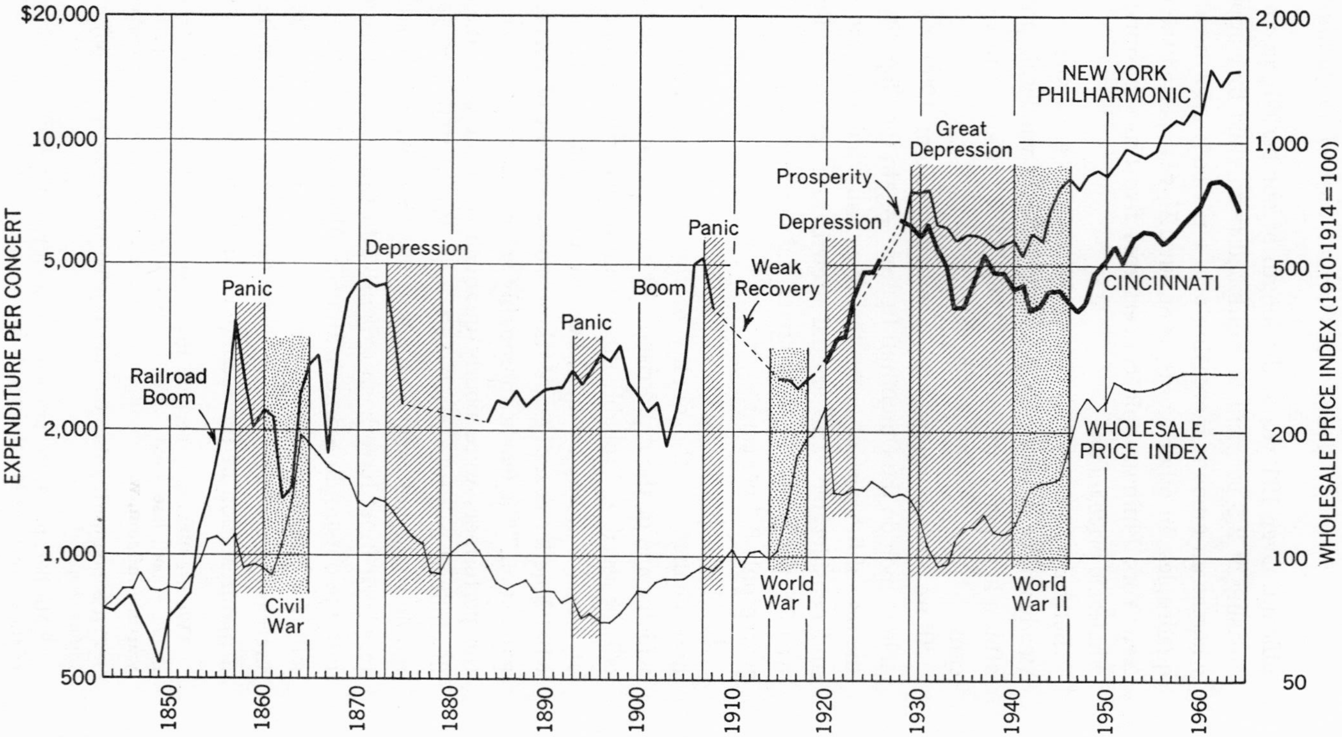

188

(*Notes on opposite page*)

general, but as a result, in part, of the peculiar history of this particular group.[12]

Prosperity, Depression and Wartime Inflation

Long-period trends, by definition, are mute with regard to the relation between fluctuations in economic activity and variations in orchestral costs. Yet to understand the economics of the performing arts it is important to see how the fortunes of an arts organization are affected by prosperity and depression, by war and inflation. Furthermore, only by relating the history of orchestral costs to contemporary economic circumstances can we tell whether the observed long-period differences in the growth of costs and general prices are an accident of the years chosen for comparison or whether they really reflect underlying economic phenomena. The length of the time series at our disposal makes this kind of cyclical analysis possible.

Our historic period encompasses the Civil War and the two World Wars. During each of the corresponding periods of wartime inflation the data go in the opposite direction from that predicted by our hypothesis — in each case the price level rose more rapidly

[12] It should be noted that changes in the nature of an orchestra's operations can bias our cost per concert growth rate downward as well as upward, depending on the direction of change and the base year used. For example, the "true" rate of increase in the costs of a given concert of the Cincinnati Orchestra between 1931 and 1964 is surely understated by comparing costs in 1931, the year in which Fritz Reiner left, and 1964. During most of the 1920's Reiner was conductor of the orchestra, and he apparently insisted on such exacting standards that the costs of the Cincinnati Orchestra almost equaled those of the New York Philharmonic. And this was at the time that Toscanini, with his reportedly astronomic salary and demanding rehearsal requirements, had pushed New York's costs to an extraordinary level!

Notes to Figure VIII–2
Between 1884 and 1905 it was customary for the Philharmonic to put on an equal number of regular concerts and public rehearsals (e.g., 6 of each in 1884 and 9 of each in 1905). Apparently, fees were collected for attendance at the latter. For this reason, and because it is difficult to separate these performances and their associated costs from the regular performances of the group, we have counted these rehearsals as part of the total number of concerts. Since public rehearsals are not mentioned after 1906, there is some question as to the validity of the segment of the graph corresponding to the period when the practice changed. Data for this graph were obtained from records of the two organizations; on the derivation of the wholesale price index see the notes to Table VIII–1.

TABLE VIII–1

Trends in Expenditures Per Concert (two major orchestras)
and in the Wholesale Price Index, Selected Periods, 1843–1964

Time Period	Average Annual Percentage Increase (compound rate)[a]		
	Expenditures per Concert		Wholesale Price Index
	New York Philharmonic	Cincinnati Symphony Orchestra	
Long-Period Comparisons:			
1843–1964	2.5		1.0
1890–1964	2.5		1.6
1920–1964[b]	3.9	2.2	0.4
Wartime Inflations:			
Civil War: 1861–1864[c]	27.0		30.0
World War I: 1915–1919	0.8		18.8
World War II: 1940–1948	4.5	–0.9	9.7
Depressions:			
1857–1860	–15.2		–5.7
1893–1897	1.1		–3.4
1920–1921	n.a.	11.0	–37.0
1929–1932 (1931–1934)[d]	–9.1	–14.7	–32.0
1929–1940	–2.3	–3.4	–17.4
"Good Times":			
1843–1857	12.1		2.8
1897–1905[e]	–0.4		3.5
1922–1928	n.a.	10.9	0.0
1948–1964	3.8	4.0	1.5

SOURCE: Orchestra expenditures per concert were calculated from data generously made available by the respective orchestras. The source of our wholesale price index for the years 1843–1951 is U. S. Bureau of the Census, *Historical Statistics of the United States, Colonial Times to 1957*, Washington, D. C., 1960, Chapter E, esp. pp. 102–3, 115–17. We use the "all commodities" series. The original source of the figures for 1843 to 1890 is George F. Warren and Frank A. Pearson, *Prices* (John Wiley and Sons, New York, 1933). The Warren-Pearson index is ideal for our purposes because it was intended to correspond with the Bureau of Labor Statistics (BLS) index, which is the primary source of data for years 1890 on. Also, the Warren-Pearson index is based mainly on New York City prices, which is fortunate since we wish to compare this series with costs and prices for the New York Philharmonic. The BLS series from 1890 to 1951 (*op. cit.*, pp. 116–17) uses

than cost per concert. Only during the Civil War did orchestral costs come close to keeping up with prices. During World War I the wholesale price index rose 18.8 per cent per year, almost doubling between 1915 and 1919, while orchestral costs hardly increased at all. During World War II and its inflationary aftermath, wholesale prices went up almost 10 per cent per year, while costs per concert of the Philharmonic rose at a rate of 4.5 per cent. There was an absolute decline in the cost per concert of the Cincinnati Orchestra, much of which can be ascribed to the fact that it increased the number of its performances sharply during this period and so reaped substantial economies of larger-scale operation.

Thus, the prediction of our basic analysis is wrong — consistently wrong — for periods of wartime inflation. There are several

Notes to Table VIII–1 continued

1926 = 100 as its base, and in order to have one continuous series we recalculated these numbers using the Warren-Pearson base period of 1910–1914 = 100. (For 1890 the Warren–Pearson index is 82 while the BLS index, with 1926 = 100, is 56.2; hence, the BLS index can be put on the Warren–Pearson base of 1910–1914 = 100 by multiplying each number by 82/56.2.) The original source of the BLS figures for years 1952–1964 is the *Economic Report of the President*, January 1965. Since this current series uses a base of 1957–1959 = 100, it was necessary to put it on the 1910–1914 = 100 base in a manner analogous to that used to transform the 1890–1951 series.

[a] Calculated on the basis of terminal years only, except that the 1964 figure for Cincinnati is the mean of the figures for 1962, 1963 and 1964; the atypical nature of the 1964 Cincinnati observation would have distorted growth rates calculated by the terminal year method.

[b] The New York Philharmonic rate applies to the period 1919–1964 because no figure was available for 1920.

[c] The New York Philharmonic growth rate is for the period 1862–1865 rather than 1861–1864. We have a choice here, because the 1862 orchestra figure is actually for the season 1861–62; and, as Figure VIII–2 shows, it is the 1862–65 period which corresponds most closely to the behavior of the wholesale price index between 1861 and 1864.

[d] Whereas the decline in the wholesale price index can be dated from 1929, the decline in costs per concert for both of our orchestras did not start until 1931. We have, therefore, calculated our "sharp" rate of decline for the orchestras from 1931 to 1934, this being the period analogous to 1929–1932 for the wholesale price index.

[e] We end this period in 1905 because, beginning in 1906, the method of counting New York Philharmonic concerts may have changed. (See the note to Figure VIII–2.)

possible explanations for this pattern. First, patrons may be less inclined to support their orchestras during wartime, and expenditures may be held down correspondingly; it might seem unpatriotic to increase orchestral expenditures markedly during a time of national crisis. Second, earnings in most salaried occupations are notoriously slow to respond to inflationary or deflationary conditions — they are "sticky" — and it may well be that the behavior of musicians' salaries during sharp inflations conforms to this pattern. This possibility will be examined in some detail in the next chapter when we analyze trends in the salaries of performers. Still a third possibility is that in wartime there tend to be shortages of many of the commodities represented in the wholesale price index, and the pressure of excess demand produces sharp increases in the prices of these commodities. Whatever the reasons, the plain fact is that during wartime inflations orchestral costs have lagged behind the wholesale price index, and the consistency of the pattern suggests that our observations do not represent mere historical accident.

Looking next at depressions, there are four periods of "hard times" covered by our data — 1857–1860, 1893–1897, 1920–1921 and 1929–1940 — and with one exception they tell a consistent story which certainly *is* in line with our hypothesis. The exceptional period is the first, the pre-Civil War Panic of 1857–1860, when the wholesale price index fell at a rate of nearly 6 per cent per year but cost per concert fell almost three times as rapidly.[13]

[13] Here we must rely on an *ad hoc* explanation. The 1856–57 season was extraordinarily successful, with receipts more than 50 per cent higher than in any previous year and much higher than in any year for nearly a decade to come. That season was the culmination of nearly ten years of sharply rising orchestral income. In 1857–58 receipts fell slightly below the amount which had prevailed in 1855–56, and there they remained for several years. As a result, payments to musicians, which were determined residually under the cooperative system, also declined. (An important general point to be noted here is that our cost figures are highly dependent on demand conditions, because musicians' incomes were determined by what was left over from orchestral receipts after payment of other expenses. But all other cost data for the performing arts share this characteristic to a degree. For example, any arts organization tends to trim its costs when its income falls. In this respect, then, all of our cost data may be considered impure, and any test of our hypotheses in which we use these figures is correspondingly imperfect.) If we look at the change in costs between 1856–57 and 1857–58 alone, what may

However, this pattern was reversed during our next major depression, the Panic of 1893 (and the longer depression period of 1888–1897).[14] Cost per concert continued to rise despite a substantial rate of decline in the wholesale price index. We come next to the brief period of depression following World War I. There is a gap here in the Philharmonic data, but we do have Cincinnati figures. Between 1920 and 1921, while the wholesale price index fell 37 per cent, the Cincinnati's cost per concert went up about 11 per cent. The great depression of the 1930's is the one slump for which we have very good orchestral data. These show a clear pattern. Costs per concert declined for both orchestras, whether we include in our calculation only the initial period of the greatest depression or take into account the entire decade of the 1930's. But for neither orchestra in neither period was the decline anywhere near so precipitous as the fall in wholesale prices.

Thus, with the exception of the very special case of the 1850's, every depression seems to have shown a pattern consistent with our analysis. Cost per concert either rose despite a falling whole-

from a longer viewpoint be regarded merely as a leveling off, looks like a precipitous drop. In addition, in 1858–59 the Philharmonic began an eight year period in which it performed five concerts per season, having offered only four concerts during each of the preceding fifteen years. Since there was no corresponding increase in orchestral outlays, this additional concert automatically caused a 20 per cent drop in expenditure *per concert*. Finally, in 1858–59 the Philharmonic moved back from the large and apparently expensive Academy of Music to Niblo's Garden. Together, these three facts explain the extraordinary drop in expenditure during the depression period of 1857–60 — a fall more rapid than that in the price level. (See Krehbiel, pp. 115–17.)

[14] It is unfortunate that our series spans only the first three years of the 1873–1879 slump. While during these years expenditure per concert dropped precipitously, this was the result of a very special set of adverse circumstances in the history of the Philharmonic.

In 1867 R. Ogden Doremus, Professor of Chemistry at New York University, accepted the presidency of the Philharmonic on the condition that membership in the orchestra be increased to 100 performers and that it hire prominent soloists (Mueller, p. 43). This caused a near doubling in cost per concert, at which level the orchestra continued to operate through 1873. At this point, however, the Philharmonic seems to have run into deep trouble, partly because of energetic competition from various sources.

Our data, consequently, show a precipitous drop in cost per concert during the next two years, and then the figures disappear altogether. It is hardly surprising that the two years for which figures exist exhibit a decrease in orchestral costs greater than the fall in wholesale prices.

sale price level, or declined less rapidly than the level of prices. In other words, *cost per concert rose relative to wholesale prices* during each of these periods.

Finally, we look at the prosperous peacetime periods in our history. Here again there is one exceptional case — the period 1897–1905 when cost per concert for the New York Philharmonic fell even though the price level was rising.[15] But during every other period of peacetime prosperity for which we have figures, cost per concert rose substantially more than the price level. This is true of the "railroad boom" of the 1850's when the annual rate of increase in orchestral costs was more than four times as high as that in wholesale prices. And it is true of the 1920's. At Cincinnati costs per concert rose nearly 11 per cent per year compounded, while wholesale prices remained virtually constant.[16]

The final prosperous period covered by our orchestral series is the interval from the end of World War II to the present. The evidence from this period is, of course, most directly applicable to the current financial circumstances of performing arts organizations, and we shall presently analyze the available data. Here it will suffice to note that once again cost per concert for both orchestras increased far more rapidly than the wholesale price index.[17]

---

[15] This is easily explained, since this period marked the final collapse of the old cooperative orchestra just before its reorganization under Gustav Mahler in 1909. Moreover, the data for this period are rather questionable, for it is somewhere in this interval that the paid public rehearsal, which we find so difficult to classify, seems to have been abandoned.

[16] This sharp rate of increase in orchestral costs may be ascribable in part to Fritz Reiner's exacting standards. Unfortunately, we lack annual observations for the New York Philharmonic during this period. However, if we calculate the growth rate of the Philharmonic's costs per concert between 1919 and 1928 — years for which we have figures — we obtain a rate of 10.2 per cent per year, a rate of increase almost exactly as high as that for the Cincinnati Orchestra. This is probably a consequence, in part, of the demanding requirements of Toscanini, who took over the baton toward the end of the decade. Note also another curious coincidence — the fact that in both orchestras expenditures per concert reached a peak in 1929, fell in 1930, and rose again to a higher peak in 1931 before embarking on a protracted decline. (See Figure VIII–2.)

[17] Cost per concert rose 3.8 per cent per year for the New York Philharmonic and 4.0 per cent for the Cincinnati Orchestra between 1948 and 1964, while the wholesale price index rose 1.5 per cent per year. If we calculate the or-

Trends in Costs on Broadway

Unfortunately, we have no continuous data series for the Broadway theater because of the absence of permanent theatrical companies. Hence we must do what we can with isolated figures assembled from a variety of sources.

The pattern, however, is unmistakable. Costs rose much more rapidly than the wholesale price index in every period for which we have figures. The single exception is the decade encompassing World War II: between 1940 and 1950 the price index went up 7.3 per cent per year, while Broadway's weekly running costs increased only 1.4 per cent per year and its production costs rose by 6.7 per cent per year. It is noteworthy that this period of wartime inflation is the same exception that we found in the orchestral data, and the explanations offered there may also apply to the Broadway theater.

Table VIII–2, which summarizes our Broadway figures, shows another curious phenomenon — production costs seem consistently to have gone up more rapidly than nightly running costs. This interesting fact, which was first noticed by Moore, will be discussed in the next chapter when we consider the components of the general cost increases in the performing arts.

The Postwar Evidence in More Detail

The period since World War II is, of course, of greatest current interest, and for this interval we have far more extensive data. These are summarized in Figures VIII–3 and VIII–4 and Table VIII–3.

Our most reliable figures are once again orchestral data. For this period we need no longer rely on two isolated case studies; thanks to the managers of the major orchestras, we have at our disposal time series for 23 of the majors. For reasons explained in Appendix

chestra growth rates by fitting a trend line to the annual observations rather than just using terminal years, we obtain slightly higher growth rates — 4.0 per cent and 4.2 per cent, respectively. Moreover, the rate of growth per concert was very steady, as shown by the R^2 of .98 for the Philharmonic and .90 for Cincinnati, where an R^2 of 1.00 means absolutely steady growth.

TABLE VIII–2

Growth in Broadway Costs and in the Wholesale Price Index, Selected Periods, 1913–1961

Time Period	Average Annual Percentage Increase (compound rate)	
	Broadway Costs	Wholesale Price Index
1913–1928:		
"Misleading Lady" — production costs	5.3	⎫ 2.2
Over-all estimate — production and running costs	5.1–8.2	⎭
1934–1952:		
"Children's Hour" — production costs	12.9	⎫ 4.7
1928–1940:		
Production costs	4.1	⎫ 1.8
Weekly running costs	1.3	⎭
1940–1950:		
Production costs	6.7	⎫ 7.3
Weekly running costs	1.4	⎭
1950–1961:		
Production costs	6.3	⎫ 1.4
Weekly running costs	5.5	⎭

SOURCE: For wholesale price index, see Table VIII–1. The growth rates for Broadway costs were calculated from several sources, in the manner explained in that table. The 1913–1928 "Misleading Lady" production costs were originally calculated by Bernheim (p. 204), and were also used by Poggi. Bernheim compared the actual costs of the 1913 production with a detailed estimate of what the production costs would have been in the 1928–29 season had the standards of the 1913 production been duplicated. Poggi made the over-all estimate that production and operating costs "more than doubled but less than tripled" between 1914 and 1928. Our average annual growth rates are equivalent to this estimate of the over-all percentage change.

The 1934–1952 estimate for "Children's Hour" comes from a paper prepared by Norris Houghton for the Rockefeller Brothers Fund study. Houghton reported that when Herman Shulman presented the "Children's Hour" in 1934 it cost $6,000 to open; when Kermit Bloomgarten revived the play eighteen years later with the same physical requirements and a cast of the same size it cost $60,000.

The estimates for the remaining periods, 1928–1940, 1940–1950, 1950–1961, come from Moore (text Table 5 and Appendix Table A–9). Moore presents only "deflated" figures; we multiplied these by the appropriate price index values in order to restore them to current dollar values. Moore's original sources are explained in detail in his manuscript; it suffices here to note that he relied heavily on Bernheim and on information collected by the League of New York Theatres.

III–2, most of our calculations are conducted in terms of a sub-group which we call our "basic eleven." For this set of eleven orchestras, costs per performance rose at an average rate of 3.2 per cent per year from 1947 to 1964.[18]

We also have detailed information about the finances of the Metropolitan Opera, obtained with the generous assistance of its management. The Metropolitan's expenditure per performance, plotted in Figure VIII–3, increased at an average annual rate of 4.4 per cent. This rate of increase was somewhat greater than that for the orchestras, and was extremely steady ($R^2 = .96$), though an acceleration can be observed between 1961 and 1963. It should be recognized that 4.4 per cent is a very rapid rate of compound growth. It means a doubling every 16 years, so that costs per performance at the Metropolitan at the end of 1964 were more than twice what they were right after the war.

Theater data on which to base trend calculations are much more difficult to obtain. We have few continuous series, and in some cases for which we do, the structure of the enterprise has changed so substantially that a direct comparison of costs over the period would be misleading. We managed to obtain two time series which may be taken to represent reasonably homogeneous activities — the American Shakespeare Festival at Stratford, Conn. and the Bucks County Playhouse, a summer theater in New Hope, Pa., both of which have been in operation for a number of years. Both experienced increases in cost per performance well beyond the growth in the price level, though a little slower than the growth rates for the orchestras.

For a number of other organizations we obtained what might be described as "spot data" — figures for several isolated years, not all of which are directly comparable. These provide the basis for

[18] The steadiness of this growth is evident from the orchestra curve in Figure VIII–3, which shows a slight dip in 1955–1957 and a steady rise thereafter until 1961. Since 1961, the *rate* of increase has been mounting. Indeed, it is noteworthy that during the four years 1961–1964 costs per performance rose faster than the average rate of increase for the entire postwar period.

The results are also highly consistent from orchestra to orchestra. While there has been some variation, and the financial difficulties of an occasional organization have forced a decrease in costs, ten of our basic eleven orchestras experienced increases in costs per performance more rapid than the rise in the price level.

FIGURE VIII–3

EXPENDITURES PER PERFORMANCE AND THE
WHOLESALE PRICE INDEX, 1947–1964

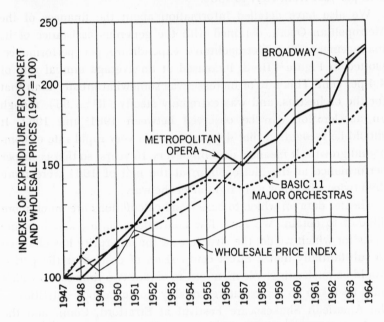

The basic data for this graph appear in Tables VIII–1 and VIII–3.

the growth rates in Table VIII–3 which are not italicized. Each of
these rates also fits the general pattern described so many times in
this chapter. The pattern holds even for the City Center Opera and
the New York City Ballet, whose costs per performance rose more
slowly than those of any other organization for which we have
data.

The over-all results, then, are sufficiently clear and dramatic.
They confirm the impression that costs in the performing arts do
indeed rise, and that they outstrip prices in the rest of the economy.
Whatever else one may conclude, it is clear that the cost problems
besetting the performing groups are no mere reflection of the rate
of inflation characteristic of the economy as a whole.

TABLE VIII–3

Growth in Expenditure Per Performance and in the Wholesale Price Index During the Postwar Period

Organization	Time Period	Average Annual Percentage Increase (compound rate)[a]	
		Expenditure Per Performance	Wholesale Price Index
Major Orchestras:			
"Basic 11"	} 1947–1964 {	3.2[b]	1.3
All 23		3.1[b]	1.3
"Basic 11"	} 1961–1964 {	4.9[b]	0.1
All 23		3.9[b]	0.1
Opera Companies:			
Metropolitan Opera	1951–1964	4.4	0.3
Opera Company A	1958–1963	5.0	0
City Center Opera	1958–1963	2.0	0
Dance Companies:			
New York City Ballet	1958–1963	2.3	0
Theaters:			
Broadway Sample	1950–1961	6.0	1.4
Regional Theater A	1958–1963	*11.2*	0
Regional Theater B	1958–1963	*6.0*	0
Regional Theater C	1955–1963	*2.5*	0.9
Summer Theater	1954–1963	*3.6*	0

SOURCE: The growth rates for the major orchestras were calculated from the compiled reports of the American Symphony Orchestra League. For definitions of the "basic 11" and "all 23," see Appendix III–2. Broadway data were obtained from Moore (see Table VIII–2 for the exact source). All other growth rates were calculated from expenditure and performance information acquired directly from the individual organizations.

[a] The italicized growth rates were obtained by fitting a trend line to the logarithm of annual observations over the period indicated. Rates not in italics were obtained simply by assuming a constant (compound) rate of growth between the terminal years, the only years for which data were available in the case of these organizations. The italicized rates are, of course, more reliable.

[b] This is a weighted average of the growth rates for all eleven orchestras, the weights being mean (arithmetic average) expenditures over the period as a whole. This gives us an over-all industry figure. We also calculated an unweighted average which tells us about a typical orchestra without regard to size. This unweighted average comes to 2.9 per cent per year. The fact

And Great Britain Once More

Having just conducted the reader through a labyrinth of American statistics, we had hoped merely to reassure him that things were similar in the United Kingdom and perhaps to report this in a footnote. On examining the British figures, however, we found a rather interesting relationship which merits some attention.

Little can be done with British data by way of long-period comparisons because most of the older records seem to have been lost during World War II. Where figures exist, some crucial piece of information, such as number of performances, is usually missing. However, we do have data for the Royal Shakespeare Theatre for the period 1949–1964. Expenditures per week (and so, we presume, per performance) grew at a rate of 9.6 per cent per year, as compared with a growth rate of 3.4 per cent in the retail price index. At the regional orchestra for which we have figures, total costs increased at a rate of 7.3 per cent per year over this period; and, since the number of concerts per year rose by only a negligible amount between 1955 and 1964, a 6 to 7 per cent growth rate in expenditure per concert seems a very conservative estimate.

At Covent Garden it is difficult to calculate a meaningful cost per performance figure since so many types of performance are given. Not only does Covent Garden offer both ballet and opera, but it also provides what are referred to as "special" and "ordinary" performances. However, since the total number of house performances actually decreased between 1951 and 1964 (from 326 to 282), the 7 per cent annual increase in total expenditures clearly understates somewhat the growth in cost per performance. Furthermore, if we exclude years with big tours, the growth rate figure for total expenditures increases to 9.3 per cent per year.

These, however, are not the most interesting observations to be made on the British figures. If we compare the rate of increase in costs with the rate of increase in the price index, we notice that at

Notes to Table VIII–3 continued

that it is slightly lower than the weighted figure suggests that expenditure per concert has grown more rapidly for the larger orchestras. Note also that the growth rate for the entire group of major orchestras has been slightly lower than that of the basic eleven alone. The difference is negligible, and in any event the rise is still far more rapid than the rate of growth of the price level.

Covent Garden, at the regional orchestra and at the Royal Shake-speare Theatre, costs have risen at an annual rate about twice as great as the rate of rise in the price index. Cost per performance rose at a rate of 7 to 10 per cent while prices went up at about a 4 per cent rate. If we now turn back to the figures for the United States, we find that *the ratio between cost and price increases was very similar.* Costs rose during the postwar period at an annual rate close to 4 per cent, while prices went up somewhere between 1 and 2 per cent, depending on which index one employs.

One cannot place too much of a burden on this very rough relationship, but it should not wholly surprise us. What it says is that after we correct for changes in the purchasing power of the dollar and the pound, real cost per performance seems to have been rising at about the same rate in both countries. If much of the rise is attributed to a structural problem in the technology of the arts that knows no national boundaries, one might have expected to find just such a result.

Economies of Large-Scale Operation[19]

Changes in the cost of most enterprises reflect not only movements in the prices of the factors of production they employ, but also changes in the scale of their operations. Experience with a number of manufacturing enterprises has taught us that in some types of activity an increase in output can reduce per unit cost. Where items can be standardized and mass produced, each unit can be provided more and more cheaply as the market expands. One may well ask whether this pattern fits the performing organizations — whether they too can benefit from economies of scale when they increase the availability of performance to the public.

Figure VIII–4 shows the relationship between cost per concert (vertical axis) and number of concerts given (horizontal scale) for one of the nation's major orchestras. For example, the dot marked 1950 indicates that in 1950, when 80 concerts were performed during the season, the cost per concert was 70 "units of real cost" (expenditure adjusted for changes in the purchasing

[19] Appendix VIII–2 contains a more technical discussion of the analysis underlying this section.

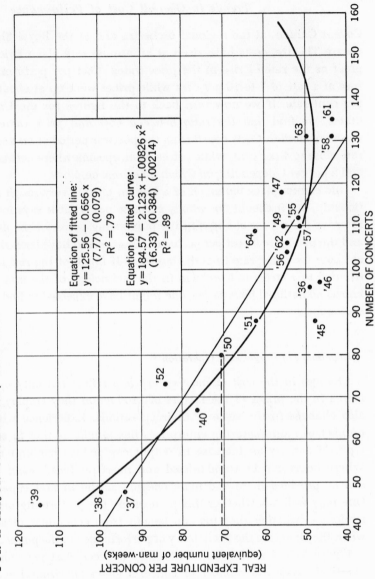

FIGURE VIII-4
REAL EXPENDITURE PER CONCERT AND NUMBER OF CONCERTS,
FOR A MAJOR ORCHESTRA, 1936–1964

Equation of fitted line:
$y = 125.56 - 0.656\,x$
$(7.77)\quad(0.079)$
$R^2 = .79$

Equation of fitted curve:
$y = 184.57 - 2.123\,x + .00826\,x^2$
$(16.33)\quad(0.384)\quad(.00214)$
$R^2 = .89$

NUMBER OF CONCERTS

REAL EXPENDITURE PER CONCERT
(equivalent number of man-weeks)

For the derivation of this graph see Appendix VIII–2.

power of the dollar to our orchestras).[20] Notice how closely the curve fits the dots representing the actual data for the years indicated. Moreover, the curve very clearly slopes downward from left to right — there are very marked and clear-cut economies of scale, though they level off (the curve flattens out noticeably after the scale of operations becomes fairly large).

This sort of analysis was undertaken for each of our basic eleven orchestras. The data for six of the eleven fell into similar patterns, though the curves were by no means identical — they were not equally steep, nor did they begin to level off at about the same number of concerts per year. Some orchestras reached what appeared to be a minimum cost level after as few as 90 concerts per year, while others still went on enjoying economies of scale until they had played nearly 150 concerts per year.[21]

What do these results mean, and how do we account for them? They suggest that up to a point the orchestras enjoy economies of large-scale operation, but that beyond this point further lengthening of the concert season will produce no further reductions in cost per concert.

Administration is one activity which offers obvious scope for such economies. A 10 per cent increase in the number of concerts performed may not require a corresponding increase in managerial personnel. If so, an increase in the number of concerts will reduce the administrative cost *per concert*.

A more important opportunity to economize is presented by the possibility of making rehearsal time cover more performances. Suppose an orchestra has been running three series of identical programs per season and decides to run four. This will not add to the number of different pieces of music performed. Each item will

---

[20] Our criterion of purchasing power was the salary of the musician, which constitutes the bulk of the orchestra's expenditures. We measured expenditures in terms of the number of musicians the orchestra could hire for one year at the relevant minimum rate if it devoted all of its expenditures to this purpose. In other words, had dollar expenditures quadrupled over a given period while the musicians' minimum annual wage had doubled, we would conclude from our calculation that the orchestra's *real* expenditures had merely doubled because they would be equivalent to only twice as many musician-years as before.

[21] See Appendix VIII–2 for a detailed presentation of all of our cost curve regressions.

now be repeated before four different audiences instead of three, and little, if any, increase in rehearsal time will be required. If rehearsal costs were $120,000 for the season, with three series the rehearsal cost per series would be $40,000, and with four series it would fall to $30,000. Here, then, is an opportunity to achieve very substantial economies.

This also suggests why the lowest cost per concert occurs at different levels of activity for different orchestras. One would surmise that the lowest unit cost corresponds to the largest number of parallel series for which the orchestra can find audiences. If one orchestra operates in a large city with many music lovers, it may, perhaps, be able to give six such concert series and thereby achieve economies up to that level of operation. But an orchestra located in a smaller, less musical metropolis may find that beyond four concert series any further expansion requires the presentation of different programs in order to attract the same subscribers back. In that case rehearsal cost per concert will rise when the number of concerts expands any further. If, in addition, these added concerts require noted guest conductors or soloists to attract audiences, it is easy to see why unit costs might cease falling. This explanation is, of course, only a hypothesis, which may or may not be valid.[22]

Similar reasoning can be applied to the stage. We know that there are some economies of scale to be obtained in the theater when the length of run of a play is increased. The production cost of a play, which encompasses the cost of rehearsals, scenery, costumes, etc., usually constitutes a very substantial proportion of the total cost for the run of that play. Consequently, as the length of run increases, the proportion of the fixed production cost that is ascribed to each week of operation declines. If a show costs $100,-000 to produce, the production costs for a ten week run would be

[22] After the preceding comments had been written we undertook a simple test of our hypothesis. For the six orchestras whose data showed a strong statistical relationship, we compared size of population in the home city with the cost-minimizing number of concerts per season. For five of the six, the ordering by population size was exactly the same as the ordering by length of season — the more populous a city, the longer the season for which its orchestra could operate without running into diminishing returns. Even the one exceptional orchestra was not far out of line with what one might have expected from our hypothesis.

$10,000 per week. By the time the show has run 20 weeks the production costs will have fallen to $5,000 a week. Thus, the longer the run, the smaller the production cost per week — which is what we mean by economies of scale.

We do not know whether the weekly running costs of a play also decline with length of run. In part this is because the requisite data are not available. The practice of classifying certain cost items sometimes as production costs and sometimes as running costs does not help matters. Things are confused even more when some of the personnel involved accept cuts in pay in order to keep a relatively unsuccessful play running, for these cuts might seem from the records to represent a decline in running cost resulting from length of run. Our data for the Bucks County Playhouse did enable us to compare the costs of the second week of a two week run with those of the first week (at that theater plays are usually given for two weeks). There the figures show that on the average the second week's operations cost 11 per cent less than the first.

Our economies of scale analysis has an implication which affects our interpretation of the cost trends described earlier in this chapter. It was stated in a previous section that for a few of our orchestras, costs failed to rise more quickly than the price level. We can now suggest a possible explanation for those exceptional cases: during the period for which our cost trends were calculated those orchestras may well have been increasing the number of concerts they gave per year, and as a result they may have achieved economies of scale sufficient to offset any real cost-increasing trends.

This is illustrated in Figure VIII–5, which reports the expenditures per concert for one of our orchestras over the period 1937–1964 (bottom curve). This curve shows that expenditures per concert rose during that period, but for the orchestra under scrutiny they rose a little less rapidly than the wholesale price index (middle curve). The top curve, however, shows how much costs would have risen had the orchestra enjoyed no economies of increased scale.[23] This curve shows clearly that had the orchestra not in-

[23] This upper curve was calculated with the aid of an average cost curve for that orchestra like the one shown in Figure VIII–5. For each year, in effect, we undid the economies that resulted from any increase in the number of concerts above the 1937 level. For this purpose we utilized the following expression: corrected expenditure per concert in year t = $(Y_{x37} / Y_{xt}) \times$ (actual ex-

FIGURE VIII-5

EXPENDITURE PER CONCERT WITHOUT ECONOMIES OF SCALE, FOR A MAJOR ORCHESTRA, 1937–1964

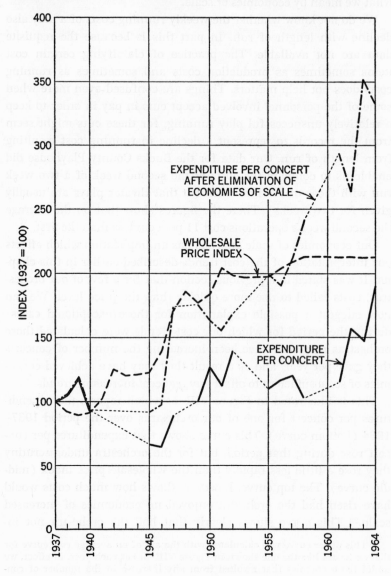

creased its scale of operations, its costs would undoubtedly have risen far more rapidly than the price level. This finding implies that in many other cases the rate of increase in cost per concert shown in our previous calculations also significantly understates the rate at which the entire cost curve has been shifting upward.

The major thrust of this chapter is summed up very simply. As our analysis in the previous chapter suggested, the real costs of performance almost always rise. These can sometimes be offset by economies of scale, and periods of war seem to constitute a consistent exception, but otherwise one can find few cases in which price rises in the economy fail to be exceeded by the state of increase in the costs of performance. This tells us clearly that inflation alone is not the villain of our story. It also indicates once more that the financial pressures upon the performing arts cannot be expected to ease with the passage of time.

penditure in year t) where $Y_{xt} = f(X_t)$ is the equation of the average cost curve for that orchestra (see boxed equation and heavy line in Figure VIII–4) so that X_t and X_{37} are, respectively, the number of concerts in the two years and Y_{x37} and Y_{xt} are the corresponding unit costs as given by the cost curve regression equation.

CHAPTER **IX**

Trends in Performer Salaries and Other Components of Cost

L ET US now examine the components of the rise in over-all costs of performance. Such an inquiry will help us to understand the source of these cost pressures and will make it easier to forecast the pattern of the future.

We begin the chapter by considering the broad components of total costs; in particular, outlays on artistic personnel as compared with all other expenditures. We then study trends in the cost of auxiliary services and equipment — scenery, stagehands' salaries, advertising, etc. Finally we re-examine performer salaries in greater detail, relating their growth to that of other incomes in the economy and considering the effects of salary changes on the supply of performers and the demand for them. In general, we shall see that performer incomes have been rising at a rate faster than that of the price level, but still have not kept up with incomes elsewhere in the economy, and that salary payments have constituted a declining portion of over-all costs of performance in recent years.

Expenditures on Artistic Personnel as a Percentage of Total Costs

Given the nature of the available data, the most consistent way to break down the costs incurred by performing organizations is to classify them into expenditures on artistic personnel and "all other expenditures." Payments to artistic personnel are the largest item in the operating budgets of performing organizations, and merit

FIGURE IX–1

EXPENDITURES ON ARTISTIC PERSONNEL
AS PER CENT OF TOTAL EXPENDITURES,
ELEVEN MAJOR ORCHESTRAS, 1937–1964

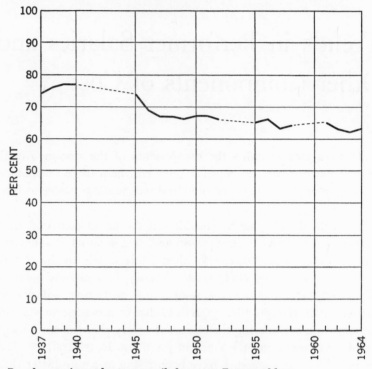

Based on major orchestra compiled reports. Data used here
are averages for the basic set of eleven major orchestras.

special attention also because performer compensations are critical for the welfare of the arts.

Costs in both of these broad categories have risen substantially,
but not always at an equal rate. The figures for one major orchestra over the whole period for which we have data — 1929–1964 —
indicate that there has been considerable variability but no obvious
long-term trends (Figure IX–2), although outlays on artistic personnel in 1964 were a slightly smaller proportion of total costs
(about 55 per cent) than they were in the 1940's (60–65 per

FIGURE IX-2

EXPENDITURES ON ARTISTIC PERSONNEL
AS PER CENT OF TOTAL EXPENDITURES,
FOR A MAJOR ORCHESTRA, 1929–1964

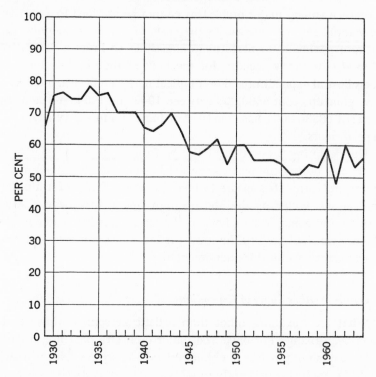

cent). Nor is there any clear-cut relation to the business cycle. For example, relative to total costs, expenditures on performers rose after 1929, but fell after the panic of 1893. Figures for another major orchestra show the same inconclusive patterns. Relative to total costs, personnel costs were high for both orchestras during the great depression.

For the postwar period, our most comprehensive and reliable figures are again those for the major orchestras. The data for our basic eleven major orchestras are shown in Figure IX–1, and Figure IX–2 shows similar data for one particular orchestra extending over a slightly longer period. Both graphs reveal a small but fairly persistent downward trend in the salaries of artistic personnel as a proportion of total expenditures. This has been offset in part by substantial improvements in fringe benefits in recent years — pensions, Blue Cross, major medical insurance and sick leave. Nevertheless, it is clear that the increase in over-all costs of performance among major orchestras cannot be ascribed to a particularly rapid rate of increase in the costs of artistic personnel. But because payments to performers constitute so large a proportion of total costs, they account for the bulk of the *absolute* increase in orchestral expenditures. For a typical major orchestra, total costs have gone up about $560,000 between 1942 and 1964, and some 60 per cent ($336,000) has consisted of increases in salary payments to performers.[1]

The declining proportion of the performer wage bill relative to total costs during the postwar period has not been confined to the major orchestras. It appears to hold for most other performing organizations, including the Metropolitan Opera, Broadway, Covent Garden and a major symphony orchestra in London. Later in the chapter we shall present the most pertinent of these data and consider the reasons for this phenomenon.

Trends in Other Types of Expenditure

What are the items other than artistic personnel whose costs have been rising? For once, the major orchestra data are of little help. It was not possible to obtain a detailed cost breakdown which could be applied consistently to all the orchestras. At best we were able to divide orchestra expenditures into three broad categories: artistic personnel costs; production expenses (including stage expenses, hall rental or operating costs, etc.); and "all other." Each of the last two classes of expenditure has increased somewhat more rapidly than personnel costs over the postwar period.

A more detailed classification of personnel costs for the Metropolitan Opera, in Table IX–1, shows that outlays on salaries of wardrobe and scenic personnel have risen much more slowly than other expenditures. There was great similarity in the rates of growth of all the other cost components, though artistic person-

---

[1] Calculated from compiled reports of the major orchestras.

TABLE IX–1

Trends in Components of Costs, Metropolitan Opera, 1948–1964

Expenditure Category	Average Annual Growth Rate[a]	R² *
Salaries:		
Artistic Personnel	5.38%	(.97)
Stage Department	6.16	(.97)
Building Operating	5.83	(.89)
Executive and Clerical	6.41	(.88)
Wardrobe and Scenic	2.96	(.11)
Total Salaries	5.62	(.98)
All Expenses	5.73	(.99)

SOURCE: Calculated from data supplied by the Metropolitan Opera Association.

[a] Calculated by fitting a trend line to the logarithms of the annual observations.

* This measure of closeness of relationship is explained in the note on semilogarithmic graphs at the end of Chapter VII.

nel costs constituted the second most slowly rising item. It is possible that the rate of increase in fringe benefits received by performers might have been sufficient to put them higher on this scale.

In the theatrical field, fairly detailed accounts are available both because of the transitory nature of the organizations and the degree of subcontracting. When a production disbands, each expenditure must be accounted for to the investors. Cost statements of this type, provided by Moore, enabled us to calculate the percentage distribution of expenditures for several Broadway productions during four different periods of time (Table IX–2).

The cast salary component of *production costs* on Broadway rose between 1928 and 1961, mainly because rehearsal pay did not become general until after the late 1920's. In spite of the trend, however, cast salaries are still a small proportion of the total initial production outlay. The largest single item in production costs — scenery — has undergone a major relative decline, as have directors' fees and outlays on crew and stagehands; on the other hand, advertising has risen most rapidly. This refers only to pre-opening advertising expenditures, which have undoubtedly risen because of

TABLE IX-2

Components of Broadway Costs, 1928–1961

	Percentage Distribution			
	1927–28 and 1928–29	1949–50 and 1950–51	1954–55 and 1955–56	1960–61
PRODUCTION COSTS				
Director's Fee	8.9	7.0	6.0	4.4
Cast Salaries	4.4	5.9	6.2	6.0
Crew and Stagehands	8.6	4.5	6.4	5.3
Scenery Designer	5.0	5.2	4.4	3.5
Scenery	30.5	28.1	23.4	22.3
Costumes	9.7	11.3	7.9	9.2
Advertising	7.0	5.5	7.0	12.0
	74.1	67.5	61.3	62.7
Remainder	25.9	32.5	38.6	37.4
Total	100.0	100.0	100.0	100.0
WEEKLY OPERATING COSTS				
Cast Salaries	51.3	41.3	36.9	37.1
Crew and Stagehands	4.5	8.0	7.3	6.4
Author's Royalties	13.5	15.4	14.8	11.9
Director and Designer	—	3.4	3.2	3.5
Stage and Company Managers	3.5	5.4	5.6	4.9
Publicity and Advertising	18.5	12.3	11.2	16.8
	91.3	85.9	78.9	80.6
Remainder	8.7	14.1	21.1	19.4
Total	100.0	100.0	100.0	100.0

SOURCE: Calculated from data collected by Moore, Ch. III.

the increased risk to which Broadway productions are subject. To minimize that risk, producers advertise more before the opening of a play in order to have as large an advance sale as possible. The miscellaneous category of production costs has also risen sharply since 1928. At that time it was made up entirely of props and electrical and sound equipment, but more recently managerial expenses, press agent salaries and legal and auditing fees have also become items to be reckoned with.

Weekly running costs on Broadway exhibit patterns not entirely similar to those found among production outlays. The share of actors' salaries has declined, and while proportional outlays on crew and stagehands rose between 1928 and 1950, they have subsequently fallen. The proportion spent on publicity and advertising, while down relative to 1928, has gone up in recent years, as has "the remainder."

Our data, in general, support the contention that the incomes of stagehands have been going up relative to the incomes of most other persons in the theater. As Appendix Table IX–A shows, the weekly minimum pay scale of stagehands increased more rapidly than the minimum scales of other Broadway theater employees between 1960 and 1965, and stagehands ranked third in rate of increase of minimum salary among the thirteen occupations for which we have data for the interval 1953–1965 (only assistant managers at musicals and wardrobe attendants experienced more rapid increases in minimum weekly pay). These comparisons do not take account of overtime payments and fringe benefits, which together constitute a significant proportion of stagehands' earnings. But neither do they include the wage rates of the "grips" — the lowest paid but most numerous category of stagehand.

Over the period 1953–1965 the rate of increase in Broadway actors' pay has placed them at about the middle of the list. They are outranked in this respect not only by assistant managers, wardrobe attendants and stagehands, but also by ticket takers, ushers and treasurers. However, the minimum scales of actors went up more rapidly than those of stage managers, department heads (stagehand and wardrobe), cleaners, porters and musicians. It is noteworthy that contract musicians performing at musical comedies are at the very bottom of the list — their pay rates rose more slowly than those of anyone else in the theater.

Since advertising outlay has risen so sharply, we investigated it in some detail. The results of a study of the amount of theater advertising lineage in the *New York Times* and the *Times'* advertising rates are presented in Appendix Table IX–B. Over the period 1957–1962 price per agate line increased about 3 per cent on the average for Broadway productions, a rate slightly higher than the rate of growth of the consumer price index (2 per cent per year)

216

FIGURE IX-3

TRENDS IN SALARIES OF ORCHESTRAL MUSICIANS, BROADWAY ACTORS, TEACHERS, WORKERS IN MANUFACTURING, AND IN THE CONSUMER PRICE INDEX, 1929–1964

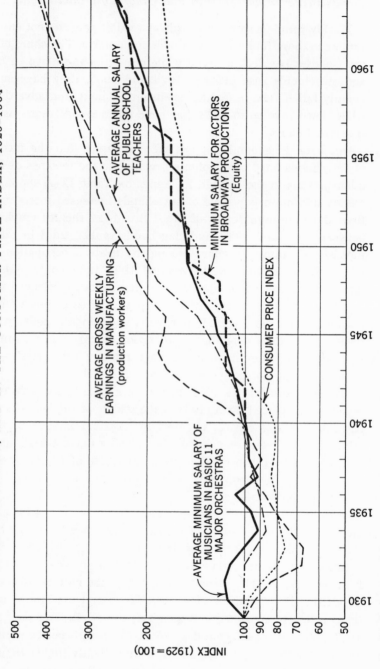

For the derivation of this graph see the notes to Table IX–3.

and about twice as large as that of the wholesale price index (1.3 per cent per year). In this period the volume of advertising went up 4.3 per cent per year on Broadway and 14.8 per cent per year off-Broadway. These last figures, however, reflect changes in the number of productions as well as variations in advertising lineage per performance. The latter increased 3.7 per cent per year on Broadway, but declined 1.4 per cent per year for the off-Broadway theater. Thus, the increased cost of advertising space, together with a growth in advertising lineage per performance, produced a rise of about 11 per cent annually in advertising costs on Broadway.

The general conclusion to which the foregoing evidence leads is that rising costs of performance can certainly not be laid to increases in performers' wage levels alone. Cost increases have been pervasive and have affected almost all categories of expenditure.

Trends in Performers' Salaries: General Comparisons

Since expenditures on performers' salaries have been rising, we are naturally led to ask how much this has helped the performer himself. Has his salary kept up with the price level and with compensation in other occupations?

Figure IX–3, our key graph, plots the course of three types of earnings: (minimum) performer salaries, earnings in manufacturing and teachers' salaries. These are expressed in index form, using 1929 as a base year, so that relative changes can be seen clearly. The consumer price index is also plotted on the diagram, as a means of showing how the various groups have fared in terms of purchasing power.[2] Table IX–3 summarizes the trends that are illustrated in Figure IX–3, and also includes data for college teachers.

There are several clear-cut conclusions to be drawn from the data:

(1) For the period 1929–1964, salaries of both Broadway actors and major orchestra musicians rose, on the average, 2.7 per cent annually. Since the annual increase in the consumer price

---

[2] Since the consumer price index is designed to measure cost of living, it, and not the wholesale price index, is the relevant measure in this instance.

TABLE IX-3

Trends in Actors' and Musicians' Salaries, in Teachers' Salaries
and in Earnings in Manufacturing, 1929-1964

	Average Annual Percentage Change[a]									
	1929–1939	1940–1948	1948–1961	1961–1964	1929–1948		1948–1964		1929-1964	
Performers:										
Broadway Actors[b]	0.0	2.3	5.0	3.6	1.0	(120)[c]	4.7	(208)[c]	2.7	(250)[c]
Major Orchestra Musicians[d]	-0.2	4.7	3.3	5.1	1.9	(143)	3.6	(177)	2.7	(254)
Others:										
Production Workers in Manufacturing[e]	-0.5	9.9	4.4	3.9	4.1	(215)	4.2	(195)	4.2	(418)
Public School Teachers[f]	-0.1	7.8	5.7	4.5	3.3	(186)	5.5	(235)	4.3	(437)
College Teachers[g]	-0.5	4.2	4.7	5.3	1.6	(135)	4.8	(212)	3.0	(286)
Consumer Price Index	-2.1	7.0	1.7	1.2	1.8	(140)	1.6	(129)	1.7	(181)

ᵃ Compounded between terminal years.

ᵇ Equity minimums for Broadway. Compiled from files of agreements and back records made available by Actors' Equity.

ᶜ Figures in parentheses are index numbers (1929 = 100).

ᵈ Between 1929 and 1937 these figures are based on an index of average remuneration paid to New York Philharmonic musicians, exclusive of recording income and other "extras." Between 1937 and 1964 the figures represent an adjusted average of the weekly minimums paid by our basic eleven orchestras. Because some orchestras failed to report every year, the raw averages could not be used; they would have seemed to decline in years when an orchestra paying relatively high salaries did not report and to increase sharply in years when a lower paying orchestra did not report. We estimated the missing salary figures by averaging the preceding and following values.

ᵉ Average gross weekly earnings. Data from Economic Report of the President, January 1965.

ᶠ Average school-year salaries. Data for years prior to 1957 are from U. S. Bureau of the Census, Historical Statistics of the United States, Colonial Times to 1957; data from 1957 on were supplied by the U. S. Office of Education. The 1962 and 1963 values are National Education Association estimates.

ᵍ Average academic year salaries. Data for 1929–1952 are from Historical Statistics of the United States. (The original source of this series is George Stigler, Trends in Employment in the Service Industries, Princeton University Press, Princeton, N. J., 1956.) The estimates for 1960 and 1965 are from the Bulletin of the American Association of University Professors, Summer 1965, p. 249. The AAUP figures are for a specially selected sample of 36 relatively high paying institutions, but this fact does not necessarily imply a similar bias in the rates of change; studies made by the AAUP suggest that, if anything, salaries at these 36 institutions have risen somewhat less rapidly than academic salaries in general in recent years.

index was only 1.7 per cent, the performers' real income went up at an average rate of about 1 per cent per year.

(2) However, the performers' minimum salary fell behind the wages of production workers in manufacturing, public school teachers and college teachers, whose respective average rates of increase were 4.2, 4.3 and 3.0 per cent per year. Looked at another way, between 1929 and 1964 performers' salaries rose to about 2.5 times their initial level; but manufacturing workers' wages rose about 4.2 times, and school teachers' pay about 4.4 times during the same period. Thus, in a relative sense, performers grew poorer over the period as a whole.

(3) We see that performers do not constitute a completely insulated group. Their pay rates are affected by general economic conditions; for example, as in most other occupations, the money wages of performers were reduced during the great depression. However, the connection between the behavior of the general economy and performers' salaries is a very loose one, involving substantial lags and variations in pattern.

(4) More specifically, performers' pay rates did not fall as much as manufacturing wages during the depression. Performers really lost out, relatively speaking, during World War II. Manufacturing earnings rose nearly 10 per cent per year during the war, as compared with 2.3 and 4.7 per cent rises for Broadway actors and major orchestra musicians. Over the postwar period the rates of increase in all the job categories on which we have reported have been fairly similar except for the musicians, who have only recently begun to catch up.[3] There is a very close parallel between the

---

[3] An interesting specific case is the off-Broadway theater, where wages are still extremely low by any absolute standards, but have been creeping up on those paid on Broadway (Appendix Table IX–C). Sixty-five dollars per week (the 1965–1967 off-Broadway minimum) is still far from affluence, but minimums have risen from 35 per cent of the Broadway levels in 1954 to about 50 per cent of the Broadway figure today. And rehearsal pay has gone up from 9 per cent ($5 per week) to roughly 60 per cent ($65 per week) of the 1965 Broadway figure ($107.50). These figures help to explain why off-Broadway earning levels have managed simultaneously to keep actors poor and yet to impose very difficult financial burdens on the producer. The decline in the off-Broadway theater in 1964–65 has been ascribed to these increases in pay rates. (See the article by Lewis Calta, *New York Times*, Oct. 17, 1964, p. 18.) But surely this argument is primarily a commentary on the shaky finances of the off-Broadway theater, and not meant to suggest that off-Broadway performer incomes have reached immodest heights.

course of performers' salaries and those of college teachers. Both ended the 1930's with about the same money wages they had at the start. Both lost out relatively during World War II, did better between 1948 and 1961 and best between 1961 and 1964. Over the period as a whole both lost out relative to manufacturing workers and to elementary and secondary school teachers.

(5) Finally, we may observe that our figures support one of the postulates employed in developing the basic analytic argument of Chapter VII. The difference between the rate of growth of manufacturing wages (4.2 per cent) and that of the consumer price index (1.7 per cent) is an annual average net increase of 2.5 per cent. This is the average annual rise in real earnings (earnings measured in dollars of constant purchasing power). It is also the approximate annual rate of increase in productivity per man-hour, so that over the entire period 1929–1964 real wages in manufacturing increased at roughly the same pace as productivity.[4]

We offer one further general comparison of trends in wages of performers with those in other occupations. The Census data which we used in Chapter V to report on incomes in professional occupations in 1959 are, in general, available for 1949, so that it is possible to determine the rate of growth of earnings in each of these occupations over the ten year period.

Musicians and actors are right in the middle of a list in which professions are ranked in the order of rate of growth in income — they are, respectively, numbers 23 and 24 out of 48 (Table IX–4).[5] The implication is that over the decade they have just about kept their place relative to other professions. It may well be argued that

[4] The comparison is not wholly valid because the work week has been shortened since 1929; *hourly* pay in manufacturing must, therefore, have risen somewhat more quickly than 4.2 per cent per year.

[5] The table refers only to males. We have a similar table for women, but since the data are less complete and show very similar results, it is not reproduced.

There is some danger of misinterpretation of these figures. The period encompassed excludes the years since 1959 when, for example, musicians' incomes, at least in a number of major orchestras, have gone up markedly. The occupational categories in the Census lists are not as cleanly defined as one might have wished; for example, the "Musicians" category is distorted not only by the inclusion of music teachers but also by the presence of players of popular music. Nevertheless, the information provided by the Census data, in its broad outlines, is most illuminating.

TABLE IX–4

Income of Men in 48 Professional Occupations, 1949 and 1959

Rank (based on percentage rise in income)	Occupational Group	Median Income		Percentage Rise in Income, 1949 to 1959	Percentage Change in Number, 1950 to 1960
		1949	1959		
1	Athletes	$2,336	$5,394	131	−64
2	Veterinarians	4,220	9,178	117	15
3	Optometrists	4,343	8,772	102	11
4*	Airplane pilots and navigators	5,263	10,514	100	92
4*	Librarians	2,294	4,592	100	91
6	Photographers	2,941	5,692	94	3
7	Dentists	6,448	12,392	92	11
8	Aeronautical engineers	4,828	9,127	89	195
9*	Funeral directors and embalmers	3,179	5,967	88	−6
9*	Natural Scientists (n.e.c.)	4,245	7,965[a]	88	60
11	Electrical engineers	4,657	8,710	87	73
12*	Chiropractors	3,471	6,463	86	16
12*	Metallurgical engineers	4,657	8,639	86	51
12*	Therapists and healers (n. e. c.)	3,011	5,591	86	35
15	Mechanical engineers	4,594	8,494	85	40
16	Physicians and surgeons	8,302	15,013	81	18
17*	Chemical engineers	5,005	8,948	79	26

17*	Lawyers and judges	6,284	11,261	79	17
19	Artists and art teachers	3,552	6,333	78	35
20*	Chemists	4,091	7,245	77	13
20*	Pharmacists	4,170	7,385	77	5
20*	Social scientists	4,446	7,868	77	76
23	MUSICIANS AND MUSIC TEACHERS	2,700	4,757	76	5
24	ACTORS	3,260	5,640	73	-28
25*	Clergymen	2,410	4,151	72	22
25*	College presidents, professors, and instructors	4,366	7,510	72	44
25*	Industrial engineers	4,519	7,790	72	137
25*	Miscellaneous engineers (except mining)	4,965	8,522[a]	72	116
29	Social and welfare workers (except group)	3,196	5,481	71	54
30	Accountants and auditors	3,977	6,758	70	21
31	Civil engineers	4,590	7,773	69	26
32*	Authors	4,033	6,745	67	115
32*	Draftsmen	3,470	5,794	67	62
34*	Entertainers	2,217	3,674	66	-19
34*	Nurses, professional	2,645	4,400	66	50
34*	Sports instructors and officials	3,300	5,519	66	53
37	Teachers (elementary and high school)	3,465	5,709[a]	65	65
38	Foresters and conservationists	2,997	4,873	63	25

TABLE IX–4 (continued)

Rank (based on Percentage rise in income)	Occupational Group	Median Income		Percentage Rise in Income, 1949 to 1959	Percentage Change in Number, 1950 to 1960
		1949	1959		
39	Surveyors	2,773	4,486	62	73
40*	Architects	5,509	8,868	61	29
40*	Personnel and labor relations workers	4,754	7,669	61	81
42*	Osteopaths	6,458	10,279	59	–21
42*	Technicians: medical and dental	2,908	4,614	59	55
44	Farm and home management advisers	4,059	6,159	52	14
45	Radio operators	4,016	5,975	49	68
46	DANCERS AND DANCING TEACHERS	2,385	3,483	46	0
47	Religious workers	2,316	3,241	40	66
48	Recreation and group workers	3,155	4,395	39	123
	All men in professional occupations	3,949	6,778	72	50

SOURCE: Compiled by Professor T. A. Finegan from U. S. Census of Population, 1960: Subject Reports, Final Report PC(2)–7A, Table 25.

ᵃ A weighted average of medians for component subgroups.

* Indicates tie ranking.   n.e.c.: not elsewhere classified.

just keeping up is not good enough for a group that had fallen behind the rest of the community over a considerable earlier period, as this merely preserves their low relative position in 1949. Some figures we gave a little earlier suggest that there has been some catching up since 1961, though we cannot be sure that this is so since we do not have comparable data for all of the other professions.

In the Census data dancers, as usual, are at the bottom of the list — only in two other professional occupations have incomes increased more slowly than in theirs.

The pattern of salaries of British performers has been similar to ours (Appendix Table IX–D). Weekly pay rates lagged behind the average weekly earnings of "operatives" (manual workers) over the 1946–1963 period (a 4.2 per cent annual increase for the former as against 6.1 per cent for the latter). The lag decreased between 1950 and 1963, and performers have improved their relative position slightly during the most recent interval for which data are available (1957–1963).

The British data, in conjunction with our American figures, bring out a fundamental point relevant to our basic analysis. They show that in Great Britain, where prices and industrial wages have been rising more rapidly than here, performers' salaries have also increased more quickly. This confirms that performing arts organizations confront a labor market which is heavily influenced by developments in the rest of the economy.[6]

Wages, Supply and Demand

The prevalence of low wages that have, at times, fallen even further behind those of the rest of the community might reasonably be expected to reduce the supply of skilled performers. It would be highly desirable to test this hypothesis by analyzing the effects of changing wage levels on the supply of and the demand for performers. Unfortunately, empirical answers are extremely difficult to

---

[6] In *real* terms, both earnings of operatives and salaries of performers have risen less quickly in Great Britain than they have here. This is noteworthy in light of the fact that productivity has increased somewhat more slowly in Great Britain than in the United States.

come by in this area. Since the real world is a hodgepodge of simultaneous occurrences, one cannot be sure whether a variation in the supply of performers subsequent to a change in wages can legitimately be ascribed to the wage change or whether it resulted from any one of the many other events which are certain to have occurred at the same time. Consequently, the materials we offer now cannot pretend to do more than hint at the nature of the underlying relationships.

We begin with some Census figures which show that between 1950 and 1960 there was a decline of 28 per cent in the number of actors (Table IX–4).[7] The number of dancers and dance teachers has remained about the same, and there has been a small increase in the number of musicians and music teachers. While these figures seem to suggest that the over-all supply of performers has been diminishing, it is hard to know what they imply about the nature of supply responsiveness. A reduction in supply may be a consequence of inadequate demand, of low earnings levels or of any number of fortuitous circumstances, and these influences cannot be disentangled from the available data.

Some evidence on supply in relation to demand is provided by a series of interviews we conducted with producers and managers. These 56 interviews involved the full range of art forms — theaters, orchestras, chamber groups, dance companies and operas. Only 4 respondents indicated that they experienced difficulty in hiring performers of satisfactory quality, 18 reported moderate difficulty and 25 reported no problem at all. All indicated that they ended up with performers who were either usually or always satisfactory. When asked whether hiring had become harder or easier over the past five years, 7 respondents indicated that it had grown more difficult, 17 that it was about the same and 13 stated that it was now easier.

It is true that one cannot always take such statements at face value. Our own response categories were at best vaguely defined. The quality of performers is difficult to evaluate, especially in com-

---

[7] In his dissertation Watts (pp. 8–9) reports that according to the Census the number of self-designated actors and actresses has been falling since 1930. This number doubled during the first decade of the century, was stable in the next decade and grew about 30 per cent during the 1920's. In the 1930's the number fell about 50 per cent; it has since been declining more slowly.

parisons extending over a period of time, and a manager is not likely to admit to having hired unsatisfactory performers. Still, there is nothing in these interviews to suggest a general shortage of performers.

Though perhaps the most important issue involved in supply is the quality of performers, the sheer number available is also of interest. On this point impressive evidence is provided by the Census counts of the number who are unemployed. These figures may be interpreted as a measure of net oversupply — the number of performers supplied minus the number demanded — with some qualifications. In two respects the Census figures probably understate the true level of unemployment in the performing arts: they do not count as unemployed those who are without professional work at the time of the Census but *are* working as waiters or in some other unrelated job; and they do not count those who have become sufficiently discouraged to leave the labor force altogether. On the other hand, many persons list themselves as actors, dancers or musicians though neither their training nor their seriousness of purpose gives much justification for their doing so, and the number of unemployed performers is enlarged in consequence. One may well question whether all would-be performers — actresses, for example — can realistically be regarded as part of the reservoir of talent available to performing organizations.

According to the 1950 Census, the unemployment rate was 18 per cent among actors and 7.4 per cent among (male) musicians and music teachers.[8] The larger proportion of unemployment among actors is ascribable in part to the scarcity of permanent companies. Since actors must change jobs often, it is only natural that many are "between jobs" at any given time. Despite this fact, an unemployment rate of 18 per cent is extremely high in comparison with the rate of roughly 5 per cent for the labor force as a whole in 1950. It represents a degree of economic hardship for the actor which is hard to duplicate elsewhere in the economy.

A comparison with the figures a decade later is even more revealing. The 1960 data, reported in Chapter V, show that during the preceding decade there was a drop in unemployment among

[8] *U. S. Census of Population, 1950: Occupational Characteristics.*

musicians and music teachers to a rate of 4.7 per cent. But by 1960 the average unemployment rate for actors had risen to an enormous 29 per cent. Here is strong evidence that the supply is still well ahead of the demand, despite a considerable decline in the number of actors reported by the Census.

Special Areas of Performer Shortage

There are reports of shortages of particular types of performer. For example, we were told that good character actors, many of whom find jobs in television and the films, are fairly hard to locate. There also seems to be general agreement that good orchestral players of string instruments are scarce.[9] Curiously, the same shortage has been reported in British and continental orchestras.[10] It is interesting that players of exactly the same instruments should be scarce in several countries simultaneously. Perhaps the universality of the shortage may be ascribed in part to the international mobility of skilled performers; they can be enticed into deficit areas from any country in which they are more abundant. Mobility has also affected the employment patterns of young American singers, who are apparently oversupplied in the United States but frequently find jobs in European opera houses.[11] Specialized performers of other types also appear to be in short supply; for example, few actors are flexible enough, by training, to work effectively in repertory.

The evidence that there is a shortage of at least some types of orchestral musician suggested to us a test which, as it turned out, revealed rather strikingly one way in which the market goes about meeting such a situation. We surmised that the shortage has helped to open the orchestral field to women, but that for a variety of reasons — perhaps prejudice, but also scheduling difficulties caused by women's family obligations — orchestras prefer to hire men. We then conjectured that the less affluent orchestras are forced to hire more women because, as a general rule, orchestras

[9] See, for example, *New York Times*, Aug. 20, 1963, p. 36.

[10] Report of the Committee on the London Orchestras, Arts Council of Great Britain, p. 9.

[11] See, for example, testimony of Anthony A. Bliss, House Hearings, II, p. 78.

employ women only when they cannot obtain men of comparable ability at their prevailing wage scales. The following table provides spectacular confirmation of this hypothesis, for it shows with what perfect regularity the proportion of women employed varies inversely with the budget of the orchestra.[12]

Size of Orchestra's Annual Budget (millions)	Number of Orchestras in Category	Women as Per Cent of Total Performers
$1.5 and over	5	3.6
$0.8–$1.49	6	11.3
$0.6–$0.79	5	19.2
$0.4–$0.59	6	27.3
Under $0.4	3	36.3

The "stars" constitute another special group in short supply. In part, this means only that the very best people in any profession are always eagerly sought after. Though this is an especially sensitive area, and though we have no hard evidence,[13] we were told by many sources that fees for stars have been going up at an exceedingly rapid rate.

One of the important factors at work here is the demand of the mass media. A star who captures the affection of the public holds very considerable economic power as a consequence of the extremely large audience to which the mass media cater.[14] If he agrees to appear in a film rather than a live play, he may increase the number of viewers (and box office receipts) by several million, and his earnings may be expected to reflect this fact. If the live performing arts wish to compete for the services of such stars, they must expect to pay dearly.

[12] These figures were calculated from information contained in the American Symphony Orchestra League report for the major orchestras, 1963–64.

[13] Even those organizations which were most willing to open their books to us balked when we broached the subject of salaries of star performers, and it is easy to see why they felt this way.

[14] The difference between the size of audiences for the living arts and for the electronic media is even greater than is sometimes recognized. It has been estimated, for example, that the few network productions of Shakespeare's plays, although they were far from successful by ordinary television standards, were seen by more persons than have seen a live performance of these plays from the day they were written. Here indeed is a revolution in output per man-hour!

Yet, on the whole, the mass media have probably caused a reduction in the demand for performers below the topmost echelon, since a single film or a record often replaces thousands of live performances. While there may be some offsetting factors, such as the increased market for the services of dancers that accompanied the advent of television, it is doubtful that the net effect of the mass media has been to increase performer incomes or professional employment.

If wages and employment in live performance decrease sufficiently, the over-all supply of skilled persons will probably also eventually fall. There must be limits to the dedication even of musicians, dancers and actors (although we have come across cases where these limits are hard to imagine). The number of actors has already been declining, and a decrease in the number of well-trained performers of other types available for the living arts is certainly conceivable.

Such a decline may ultimately produce a serious problem for the mass media as well, for the living arts serve as an important training ground for the performers needed to produce recordings, films and television programs. Perhaps the mass media will yet have to learn to contribute more directly to the financial health of live performing groups. Motion pictures and television cannot afford much experimentation and failure, as the penalty for not attracting the public is as extreme as the reward for pleasing it. Yet first-rate talent can be developed only if there are opportunities to experiment and freedom to fail. Since the live performing arts do perform these essential functions for the mass media, it may not be far-fetched to suggest that the mass media may some day undertake to compensate them.

Remarks on Union Activity

The performing arts are one of the most highly unionized sectors of the economy, the spectrum of membership including such diverse personnel as stagehands, ticket takers, press agents, musicians, actors and business managers. While in many fields, such as the automobile industry, a single union represents the great majority of the unionized employees, workers in the performing arts are organized into a large number of independent craft unions. The main unions in this field include Actors' Equity, the American Federation of Musicians, the American Guild of Musical Artists (AGMA), the American Guild of Variety Artists (AGVA), the Theatrical Protective Union and the Directors and Choreographers Guild.

The craft union structure of its labor organizations means that managements must deal with several sets of union negotiators, and that some performers may belong to several unions at the same time.[15]

Perhaps a more important consequence of craft unionism is that rather rigid lines are drawn between different kinds of work, and the exclusive right to each of its job functions is carefully protected by each craft. Irritation is often caused when an actor or a director is not permitted to move a chair on a set, this being the exclusive province of the stagehand.

The long history of unionism in the performing arts[16] is attributable to several causes. The relatively chaotic and impermanent nature of the operation of many organizations in the industry has meant that unions such as Actors' Equity have served to introduce a degree of stability to the industry. Thus, they have played a role similar to that of the unions in the needle trades. Economic hardship and poor working conditions have, no doubt, also served to spur unionism, as has the concern with social problems which has long been characteristic of artists.[17]

Today, the unions in the performing arts, like most other labor organizations, concern themselves mainly with improvements in

[15] We were told, for example, that during a brief visit one foreign performer who worked in opera, appeared briefly off-Broadway and made a few television appearances, had to be a member of AGMA (for his work in opera), Equity (for his stage appearances), the American Federation of Television and Radio Artists (for his television appearances), and that, had he made a movie, he would also have had to join the Screen Actors Guild.

[16] The American Federation of Musicians was founded in 1896 and Actors' Equity in 1913. (See Leiter.)

[17] Actors' Equity was a pioneer in the struggle against discrimination. As long ago as 1947, because of some highly publicized incidents in the nation's capital, it added a clause to its rule book specifying that "the actor shall not be required to perform in any theater in Washington, D.C. where discrimination is practiced against any actor or patron of the theater by reason of his race, color or creed."

the wages, employment opportunities and working conditions of their members. They pursue these objectives not only through collective bargaining, but also by working to stimulate greater public interest in the arts and more governmental support.

The unions have sought to publicize the inadequacy of performers' earnings levels, a judgment generally shared by performer and management alike. Though standards of fairness are not easily defined, few persons in the performing arts feel that compensation levels are adequate, and hardly anyone seems to argue that the issue ought to be left exclusively to the market forces of supply and demand.[18] Managements usually argue only that they cannot afford to pay better. Ultimately, the level of wages is heavily influenced by the general financial state of the performing organization. The dilemma posed by what are considered to be the requisites of justice and the limitations imposed by financial constraints was nicely summed up by one prominent Broadway producer when, in commenting on the outcome of negotiations with Actors' Equity, he remarked, "My colleagues and I feel that this was a very fair settlement. We can't afford it, but it is a fair settlement."[19]

In some cases unions have attempted to help both performing and non-performing personnel by imposing work rules that are often denounced as "featherbedding." Unfortunately, the subject is more elusive than might be thought, and our rather intensive efforts at documentation brought meager results. In our discussion of this subject we must, therefore, rely on the views of persons more closely acquainted with the field.

It is easy enough to provide illustrations of the sort of practice that is alleged to occur.[20] A particularly forceful statement appeared in a newspaper article written by a Broadway producer. There he suggested that

> . . . to bring back to its doors the men and women who love and should go to the theater . . . [one should answer] some pertinent questions, such as, why does it cost as much to move a one set

[18] For an exception see the statement by Sigmund Spaeth, House Hearings, II, p. 169.

[19] *New York Times,* June 7, 1964, p. 31, quoting David Merrick.

[20] Featherbedding is not a new problem for the theater. Poggi, (Chapter 10, p. 17) gives examples going back nearly fifty years.

show four city blocks as to ship an entire householder's goods from New York to far away Tibet; why a play with two people requires 22 stagehands; why a performance starring two entertainers, one a pianist and the other a monologist, who appear in dinner jackets, requires a wardrobe mistress; why an actor signed for a run-of-the-play contract, but who on the second day of rehearsal is relieved of the role, must necessarily be paid $1,700 a week for the entire run, while this artist is doing work in television and in films; why it costs as much to build and paint on canvas a one set interior, as it does to build a seven-room house; why a straight play's producer must employ four standby musicians who are paid *not* to play.[21]

If nothing else, this statement illustrates what a tremendous irritant "featherbedding" practices have been to theatrical management and helps to account for the disproportionate amount of time that is sometimes spent in dealing with union representatives on such matters.

But perhaps the most illuminating evaluation of the subject was written by A. H. Raskin of the *New York Times*. In a background paper written for the Rockefeller Brothers Panel, he first reminds the reader of the example

> . . . provided in the 1961 season by "An Evening with Mike Nichols and Elaine May" at the Golden Theater. With only two performers, the show had fifteen stagehands. This automatically stirred memories of the parade of eleven carpenters, electricians, property men, and grips Victor Borge used to call up for a bow at the final curtain of his one-man show of comedy and piano improvisations in the period from 1953 to 1956. The procession of unionists battening off Mr. Borge's talents never failed to send the audience home chuckling, but also vaguely disquieted.
>
> However, Alexander H. Cohen, producer of the Nichols and May show, saw nothing either funny or excessive about his fifteen-man stage crew. He considered every man necessary from the standpoint of the artistic integrity of the production, even though he was aware that eight men could readily have been dropped if the settings were laid out differently. . . .
>
> What the producers find especially galling about . . . payments for work not done is that . . . [some of the unions have] no unemployment problem. Since the advent of television, . . . [one of them] has had more jobs than members, and employers assert that "moonlighting" — the practice of holding two or three jobs at the same time — is widespread. The union not only maintains a tight rein on the admission of new members, but it cracks down on any producer who seeks to have a stagehand perform work in more than

[21] Joel Schenker, *New York Times*, June 21, 1964, Section 2, p. 3.

one department classification. This means that a man whose sole task is to push a light switch once an evening cannot be used to move a chair offstage in another scene a half hour later. If he has anything to do with lights, he is an electrician and cannot also serve as a prop man. . . .

Despite the vast amount of grumbling among producers about the multiplicity of extra costs for stagehands, many admit privately that the shows that get hurt most in this regard are usually those in which the employer has been insufficiently vigilant in protecting his own interests. If he determines his needs carefully and makes it plain to the union that he will resist any overcharges, he can often temper the overexuberance of a business agent eager to saddle him with more men than the rules require. . . .

He concludes:

I can think of nothing less useful than a repetition . . . of the sterile, and largely baseless, complaint that high union wages and restrictive union rules represent a principal obstacle to the financial health of professional groups in the performing arts. It is undoubtedly true that the standards built up to protect those with jobs would cheerfully be waived by younger artists of talent who would like an opportunity to demonstrate their ability. It is also true that experimental groups often find manpower and other requirements imposed by unions representing stage hands, electricians, etc., an obstacle. But if the groups are determined enough they usually can obtain waivers. Similarly, in the professional theater, music, and opera, where producers stand up with sufficient vigor for their rights, abuse is much less frequent than where submission comes without even the appearance of a fight.

Unions in the arts — in common with those in social agencies, hospitals, and other nonprofit organizations — reject the notion that their members should be expected to make what is, in effect, a charitable contribution to keep worthy organizations afloat. Nevertheless, when they are convinced of the genuineness of the financial emergency, modifications of rules and even of union scales are made with the agreement of unions and their members.[22]

In trying to account for movements in wages one would normally look to three types of influence: the general economic situation, which pulls wages in most fields along with the remainder of the economy; the nature and extent of union activity; and special circumstances affecting the particular field of endeavor, in this case the presence of the mass media and shortages of particular skills. In this chapter we have commented briefly on each of these

[22] Raskin, "Labor as Performer and Practitioner in the Arts."

types of influence. In looking at performer earnings from these various angles, however, one runs some risk of losing sight of the two main conclusions to which this chapter points:

(1) Artists' earnings are not the only component of cost of performance that has been rising. Indeed, other costs have grown more rapidly. In recent years, at any rate, expenditures on artistic personnel have been a declining portion of the total expenditures of the typical performing organization.

(2) While the money wages of performers have risen and have increased more rapidly than the price level, for long periods they have lagged well behind those in other occupations. Thus, in relative terms, performers have grown poorer over the rather long period examined. Only in the last few years do they seem to have stopped falling further behind.

CHAPTER X

Factors Affecting Demand and Earnings

HAVING completed our discussion of the cost side of the economics of the performing arts, we come to the second major aspect of their finances — their receipts. In this chapter we shall examine the elements which affect the demand for the performing arts and the income received by them. We shall discuss the effects on their income of general economic conditions, of the mass media, and of the number of contemporary works presented. Only one major ingredient in the determination of earnings, the price of tickets, will be postponed until the next chapter.

Before discussing the factors which determine attendance, we shall review the current state of affairs. Specifically, we begin by considering the extent of excess capacity in the performing arts — the proportion of unsold seats at a typical performance.

Attendance and Unused Capacity

Data on attendance in relation to capacity provide a direct measure of the current balance between supply and demand in live performance. This information is a necessary element in any evaluation of the performing organizations' policies on pricing, promotion and programing. Unsold seats may be considered to pose a challenge to an organization's management — an opportunity to expand revenues without a commensurate increase in expenditures.

We therefore investigated, for a number of American organiza-

237

tions and a few British groups, the relationship between attendance and capacity in 1963–64. The results (summarized in Table X–1) show that there is substantial room for increases in audience requiring no rise in performance costs. The few exceptions are the Metropolitan Opera, which has had few empty seats indeed, having operated at a very exceptional 97 per cent of capacity, some hit Broadway productions and several of the major orchestras. But in the other cases, all of the percentage capacity figures presented in this table show a considerable excess of capacity over demand. At the average major orchestra concert, about one quarter of the seats were unsold, and in London the ratio was one third. On Broadway roughly one third of the seats were unused, and at the average straight show the house was more than 40 per cent empty.

TABLE X–1

Attendance as Per Cent of Capacity,
by Art Form and Night of Week, 1963–64

Art Form	Average	Weekend Average Less Weeknight Average[a]
Major Orchestras:		
United States[b]	78	+11
London[c]	68	
Broadway Theater:[d]		
Musicals	75	
Straight Shows	57	
Total	67	+24
Regional Theater in U. S. (survey results)[e]	77	+ 7
Opera:		
Metropolitan[f]	97	+ 2
Other U. S. Operas (survey results)[e]	71	+24
Covent Garden[g]	81	

SOURCE: Broadway figures based on data from *Variety;* others calculated from data supplied by individual arts organizations. See footnotes below for more detail.

[a] "Weekend" is defined here as Friday, Saturday, Sunday, and "weeknight" as Monday through Thursday. All of the results in this column are based on

Table X–1 also shows how much smaller are unused capacities on weekends. For example, attendance at performances of the major orchestras was 11 per cent higher on Fridays, Saturdays and Sundays than it was on other nights of the week, and Broadway attendance increased 24 per cent on the weekend.[1]

In interpreting figures of this kind, it is important to recognize that no industry can easily achieve full use of capacity, and that to do so would often require decisions which were unacceptable on other grounds. In the case of the performing arts it might be necessary, for example, to eliminate performances whose content and timing are least popular. Later in this chapter we shall present a detailed analysis of the box office consequences of the performance of relatively unknown works. The elimination of performances on unpopular nights of the week could also have its drawbacks. One orchestral manager reported he had once considered

---

[1] Figures reported in *Variety* indicate that attendance as a percentage of capacity varies seasonally in the Broadway theater. It is lower in the fall and winter months; but this probably reflects the effect of the holidays and the timing of new openings. In the fall and winter, recently opened but unsuccessful productions pull down the average percentage of capacity sold, but by spring many of these shows will have vanished from the list of offerings.

Notes to Table X–1 continued

data collected for our audience survey performances, except in the case of the Metropolitan Opera.

b Regular series subscription concerts only. The figure given is the arithmetic mean of percentage-of-capacity figures for our basic eleven orchestras. The interquartile range is 70.3 per cent to 87.1 per cent.

c For all concerts given at Royal Festival Hall. Data from a paper by T. E. Bean, General Manager of Royal Festival Hall, published as Appendix B of the Goodman Committee Report.

d Calculated as follows: the actual dollar gross as a percentage of capacity gross was calculated for each Broadway show running during a single week in each month from September through June of 1964–65 from data published in *Variety*. Generally the second week in each month was used. An average for each month was then calculated for musicals, straight shows, and all shows combined. The averages for these monthly sample weeks were then combined into season averages, with the number of "theater weeks" in each sample week serving as weights.

e See the list of organizations surveyed (Appendix Table IV-B) for the organizations included in this average.

f Box office receipts as a percentage of capacity gross.

g Based on box office summary statements. The weekday average is for Monday through Thursday nights and the weekend average is for Friday and Saturday nights only. Matinées are excluded.

dropping his poorly attended Sunday matinées until he realized that some of his largest contributors preferred to go to them. Since a reduction in the number of performances also makes life harder for the performer, it is not a decision that is taken easily. For all of these reasons, there will continue to be times when attendance is low.

But while universal capacity audiences may represent an unattainable goal, a great deal can be done to expand audience size. Increased ticket sales are, no doubt, a desirable end in themselves, and they can also make a very substantial contribution to the finances of the organization. If ticket sales to a performance are raised from 80 to 88 per cent of capacity, it is clear that the revenues from that performance will have risen 10 per cent (assuming average ticket price is constant), and that *there will be virtually no offsetting increase in cost.*

Yet increased attendance offers no cure-all for the financial problems of the arts. Even organizations such as the Metropolitan Opera and the most prosperous major orchestras, which operate close to capacity, still have substantial gaps between income and expenditures. A larger audience would, of course, ease the difficulties of organizations that are operating below capacity, but it would not solve their problems either. For the major orchestras as a whole, average excess capacity was 22 per cent in 1963–64. If box office receipts were to increase in proportion to size of audience (i.e., if there were no fall in average ticket price), earnings from this source could be raised at most about 20 per cent. However, for the average major orchestra, the gap between concert income and expenditures amounts to about 69 per cent of its income.[2] *Thus, even if every major orchestral concert were sold out, the consequent increase in receipts would cover much less than one third of the total financial gap.* In any event, even if 100 per cent attendance were feasible, one cannot go on from there to 105 per cent of capacity. Increased attendance is not an effective avenue for escape from a gap which can be expected to grow progressively with the passage of time.

---

[2] The average gap was $374,000. The average amount of earned income from concerts was $544,000.

But while it is no financial panacea, near capacity attendance is certainly desirable and fully merits the effort required to achieve a closer approximation to it. In the near future, audience promotion is likely to become an even more important activity for many performing groups. With the widespread adoption of a year long season, a larger audience will have to be found for the increased number of performances. While additional performances produce some rise in attendance, our data suggest that a 10 per cent increase in the number of performances by itself increases the audience by less than 10 per cent.[3] Thus, the new vogue for lengthened seasons is likely to increase the number of unsold seats, and thereby aggravate the pecuniary problems of the arts unless there is a marked rise in demand.

In the remainder of this chapter we shall, therefore, consider the variables which affect the demand for performance. Some of these, such as the state of the economy and the competition of the mass media, are beyond the control of the performing organizations. But others, such as promotional activity and the nature of their programs, are entirely subject to their decisions.

Trends in Demand and the Effects of Recessions

In this chapter we shall report only recent data on the state of demand. We shall reserve discussion of the earlier history of earnings and our older figures for the New York Philharmonic and the Cincinnati Orchestras until Chapter XII, where we bring together our cost and income information and discuss trends in the income gap.

Figure X–1 shows the course of box office receipts on Broadway and earned income of the major orchestras since 1937, the starting point for both these series. It also shows the pattern of over-all expenditures on admissions to live performance of every variety as reported since 1929 by the *Survey of Current Business* and the pattern of total personal consumption expenditures for the population as a whole. The graph shows a fairly steady rise in all of these series, with some leveling off in over-all admissions

[3] See Appendix X–1.

FIGURE X-1

EARNED INCOME OF MAJOR ORCHESTRAS, BROADWAY
AND ALL LIVE PERFORMING ARTS, 1929–1964

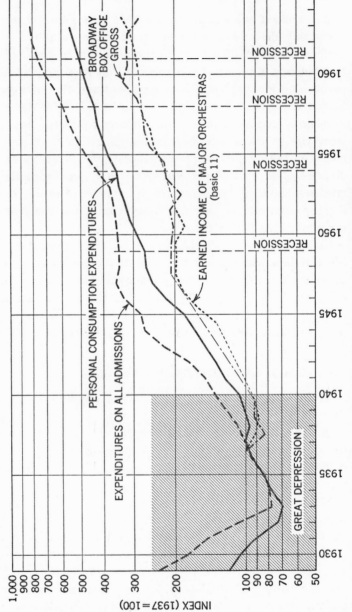

This graph is based on data from Appendix Table III–A, Major Orchestra Compiled Annual Reports, and *Variety*.

242

and Broadway receipts in the last few years. It is interesting that orchestral and Broadway incomes have followed an extremely similar path, and that both have lagged somewhat behind personal consumption expenditures and over-all expenditures on admissions. The fact that orchestral and Broadway earnings have not kept pace with personal consumption confirms our earlier conclusion about the behavior of these variables (Chapter III). The relatively slow growth rate of Broadway and major orchestra earnings, as compared with the rate of increase in total admissions, is evidence of the increasing importance of semi-professional and amateur activity.

The graph also enables us to draw conclusions about the sensitivity of receipts to recessions in business activity. During the great depression, over-all admissions fell off markedly and reached their nadir in 1933. Although this downward movement can be ascribed in part to other causes, the fact that general consumption expenditures behaved in a similar fashion, and terminated their descent in the same year, leaves little doubt that the depression had a strong impact on the arts.

Since World War II there have been four mild recessions: in 1949, 1954, 1957–58 and 1960–61. The rate of increase in total personal consumption expenditures was dampened by each of these recessions, but expenditures on admissions to the arts were unaffected, as Figure X–1 shows. This may be somewhat surprising, for one might have thought that a "luxury" item such as attendance at the theater would be the first to suffer in an economic downturn. But the fact is that the sort of mild recession we have experienced since the war has had very little effect on the earnings of the professional, high income level families who, as our surveys show, constitute the bulk of the audience for the performing arts. Had there been more blue collar workers in the audience, it is possible that recessions would have been felt more strongly at the box office.

The Mass Media and the Audience for Live Performance

The classic example of the effect of the mass media on the audience for live performance is that associated with the advent of the movie industry and the subsequent introduction of the "talkies."[4] We recall that activity on "the road" — traveling theatrical companies from New York — started its decline about 1908, some two decades before Broadway began to experience difficulties. The decline became precipitous during the same decade (1910–1920) that movies were first exhibited commercially on a large scale. While the movies undoubtedly attracted many people who had never been to a live performance,[5] they must also have lured many persons away from the theater, for it is hard to believe that the simultaneous drop in attendance at live performance was largely coincidence.

There were many reasons for this massive switch on the part of the audience. Rising costs, particularly those involved in transporting theatrical companies, were driving some theater houses out of business, and at least some were soon turned into movie houses.[6] The difference in ticket prices was probably even more important. In the 1920's admission to a movie theater cost from $ .25 to $ .75, while a theater ticket cost about five times as much. The individual's demand for entertainment was probably stimulated by a general decrease in the number of work hours. Since he had only a limited amount to spend on entertainment, it may be that only the relatively inexpensive cinema was able to supply his increased entertainment demands without taking him beyond his budget.

In view of the steady decline of "the road" after about 1908, the continued prosperity of its parent, the New York theater, seems distinctly anomalous. One reason why Broadway alone continued to thrive for so long is that the prosperity of the 1920's was largely confined to cities. We also surmise that the quality of live performances in rural areas had never been particularly high, so that they were more vulnerable to competition. At the same time an outstanding generation of American playwrights, O'Neill, Rice and Anderson among others, brought a new vitality to the New York stage, and this too helped prolong its prosperity.

[4] Here Poggi's discussion has been invaluable, and the next few paragraphs lean heavily on his analysis.

[5] Bernheim (p. 87) points out that in 1925 motion picture attendance was at least 56 times the maximum possible weekly attendance at the legitimate theater in the peak season of 1901.

[6] Poggi, p. 58 ff.

But even in New York, theatrical activity began its decline in 1927. The date is noteworthy, for it indicates that Broadway's troubles antedate both the great depression and the advent of the "talkies." Probably by then the combination of rising costs and the competition of the silent movies had begun to take their toll.

In many ways television after World War II played a role very similar to that of the movies in the previous postwar period. The rate of growth of the television industry from its commercial beginnings in 1948 is indicated by the fact that the number of families owning television sets rose from one half of one per cent of all households in 1948 to 30 per cent in 1952 and 84 per cent in 1962.[7]

The effect of this development on the size of the audience for the live performing arts and for motion pictures is hard to quantify, but if we look back at Figure X–1 we see a very pronounced leveling off of expenditure on the performing arts between 1948 and 1952. Though total consumer expenditures in this period went up about 23 per cent, the amount spent on admissions rose only 5 per cent, the Broadway gross increased 1 per cent and the earned income of the major orchestras remained just about constant. It is hardly plausible that this state of relative stagnation is totally unrelated to the increase over the same period in the number of families with television sets from 0 to 30 per cent of the total. And, in all likelihood, ownership of television sets among the high income families who are the bulk of the audience for the live performing arts rose far more rapidly during the early days of television when sets were quite expensive. In sum, it seems clear that the mass media have made inroads into the audience for live performance.[8]

In evaluating the consequences of the advent of the mass media, the effects on the quality of performance must be considered carefully. Although there is obviously a different experience in-

[7] U. S. Bureau of the Census, *Historical Statistics of the United States: Colonial Times to 1957*, and *Continuations to 1962;* data on number of television sets from Series R–98, and number of families and unrelated individuals from Series G–118.

[8] The connection between record sales, which grew about fourfold between 1952 and 1963, and the size of the orchestral audience is much less clear-cut. There is no obvious statistical relationship. It has even been argued that record sales may stimulate attendance at concerts.

volved in watching a live performance and watching the same performance on TV, the mass media have not changed the nature of the final product as significantly as may at first appear. The view that the decreased number of plays currently offered in live performance represents a very great decline in the output of "art" is a romantic notion for which the evidence is tenuous. If one examines the plays and other live presentations that constituted the bulk of American theatrical offerings between the turn of the century and the end of the 1920's when the number of new productions was at its height, one sees that the day-to-day offerings of the mass media have at least in part replaced their own kind.[9] A substantial part of earlier live performance was vaudeville, and even the legitimate theater contained a high proportion of items which might not enchant our contemporary critics. Today the mass media make available to the general public — which includes a new rural audience — vaudeville and other forms of entertainment, light and otherwise, in far greater abundance than was provided for them in the "golden age." And it is probable that the typical "canned" performance satisfies higher critical standards than its precursor, while offering the advantages of ready accessibility and unlimited audience capacity.

The fact that many of the more routine kinds of performance once found on the stage are now provided by the mass media can be regarded as a sensible application of the principle of comparative advantage. The mass media, though they often present entertainment of extremely high caliber, are basically vehicles for what is, in effect, assembly line entertainment. It is certainly arguable

---

[9] Poggi (pp. 274–75) points out ". . . the remarkable resemblance between the ways in which plays were put together between 1870 and 1910 and ways in which movie scripts were assembled after 1910. The professional playwright of the early period usually wrote 'on order' for a producer, developing an idea proposed by him, or adapting one of his own ideas to fit a particular star. Sometimes the producer turned an author's manuscript over to one or more other writers in order, as John Golden put it, 'to infuse freshness of viewpoint into the play' . . . The parallels between these practices and those employed later in the movie industry are almost perfect. . . . The basic assumptions were the same: that scripts were manufactured to suit the preconceptions of a vast national audience; that the producer, being a highly sensitive 'barometer' to the public taste, could help a writer make the necessary adjustments in his scripts; and that the final test of a dramatic work was acceptance by the greater number."

that the decline of *live* performances of this kind has been no great social loss. For these performances, the great cost per viewer involved in retaining the archaic technology of live presentation is probably not justified from the point of view of the public welfare. Furthermore, while the movies and television have assumed the task of satisfying the demand for mass entertainment, much of the individually thought-out theatrical activity which may or may not have a wide appeal has been left to the legitimate theater. It is here, as with any other product in which craftsmanship and imagination are of the essence, that a very real loss may be occasioned by the adoption of mass production techniques.

The vitality of live performance in this country is undoubtedly desirable from an aesthetic viewpoint, and is absolutely essential if for no other reason than to provide new material and trained personnel for the insatiable mass media. But in our zeal for the irreplaceable quality of live performance we must not ignore the fact that in more standardized types of entertainment, and even in some types of performance meeting the most exacting artistic standards (e.g., recordings of music), the mass media have made a very significant net social contribution by providing performances more cheaply, more conveniently and, sometimes, of higher quality than have ever before been widely available.[10]

Earnings from Broadcasting and Recording

If the mass media have made things more difficult for the living arts by limiting their income from ticket sales, they have provided some compensating earnings to the performing organizations in the form of payments for movie rights and fees for broadcasting and recording. From the point of view of the industry as a whole, as we saw in Chapter VI, payments from these sources are comparatively small and very unevenly distributed. In 1963–64 only three of the major orchestras derived sizable sums from such

[10] We must not lose sight of the fact that the film is also a vital art form in itself. There are those who believe that at the moment the "art film" is a focus of creativity more significant than much of the live theater. On the other hand, there is a great deal of criticism of the mass media, and of television in particular, for having failed to make full use of their potential for the dissemination of the arts.

sources. In fact, many major orchestras earned more from these sources in earlier years (even in absolute dollar amounts) than they do now. Since the purchasing power of the dollar was higher at that time, the real decline has been even larger than the figures suggest. Specifically, the compiled reports of the major orchestras show that in 1946–47, 17 major orchestras earned at least $1,000 net from recording and broadcasting, while only 10 earned this much in 1963–64; and 7 orchestras netted $30,000 or more from this source in 1946–47, but only 3 did so in 1963–64. Although the reports do not give comparable figures for any length of time for the three orchestras that do obtain substantial sums from recording and broadcasts, the available data suggest that even for these three organizations revenue from these sources has grown slowly and has constituted a declining portion of total income.

In Great Britain the decline in recording income has had a major impact on orchestral finance. According to the Goodman Report[11] one of the London orchestras (the New Philharmonia) was founded in 1946 for the express purpose of recording for Electric and Musical Industries, Ltd., but now that recording income has waned the orchestra has run into serious financial difficulties. The decline in recording opportunities has also had adverse effects on the finances of the Royal Philharmonic.

This decline can plausibly be ascribed to two influences, the satiation of the record market and the fact that musical performance makes poor television programing. After the war, with the development of high fidelity recording techniques, the record companies found it necessary to build up a completely new library of recordings of the standard works. This created a great deal of employment, but its effects were transitory. While the number of performances available on records has grown, the rate of new recordings seems to have fallen. And where once orchestral performances constituted a standard part of radio programing, live broadcasting has been largely driven from the air waves by television. Because an orchestral performance is visually uninteresting, and because the small speakers with which television sets are equipped give rather poor sound reproduction, musical performances have never

[11] Report of the Committee on the London Orchestras, Arts Council of Great Britain, p. 4.

become a staple of television programing, even during the Sunday afternoon hours which have been described as the networks' "cultural ghetto."

In opposition to this general trend the income which theaters derive from the mass media has been increasing. Gross income from the sale of film rights amounted to a little more than $2½ million in 1955 and rose fairly steadily thereafter to nearly $5½ million in 1964.[12] Once again, however, the benefits are somewhat unevenly distributed; that is, the bulk is being obtained by a very few organizations. Yet even for the less successful plays and musicals, the sale of movie rights, often arranged before the opening of the production, frequently makes the difference between solvency and financial catastrophe, and in many cases provides substantial benefits to the playwright.

Variables Subject to Managerial Decision: Advertising and Promotion

The performing organizations have little control over the prosperity of the economy or the competition of the mass media. But they can influence demand by a variety of means, among them advertising and promotion.

Here the term "advertising" should not conjure up visions of televised nightmares depicting stomach pills dropped into phrenetic digestive tracts. Advertising and promotion can take far more palatable forms, and can certainly be extremely useful in stimulating demand. Moreover, they encompass a variety of activities which the layman rarely thinks of as advertising.

One class of long-range promotion program involves special children's concerts and inexpensive tickets for students, each of which is expected to build audiences for the future.[13] Similarly, con-

---

[12] Specifically, the figures supplied by a reliable but anonymous source were as follows (in millions): 1955, $2.59; 1956, $2.35; 1957, $2.37; 1958, $3.30; 1959, $3.46; 1960, $4.83; 1961, $4.27; 1962, $4.72; 1963, $3.88; 1964, $5.46.

[13] Given the high degree of mobility which characterizes the American population, a child who is taught to enjoy music in Philadelphia may very well grow into an adult who attends concerts in Los Angeles or some other city. Thus, considered purely as a financial investment, this sort of promotion is not likely to be good business for any one organization though it may be of extreme importance for the Nation's arts as a whole.

struction of a new cultural center with attractive auditoriums and the attendant fanfare of publicity serve in part as a promotion device. The Los Angeles Orchestra doubled its gross receipts in its first season at its new home, though it remains to be seen how much of the increased audience will remain as the novelty of the buildings declines.

Promotion in the arts consists of fund drives, women's auxiliaries, organized benefit performances, sales of baked goods, linens and works of art, and a multitude of other activities which may be nearly as time consuming as the work of the musicians themselves. "Get me 50 women and a tea pot," said a wag, "and I will give you a new symphony orchestra." It has even been argued that if fund raising were not so dominating a concern for many organizations, a sizable block of the audience might drift away. For some persons the pre-concert dinners and other opportunities to participate in community-wide drives associated with the performing group constitute one of its principal attractions. Having participated in such functions, they feel they really should buy tickets themselves and attend some performances.

A most interesting illustration of the potential effects of promotion is the work of Danny Newman, of the Chicago Lyric Opera. He has served the Theater Communications Group as consultant for regional theaters throughout the United States and Canada and, through the Ford Foundation program in Humanities and the Arts, has helped a number of opera and ballet companies. Newman urges that investment in audience building is every bit as important for a performing organization as is the construction of an auditorium. Among other approaches, he urges large-scale but selective mailings and reliance on large volunteer groups to sell tickets directly, run meetings, conduct telephone campaigns and sell blocks of tickets to industrial concerns and other groups.

Newman is a very strong advocate of the subscription series, a device currently used most effectively by the major orchestras, the Metropolitan Opera, the regional theaters, many out-of-town theaters and other performing groups. He believes that full-scale efforts should begin six months before the start of the season, and he relies on a mounting sense of excitement as an element important in producing his results. He has increased the size of subscription audiences by as much as 300 per cent in a single pre-season campaign, and gains of 200 per cent have not been uncommon. Of 14 organizations with which he worked recently, 10 recorded gains of at least 160 per cent; the smallest increase in audience was 48 per cent. All of this shows what can be achieved by determined effort.

Advertising, too, can be very helpful. Some evidence of this was obtained from our audience surveys, in which one of the questions asked was: How did you hear about tonight's performance? The answers show quite clearly that newspaper advertising is one of the primary sources of information for potential members of the audience.[14]

Methods of Ticket Distribution

Audience size can also be affected by the ease with which tickets are obtainable. This has been a particularly controversial issue for the New York commercial theater, whose system of ticket distribution is a model of perfection in its inefficiency. The actual tickets are allocated, and often delivered directly, to the various brokers. There is no clearing house which can tell the consumer on a single inquiry what tickets are available for what plays, at what prices and for what performances. There is no pooling of information about the tickets even to a single play, and as a result, before a playgoer can determine if and where there are unsold seats, he often must go from box office to box office and possibly from broker to broker. Even the producer or the theater owner may have no way of knowing the size of his audience until just before a given

---

[14] Appendix Tables X–A and X–B, respectively, summarize the results by art form for the country as a whole and for New York City alone. Our surveys also provided what is probably the first extensive set of figures on audience overlap. These figures, showing to what extent people who patronize one art form also attend performances of others, are relevant to advertising decisions for many reasons. Information of this sort tells managements whether they must appeal to the same individuals as well as to the same type of individual, and thereby can help them decide whether common advertisements for several art forms make sense. It indicates whether it will pay one art form to advertise in another's programs. It enables managements to decide better how important it is to avoid conflicts in scheduling dates. In Chapter IV we have already discussed our findings on audience overlap in fairly general terms, and detailed figures are provided in Appendix Tables X–C and X–D.

performance, for under current arrangements the broker retains the right to return tickets to the theater up to 6:30 or 7:30 on the evening of the performance.[15]

Several remedial measures are either being tried or considered. The Shubert Theater chain (the largest in New York) and R. H. Macy and Co. (the largest department store) established a central ticket office in March 1964 in Macy's main store and at several suburban branches. At these locations one can purchase, at box office prices, tickets to any of the Shubert Theaters and to several others (including a few off-Broadway theaters) that have asked to be represented. Each theater pays a monthly charge to defray the costs of operating these distribution points.[16]

Though the Macy experiment has been criticized by some persons as a self-destructive arrangement in which the theaters subsidize the most effective competitor of the ticket brokers, who are Broadway's regular retailers, it has also been heralded as a means for recovering a lost audience.[17] We conducted a survey of ticket purchasers at these box offices in order to compare the composition of this group with that of the Broadway audience as a whole.[18] While (as shown in Appendix Table X–E) they turn out to be very similar in age, occupation, education and income, two differences are noteworthy. There is a much higher proportion of women among the Macy-Shubert box office customers (61 per cent, as compared with 43 per cent among the Broadway audience as a whole), and more of Macy's ticket purchasers were drawn from among those persons who were infrequent theatergoers. Thus, while the new box offices seem not to have reached a new *kind* of audience, they have apparently reached a larger group than had been attending before. Incidentally, many Macy respondents volunteered favorable comments on the new system of

[15] Lefkowitz, Hearings, I, from testimony given by Leland Hayward.

[16] The very reasonable proposal of a central ticket office certainly has all the dignity imparted by age. Poggi (p. 40) reports that a serious altercation between Lee Shubert and E. L. Erlanger broke out in 1923 over Shubert's advocacy of a central ticket office. See also *Variety*, July 28, 1923, p. 1.

[17] *New York Times*, March 12, 1964, p. 40.

[18] The survey was carried out in the spring of 1964. A shortened form of our audience questionnaire (see Appendix Table X–E for its text and for a brief discussion of our procedure) was prepared, as it was felt that a customer standing at a tiny counter would not want to write very much.

ticket distribution, in marked contrast to reactions encountered during some of our other surveys in New York.

A further innovation currently being considered is the installation at various locations of electronic equipment which could provide instantaneous information on the availability of tickets to any show, and enable patrons to reserve seats from a distance, perhaps with the aid of a credit card.[19] This is a promising proposal and might greatly facilitate the entire operation of ticket buying.

However, for this purpose the only really indispensable instrument is the telephone. If one wishes to purchase tickets to just about any type of performance in London, he steps into one of the many ticket offices scattered throughout the city. The agent telephones the chosen theater box office, finds out what tickets are available and, if the price, date and location are satisfactory to the customer, reserves the seats at once. The customer pays in cash, and is given a chit on which his seat numbers are written. While it is true that the ease of ticket buying in London can be explained largely by the fact that performances can afford to run there with smaller audiences in proportion to capacity, the difference is surely to be ascribed at least in part to differences in ticket distributing arrangements.

It is difficult to attribute the failure of our own commercial theater to adopt so simple a system to anything but lack of imagination or to the opposition of narrow interests, some of whom may even fear the loss of the scalper's profits which the current system facilitates. Often, the grounds for opposition are more mundane. One manager commented that he would be reluctant to join a central box office because, under the present system, when a performance of his organization is sold out his own ticket seller tries to push a performance of the same group on another night instead of the performance of a competing organization.

Contemporary Works: The Economics of "Adventurous" Productions

As we have seen, size of audience depends on a variety of considerations, including general economic conditions, the competition of the mass media, promotion and the ease with which tickets

---

[19] Howard Taubman, "How to Civilize Ticket Sales," *New York Times*, May 23, 1965, Section 2, p. 1.

can be obtained. The specific production or program offered, however, may have a greater influence on attendance than any of these other factors.

Thanks to cooperative managements, we were able to collect attendance figures for individual operas from the Metropolitan Opera for 1962–63, the New York City Opera for 1961–62 and the fall of 1962, and from Covent Garden for 1957–58 through 1963–64. In addition we obtained some case-study figures from the Chicago Lyric and the Santa Fe Operas. We next compared attendance when contemporary works were being performed with attendance on other occasions. "Contemporary" operas were defined arbitrarily as those written after World War I, a definition which has the advantage of objectivity, though "adventurous" is, in at least a few cases, something of a misnomer.

We found that ticket sales at the Metropolitan fell from their usual 97 per cent to 89 per cent of capacity when a contemporary work was performed. At the New York City Opera the corresponding decline was from 65 to 39 per cent of capacity, and at Covent Garden there was an average reduction from 83 to 67 per cent of capacity.[20] On the basis of our figures it may be estimated that a single performance of a contemporary opera results in a foregone revenue loss of nearly $2,500 at the Metropolitan, nearly $4,000 at the New York City Opera, and over £400 at Covent Garden.[21] At the New York City Opera, operating at City Center, we were told in an interview that the maximum capacity gross was over $11,-000, but contemporary operas usually grossed between $2,000 and $5,000 per performance, and a $5,000 or $6,000 gross was considered a tremendous success.

---

[20] Our data and findings are reported in more detail in Appendix Table X–F. These are, of course, only averages, and there are exceptions. The Sante Fe Opera has done well with "Lulu" and several Stravinsky works, and a contemporary work is sometimes well attended when tickets are sold as part of a subscription series or when an outstanding soloist is involved.

[21] These estimates utilized data on capacity gross obtained from the various performing organizations, i.e., figures indicating the total amount that would be earned at a performance if every seat in the house were sold. In these calculations it was assumed that a reduction in attendance would have a proportionate effect on ticket sales in every price category. Where capacity gross varied by night of the week or for any other reason, a weighted average figure was utilized.

Nor is this the end of the financial difficulty caused by the production of such works. In part because contemporary works are often presented by the company for the first time, and in part because they are characteristically difficult to perform, they may require a substantial expenditure on extra rehearsals as well as associated production costs. And since the piece is usually given only a few times, these production costs cannot be spread over a considerable number of showings.

Adventurous works cause similar financial problems in other art forms. In the theater, "adventurous" is not synonymous with "contemporary." True, the "theater of the absurd" and other experimental plays are not generally a blessing to the box office. But neither are the classics. Apparently the bulk of the theatergoing public wants new plays, but plays which place little strain on conventional attitudes.

We have few data on this subject pertaining to the theater generally, but we have figures extending over a ten year period (1953–1963) for the Bucks County Playhouse, which, as a matter of policy, has been putting on several new plays each season. The new shows ordinarily constitute a little less than one third of the theater's offerings. Even though none of these productions was radically experimental, they did more poorly at the box office than the tried and true productions in 7 of the 10 years reported. The difference was small, however — on the order of magnitude of 5 per cent over-all. Cost data for the Bucks County Playhouse for both types of productions show that running costs for the premieres were higher in every year, the difference amounting to about 5 to 10 per cent. Here we see again the double financial pressures besetting new productions.

Finally, we may look at the orchestral situation. We have no American data, but excellent British figures were prepared by the Royal Festival Hall for the Goodman Committee. The results are summarized in Appendix Table X–G. In this case "adventurous" programs are defined most conservatively, as any in which at least one piece is not part of the standard repertoire. Even so, adventurous programs reduced attendance by about 20 per cent of capacity on the average. Furthermore, this holds for all orchestras performing at the hall, and for all seating price categories.

While we have no corresponding figures for the United States, we suspect that the effect on audience size of the inclusion of a contemporary work on a program is somewhat less drastic than it is in England. There are two grounds for this surmise. First, American orchestras operate closer to capacity, so that at least some audiences in this country may be forced to purchase tickets to performances which are partially contemporary if they wish to hear the orchestra at all. Second, American orchestras sell tickets in subscription series, a procedure which has only recently even been proposed for London orchestras. The practice of selling subscriptions clearly gives the ticket purchaser less choice — if a concert containing contemporary works is part of a set of concerts offering more standard works, he can less easily avoid purchasing a ticket to it. But whether our guess is or is not valid, the path of the contemporary composition in this country is not usually smooth. It is often argued that the repertoire still consists primarily of revered standard works, and that even those contemporary composers who are played are likely to be represented by their "safest" and most conservative works — pieces for which they themselves have little affection. Like token integration, such token representation of contemporary pieces in the musical repertoire conceals a problem instead of solving it.

To be sure, in determining program content a performing group must take into account the likely economic consequences as well as its own beliefs about the relative merits of the works it is considering. It has been suggested by one manager that any musical organization which does not play new works cannot maintain its reputation among other musicians. But an organization which pursued an art-for-art's-sake approach and disregarded the type of audience response that we have documented might well be committing financial suicide — a fact largely ignored by critics of conservative programing.[22] On the other hand, if new plays, operas

---

[22] Though most published criticism of their programing objects to the conservatism of the performing groups, those who dislike contemporary music are also vehement in their criticism. In the course of our audience survey we received a number of unsolicited comments denouncing performances of contemporary music as a blight on the art and an offense to the audience. Another example is provided by an article in a right-wing publication which condemns the sandwiching "between . . . acceptable compositions of some out-

and musical compositions are not performed, they may not long be written and the arts will lose their vitality. The problem, then, will probably not be solved by the individual organizations; they cannot fairly be criticized for hesitating to embark on a path which may be catastrophic financially. Instead, it must be solved by all organizations together, and ultimately by society itself. The Ford Foundation's program of financial assistance for the presentation of contemporary works may illustrate the type of support required.

There are several morals to this chapter. First, the financial problems of the arts will not be solved by increases in audience demand alone. Unused capacity in the arts is substantial, but even if the audience grew enough to eliminate unsold seats completely, many performing arts organizations would find that the increased revenue still fell far short of their current income gap. If demand grows beyond this level, we cannot rule out the possibility that the resulting rise in costs will exceed the income gained in the process. Second, we conclude that audience size can sometimes be stimulated by means requiring sacrifices of principle, such as the avoidance of contemporary works, sacrifices which some organizations may be unwilling to accept. Yet despite these reservations we conclude that stimulation of demand is important. It may become a matter of absolute financial necessity as performing seasons are lengthened. And, above all, the desirability of increased audiences will be accepted as an article of faith by all those who believe in the importance of the arts for society.

Having, therefore, considered a number of the elements affecting audience size and the earnings of performing organizations, we turn to the most crucial income variable of all, the level of box office prices. This is the subject of the next chapter.

pourings of more or less raucous dissonance," describing this practice as "a violation of cultural freedom." William H. Chamberlin, "Musical Forced Feeding," *The Freeman*, June 1965, p. 11.

CHAPTER **XI**

Ticket Prices

THIS CHAPTER treats a variety of subjects connected with the pricing of tickets. It reports current levels and trends in ticket prices, comparing these with the behavior of the price level in general and with the cost of live performance. It reports also on the expenses other than ticket purchase which members of the audience typically incur when they attend a performance — expenditures on transportation, meals, baby-sitting, and so on. It next examines the effects of ticket pricing on audience composition, and deals, finally, with speculation and ticket scalping — topics which have received no little notoriety.

TRENDS IN TICKET PRICES AND RELATED COSTS

Current Ticket Prices

Again, our primary interest is in long-run prospects rather than just the current, no doubt transitory, state of affairs. We will begin, however, with a brief review of current ticket price levels.

As Figure XI–1 shows, average ticket prices for the different art forms span a considerable range, with the more expensive opera companies and Broadway hit musicals at the top of the ladder, each charging about $7 to $8 per seat. Major orchestra subscription series tickets are the bargain of the performing arts, with an average ticket price of about $2.50 per concert. There is a clustering of activity at the $3 to $4 level, with every art form represented in that range — an indication that considerable performing activity is still available at very reasonable prices. Certainly in New York City one can attend outstanding dance recitals, musical and

259

FIGURE XI-1

THE TICKET PRICE LADDER: AVERAGE TICKET
PRICES, VARIOUS ORGANIZATIONS, 1964–65

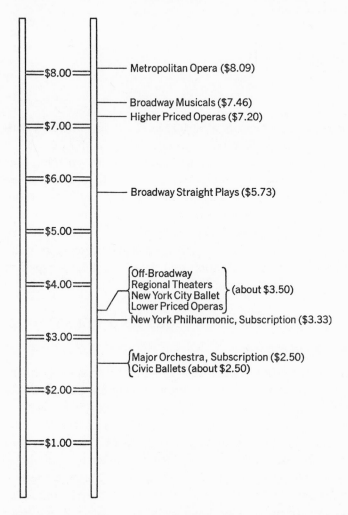

Average ticket prices were obtained by dividing capacity gross
by the total number of seats in the auditorium. This procedure
automatically yields an appropriately weighted average because it weights any ticket price category in proportion to the
number of seats available at that price. The basic data were
supplied by individual organizations in each case.

operatic performances, and fine theater, at prices averaging no more than $4.00 per ticket.

Of course, these prices are only averages; the actual range is considerably wider. The tickets for one Broadway musical have exceeded a $10.00 top; Metropolitan Opera prices range from $12.00 in the front of the orchestra to $2.50 for the high altitude seats in the family circle. Many seats at Broadway and off-Broadway performances are, in fact, disposed of below their nominal prices. The device employed by less successful productions, and even by hits when their audiences begin to fall off, is the "twofer," which entitles its holder to purchase two tickets for the price of one. Special student prices are sometimes arranged. Consequently, ticket prices as low as $1.50, or less, for some types of professional performances are not unknown.

Other Costs of Attendance

Though we often speak of the cost of a ticket as "the price" of an evening at a live performance, obviously, the typical member of the audience incurs other expenses as well. The level of associated costs — baby-sitting fees, transportation outlays, etc. — can affect attendance as surely as ticket prices do. Needless to say, these cost figures are harder to obtain than are the ticket price data. Before the completion of the Twentieth Century Fund audience survey no systematic information seems to have been available on associated costs for the performing arts as a whole.[1] Since this is so important a lacuna, we devoted a considerable part of our audience questionnaire to the subject.

Our results for the United States as a whole are summarized in Table XI–1. They indicate that over 90 per cent of attendees made some sort of non-ticket expenditure: 88 per cent of the audience spent something on transportation, 31 per cent ate at a restaurant and 15 per cent had to pay a baby sitter.

[1] Moore conducted a survey in which he asked about the anticipated cost of the evening, and he provides insights into the differences between New Yorkers and suburbanites, the effects of expense accounts, and so on (Chapter V). Aside from this survey there exist only scraps of information, such as the report by a television program that traced a hypothetical suburban couple through an evening of theater attendance, and after itemizing the costs, arrived at a total of $48.96 for the two persons together.

TABLE XI–1

Ticket Expense and Associated Costs of Attendance at Live
Performances, United States, 1963–64

Expense Category	Per Cent Incurring Each Expense	Average Spent Per Person		Per Cent of Total Expense
		By Persons Incurring Each Expense	By All Who Paid for Own Tickets	
	(1)	(2)	(3)	(4)
Public Transportation	26	$1.42	$0.37	5.4
Auto Transportation[a]	65	1.60	1.06	15.5
Total Transportation	(88)	(1.59)	(1.43)	(20.9)
Restaurant	31	4.42	1.43	20.9
Baby Sitter	15	1.97	0.31	4.5
Total Non-ticket Expense	92	3.31	$3.16[b]	46.3
Ticket Expense[c]	100	3.66	3.66	53.7
Total Expense			$6.82	100

SOURCE: Twentieth Century Fund audience survey. This table is based on
23,556 responses.

[a] Figured at $.10 per mile plus parking.

[b] Detail does not add exactly to total because of rounding.

[c] Excludes persons who reported ticket expenses in excess of $10 per seat. The
number who did so is small, and most of them apparently named the
amount they paid for an entire season's subscription.

The average expenditure of persons who incurred some type of
non-ticket cost was $3.31. Dining out was the most expensive item,
with an average restaurant cost of $4.42 for persons who incurred
this type of expenditure. Including in our calculations all respondents, whether or not they incurred any "associated" costs, we obtain an average non-ticket cost of attendance, totaled over all items,
of $3.16. Since our average ticket cost comes to $3.66, non-ticket
costs constitute 46 per cent of the total cost of attending a performance ($6.82). This means that if ticket prices were reduced by, say,
10 per cent, the cost of attendance would go down only about 5 per
cent.

It is interesting to compare costs of attendance in New York
(presented in detail in Appendix Table XI–A) with those for the

United States as a whole. The total cost of attending a performance in New York was higher; it averaged $8.68 per person as compared with the national average of $6.82. There was also some difference in the relative importance of the various expenses. Whereas only 26 per cent of respondents throughout the country utilized public transportation, 54 per cent of New Yorkers did so, and the proportion reporting use of private automobiles was naturally reversed. New York attendees were more apt to go to a restaurant and paid more for baby sitters if they hired them. But more striking are the similarities between New York and the country as a whole. For New York attendees transportation costs were 18 per cent, restaurant costs were 25 per cent, and total non-ticket costs 47 per cent of the total; for the country as a whole the respective figures were 21, 21 and 46 per cent.

If New York is compared with London, the surprising pattern of similarity described in earlier chapters also is found here. (See Figure XI–2 and Appendix Table XI–A.) Thus, 57 per cent of the audience incurred public transportation costs in London compared with 54 per cent in New York. Forty per cent went to a restaurant in London and 42 per cent in New York. Only the use of baby sitters is radically different: 12 per cent of the New York audience used them as compared with 5 per cent of London attendees, many of whom probably employed household help on a more regular basis.

Our data also show that people who attend free concerts spend much less on other items. On the average, their non-ticket outlays were $1.53 per person, or only one half as much as was spent by audiences at performances where an admission fee was charged. This suggests that perhaps free concerts are attended by lower income groups, a hypothesis we will explore later in the chapter.

In New York City there is not much variation in the breakdown of total attendance costs by art form (Appendix Table XI–B), with ticket prices ranging between 51 and 57 per cent of the total. For the country as a whole tickets run from 50 to 60 per cent of the total. Both in New York and throughout the country non-ticket expenditures are highest among theatergoers. This was particularly true of members of the Broadway audience, 53 per cent of whom went to a restaurant, at an average cost of $6.29 per person.

FIGURE XI–2

TICKET EXPENSE AND ASSOCIATED COSTS OF
ATTENDANCE AT LIVE PERFORMANCES,
NEW YORK CITY AND LONDON

(percentage distribution of total expenses by type)

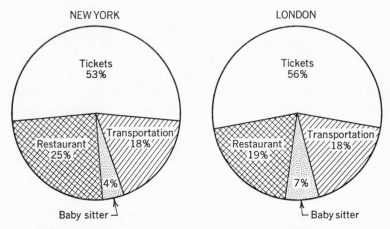

The basic data for this graph are contained in Appendix Table XI–A.

Thus, today, supplementary attendance outlays constitute nearly
half the cost of going to a performance, and since the items involved are services, we should expect their costs and, hence, their
prices to rise more rapidly than prices in general. Between 1953
and 1961, restaurant prices increased 2.4 per cent per year, while
the consumer price index was rising at a rate of 1.4 per cent.[2]
During 1947–1961 the price index of private transportation went
up at a yearly rate of 2.9 per cent and *public transportation prices
rose 6.3 per cent per year,* while the consumer price index advanced
at a rate of 2.1 per cent. As a result of such trends in the costs of
services, even if ticket prices were to remain constant, related costs
would continue to make attendance ever more expensive.

[2] U.S. Department of Labor, Bureau of Statistics, *Consumer Price Index,*
September 1962, Table I. All of our figures on trends in non-ticket costs come
from this source.

Trends in Ticket Prices

We have what appear to be accurate ticket prices and capacity gross figures for Covent Garden in 1760. Comparing these with current prices at the Royal Shakespeare Theatre, we see that the cost of admission went up between 0.6 and 0.8 per cent per year, while the price level rose at an average annual rate of 1 per cent.[3]

The slow increase in ticket prices over this period reflects in part the very high ticket prices of the eighteenth century English theater (which also extended to the colonies, as we saw in Chapter II). At that time a day laborer received 2 shillings or less for a day's work, and a journeyman earned about 3 shillings a day. Admission to the cheapest seat at Covent Garden and Drury Lane, for a time the only theaters licensed under an act of 1737, cost one shilling. The semi-legal "minor" theaters charged sixpence for their lowest-priced tickets — a quarter of a day's wages for a laborer. In the eighteenth century, admission costs amounted to a far higher proportion of a workman's income than they did in Elizabethan times or than they do today, yet working people seem to have loved the theater, and to have felt so strongly about it that serious and prolonged rioting arose at one point over theater prices.[4]

Other British figures permit us to make comparisons between current ticket prices and those prevailing in the late 1880's or early in the twentieth century. They all show ticket prices to have risen with a curious degree of consistency, at just about the same rate as the retail price index.

[3] These and other British ticket price data are summarized in Appendix Table XI–C. The differences just mentioned between movements in the price level and in ticket prices may seem minor, but it must be remembered that a 200 year period is involved. Over so long a period the cumulative effect of apparently small differences can be considerable — the 1 per cent per year rise in the price level amounts to a 7.6-fold increase between 1760 and 1964, while an annual growth rate of 0.8 per cent in ticket price compounds to only a 5.1-fold rise over that period, and a growth rate of 0.6 per cent is equivalent to a 3.3-fold increase.

[4] The preceding historical discussion is based on Pedicord, Chapter II. The riots arose out of attempts to abolish the custom of "half-price" — a reduction in ticket price after the third act of the principal item, for those who attended only the lighter and far more popular "afterpiece." This normally began after 7 P.M. when working people could attend after completing their 13 to 15 hour workday. At that point in the performance, "the seats, hitherto comparatively empty, were invariably filled to capacity." (Pedicord, p. 30.)

Turning now to the United States, we look first at trends on Broadway. Figure XI–3 shows the pattern of top prices (including tax) for straight shows and for musicals, and compares these with the consumer price index (CPI). The most noteworthy feature of this graph is the very close parallel between the behavior of the CPI and ticket prices between the mid-1930's and the mid-1950's. After about 1956, however, Broadway prices began to rise relative to the price index. Between that year and 1960 the top price for straight shows went up 23 per cent and that for musicals rose 30 per cent, while the CPI increased only 8 per cent. Since 1960 the rate of growth of ticket prices has slowed down to about that of the price index, and has perhaps even fallen a bit behind it.

Figure XI–4 shows average ticket price data for several major orchestras. The movement of ticket prices and the behavior of the CPI tend to be very similar from 1942 on, except for 1962–1964 when prices charged by the eleven orchestras increased sharply. Our three-orchestra average lagged during the mid-1950's but then gathered sufficient momentum to catch up with the price index by 1963.

Figure XI–5 indicates that ticket prices at the Metropolitan Opera have risen much faster than the CPI. These data, however, relate only to the postwar period, when ticket prices in general increased with unusual rapidity.

Ticket prices in Great Britain in recent years have behaved in a fashion similar to those in the United States. Orchestra prices have risen at roughly the same rate as retail prices, while the rise in the prices of all other performances has far surpassed the rise in the price index.

Table XI–2 (p. 270) provides a summary of the relationship between ticket price movements and movements in the CPI during the postwar period. It shows that there is some limited justification for the complaints that ticket costs have been rising, though the rise in ticket prices in comparison with purchasing power is a rather recent phenomenon.

Trends in Ticket Prices and in Cost Per Performance

Whether ticket prices have or have not gone up faster than the consumer price index is not of crucial importance for the finances

FIGURE XI-3

TOP BROADWAY TICKET PRICES AND THE CONSUMER PRICE INDEX, 1927–1965

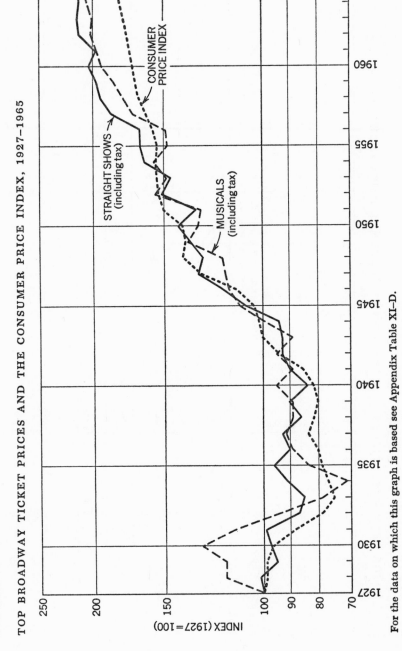

For the data on which this graph is based see Appendix Table XI-D.

FIGURE XI–4

MAJOR ORCHESTRA TICKET PRICES AND THE CONSUMER PRICE INDEX, 1928–1964

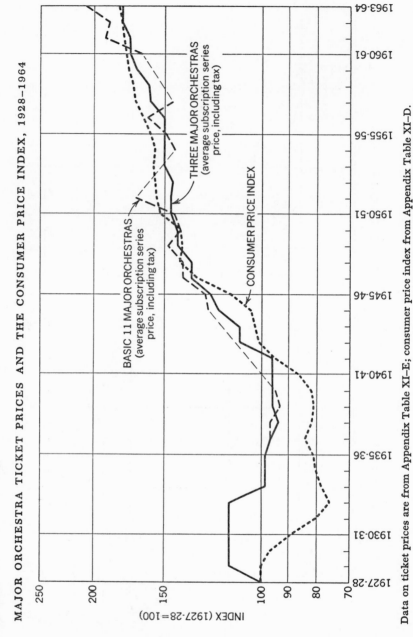

Data on ticket prices are from Appendix Table XI–E; consumer price index from Appendix Table XI–D.

FIGURE XI-5

METROPOLITAN OPERA SUBSCRIPTION TICKET PRICES
AND THE CONSUMER PRICE INDEX, 1951–1965

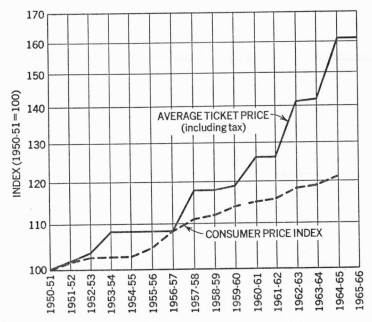

Data on ticket prices were supplied by the Metropolitan Opera.

of the performing groups. For them the critical issue is the rise
relative to cost per performance, for it is this relationship between
prices and costs which influences the course of the income gap.

The ticket price measure that is relevant here is the price net of
the admission tax. The wartime federal admissions tax was eliminated for orchestras and operas before the 1952–53 season, was
reduced for the theater from 20 to 10 per cent in April 1954, and
was eliminated altogether at the end of 1965. However, the organizations involved often did not pass on the savings, with the
result that during the postwar period ticket prices excluding tax
have risen at a faster rate than ticket prices including tax.

For the long interval for which we have data on the British theater the comparison is simple. In Chapter VIII we saw that between
1775 and 1964 cost per performance in the British theater rose

TABLE XI–2

Postwar Changes in Ticket Prices (including tax) and in the Consumer Price Index, United States and Great Britain

Organization and Time Period	Average Annual Percentage Increase (Compound Rate)[a]	
	Ticket Prices (including tax)	Consumer Price Index[b]
UNITED STATES		
Broadway:		
Top Price, 1947–1964:		
Straight Plays	3.5	2.0
Musicals	4.1	2.0
Average Price, 1950–1965:		
Straight Plays	2.9	1.8[c]
Musicals	3.8	1.8[c]
Major Orchestras:		
Composite Three-Orchestra Average, (N.Y., Cin., Pitt.), 1947–1964	1.7	2.0
Basic 11 Major Orchestras — Average Subscription Series Price, 1947–1963[d]	2.2	2.0
Metropolitan Opera — Average Price, 1951–1964[e]	3.0	1.8
GREAT BRITAIN		
Theater: Stratford-on-Avon — Top Price, 1947–1964	6.4	3.8
Orchestras:		
London Orchestra, Promenade — Top Price, 1947–1964	3.1	3.8
Regional Orchestra — Top Price, 1955–1964	3.4	2.9
Opera: Covent Garden — Average "Ordinary" Price, 1951–1964	5.1	3.4
London Ballet Company — Top Price, 1955–1964	6.5	2.9

SOURCE: Broadway top prices from Appendix Table XI–D. Broadway average prices for the years 1950–1961 were calculated by Moore from January averages in *Variety* by dividing weekly capacity gross by number of seats x 8 (performances). We made similar calculations for 1962–1965, also on

about 1.4 per cent per year. At the same time ticket prices went up about 0.8 per cent per year. Costs in 1964 were 13.6 times their 1775 value, while ticket prices had multiplied to only 5.4 times their 1760 value.

More recent American figures (Table XI–3) show that between 1950 and 1965 Broadway costs per performance grew 6 per cent per year, while ticket prices advanced only 3 per cent a year.

The situation is somewhat different in the case of the basic eleven orchestras, as is shown in Figure XI–6. From 1947 (by which time the 1937 relationship between costs and ticket prices had been restored) to 1951, the ticket price index lagged slightly behind costs, but it spurted and caught up in 1952. Over the period as a whole the two series have risen at almost precisely the same rate.

Ticket prices for the New York Philharmonic and the Cincinnati Orchestra have moved upward by steps. Both took their largest jumps between 1952 and 1953. These are the years in which the federal admissions tax was removed, and the amount that had previously been paid in tax reverted to the organization. Even so, the ticket price index has lagged behind costs in the postwar period. In the case of the Cincinnati Orchestra this disparity is especially

Notes to Table XI–2 continued

the basis of January data published in *Variety*. Because capacity gross figures from *Variety* are net of all taxes, we adjusted them to include the federal tax of 20 per cent for 1950–1954 and 10 per cent for 1955–1965, and the city tax of 5 per cent for 1955–1965. (The city tax was "repealed" in 1961, in the sense that the monies since then have been diverted to an industry-wide pension and welfare fund, but this of course makes no direct difference to the ticket purchaser.) Major orchestra prices from Appendix Table XI–E. Metropolitan Opera and British prices from individual organizations.

[a] Calculated on the basis of terminal years only, except as indicated in notes d and e.

[b] Retail price index used for Great Britain.

[c] We estimated the value of the consumer price index in 1965 at 182, on the basis of the ratio between its January–June values in 1965 and its January–June values in 1964.

[d] Because of the erratic nature of this series (see Appendix Table XI–E), we used an average of 1962, 1963 and 1964 values as our terminal year observation, treating it as the 1963 value.

[e] Estimated on the basis of a trend line fitted to annual observations.

TABLE XI–3

Postwar Changes in Ticket Prices (excluding tax) and in
Costs Per Performance

	Average Annual Percentage Increase (Compound Rate)[a]	
Organization and Time Period	Ticket Prices, Excluding Tax	Expenditures Per Performance
Broadway: Straight Plays — Average Price, 1950–1965	3.0	6.0
Major Orchestras, 1947–1964: Basic 11 — Average Subscription Series Price	3.3	3.2
New York Philharmonic — Front Orchestra Price	3.7	4.1
Cincinnati Symphony — Front Orchestra Price	2.5	3.6
Metropolitan Opera — Average Subscription Price, 1951–1964	3.2	4.4

SOURCE: Same as Table XI–2, except that ticket prices net of taxes were used.

[a] Calculated by fitting trend lines to annual observations, except in the case of expenditures per performance on Broadway, where lack of a continuous cost series required that growth rates be calculated between terminal years.

clear: ticket prices rose at a rate of 2.5 per cent while cost per concert went up 3.6 per cent per year. At the Metropolitan costs increased more than 1 per cent per year faster than ticket prices.

EFFECTS OF TICKET PRICE DECISIONS

Ticket Prices, Demand and Box Office Revenues

We inquire now into the logic behind ticket pricing decisions. A basic conflict complicates these decisions: while the typical performing organization wishes to attract as large and as variegated an audience as possible, it also wants to use box office income to minimize its financial difficulties. The price policy that serves the one goal may not always promote the other.

Even if the objective of pricing policy were purely deficit mini-

FIGURE XI–6

TICKET PRICES AND EXPENDITURES PER CONCERT,
BASIC ELEVEN MAJOR ORCHESTRAS, 1937–1964

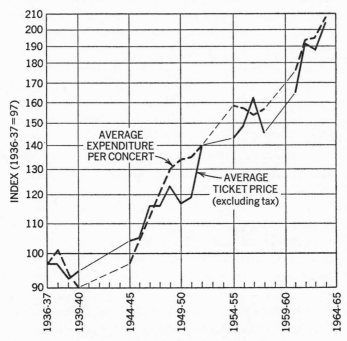

The data used here were obtained in the same way as the data
presented in Appendix Table XI–E; see the notes to that table.

mization, the implications for pricing decisions would not be auto-
matic, for here a second conflict arises which is not always recognized. An increase in box office price does, of course, raise receipts
per customer, but it is also likely to produce a decrease in the number of customers. Therefore, it is not always clear in advance
whether a ticket price rise will increase or reduce total receipts. For
example, suppose a theater charges $4.40 for all seats, and that it
draws an average audience of 2,000 persons. If the ticket price
were raised to $5 and audience size consequently dropped below
1,760 (the break-even point), receipts would actually decline. As a
general rule, if the percentage decrease in audience is smaller than
the percentage rise in ticket price, revenues will go up when prices

are increased, but if the percentage decrease in audience is greater than the price rise, revenues will decline.[5] If the percentage change in audience size is more than that in ticket price, we say that demand is *elastic* (highly responsive to price changes), while if audience size varies by a smaller percentage than prices, the demand pattern is called *inelastic*. Thus, price increases are certain to pay off financially only if demand is inelastic.

Unfortunately, the only way to arrive at reliable estimates of demand responsiveness is by elaborately controlled experimentation. The obvious statistical methods do not work because other influences are simultaneously being felt whenever price changes occur in practice, and it is extremely difficult to determine what part of the demand change represents a response to the price variation alone. Indeed, naive statistical tinkering often leads to spurious relationships. For example, during the period when the off-Broadway audience was growing, ticket prices were also going up; a standard statistical correlation might have suggested to the unwary that rising ticket prices bring in larger audiences.

In this section, therefore, we shall not attempt to offer definitive estimates of demand responsiveness.[6] Instead we will provide bits of evidence which suggest that demand for performance does respond to price changes, but that it is probably inelastic. We will then try to account for the observed behavior of ticket prices reported in previous sections.

A comparison of attendance in relation to capacity with ticket prices (before taxes) for the basic eleven major orchestras offers some evidence of a negative relationship between the two. Ticket prices rose sharply in 1949 and the percentage of capacity fell the next year; prices fell in 1950 and the percentage of capacity rose. Prices jumped in 1957 and the percentage of capacity fell, and the reverse was true in 1958. Over the 1961–1964 period prices rose very sharply and the percentage of capacity fell (though this can be

[5] The rule as stated is accurate if changes are calculated as a percentage of the *average* of initial and final values. In our illustration the ticket price rise was $5 − $4.40 = $0.60. The average price was $4.70, and as 60 is about 13 per cent of 470, ticket price went up by nearly 13 per cent. The percentage change in audience should also be calculated from its average value.

[6] For statistical estimates of elasticity of demand see Moore, Chapter 6, and Birkenhead.

ascribed in part to increases in length of season). The persistent correspondence between ticket prices and demand, even in these crude data, with a fall in demand following a rise in prices, and vice versa, must represent either an incredible series of coincidences or a very real relationship. There is only one exceptional case over the entire period: in 1952, when prices rose substantially, the percentage of capacity just held its own (Appendix Table XI–F).

A better opportunity to study the relationship systematically is provided by records for the New York Philharmonic and the Metropolitan Opera, which allow us to pinpoint the dates of the price increases and study their effects. In the case of the New York Philharmonic a comparison of attendance per concert in the year price increases were instituted with attendance in the previous year provides evidence of a weak relationship.[7] Attendance fell in four of the seven cases when prices were increased. Since attendance fell only nine times in the 27 years for which we have figures, the evidence suggests that price increases have tended to lead to at least short-term declines in attendance. The Metropolitan Opera figures (see Appendix Table XI–F) show a similar relationship. During the period for which we have attendance data price increases occurred in four different years: 1958, 1961, 1963 and 1965. In three of these four cases attendance as a percentage of capacity fell temporarily, and it did not fall in any other year.

It seems, therefore, that price rises do tend to inhibit the size of audiences. But there is also a second important conclusion to be drawn: this inhibiting effect is small (and perhaps transitory). In all but one of the cases the percentage decline in attendance was smaller than the percentage rise in prices.[8]

[7] Attendance was estimated by dividing receipts per concert by an index of ticket prices.

[8] Of course, this result may be ascribable in part to upward trends in audience demand, something we could not measure and allow for because both the Metropolitan and the Philharmonic play to near-capacity audiences.

Our case histories also suggest two other illuminating generalizations: first, that price increases tend to occur when attendance has been rising, and second, that they are usually instituted in years when total expenditures have gone up. This is important because it indicates that price policy in the performing arts can be influenced strongly by financial pressures as well as by considerations of size and composition of audience. Managers often know in advance when expenditures are going to rise, and this forces them to think about raising prices and, of course, offers some justification for their doing so.

A different sort of evidence on audience reaction to ticket prices was provided by our audience surveys. In order to obtain some information on unsatisfied demand we asked respondents whether they had tried to buy either cheaper or more expensive tickets than those they actually purchased. The findings are summarized by art form in Appendix Table XI–G. In general we found that surprisingly few persons tried to purchase less expensive seats. The largest figure for any type of performance was 17 per cent, and this occurred off-Broadway where theaters are so small that the more expensive seats offer virtually no advantage. Of all respondents, only 11 per cent had sought cheaper tickets and 5 per cent had tried to purchase more expensive seats. At the ballet, where prices are generally low, the number of persons seeking higher priced seats actually exceeded the number who wanted less expensive ones. Thus there is no indication here of great audience dissatisfaction with current ticket prices.

There have, of course, been complaints that ticket prices are too high, but there is little evidence of substantial price resistance. Indeed, interviews with several persons with long experience in the theater elicited the opinion that reduced ticket prices rarely, if ever, increase audience size. Various experiments with low ticket prices over the years seem to have failed to increase audiences substantially. Dore Schary recounts that his production "Sunrise at Campobello" could not attract customers for the last three rows of the second balcony, where tickets were priced at $1.85. According to Schary, he took the advice of "a very old and wise manager" who suggested that the price be raised to $2.20, whereupon the balcony tickets were sold out.[9] Proponents of this view suggest that one should not be misled by such phenomena as the demand for "twofers" or the 70,000 people in attendance at the New York Philharmonic's free concerts in Central Park. Here, they say, the lure is not the low prices, but the "something for nothing" psychology, a strategy sometimes used in a different form when tickets are advertised at high prices and sold at a discount through special deals.

[9] House Hearings, II, p. 162.
One reader took exception to the preceding discussion, writing that the effect of low prices can be tested adequately only in conjunction with a new approach to audience building and theater operation: "The fact is that the present audience is extremely limited, is an expense account audience and, of course, does not want the bad balcony seats. . . ."

If it is true that demand is relatively unaffected by price change, why have prices not risen more frequently and more rapidly? In Chapter VII we pointed out that in the arts, as in education, high prices are thought to conflict with the requirements of social responsibility; hence, managements attempt to avoid them as long as possible. There is also some fear (disclosed by our interviews) that increased prices would lead to a decline in contributions, though at least one person in a managerial position told us that contributions were not affected when his organization raised its ticket prices. In any event, none of these explanations seems adequate by itself. Despite similar predilections and a similar dependence on contributions, tuition charges for higher education have increased much more rapidly than ticket prices. Even in subsidized public institutions tuition charges rose more than 5 per cent per year during the period 1948–1964, and in private institutions the rate of increase was more than 7.2 per cent per year.[10] Meanwhile, the annual increase in ticket prices was a little over 3 per cent on Broadway and under 2 per cent per year for orchestras, for which we have our most dependable data.

The answer must lie in economic conditions, and here the difference in the circumstances of artistic and educational institutions is quite marked. There are special economic circumstances which restrain ticket prices. Unlike outlays on education, expenditure on tickets is not generally considered an investment from which a pecuniary return can be expected. Therefore, managers of performing arts organizations are doubtless more fearful of buyer resistance to price increases, a feeling which must be reinforced by the existence of unused capacity.[11]

The arts are also subject to more direct competition than is education. To some extent audience demand depends not only on the

[10] Tuition figures are from American Council on Education, Office of Statistical Information and Research, *Fact Book on Higher Education*, Washington, 1963, pp. 217–22.

[11] One particular problem faced by performing groups and not by suppliers of most other goods and services is the fact that everyone can see for himself when sales are going badly. If a breakfast cereal is not selling well its customers need not know how unpopular a choice they are making, but an empty auditorium speaks eloquently of the state of demand for the performance. To the extent that sales breed further sales this is a serious handicap for the performing group, and one which must be considered very seriously when a price rise is contemplated.

price of performance but also on the relative cost of substitute goods, in this case the price of the services provided by the mass media. Although the price of admission to the movies has been going up over the years, this is not true of the cost of enjoying other mass media. The cost of television receivers *fell* about 20 per cent between 1951 and 1961.[12] While there is no official index of phonograph record prices, such comparisons are not too difficult to obtain. For example, in 1927 Beethoven's Ninth Symphony required both sides of eight 12 inch records and cost $2 per record.[13] Today the same composition requires only both sides of two long-playing records selling at $4.00 each, so that even at list price,[14] and neglecting the fact that today one obtains a better product, the price of this recording has been cut in half. As productivity gains in manufacturing bring down costs, the competitive problems of the performing arts are increased.

These observations help to explain why performing groups have not increased admission prices more rapidly. In effect all these arguments show that even if the demand for tickets is not reduced much by price increases (it is inelastic), this demand is nevertheless likely to be affected more adversely than is the demand for higher education by a similar percentage rise in tuition.

Some Notes on Price Schedules

Unfortunately, there is little systematic evidence on what has happened to relative ticket price — prices of front row seats versus balcony seats, prices on week nights versus weekend prices. There has been some tendency toward a narrowing of the range of available prices, with the cost of the lower-priced seats rising most rapidly. Of 12 American and British organizations and groups of organizations for which we have data, the ticket prices of the

[12] Bureau of Labor Statistics, *Consumer Price Index,* September 1962, Table 1.

[13] "LP Records Set Stage for Classical Music's New Era," *Music Business,* Vol. IX, No. 19, December 12, 1954, p. 46.

[14] The real fall in price is undoubtedly understated by these figures because most long-playing records are currently available at about 20 per cent below list price, while such discounts do not seem to have been widely available in the 1920's.

cheapest seats increased most rapidly in 7; in 3, prices of the most expensive seats went up fastest, and in 2 the relationship fluctuated. The range of choice has also been decreased in another way: seats which once were inexpensive have been incorporated into more expensive categories. Like the smaller candy bar, this is an easy means of disguising price increases. One producer stressed the fact that he had been able to keep his ticket prices from rising for a considerable number of years, yet pointed out that during this time he had been "upgrading" low-priced seats in his theater through price reclassification.

Nevertheless, there is evidence that the relative demand for the more expensive seats is growing, while the demand for cheaper seats declines. One investigator performed a most illuminating calculation utilizing Broadway data. Over the seasons 1950–51 to 1959–60 he compared the average price of all available tickets ("average capacity price") with the average price of the tickets actually bought ("average actual price"). He found that in every year the latter was the larger figure, meaning that the proportion of high-priced tickets which theaters managed to sell was greater than the corresponding proportion of low-priced tickets. Even more significant is his finding that the average actual price increased far more rapidly than the average capacity price. This implies that the relative demand for high-priced seats was growing more rapidly than the number of high-priced seats available.[15]

While many organizations were narrowing the range between low-priced and high-priced tickets, they also indicated a reluctance to vary prices from performance to performance, so that many theaters have just two or three sets of seat prices — one for week nights, one for weekend evenings and one for matinées. The difficulties of advertising a more complex price schedule may account in part for this decision, but one also has the impression that at least some of the persons involved seem to consider the morality of such price variation to be somewhat suspect: they are uncomfortable at supplying what seems to them to be the same product at widely varying prices. Economists maintain that there is no reasonable ground for this discomfort. A product supplied at a dif-

[15] Wunderlich, p. 32.

ferent time and in a different place is a different item. A performance on Saturday night when the typical audience member can
conveniently indulge in a late night is different from a performance on Tuesday evening. The former is in shorter relative supply
and is more valuable to most potential customers. It is no more
immoral to charge high evening prices as compared to those at
matinées than it is to charge more for Christmas trees in December
than in June.

But, such ethical issues aside, a narrowing of price range may
well be detrimental to everyone. It affects the performing organization by reducing its income, perhaps weakening its public image
and narrowing the audience that can afford to attend. The Broadway theater is not really making it easier for less affluent persons
to attend when it raises the price of its cheapest seats and protects
the sanctity of the "$10 top." At best it is merely making the most
expensive tickets available at a price below the market clearing
level to those persons who can well afford to pay more. At worst,
when top seat prices are kept down artificially, the arts lose potential income, and the money is appropriated by a black market in
which the public is forced to pay a full market price for these tickets
all the same.

A larger price differential for popular productions among different nights of the week might also increase the revenue of the
performing organizations. The fact that a so much larger proportion of capacity is normally filled on weekend evenings suggests
that pricing differentials by night of the week and between mati-
née and evening can profitably be widened to the general benefit.[16]

---

[16] Unfortunately, a stronger argument requires recourse to a bit of mathe-
matics. Assume that when a theater is filled, elasticity of demand is always
less than unity. Then at each performance the revenue maximizing price, P_t,
should exceed $P_{t\ cap}$, the price at which the theater would be filled, by an
amount which varies inversely with elasticity of demand on a particular night.
Thus, $P_t - P_{t\ cap}$ should probably be smallest toward the beginning of the week
when people are more likely to come in order to save money than because of
pure preference. However, the resulting excess capacity may not vary much
over the week. Indeed, if the percentage difference between P_t and $P_{t\ cap}$, i.e.,
$(P_t - P_{t\ cap})/P_{t\ cap} = \%\Delta P_t$ is assumed to be inversely proportional to elasticity of demand on night t, excess capacity will be constant throughout the
week. To see this, let r be any other performance, and a_r be attendance on
night r, then, by definition,

By reducing unused capacity at less popular performance times, revenues can be increased and a larger audience can be served.[17]

Ticket Prices and Audience Composition

The effect of increased cost of admissions on the nature of the audience — on the presence of lower income groups, younger persons or special groups such as students — is clearly a very important issue. It was the cause of controversy between the New York City Center and Lincoln Center in 1964–65. The former has always followed a low ticket price policy, and argued that in its new location at Lincoln Center this policy had to be guaranteed for the indefinite future in order to attract groups that would otherwise be excluded from the audience.[18]

At the heart of such discussions lies a question of fact: do low ticket prices really have much effect on the make-up of the audience? Our audience surveys provide the first systematic evidence on the subject. In analyzing the survey results we classified respondents according to ticket price paid and compared the resulting audience profiles (summarized in Appendix Table XI–H).

Note 16 continued

or

$$\frac{\% \Delta P_t}{\% \Delta P_r} = \frac{E_r}{E_t} = \frac{\% \Delta a_r / \% \Delta P_r}{\% \Delta a_t / \% \Delta P_t}$$

$$1 = \frac{\% \Delta a_r}{\% \Delta a_t}$$

so that on both nights attendance would be the same percentage of capacity. This, then, is probably not too bad a rule of thumb: attendance on all nights should be about the same proportion of capacity.

[17] There is one point at which a revenue-maximizing ticket price policy clashes with what may be considered the requirements of the public welfare. If an organization is trying to increase its ticket revenues, the probability of turning away a customer for an expensive seat should be kept as close to zero as possible. Good strategy then calls for the organization to keep a far higher proportion of its excess capacity in its expensive seats; that is, a row which is on the borderline between two seat prices should always be assigned to the more expensive category if there is comparatively little excess capacity in high-priced seats.

[18] See, for example, an article by Alan Hughes in the *New York Times*, January 24, 1965, Section 2, p. 11.

By now the reader may have become weary of the "astonishing regularities" which the authors find so gratifying, but these results surely constitute another and rather fine set. While it is true that the proportion of blue collar workers is low in any seat category, and that there is no clear general relationship between ticket prices and education or frequency of attendance, yet:

1. Lower prices do attract a younger clientele. In almost every case, for every art form, a rise in ticket price produces a rise in median age of the audience group.

2. Students usually buy lower-priced tickets. In almost every case, for every art form, the proportion of students drops sharply as ticket prices rise.

3. Except in Great Britain, teachers usually purchase inexpensive tickets with the same degree of regularity shown by the students.

4. In the United States the proportion of persons in professional occupations falls and the proportion of managerial personnel rises with almost perfect regularity as ticket prices increase.

5. There is a perfect relationship between median family income and ticket prices: *the lower the family income, the less expensive the seat purchased.* The perfect regularity of this important relationship is shown in Figure XI–7.

We also have data indicating how audience composition is affected when no admission is charged (Appendix Table XI–I). In general, free performances draw the same type of audience as is attracted by lower-priced tickets — younger, more students and lower incomes. But there are several noteworthy differences. The proportion of teachers and professionals in the audience at free "open air" performances is somewhat smaller than at other performances. More important, the general level of education is clearly lower (though still very high, with four years of college as the median educational attainment of males), and the proportion of blue collar workers is increased significantly, though it still remains well under 10 per cent of the audience. While still well above the figure for the population as a whole, median family income at free performances is much lower than that at paid performances: $9,400 at the former, $12,300 at the latter.

FIGURE XI-7

RELATION BETWEEN TICKET PRICE PAID AND
FAMILY INCOME, U. S. AUDIENCE, 1963-64

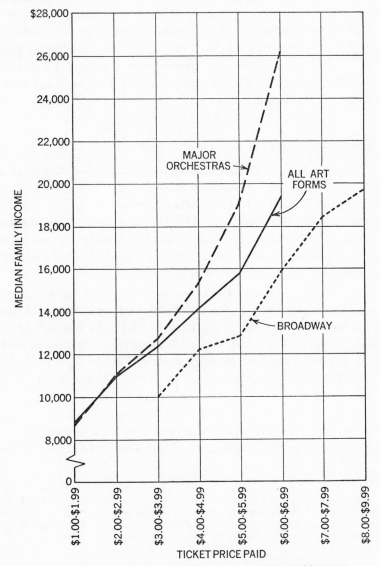

TICKET PRICE PAID

The basic data for this graph are presented in Appendix Table XI-H.

Our results on audience composition lead to two very clear-cut conclusions: first, the advocates of low ticket prices are right when they suggest that lower ticket prices bring in a less well-to-do, younger audience composed more heavily of students and members of the professions. The evidence in this regard is indisputable. Second, while low prices do diversify the audience to some extent, they do not metamorphose the performance into "art for the people." Even at free performances the audience is relatively well educated, of relatively comfortable means, and is composed primarily of members of the professions.

Speculation and the Sub Rosa Ticket Market

Whenever a production on Broadway attains the status of a "hit" (and sometimes when it achieves only a modest success), tickets to it become scarce. However, the box office price of the ticket normally rises very little if at all. As a result, would-be patrons frequently have to purchase tickets many months in advance, and anyone who wants to attend without much delay must be prepared to pay a premium to the speculators.[19]

Ticket scalping is not new. Documented cases of "scalping" occurred in London early in the eighteenth century.[20] In the United States we know of cases going back to 1850, the date of Jenny Lind's appearance at Castle Garden.[21] Since then newspapers have published denunciations, hearings have repeatedly been held and various sorts of legislation passed in order to curb speculation and to limit ticket prices. Most recently, in 1963, a set of hearings on the subject was conducted in New York City.[22] Since a banker's books must be beyond reproach, it was only natural that reliable banking firms in New York City kept detailed records of their ex-

---

[19] It should be made clear that "speculator" is not intended here as a term of opprobrium. In many fields the speculator serves an extremely useful function. His main job is to undertake (for a fee) risks which others wish to escape. When a speculator buys tickets to a production before it opens, he is, in effect, reducing the risk to which the producer is subject. His profit, if the show proves to be a hit, is his fee for bearing the risk.

[20] Stone, p. ciii.

[21] Bernheim, p. 186.

[22] Lefkowitz Hearings.

cess payments for theater tickets required to entertain important clients. These accounts provided the bulk of the systematic evidence offered at the hearings, and the listing of these overpayments for Broadway theater tickets occupies nearly twenty pages. It is also reported in the record of the hearings that the Columbia Broadcasting System, which was the sole financial backer of the Broadway production of "My Fair Lady," frequently had to spend $300 to $400 a week at the scalpers' to supplement its allotment of tickets to this production.[23] Moore has estimated that *sub rosa* payments on tickets, generally called "ice,"[24] amount to some $2 million annually.[25]

Despite all the hearings, regulations and accusations, as Bernheim concludes,[26] "War on ticket speculation — that time-worn battle cry — has never been successful, whether the war was waged by those within the theater business, or by forces from without."

How can one explain this melancholy history? As a matter of fact, to the economist it comes as no surprise. The phenomena we have just summarized constitute a documentation of one of his most fundamental principles. When an item is available in only relatively small quantities some means must be found to allocate the available supply among those who desire it. There are two main ways in which the allocation process can operate: through the price mechanism or by means of a rationing process. The price system favors the allocation of items in short supply to two classes of people: those who want it badly, and who, therefore, are willing to pay a high market price; and the wealthy, for whom price is not much of an obstacle. A system of rationing is usually instituted to avoid favoring the wealthy. But to the best of our knowledge

[23] Lefkowitz Hearings, I, p. 20 ff.

[24] Strictly speaking, "ice" designates illegal payments to theater personnel in the course of acquiring tickets. Thus, speculative profits and "ice" are not synonymous. No one seems to be sure of the origin of the term. The most frequent explanation is that some dishonest politician had hit upon the device of listing as "Incidental Campaign Expenses" monies whose disbursement he would rather not explain. (Moore, Chapter 5.)

[25] The accountant who reported on the bank records of ticket overpayments at the Lefkowitz Hearings (I, p. 20 ff.) placed the figure at $10 million, but the basis for his guess was not explained.

[26] pp. 187–88.

there has been no case in history when such a program of rationing was not accompanied by a black market which provided commodities to those who were willing and able to pay for them.

Those who seek to impose prices for the arts which they feel approximate the requisites of justice[27] wish to prevent the price system from working, but they provide no alternative system of ticket rationing. The results are inevitable. When a production is a success there are limits to the extent to which its seating capacity can be extended. With supply inflexible and the demand for tickets in excess of the supply, someone will inevitably offer a premium for tickets, and it is equally certain that someone will be willing to accept it.

Nor is this necessarily undesirable — indeed, as we have maintained, it is part of the normal allocation process. Suppose only one seat is left for a particular performance and two persons wish to buy it — a visitor to New York who will have no other opportunity to see the show and a native New Yorker who can attend almost any performance. If the two contenders have roughly equal incomes, the visitor will offer to pay more because the seat at this particular performance is of greater value to him; and we see nothing "immoral" in this act. Things go wrong only when someone tries to maintain a "just price" artificially, either through legislation or through self-denial on the part of the supplier in response to a questionable notion of public virtue. If those who supply the product are unwilling or unable to collect what would normally be its market price, invariably someone else will volunteer to take their place. The speculator who had nothing to do with the production will then reap the rewards which would otherwise have gone to those who contributed their labor and resources to the performance.

In fact, legal regulation of prices has two predictable consequences:

---

[27] Incidentally, some of those who believe in the imposition of "moral" ticket prices seem to feel that brokers' fees are rather questionable exactions. But since brokers do presumably provide a service — convenient ticket distribution — there seems to be no good reason for them to provide it free, nor does there seem to be any good reason why the price for their service should be set at a maximum of $1.50 per ticket as the New York law currently requires, instead of being determined by market forces.

(1) the stricter the regulation, the more unsavory the characters of those who will supply the demands of the market, since only the unscrupulous will be prepared to flaunt strong laws and take the risks involved;

(2) the stricter the regulation, the higher the premium which the public will pay, because the high risk will keep down black market supplies and cause the suppliers to demand higher payment for the additional danger in which they place themselves.

The parallel with the history of Prohibition and other attempts to regulate public virtue is all too obvious. As always, the legitimate supplier and the consumer are the ones who suffer — the former because receipts are diverted to those who contributed nothing to the production process, and the latter because he must pay prices even higher than those which an unregulated market would have charged. It is the investor, the author, the performers, and (usually) the producer and the theater owner who sustain the real losses.

Until 1966, federal regulations[28] made it virtually impossible for a theater to raise or lower its prices quickly. If one ticket was sold in advance at $7.50, all other tickets for that row at that performance had to be sold at $7.50 at the box office. Consequently, a theater that wished to reduce its prices would have had to wait for a very long time — beyond the period for which it had already sold any tickets in advance — or it would have had to find the holders of such advance sale tickets and make refunds to them.

Many peculiar and restrictive laws still plague the sale and pricing of theater tickets. For example, a regulation issued by the New York City Department of Licenses prohibits theaters from providing any financial incentives to brokers for the sale of their tickets. But happily the federal regulations that most effectively pre-

---

[28] See 1954 Internal Revenue Code, Section 4231, Regulation 101.10 under Section 4231 (4) and (5). These laws seem to have had their origin in 1917 when Congress was looking for new sources of revenue. Senator Charles Thomas of Colorado, who was a member of the Finance Committee, was shocked at the premium he was required to pay for his theater tickets while on a visit to New York. At his instigation a number of "reform and punitive measures" were passed along with the excise tax. (*New York Times,* December 2, 1964, Section 2, p. 5.)

vented ticket price reductions have recently been dropped, and there are reports that the Broadway theaters are planning a more flexible system of prices.[29] This move can only be welcomed as the end of another "noble experiment" — an attempt (as the *New York Times* once put it) to repeal the law of supply and demand.[30]

It is important to recognize that pricing on a free market basis is a two-way street. Just as it will raise prices for a hit, it will bring down the admission charges for a less successful production.[31] In doing so it can enlarge the audiences for precisely those productions in which there *is* room for more people, and whose cast would frequently welcome an increased audience on almost any terms. This is part and parcel of the allocation process, which works to increase demand where demand is short, just as it works the other way where demand exceeds the available supply.

While the strong stand on policy we have taken in this section represents a departure from the purely analytic preoccupation of most of this book, it has also served an analytic purpose. It has offered an explanation of two of the problems which plague the theater — the paradox of the simultaneous scarcity of both seats and customers, and the catastrophic failure of all the attempts made to impose virtuous pricing on a market in which demand and supply are not always in balance. It has been shown that both of these are man-made problems which have been created by artificial regulation and misguided notions of equity. They can be dealt with effectively only by the elimination of any further attempts to impose pricing "justice," and not by still more complex legislation, stronger penalties or exhortation against the (usually

[29] Milton Esterow, "Theaters' Prices Will be Flexible," *New York Times*, June 24, 1965, p. 1.

[30] For views similar to many of those expressed in this section, see Wharton's report.

A sort of half-way proposal by Attorney General Louis Lefkowitz would set aside a small number of seats to a hit production at $25 each and put them on sale only at the last minute (*New York Times*, June 21, 1964, Section 2, pp. 1–2). Even this scheme seems to us unnecessarily restrictive and artificial.

[31] In the 1920's and early 1930's a number of cut rate ticket agencies flourished, and ticket price cutting was an established practice. (See Bernheim, pp. 195–97.) Apparently, the last of the cut rate agencies discontinued this part of its operations in 1938. According to its manager the decrease in Broadway activity made it uneconomic for the agency to deal in anything but tickets that could command the broker's premium.

unnamed) evil individuals who are often blamed for any economic mischance.

This chapter has examined several ramifications of ticket pricing. Taking our subjects in reverse order, it examined the effects of regulation of ticket prices, pointed out its indissoluble connection with scalping, and argued that a free market in tickets may well reduce as many ticket prices as it raises. We also investigated the effects of prices on audience composition and showed that the less expensive tickets at a given performance attract a slightly younger, considerably less affluent audience, composed of a larger proportion of students and persons in professional occupations. We discussed the principles of ticket pricing and the effect of prices on level of demand, and concluded tentatively that demand for tickets is relatively unresponsive to price changes. Nevertheless, competitive pressure, as exemplified by the reduced cost of phonograph records and television receivers, as well as the principles of pricing "justice" held to by performing organizations, have limited price rises. Thus, theater ticket prices have for long periods risen more slowly than the price level. While in the postwar period they have frequently gone up more rapidly, they have still not managed to keep pace with increases in cost per performance.

The very significant implication of this last finding for the arts' financial gap is the subject of the following chapter, which is the climax of this part of our study.

CHAPTER **XII**

Trends in the Income Gap

T HIS CHAPTER, though the briefest in the book, is one of the most important. It reports the most significant conclusions which we have derived from our financial data, and in the process seeks to develop a unified pattern from the many pieces of information which have been presented. It undertakes to answer the basic factual question: Have the income gaps of the performing organizations grown larger, and, if so, at what rate?

Trends in Earned Income, Expenditures and the Financial Gap

The data used in this chapter pertain to five organizations or groups of organizations: the New York Philharmonic (from 1895), the Cincinnati Orchestra (since 1920), the Metropolitan Opera (since 1951) and the basic set of eleven major orchestras (since 1937). Unfortunately, we have no theatrical data. The regional theaters are almost all too new to provide significant trend information, while annual "gap" figures have no obvious meaning for Broadway and off-Broadway.[1]

The data are described in six graphs and an appendix table, which we can discuss simultaneously. Figure XII–1 shows the available data on earned income and total expenditures for the New York Philharmonic since 1895. The Philharmonic data for the nineteenth century and the first decade of the twentieth are, unfortunately, largely useless for our present purposes. During this

---

[1] It would have been highly desirable to have figures from which one could judge profit trends on Broadway. The League of New York Theatres is making efforts to provide better data, and has begun to collect some figures for recent years.

period, when the orchestra operated as a cooperative and all earnings in excess of expenditures were shared out among the musicians, orchestral earnings *had* to be identical with *net* operating income (except for occasional unimportant additions to or withdrawals from reserves kept in a savings account). This correspondence is seen very clearly in the pre-1910 portion of the graph. What the experience of the New York Philharmonic during this early period does show is that there was a time when an important orchestra was able to operate in the main on a profit-making basis.[2]

Even where the cooperative system was not employed (Figure XII–1 after 1910 and Figures XII–2, XII–3, XII–4 and XII–5), there is a clear parallelism between movements in earned income and expenditure.[3] Again, this undoubtedly represents a combination of interactions. When public demand for tickets caused an increase in the funds available to organizations, performer salary levels were increased; and when pressure from the performers forced a rise in remuneration levels, ticket prices were usually increased or extra performances were put on to raise the necessary funds.

The bottom sections of Figures XII–1 to XII–5 show how earned income has varied over time as a percentage of expenditure. The last three of these graphs seem to show a declining ratio of income to expenditure. Yet there is a great deal of fluctuation, and the trend is not always clear-cut, particularly for the Metropolitan Opera and our basic set of major orchestras in the early postwar period. This need not mean that there has been no clear trend in the income gap. On the contrary, in every organization for which we have data, *the income gap has been growing, and it has been doing*

[2] We say "in the main" because there is evidence that, even during this early period, some musicians in the Philharmonic and their friends were contributing services. Moreover, at least a small part of the fees and dues collected from the "subscribers" and "associate members" should, no doubt, be regarded as a contribution to the Society, and not just as the purchase of the right to attend concerts and public rehearsals.

[3] The use of a semi-logarithmic scale produces a seriously misleading impression in Figure XII–1. It looks as though the Philharmonic's income gap has been growing constantly smaller and has all but vanished in recent years. However, this illusion is only a result of the fact that semi-logarithmic scales compress the higher values on a graph. See Chapter VII, pp. 176–179.

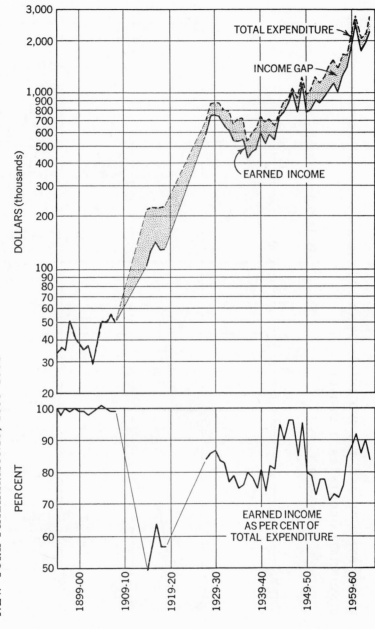

Basic data for this graph were supplied by the New York Philharmonic Orchestra.

FIGURE XII-2

TOTAL EXPENDITURE, EARNED INCOME, AND INCOME AS PER CENT OF EXPENDITURE, CINCINNATI ORCHESTRA, 1920–1964

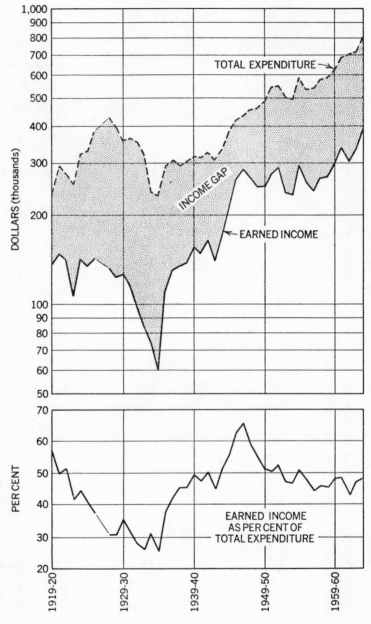

Basic data for this graph were supplied by the Cincinnati Symphony Orchestra.

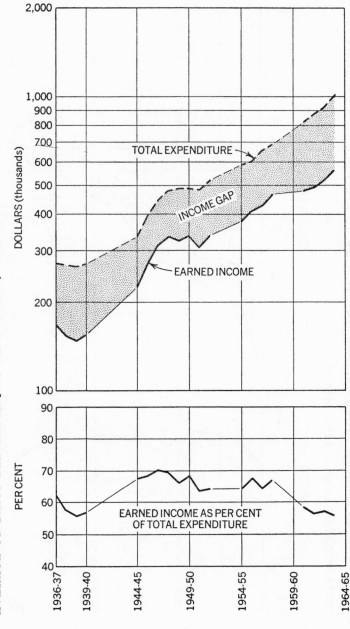

FIGURE XII-3

TOTAL EXPENDITURE, EARNED INCOME, AND INCOME AS PER CENT OF EXPENDITURE, AVERAGE OF BASIC ELEVEN MAJOR ORCHESTRAS, 1937–1964

DOLLARS (thousands)

TOTAL EXPENDITURE

INCOME GAP

EARNED INCOME

PER CENT

EARNED INCOME AS PER CENT OF TOTAL EXPENDITURE

Data for this graph were obtained from compiled reports of major orchestras.

FIGURE XII–4

TOTAL EXPENDITURE, EARNED INCOME, AND INCOME AS PER CENT OF EXPENDITURE, METROPOLITAN OPERA, 1951–1964

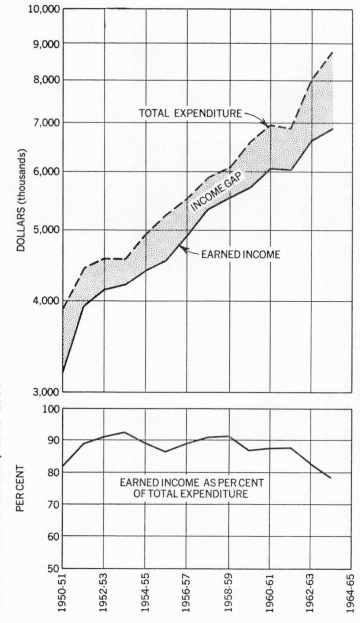

This graph is based on data supplied by the Metropolitan Opera.

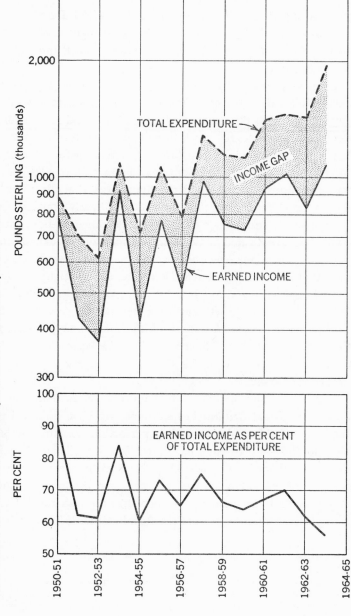

FIGURE XII-5

TOTAL EXPENDITURE, EARNED INCOME, AND INCOME AS
PER CENT OF EXPENDITURE, COVENT GARDEN, 1951-1964

This graph is based on data supplied by Covent Garden.

so quite steadily. This is shown in Figure XII–6. Despite some ups and downs in the graph (in part the consequences of intermittent tours), the tendency for the income gap to grow is quite obvious in this last graph.

Even when earned income does not decline as a proportion of expenditure, if both rise at the same compound rate, so does the gap. If income is 60 per cent of expenditure, and both income and expenditure double, the gap will still be 40 per cent of expenditure, but in dollar terms it will be twice as large as before. For example, in 1951 the Metropolitan Opera's earned income was 82 per cent of its expenditure, and in 1963 the figure was virtually the same — 83 per cent. Yet during that time its gap nearly doubled, growing at an average annual rate of 5.8 per cent. Since, in fact, earned income has constituted a declining proportion of expenditure for many organizations over the postwar period, we would expect that over that interval gaps have risen quite substantially. To test this assertion we fitted trend lines to our postwar gap statistics and found the annual growth rates for the income gaps to be 5.2 *per cent per year for the New York Philharmonic, 4.7 per cent for the Cincinnati Orchestra, 6.9 per cent for the basic eleven major orchestras, 8.2 per cent for the Metropolitan Opera and 9.2 per cent for Covent Garden.*[4]

Gaps have also increased in countries other than the United States and Great Britain. For example, we have financial records for three of the leading Swedish performing organizations going back to 1947–48. In each case attendance has been virtually stationary, and while the Swedish price level has been rising during the postwar period at 3.9 per cent per year, the income gap of the Royal Opera in Stockholm has been growing at a rate of 10.5 per cent per year, and the gaps of the Royal Dramatic Theater in Stock-

---

[4] See Appendix Table XII–A for details of the calculations, including the tables involved.

The *real* rate of growth of Covent Garden's gap is actually lower than that of the Metropolitan Opera's because the price level in Great Britain was growing about twice as quickly as ours over this period. In constant dollars the annual growth rates in the gaps are very roughly: New York Philharmonic, 4.5 per cent; Cincinnati, 3 per cent; basic eleven orchestras, 5 per cent; Metropolitan Opera, 7 per cent; and Covent Garden, 6 per cent.

FIGURE XII–6

THE INCOME GAP: BASIC ELEVEN MAJOR ORCHESTRAS,
METROPOLITAN OPERA AND COVENT GARDEN, 1948–1964

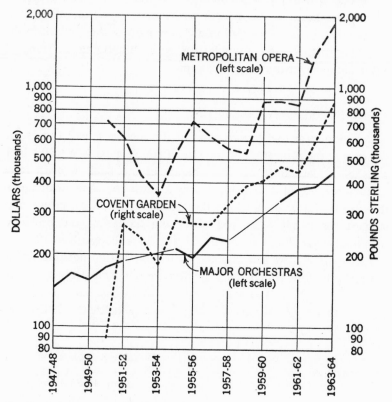

For the data used, see Appendix Table XII–A.

holm and the municipal theater in Malmö have increased at annual
rates of 19.5 and 12.5 per cent respectively.[5]

The reader will recall that up to this point a 4 per cent annual

[5] The data on performing groups in Sweden were supplied by the Swedish
Centre of the International Theater Institute. The data for the Royal Opera are
for 1947–48 to 1963–64. Figures for the Royal Theater span 1947–48 to 1962–
63 and those for the Malmö municipal theater are for 1947–48 to 1964–65.
The index of prices used is the Consumer Price Index (Cost of Living Index)
for 1947–1964, from United Nations, *Monthly Bulletin of Statistics*.

growth rate seemed rather sizable. In fact, not one of our calculated gaps has been growing as slowly as this. It should be noted that an amount growing at 5 per cent per year doubles every 14 years, while one growing at 8 per cent doubles every 9 years. Thus the figures suggest that the typical performing organization's gap is compounding at a very rapid rate. These figures, then, quantify the rate of growth of the financial pressures impinging on some of our leading performing organizations.

Some Indications of a Growing Gap

Calculation of the growth rates of the income gaps is an essential step in the projection of the size of future gaps — a task which we shall undertake in the last chapter of this book. Growth rates by themselves, however, convey only a stark and skeletal image of the underlying realities which they reflect. A few illustrations may suggest somewhat more concretely the nature of the problems which arise out of a growing gap, and indicate their universality.

Perhaps the most sensational illustration of the fact that the financial pressures which beset the arts are not exclusively an American phenomenon is provided by a 1965 news story headlined "Operas in Italy May Face Closing,"[6] in which Robert C. Doty reported:

> The Rome Opera and many of the other major Italian companies may have to face the threat of a close-down early in August unless the Government can raise the equivalent of $5.6 million to meet July payrolls.
> Massimo Bogianchino, artistic director of the Rome Opera, now holding its summer season in the ruins of the Baths of Caracalla, said the salaries of more than 400 orchestral and choral musicians, dancers, technicians and office workers — nearly $200,000 — could not be paid this month without state help. . . .
> Almost all of the 13 major operatic and symphonic companies in Italy were in similar straits, Mr. Bogianchino said. . . .
> Opera-going is a deeply ingrained Italian tradition, and interruption of the supply of Puccini, Verdi, Mozart and Donizetti would be almost as great a public disaster as a utility strike.
> Yet the opera patrons here are no more able to foot the entire bill for their favorite entertainment than are their fellow enthu-

[6] *New York Times,* July 26, 1965.

siasts in New York and the current crisis is a symptom of a chronic disease — deficit.

In New York and many other American cities, the deficit is filled by rich, individual contributors. In Italy, the state is the patron, appropriating annually more than $18 million for subsidies to music. But, with lavish Italian production standards and rising wages and other costs, the 13 major state-subsidized organizations have built up debts of more than $22 million.

Similar problems have arisen in Great Britain. In its 1952–53 annual statement, the Arts Council of Great Britain reported:

> The year which ended last March was an anxious one for many of the bodies with which the Arts Council is associated. The cost of producing the arts continues to mount, and several wages awards had to be met by the Symphony Orchestras and the Grand Opera and Ballet Companies. . . . The losing battle in which some of the Repertory Theatres are engaged called for emergency action. *It must be emphasized that most of these anxieties were not provoked by a falling-off in audiences, but rather by the inexorable increase in the costs of presentation.* In such circumstances the providing bodies, and especially the major ones, are confronted with a dilemma. If they decide to economize by, let us say, reducing the number of new productions in opera, ballet and drama they run the risk of a decline at the box-office. There is a limited audience for any given opera or ballet or classical play; and the programme must be frequently changed if attendances are to be maintained. Morton's Fork is a familiar phenomenon in administering the arts.
>
> With the aid of a supplementary vote from Parliament, and the use of its 1951 Festival reserve fund, the Arts Council was able to stave off disaster. For the present year its grant has been substantially increased by Parliament and, at least, breathing-space has been secured.[7]

Since Great Britain is now behind the United States in man-hour output in manufacturing, and hence in manufacturing wages, one might surmise that the cost pressures on British arts organizations are correspondingly lower; and the relatively narrow financial gaps exhibited by a number of organizations whose data we have examined would appear to bear this out. But with productivity rising progressively in the British economy it is only a matter of time before the financial problems of British performing organizations become as serious as ours. Travelers have often commented in the

[7] Arts Council of Great Britain, *The Public and the Arts*, Annual Report for 1952–53, pp. 14–15. Italics ours.

past on the relative aura of prosperity which surrounds the British commercial theater. The large number of new productions offered and the relatively low ticket prices have been cited as evidence. But if our analysis is valid, the unsubsidized West End should not remain immune for very long from the problems which have beset Broadway for some time, and which recently undermined the off-Broadway theater. As wages rise in the British economy, costs of theatrical production will be forced upward, and the increased risk and profit squeeze will be on. Indeed, oral reports indicate that such pressures are already beginning to be felt, and that the British commercial theater will, regrettably, soon join the international brotherhood of arts in perpetual crisis.[8]

What is being done to meet the challenge which a rapidly growing income gap poses for the economic viability of the arts will be considered in the next few chapters, in which we examine sources of contributed income.

[8] Since this was written we found an article which reported that "As far as the rank and file West End theaters were concerned this (1963–64) was one of the most disastrous seasons since before the war. Of twenty-three straight plays only five achieved lengthy runs." (*Theater World Annual*, No. 15, p. 19.) Further investigation confirmed that in London, though there was a sharp increase in 1963–64 in the number of plays performed, the total number of performances and the number of performances per production have declined fairly steadily over the past five years. The number of performances fell from a high of nearly 17,000 in 1954–55 to to a little over 11,000 in 1961–62 and a little over 9,000 in 1962–63 (see Appendix Table XII–B).

Incidentally, if off-Broadway plays are included, the sheer volume of theatrical activity is considerably greater in New York than in London. In 1962–63, for example, 83 different plays were running in London, while in New York 71 were running on Broadway and 131 off-Broadway.

PART III

SOURCES OF
FINANCIAL SUPPORT

CHAPTER **XIII**

Contributions by Individuals

IT IS impossible to evaluate potential philanthropic support of
the performing arts without examining private philanthropy in
general. One reason for this is the paucity of data on gifts to the
arts alone; patterns of giving to the arts can only be inferred from
the behavior of contributions to other recipients. Second, the record
of contributions to the performing arts, even if it were available,
would tell us no more than the data on the income gaps of the performing organizations which we have already examined. The two
figures would virtually coincide because the gaps have usually been
offset almost exactly by contributed income. Since few performing
organizations have actually gone out of business, they must, by and
large, have taken in no less than they spent; and, being non-profit
groups, they would generally not have spent less than they took
in. Most important, the record of giving for all purposes describes
the available pool of philanthropy from which the performing arts
must draw, and the long-run financial state of the arts can, therefore, be inferred only from an examination of what is happening
to the size of that pool.

Private Philanthropy in General

It is not easy to define "philanthropy" operationally. We shall
use the term in the customary sense of "private giving for public
causes as distinguished from person-to-person giving or tax-fi-

TABLE XIII–1

Estimates of Private Philanthropy in 1964, by Source

Source	Estimate A, including itemized individual contributions only[a]		Estimate B, including an estimate of total individual contributions[a]	
	Amount (millions)	Per Cent of Total	Amount (millions)	Per Cent of Total
	(1)	(2)	(3)	(4)
Individuals:				
Living Donors	$ 8,400	77	$11,000	82
Bequests	1,050	10	1,050	8
Subtotal	$ 9,450	87	$12,050	90
Corporations	580	5	580	4
Foundations	850	8	850	6
Total	$10,880	100	$13,480	100

SOURCE: Estimated by taking the relatively "hard" estimates for 1961 and 1962 (see Appendix Tables XIII–A, XIV–A and XIV–C and U. S. Treasury Department, Internal Revenue Service, *Statistics of Income, Estate Tax Returns*), and multiplying by the percentage increase in the Gross National Product between 1962 and 1964 (12%).

[a] We present separate estimates for contributions of individual donors, Estimate A using only the actual amount reported on itemized tax returns and B including an additional amount of contributions imputed to persons taking the standard deduction.

nanced projects."[1] Unfortunately, no reliable estimates of philanthropic giving more recent than 1962 are available. To provide an indication of the relevant orders of magnitude in 1964, we have simply increased the 1962 figures in proportion to the growth in Gross National Product (G.N.P.) between 1962 and 1964 (Table XIII–I).

We estimate that between $11 and $13½ billion was contributed from private sources for all philanthropic purposes in 1964. In-

[1] *Giving USA*, Annual Reports of the American Association of Fund-Raising Counsel, 1964 ed., p. 7. For an extended discussion of the definitional problems, see National Bureau of Economic Research, proceedings of a conference on *Philanthropy and Public Policy* sponsored by the Merrill Center for Economics at Amherst, 1961, published in 1962.

dividual donations from living donors and from bequests accounted for roughly 90 per cent of the total. Foundations are responsible for 6 to 8 per cent of total private philanthropic contributions and corporations for 4 to 5 per cent. This does not mean, of course, either that individuals are the fastest growing single source of contributions or that they provide anything like 90 per cent of the funds given specifically to the performing arts.

On the basis of detailed information on sources of contributions supplied by many of the arts organizations we studied, we know that, except when one of them receives a large foundation grant — and often even then — contributions of individual donors do constitute the backbone of their support. Together, the 25 major orchestras received contributions from all sources, excluding endowment, of about $6.8 million in 1963–64. Of this, about 84 per cent ($5.7 million) came from maintenance fund campaigns, the receipts from which consist predominantly of gifts from individuals but also include business gifts. In addition, the orchestras received "special projects" income of $670,000, which is also a form of individual contribution. Looked at the other way, grants from foundations and government to the major orchestras amounted to only $400,000, or 6 per cent of all contributed income. Of course, the $85 million Ford Foundation grant to the orchestras announced in the fall of 1965 will make a noticeable difference in this pattern.

The importance of the individual donor is equally apparent in the case of the Metropolitan Opera, which received $1.6 million in donations in 1963–64, almost all of it from individual givers. Roughly 20 per cent came from subscribers, who were requested to consider contributing 20 per cent above the cost of their seats (about 55 per cent of them now do send contributions); two fund raising arms, the Metropolitan Opera Guild and the National Council, contributed about 20 per cent, and miscellaneous individual contributions accounted for most of the remaining 60 per cent. Other operas also rely heavily on individual supporters.[2]

Foundation grants have played a larger role in the case of the regional theaters, but many of these organizations have had to match their grants with private contributions and have succeeded

[2] Rockefeller Panel Report, p. 73.

TABLE XIII–2

Per Cent of Audience Contributing to Performing Arts
Organizations Regularly, Occasionally, Rarely, by Art Form,
United States

Audience	Regularly	Occasionally	Rarely
Theater:			
Broadway	6.4	19.0	74.6
Off-Broadway	12.5	24.1	63.4
Regional	10.2	20.9	69.0
Major Orchestras	23.1	25.1	51.8
Opera	17.1	26.9	56.0
Ballet	10.3	22.7	67.0
Ensembles	7.6	19.0	73.4
Average, All Paid Performances	15.6	23.1	61.3
Free Open-Air Performances	7.2	21.8	71.1

SOURCE: Twentieth Century Fund audience survey.

in doing so. Here again individual donations provide the major share of contributed income.

Our audience survey also produced evidence on individual giving. We did not ask for specific amounts, suspecting the trust-worthiness of respondents' memories, but we did ask if respondents contributed to performing arts organizations regularly, occasionally or rarely. To discourage people simply from saying they contributed whether they did or not, we requested them to list the organizations to which they had made donations in the last 12 months.[3] Roughly 40 per cent of our respondents said they contributed either occasionally or regularly, and 15 per cent said they gave regularly. As Table XIII–2 indicates, orchestral audiences contained the largest proportion of contributors, while persons who

[3] Almost everyone who said he contributed listed at least one organization, and many listed more. Of course a person can always make up a name, but this seemed to us less likely than his just checking a box.

attended Broadway productions contributed less frequently than any other segment of the total arts audience surveyed. These results are just what one might have expected — they reflect the effectiveness of fund raising efforts by orchestras and the fact that Broadway, consisting as it does of commercial enterprises, does not solicit donations. The considerable number of persons who contribute regularly among audiences of all sorts is additional evidence of the great importance of individual giving to the performing arts.

Trends in Total Giving by Living Donors

Information on individual giving for almost five decades, derived from individual federal income tax returns, is compiled in Appendix Table XIII–A. This information in its raw state is affected by changes in the provisions of the tax laws. In the early years of the income tax many more persons than today were exempt from filing, which would make a comparison of trends in contributions reported on tax returns with trends in the Gross National Product very misleading. Reported deductions claimed for charitable contributions would seem to rise relative to the G.N.P. simply because the tax base was broadened, as happened at the beginning of World War II. A way of avoiding this kind of distortion is to relate contributions, not to G.N.P., but to total adjusted gross income of all individuals (their gross total income less business deductions as reported for tax purposes),[4] for as tax coverage broadens, both adjusted gross income and the volume of deductions rise.

A first impression of trends in deductions for contributions is provided by the broken upper curve in Figure XIII–1, which shows reported contributions as a percentage of adjusted gross income. We see that philanthropic contributions amounted to roughly 2 per cent of adjusted gross income from 1917 to 1940, and that there

---

[4] For a fuller discussion of the definition of adjusted gross income, see C. Harry Kahn, *Personal Deductions in the Federal Income Tax*, National Bureau of Economic Research, Princeton University Press, Princeton, N.J., 1960, pp. 8–9, 17. Kahn points out that the concept differs from the Commerce Department's concept of "personal income" primarily because it includes net capital gains and losses and employee social insurance contributions, and excludes a large part of military pay, social security benefits, interest on state and local bonds and most income in kind.

FIGURE XIII-1

INDIVIDUAL PHILANTHROPIC CONTRIBUTIONS AS PER CENT

OF ADJUSTED GROSS INCOME, 1917–1962

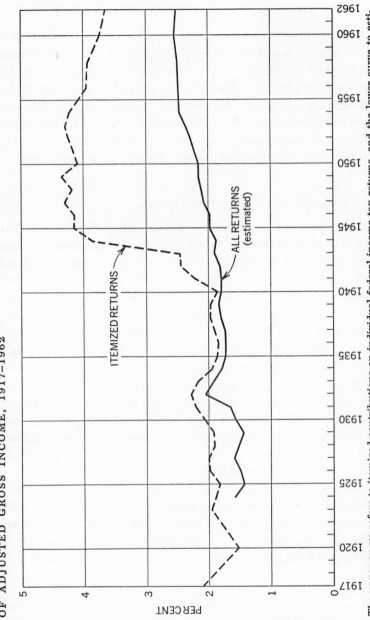

The upper curve refers to itemized contributions on individual federal income tax returns, and the lower curve to estimated total contributions. The latter data take into account the use of the standard deduction by some taxpayers in more recent periods, as well as the fact that a smaller proportion of the population filed in earlier years. Appendix Table XIII–A contains the basic data.

was no clear trend during that period. But after 1940 the proportion jumped sharply to about 4 per cent, reached a high of 4.34 per cent in 1949, and then declined gradually to 3.64 per cent in 1962.

Unfortunately, however, these apparent trends are also misleading and further adjustment of the statistics is required. In the early years there was no allowance for deductions unless these were itemized, and practically every return showed itemized deductions. The standard deduction, which permits the taxpayer to deduct a fixed proportion of his income (up to a certain limit, currently $1,000 for a married couple filing a joint return), instead of itemizing deductible items, was introduced between 1941 and 1943 and was made widely available in 1944. The introduction of this option explains why in 1941, 60 per cent of all income tax returns showed itemized deductions but by 1944 only 18 per cent of all taxpayers itemized. Obviously, persons who make large contributions are more likely to file itemized returns than are persons who contribute little. Hence, the smaller the proportion of persons who itemize their deductions, the larger will be the *apparent* rate of contribution.

When the data are revised to allow for the donations of individuals taking the standard deduction,[5] as in the heavier curve in Figure XIII–1, we see that both the apparent 1943–44 jump in the upper curve in this graph and its subsequent decline are largely manifestations of variations in reporting associated with the use made by taxpayers of the standard deduction, and have little to do with the underlying trends. The adjusted series shows that total contributions as a percentage of adjusted gross income displayed a modest but rather steady upward trend from the 1920's to the mid-1950's, the contribution rate rising from about 1½ per cent in 1925 to just under 2½ per cent in 1954. Since 1954 the contribution rate has increased only slightly.

Similarly, the behavior of the contribution rate in recent years can be understood only in the context of the changes in the tax provisions regarding the limit on deductions for contributions which took place in 1952 and 1954. The limit was raised from 15 per cent

---

[5] In making this adjustment we have followed the procedure designed by Kahn (Chapter 8), who revised the figures through 1956.

of adjusted gross income to 20 per cent in 1952, and then to 30 per cent in 1954.[6] Hence, it is not surprising that the most pronounced increases in the contribution rate occurred between 1950 and 1954. The fact that the contribution rate has increased so little since 1954 means that the dollar volume of contributions has gone up only slightly faster than incomes in general — at an average annual rate of 5.6 per cent.

Which Income Classes Provide the Most Money?

We ask next whether it is the rich or the poor who do most of the giving. The answer is clear. It is the poor and the lower-middle income groups. Even if we consider only itemized contributions, which under-represent the giving of lower income groups, we find that persons with adjusted gross incomes below $3,000 per year gave 4.7 per cent of the total in 1962, and persons with incomes under $10,000 per year gave 55.8 per cent of the total. (Appendix Table XIII–B). At the other end of the income scale, taxpayers with incomes of $100,000 or more provided only 6.3 per cent of all itemized contributions. When we correct even very roughly for contributions made by persons who filed non-itemized returns, the percentage given by the group having incomes over $100,000 falls to 4.8 per cent of the total, while the share contributed by those with incomes below $3,000 rises to the impressive figure of nearly 8 per cent.

Of course, the main reason the lower income groups provide so large a percentage of the total is that their ranks are so numerous. In 1962, of the total of $350 billion of adjusted gross income, 8.5 per cent was reported by persons whose incomes were less than $3,000, 23.2 per cent by persons receiving less than $5,000 and 66.6 per cent by persons receiving less than $10,000. Less than 2 per cent of this income was received by persons in the above

---

[6] To be eligible for the full 30 per cent, the taxpayer must contribute at least 10 per cent of his adjusted gross income to specified types of organizations. The effect of such tax incentives on contributions is discussed more fully in Chapter XV in the section dealing with federal support of the performing arts.

$100,000 class, and so it is easy to see why they did not dominate the nation's giving.[7]

The relationship between the percentage of adjusted gross income contributed and the donor's income class provides a measure of the relative generosity of the different income groups. The data are plotted in Figure XIII–2 and recorded in Appendix Table XIII–C. Contrary to what one might have expected, the over-all contribution rate does not rise sharply or even steadily with income. The curve for 1943 shows that lower income groups devoted a somewhat larger proportion of their adjusted gross incomes to contributions than did many middle and upper income groups. Indeed, the lowest contribution rate was that of persons in the $10,000–$24,999 class — a very considerable income level in 1943. It is only beyond the $50,000 level that contributions begin to climb with income. Essentially the same picture held for 1962.

Thus the pattern of individual giving can be ascribed both to the large absolute number of relatively impecunious individuals and to the fact that they give at least as high a proportion of their income as many wealthier groups. We shall see presently that much of the giving of the lower income groups can be ascribed to the influence of the church.

While lower income groups give a great deal collectively, the average dollar amount given by each member alone is very small. For example, persons with incomes under $5,000 a year contribute well under $200 each on the average, and since this amount usually represents several donations, the average gift must be considerably smaller than this. Fund raising being so expensive and time consuming an activity, it is easy to see why much of it is aimed at high income persons, despite the fact that they account for a small proportion of total giving. The point is that one is likely to get more money per dollar of fund raising effort from a wealthy person because his average donation is considerably larger. The success of the churches in raising money from lower income groups is attributable in no small measure to their ability to handle small gifts economically.

[7] U.S. Treasury Department, Internal Revenue Service, *Statistics of Income, Individual Income Tax Returns,* 1962, Table 1.

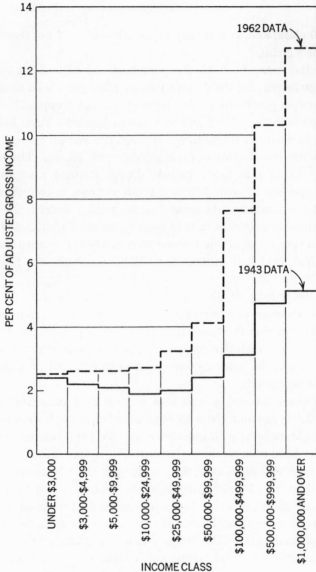

FIGURE XIII-2

INDIVIDUAL PHILANTHROPIC CONTRIBUTIONS:
PROPORTION OF INCOME CONTRIBUTED, BY INCOME CLASS, 1943 AND 1962

PER CENT OF ADJUSTED GROSS INCOME

1962 DATA

1943 DATA

UNDER $3,000

$3,000-$4,999

$5,000-$9,999

$10,000-$24,999

$25,000-$49,999

$50,000-$99,999

$100,000-$499,999

$500,000-$999,999

$1,000,000 AND OVER

INCOME CLASS

Both sets of data are estimates for all individual federal income tax returns. The 1943 set is the more reliable, because in that year the standard deduction was available only to persons with incomes below $3,000 and it was necessary, therefore, to estimate contributions for only this lowest income group. In fact, half of the members of this group happened to elect to report their contributions. (See F. Emerson Andrews, *Philanthropic Giving*, Russell Sage Foundation, New York, 1950, p. 53.) For the data on which the graph is based see Appendix Table XIII-C.

314

Activities Supported by Different Income Classes

Before examining which activities are supported by the different income groups, it is appropriate to see how the total flow of philanthropic giving is divided among the various claimants. The dominance of religious groups is the single most striking characteristic of the distribution of individual contributions by type of recipient as reported on 1962 tax returns. In that year 79 per cent of those who filed itemized returns gave some money to religious activities. "Other charitable organizations," which include Community Chests, the American Red Cross, the American Cancer Society and similar organizations, was the second most popular category, receiving contributions from 69 per cent of all donors. Hospitals and educational institutions ranked much lower in this respect, with gifts to each by only 4 and 6 per cent of all contributors. (See Appendix Table XIII–D.) Undoubtedly, the arts would fall even lower in the list if the data were available. Sixty-one per cent of *itemized* contributions went to religious organizations (Appendix Table XIII–E), and the percentage is undoubtedly higher for persons taking the standard deduction. The category of recipients which includes Community Chests and the Red Cross received 14 per cent of all itemized contributions. Educational institutions received less than 4 per cent, and hospitals only 1.5 per cent of the total. Twenty per cent of the total, or roughly $1.5 billion, went to "other organizations," a category defined to include organizations "not elsewhere classified or not specifically stated . . . including literary, educational and scientific foundations, libraries, museums and zoos."[8] Apparently, performing arts organizations are also included here, but from these statistics there is no way of telling what fraction of the $1.5 billion they received.

On the basis of a detailed analysis of tax returns made available by the Internal Revenue Service for the first time in January 1965, it is possible to determine which income groups support education, which provide church funds, and so on. Table XIII–3 and Appendix Table XIII–D summarize a mine of fascinating information indicating which income groups serve as the leading patrons for each major type of non-profit activity. As the text table indicates, reli-

[8] *Statistics of Income*, 1962, p. 8.

TABLE XIII–3

Percentage Distribution of Individual Philanthropic Contributions to Each Type of Recipient, by Income Class, 1962[a]

Adjusted Gross Income	Per Cent from Each Income Class					
	Religious Organizations	Comm. Chest, Red Cross, etc.	Hospitals	Educational Institutions	"Other"	All Organizations
Under $3,000	5.6	3.5	1.2	1.1	3.9	4.7
$3,000–$4,999	13.0	9.6	2.9	1.8	9.6	11.3
$5,000–$9,999	44.5	39.2	12.2	14.0	32.5	39.8
$10,000–$24,999	27.6	28.7	18.8	18.3	22.0	26.2
$25,000–$49,999	5.8	8.7	20.3	15.8	8.7	7.4
$50,000–$99,999	2.3	5.4	17.1	15.9	7.1	4.4
$100,000–$499,999	1.0	3.9	19.1	22.9	10.0	4.3
$500,000–$999,999	0.1	0.6	3.8	4.3	2.1	0.8
$1,000,000 and Over	0.1	0.5	4.6	5.9	4.2	1.2
Total, All Income Classes	100	100	100	100	100	100

SOURCE: Appendix Table XIII–D.

[a] Based on itemized federal income tax returns only.

gious organizations depend on lower income groups; in 1962 over 60 per cent of their total came from donors with income under $10,000, and the proportion would be substantially greater if non-itemized returns were included. The pattern for Community Chests *et al.* is similar. Hospitals and educational institutions rely much more on the upper-middle classes and the wealthy. Figure XIII–3 shows that the largest portion of gifts received by educational institutions comes from individuals in the $100,000–$499,999 per year income class, who alone provided 23 per cent of the total in 1962. The less than 350 taxpayers declaring incomes of a million dollars or more in 1962 provided 6 per cent of the educational total by themselves.

We can learn very little about the performing arts from the data in the "other" category. This miscellaneous group is probably subject to a relatively large amount of misreporting and, to complicate

FIGURE XIII–3

INDIVIDUAL PHILANTHROPIC CONTRIBUTIONS
RECEIVED BY EDUCATIONAL AND RELIGIOUS
INSTITUTIONS: PER CENT RECEIVED FROM
DIFFERENT INCOME CLASSES, 1962

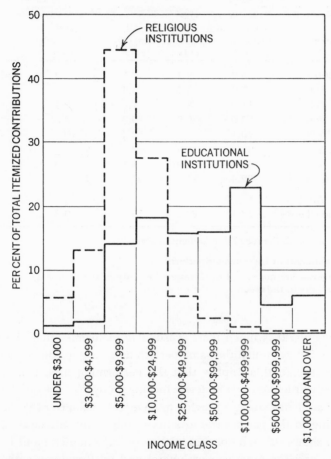

The data are based on itemized federal income tax returns.
For the percentage figures see Table XIII–3, and for the absolute figures Appendix Table XIII–D.

matters further, includes such varied items as zoos and family
foundations. The pattern of giving to this "other" category probably
has little relevance to the performing arts, surely one of its smaller

TABLE XIII–4

Per Cent of Audience Contributing Regularly to Performing Arts
Organizations, by Family Income Class, United States and
Great Britain, 1963, 1964

| | United States | | | Great Britain | |
Family Income Class	Major Orchestra Respondents	Off-Broadway Respondents	All Respondents[a]	All Respondents	Family Income Class[b]
Under $3,000	5.0	2.4	3.7	5.2	Under £1,400
$3,000–$4,999	7.6	6.4	5.4	5.1	£1,400–£2,529
$5,000–$6,999	11.0	8.1	7.9	8.4	£2,530–£3,359
$7,000–$9,999	15.0	8.3	9.3	8.3	£3,360–£4,899
$10,000–$14,999	20.1	7.9	13.4	10.1	£4,900–£6,999
$15,000–$24,999	28.5	13.5	18.8	⎫	
$25,000–$49,999	42.9	21.9	31.1	⎬ 16.0	£7,000 or Over
$50,000 and Over	62.4	33.7	44.5	⎭	
Average, All Income Classes	23.1	12.5	15.6	9.8	

SOURCE: Twentieth Century Fund audience survey.

[a] Except respondents at free open-air performances.

[b] These categories are not meant to correspond exactly to the U. S. categories; we are interested mainly in the ordering of the relationship.

components. It is much more reasonable to surmise that giving to
the arts follows much the same pattern as giving to educational institutions, and this implies that the performing arts, too, obtain
relatively little money from lower income groups.

Our audience surveys provide more direct evidence of variations
in giving *to the performing arts* according to income class. Table
XIII–4 shows this relationship in the over-all American and British
results, and for American orchestral and off-Broadway audiences
separately.

The results are strikingly regular and show a very steady rise in
the proportion of regular contributors as incomes increase. Thus,
as we surmised, the pattern of giving to the arts by income class is

similar to the pattern of contributions to education: there is a strong positive relationship between income and contributions. A similar relationship is revealed by the British data, though in the British case the association between income class and percentage contributing regularly is not nearly so strong.

The Large Donors

The findings just reported show that the performing arts have a special interest in the number of high income recipients as well as in their giving propensities, subjects which we shall examine in this section.

We do not mean to imply that small, low-income donors are unimportant. It has been pointed out many times that the day when a performing organization could depend on a single family for its support is long past. There was a time when the Cincinnati Orchestra could expect the Tafts to meet its deficit automatically, but today it counts more heavily on many small donors, just as do symphony orchestras elsewhere in the country. The American Symphony Orchestra League reports that 85 per cent of all contributions to orchestras are in amounts under $100. Of 4,882 contributions to the Boston Symphony in 1963–64, 4,407 were of $100 or less.[9] Small contributions, moreover, provide a basis for community-wide interest in the arts and a focus for enthusiasm that can increase ticket sales and pave the way for public support. But from the standpoint of total receipts, big gifts are apparently still of paramount importance to most performing arts organizations.

In examining trends in giving by high income recipients, we need to look at trends both in the total income at their disposal and in contribution rates. We begin with the income tax data, asking whether government policies since the New Deal, principally the extension of progressive taxation, have in fact reduced the number of top income receivers.

Of special interest are the members of the very top group — those with incomes of $1 million or more in a year. Their numbers

[9] Rockefeller Panel Report, p. 72.

are small indeed, for even many millionaires might in any particular year receive much less than a million dollars in income. The relevant data are presented in Appendix Table XIII–F.[10]

The number of million dollar returns (342 in 1962) is still below the peak of 513 reached in 1929, though the number has been rising fairly rapidly since 1942. In interpreting this observation and many other related pieces of information in this chapter, one must not forget that there is today a greater tax incentive to obtain income in non-taxable (and hence non-reportable) form and that in consequence the number of million dollar income receivers is probably greater than the figures suggest. On the other hand, the decline in the purchasing power of the dollar means that a million dollar income today is really much less than it was 35 years ago; thus, even if the number of returns reporting a million dollars had regained its 1929 level, this might still represent a substantial decrease in the number of people with very high incomes. In 1929, in fact, individuals with incomes of a million dollars or more had a combined after-tax income of over a billion dollars; in 1962 the comparable figure was only about a third of this. Their after-tax income as a percentage of all United States disposable personal income is the best indicator of how these people have fared in relation to the rest of the community. (See Appendix Table VIII–F.) In 1929 the 513 persons in the million-and-over category received 1¼ per cent of the nation's entire disposable personal income. This proportion fell precipitously during the depression to 0.04 per cent in 1932 and reached a low of one one-hundredth of one per cent of the nation's disposable income in 1943. However, the proportion has risen again in the postwar period and has recently gone up to about one tenth of one per cent of the total.

Since persons having million dollar incomes are a very small part of the wealthy segment of the community, let us consider two

[10] The trend may be distorted slightly by the institution of the joint return in 1948, but one cannot be sure of the direction of this bias. If Mr. A received $800,000 and Mrs. A $400,000, and they filed separate returns, neither would appear in the million-dollar-and-over category; the option of joint filing, if used, would then increase by one the total number of returns in that income category. If Mr. B and Mrs. B each received an income of $2 million, the system of separate filing would produce two returns in the million-dollar-and-over category but use of the option of joint filing would produce only one.

broader groups — the upper 5 and the upper 20 per cent of the nation's families in terms of total personal income (Appendix Table XIII–G). From 1929 to the end of World War II, their share of family personal income declined markedly. Since then there has been a much more gradual but still noticeable decline in the share of the top 5 per cent, while the share of the top 20 per cent has stayed remarkably constant. Similar official figures are not available for years before 1929, but Simon Kuznets has provided estimates for earlier periods. These make clear that the late 1920's was a peak period for the top income recipients, and that the upper 5 per cent group accounted for about as large a proportion of total income in 1940 as at the beginning of the 1920's. From a long-period point of view, then, there has been some decline in the proportion of income going to the upper income groups, but the reduction has not been nearly as sharp as a set of figures beginning with 1929 would suggest.[11]

Whatever one may think on general grounds about the virtues of the long-run tendency of the income distribution to flatten out somewhat, it is bound to have an adverse effect on private giving to the performing arts. If the bulk of such giving comes from the well-to-do, anything that limits the disposable incomes of this group is likely to reduce contributions.

Of course, increases in the contribution *rates* of the top income groups can offset any tendency for their share in income-after-taxes to decline, and in fact the contribution rates for these groups are much higher now than they were prior to the 1950's. Itemized contributions of persons reporting incomes of $500,000 or more represented 12.3 per cent of their adjusted gross incomes in 1962, compared with 6.6 per cent in 1949; and the contribution rate for those in the $100,000–$499,999 category was 7.8 per cent in 1962, compared with only 4.6 per cent in 1949 (Appendix Table XIII–H). It is essential to recognize, however, that almost all these sharp increases occurred between 1949 and 1954, during which period the

[11] See Simon Kuznets, ed., *Income and Wealth in the United States, Trend and Structure,* Bowes and Bowes, Cambridge, England, 1952. Kuznets used before-tax figures. Long-term data on the after-tax income distribution are not readily available; however, the increase in income tax rates through the years is certain to have reduced the share of top income groups in total family personal income even more sharply than the before-tax figures show.

tax law was changed twice to provide greater incentives for private contributors.

As tax incentives have been roughly constant since 1954, this is the relevant period for an assessment of underlying trends, and the combined effect of changes in the income share of top bracket tax-payers and changes in their contribution rates during these years is what interests us. The method we used to estimate trends in con-tributions for the top income group is explained in Appendix XIII–1. Our estimates suggest that over the period 1954–1962 the contributions of the top group increased at an average annual rate of 5.8 per cent — a rate almost exactly equal to the rate of in-crease in total contributions (5.6 per cent). Between 1958 and 1962, moreover, the contributions of the top income group in-creased at a considerably slower rate. Over this interval they went up only 3.8 per cent per year, compared with a growth rate for total contributions of 5.3 per cent. The significance of these findings for the future of the performing arts will be considered in some detail in the last chapter of this book when we project the over-all income gap and contributions from all sources to 1975. No projection is required, however, to note that the apparent failure of top income groups to increase their giving as rapidly as contributors in general in the last few years is hardly a good omen for the performing arts.

Bequests

Bequests are a very important and too often neglected compo-nent of individual giving. They provide 8 to 10 per cent of total pri-vate philanthropy. There has been a very appreciable growth in charitable bequests in the postwar years, from about $200 million in 1947–48 to nearly $1 billion in 1961. This can be ascribed both to an increase in the value of estates and to a rise in the proportion of estates which is devoted to philanthropic purposes. (See Ap-pendix Table XIII–I.)

We have assembled no detailed figures on the distribution of be-quests according to recipient,[12] but one may reasonably assume

---

[12] But see F. Emerson Andrews, "Bounty from Beyond," *Harper's*, Vol. 225, August 1962, p. 65.

that the performing arts receive a higher proportion of bequests than they do of gifts by living donors in top income categories. After all, the will is primarily an upper bracket instrument, and we have suggested that it is primarily the wealthy who provide funds to the arts, just as they do to education and hospitals. As with income, there was some decline in the share of wealth held by the very rich between 1929 and the end of World War II, but between 1945 and 1956 this share increased somewhat.[13] The rise may explain the recent spurt of bequests. Certainly our figures offer no support for the idea that the large accumulations of wealth have dried up as sources of philanthropy.

Determinants of Individual Giving: Fund Raising Activities

Giving to the performing arts may be regarded as determined by five major factors — total income in the economy; its distribution; tax incentives for contributions in general; the relative "needs" of arts organizations as compared with those of other non-profit groups; and the effectiveness of the specific fund raising activities. We have already discussed income and its distribution. Our detailed examination of tax incentives will be deferred until the chapter on government support, and the relative needs of the arts will be considered after we have examined the support provided by corporations and foundations. Here we will focus on the fund raising activities of the arts organizations.

No doubt many individuals avoid giving to the arts because several important points have never been made clear to them: that most performing organizations are not profit-making institutions; that the arts play an important role in society beyond the mere provision of "entertainment"; and that wealthy patrons no longer stand ready to cover deficits automatically. A study of a well-known educational television station which was recently operating under serious financial pressures indicated that most of its audience was unaware of its need for funds. If they realized the non-commercial status of educational television stations, they thought perhaps that

[13] Robert J. Lampman, *The Share of Top Wealth-Holders in National Wealth, 1922–56*, National Bureau of Economic Research, Princeton University Press, Princeton, N.J., 1962, p. 276.

money was amply provided by the government or educational institutions.

The Metropolitan Opera and a few other operas, the major orchestras and certain repertory theaters have established concerted
and systematic fund raising procedures, but many performing organizations have failed to do so. This is certainly true of a number
of dance organizations, and the lack of effective fund raising efforts
certainly has not helped their finances.

To conduct a successful campaign it is very helpful to know
whom to go after. In this connection some of our audience survey
results can once again be helpful. Appendix Tables XIII–J and
XIII–K provide profiles of the major orchestra and off-Broadway
audiences tabulated by frequency of contribution. Education and
profession are obviously highly correlated with income level so that
these profiles are heavily colored by the central fact that higher income groups give more to the performing arts. Further analysis is
required, for example, to find out what difference occupation makes
at any given income level. One of the most interesting findings
to emerge from the analysis provided in the tables is the fact that
members of the managerial class are more likely to contribute regularly than other occupational groups. For example, 35 per cent of
all managers earning between $10,000 and $15,000 contribute
regularly, which is more than twice the proportion of regular contributors among teachers and professionals generally in that income bracket. Contributions are shown to go up with frequency of
attendance — hardly a surprising result. Also, persons with graduate education contribute less frequently than persons with high
school education in the same income bracket.

The Role of Community Arts Councils

One of the most recent developments affecting the contributions
received from individuals and from corporations by the performing
arts has been the growth of community arts councils. These merit
attention because of their great potential importance for the arts.

Arts councils are of two general types: so-called community
councils, and official councils formed by states and municipalities.

The next chapter will discuss the state and municipal varieties, whose responsibilities may include the administration of government financial and technical assistance programs, the arrangement of tours by performing organizations and the collection and dissemination of information on matters affecting the arts. We shall concern ourselves here with community councils. These are usually private groups composed of individuals and performing organizations or, in some cases, only the relevant organizations, "banded together to share services and solve common problems."[14] Though their programs vary, they typically undertake pooled managerial, administrative and promotional duties for their constituent groups. Fund raising has not been the primary activity of most such councils up to now. They have usually concentrated their efforts on audience development and coordination of the schedules of their constituent organizations. However, a number of them have organized annual united fund raising campaigns for cultural activities in their communities similar to the united drives run for the benefit of health and welfare services. As the Rockefeller Panel Report points out,[15] in 1964 only 9 of the 472 cities reporting to the United Community Funds and Councils of America included support for the performing arts, and most of that was probably devoted to community schools and neighborhood centers.

The community arts councils are a recent phenomenon, having emerged on a significant scale only after World War II. Only 8 councils were formed between 1945 and 1950. By 1955 there were 25, a number that had grown to 50 in 1960, and today (1965) according to Ralph Burgard, Executive Director of the Arts Councils of America, some 250 such councils are in operation.

Only some 12 of these organizations have so far engaged in united fund campaigns despite the considerable publicity this aspect of their work has received. This highly organized approach to fund raising is not without disadvantages. In some cases the constituent groups may be tempted to relax their efforts when cam-

---

[14] *Arts Councils of America,* booklet issued by Arts Councils of America, New York City.

[15] p. 78.

paigns are in the hands of a central agency, and many organizations then suffer instead of one if a project fails. At the end of a united campaign the constituent groups may feel short-changed by their share of the total receipts, and bitter feelings among the participants may result. In addition, the directors of any such large effort tend to support old, established organizations, with whom they can deal in a business-like manner. Not only may there be less money available to young, untried experimental groups, but because a donor is likely to feel that the contribution he makes to a united drive fulfills his responsibility toward cultural activity in the community, these groups may have less chance than otherwise of securing the backing of some well-to-do individual. As one authority said to us, "Community Chest drives came about not by willing cooperation among the fund-raising organizations, but rather in response to the pressure of enraged citizens who were just tired of being besieged by so many fund raisers."

Yet there is a great deal to be gained by united fund raising. It is constantly stressed as a means whereby performing arts organizations can obtain more money. The dozen communities which by 1964 had used this approach seem, in general, to have had quite satisfactory results. And since the performing arts are excluded from most current United Fund efforts, if they are to undertake such an approach they must organize it themselves.

The Winston-Salem Community Arts Council may perhaps be regarded as a prototype. Winston-Salem, an industrial city of about 100,000 population in the Piedmont region of North Carolina whose main industries are tobacco, textiles and electronics, was one of the first cities in the country to establish a United Fund. It has an outstanding philanthropic record; no community-wide fund drive has ever failed. Member groups submit their budgets about six months before the start of each fiscal year. A budget committee, composed of businessmen, community leaders and persons especially interested in the cultural life of the community, determines how much money it thinks it can raise, and then, in a series of meetings with representatives of the member groups, their budgets are trimmed to fit the total. In its first few years the Council raised money through a musical comedy presentation, but more recently it has undertaken straight fund raising. Its collections rose steadily from $22,000 in 1952 to $73,000 in 1964.[16]

Another such group, the United Fine Arts Fund of Cincinnati, also reports encouraging results, with contributions rising from $249,000 in 1949 to $418,000 in 1963.

Thus, united fund raising efforts can be effective if the leaders are careful to avoid the reported tendency of community arts councils to sponsor the routine and shy away from experimental efforts. If these groups can also maintain the autonomy and zeal of their constituent organizations, they may prove an important financial instrument for the performing arts. Fund raising is a difficult task, and arts councils can perhaps provide a vehicle for more skillful planning, execution and coordinating of fund raising efforts for many small institutions which, left to themselves, might find it too difficult a task.

Despite an abundance of data on contributions, we have no way of obtaining a reliable estimate of individual giving to the performing arts. As a mildly educated guess we would hazard that in 1964–65 individual giving to support live performance amounted to between $50 million and $75 million in all. From what we know of individual giving to support the construction of cultural centers and about contributions toward the operating costs of the performing organizations, we are certain that the amount could not have been much below $50 million. Moreover, we know that $274 million in individual giving to education was reported on itemized federal income tax returns in 1962, and it seems most implausible that contributions to the performing arts would have been as much as 25 per cent of this amount. This gives us the upper limit of our estimate of total contributions to the performing arts.

Several firmer and, for the long run, more important conclusions emerge from the statistics presented in this chapter: that the

[16] According to Ralph Burgard, most budget committees work in a slightly different fashion: they first hold interviews with representatives of their member groups, and adjust requests in terms of their evaluation of the need of the groups; if these adjusted figures add up to what seems a reasonable sum in view of the preceding year's campaign yield, this total is taken as the current goal.

performing arts obtain the bulk of their support from upper income groups; that the share of these groups in the nation's income and wealth has slowly been declining, though the rate of decline seems to have slowed appreciably since World War II; and that the philanthropic contributions of wealthy individuals taken as a group have increased less rapidly than the philanthropic contributions of individuals in general since 1954. Taken together, these facts suggest that for any significant expansion in individual giving to the arts, skillful exploitation of fund raising opportunities will be required.

CHAPTER XIV

Private Institutional Support

THOUGH the individual donor is by far the nation's most important source of philanthropy, other sources are by no means unimportant, and in some cases they have played a crucial role. This chapter discusses private institutional supporters and potential supporters of the arts — corporations, labor unions, universities and foundations — their record of giving in the past and their likely role in the future. Once again, to determine the potential magnitude of philanthropy to the arts from these sources we will have to examine giving for related purposes as well as the amounts contributed to the arts.

The Corporation as Donor

We have seen that corporations provided roughly 5 per cent of total private philanthropy in 1964. In fact, their role is more important than this figure suggests, for their contributions have been growing significantly and there is considerable potential for expansion. Since 1937 contributions have gone up from $30 million to $512 million in 1962. They have risen faster than corporate profits. In 1936 corporate giving amounted to less than one half of one per cent of profits, and today it is well over one per cent. (See Appendix Table XIV–A.)

Behind these figures lies a moderately long history involving a number of issues of principle and law. Corporate support of philanthropic enterprises goes back to the end of the nineteenth century when the railroads contributed funds to the YMCA's, presumably to help provide lodgings for railroad employees in transit.

Some of the country's early fund raisers received their training here. The earliest example of more widespread corporate support occurred during World War I with the first "high pressure" Red Cross drive, much of whose leadership was supplied by Morgan bankers.

With the great depression and the changed attitudes toward business which accompanied it, there was an increase in pressure for corporate giving as part of the social responsibility of business. In 1935 the Internal Revenue Code introduced a tax provision permitting the deduction of charitable contributions for corporate income tax purposes up to a maximum of 5 per cent of taxable income. This provision seems to have been opposed mildly by President Roosevelt, who was nevertheless persuaded by the leaders of the community chests and councils not to veto the act.[1]

In determining a contributions policy, corporations face a serious problem of principle. Presumably a corporation is run primarily in the interests of its stockholders. It is clear to everyone how a scholarship to an engineering student who promises to come to work for the firm after graduation might serve stockholder welfare. But the stockholders' stake is less obvious in the case of an unrestricted grant to a school of engineering, only a few of whose graduates might be expected to be associated with the company, and the connection between stockholder welfare and corporate support for a symphony orchestra is even more subtle. Not only is there a moral issue of the propriety of such a use of corporate funds; there are also some strategic and legal problems. No management wants to do anything that incurs strong stockholder opposition, and, though what experience there is seems to indicate that this fear is groundless, many executives have voiced concern that large corporate gifts would arouse ire in these quarters.[2]

The legal issue is whether corporate charters permit the use of any of the company's income for philanthropic purposes that provide no direct benefit to the firm. Various court decisions, notably that in the Smith case of 1956, have established the corporation's

[1] On these historical matters see Scott M. Cutlip, *The Changing Role of American Corporate Philanthropy*, report on a 1961 public relations conference, University of Wisconsin, October 10, 1961, Introduction.

[2] Rockefeller Panel Report, pp. 90–91.

right to make such gifts. In the Smith case, in order to provide a legal test of the issue, it was arranged for a stockholder to challenge a gift to Princeton University by a New Jersey manufacturing company producing, among other things, fire plugs. The suit was decided in favor of the university by the New Jersey Superior Court, and the decision was unanimously upheld by the State Supreme Court. The fact that the case was decided on the basis of the common law encouraged corporations in all states to feel that they were on firm legal ground when they made their gifts. Most states now authorize corporations to make certain kinds of gifts, and Congress has amended the National Banking Act to provide the donative power to national banks. The argument used to rationalize these decisions is that the firm cannot operate effectively in a poorly functioning society and that, therefore, charitable contributions relate to a legitimate area of corporate concern.

The recent history of corporate giving has been affected by these and other legal and economic developments. During World War II corporate giving rose sharply from about 0.4 per cent of profits in 1943 to 1.25 per cent in 1946. (See Appendix Table XIV–A.) This increase was almost certainly, at least in part, a consequence of the high federal taxes imposed on profits during this period, which made it cheaper for corporations to make gifts. At a 50 per cent tax rate a million dollar gift may be interpreted as costing a corporation $500,000, while in 1944 the same gift taken from "excess profits" under the 95 per cent tax rate would have represented only $50,000 in after-tax profits. It is not equally clear how much of the postwar return to high levels of giving (from about 0.7 per cent of profits in 1948 to nearly 1.1 per cent in 1961) is to be attributed to the permissive court decisions we have described, but obviously gifts would have been considerably reduced in their absence. Some of the growth in donations must also be credited to the general tendency among corporations to increase their participation in community aid as a way of making clearer the extent to which they "belong" in society.

In addition to direct giving, the business community has increasingly undertaken the establishment of company foundations. These grew in number from 20 before 1939 to over 1,500 by 1962, more than 60 per cent of which were set up in the high tax years during World War II and the Korean War. Some company foundations have assets exceeding $10 million. For recipients, the advantage of the foundation arrangement is that it stabilizes company giving. Even in years when company profits are low the foundation can continue its donations out of the tax-exempt reserves paid into it in more profitable years.

Corporations have been formalizing their giving in other ways as well: through the establishment of contributions committees, the assignment of full-time employees to deal with contribution matters and through the preparation of explicit contribution budgets. According to a 1963 survey of the American Society of Corporate Secretaries, 79 per cent of its respondents now prepare such a budget annually, an increase of about 15 per cent since 1956.[3]

While the upward trend in corporate giving is impressive, corporations still have a long way to go before they come close to the 5 per cent ceiling on deductible contributions provided for in the federal tax law. In the most recent years for which data are available, contributions have been just over 1 per cent of taxable income — whether they will ever reach 5 per cent is certainly an open question.

The Corporation and the Arts

Health and welfare have been the traditional "safe" areas for corporate support, and just as individuals can be said to have specialized in religious giving, corporate gifts have until recently been directed primarily to recipients of the community chest variety. However, while the attractiveness to the corporation of such gifts remains strong, in 1962 corporate gifts to education surpassed them for the first time in total amount received, though not in number of contributions.[4] There was little business aid to education before 1948, but the pressing needs of the nation's educational institutions, the effective presentation of their case and the corporation's obvious interest in their effectiveness led to an in-

[3] *Corporate Contributions Report,* 3rd ed., March 1965.

[4] National Industrial Conference Board, wall chart No. 250, 1961, and John H. Watson, III, "Report on Company Contributions for 1962," *Business Management Record,* October 1963, p. 25.

crease in the allocation of corporate gifts to educational institutions from 14 per cent of the total in 1947 to 42 per cent in 1962.

In the aggregate, the arts have received very little corporate support. The available data (Appendix Table XIV–B) indicate that civic and cultural activities together received 5.3 per cent of corporate giving in 1962, and this category clearly includes considerably more than the performing arts alone. Estimates of the portion going to the performing arts range from about 3 to 4 per cent[5] of the total of $580 million given by the corporations in 1964 — somewhere between $17 and $23 million, with the lower of these figures the more plausible. Roughly half of the nation's large corporations give something to the arts, but most of them give very little; about half of those contributing allocate less than 1 per cent of their total donations to this purpose.[6] Some companies do give more — two companies are reported to have devoted at least 50 per cent of their contributions to the arts, and grants up to 10 per cent of the total are somewhat less rare.

Several arts organizations have managed to derive a significant portion of their support from corporate sources. The United Arts Fund of Cincinnati in 1963 received 46 per cent of its funds from company or corporate gifts and another 16 per cent from money collected at the place of business from executives and employees. In 1959–60 at least 10 of the nation's leading orchestras received 20 to 60 per cent of their support from business sources.[7] Several cultural centers have also benefited from sizable business gifts.

Stimulation of Corporate Support

There are various levels on which management's interest in the support of the arts can be aroused. In some cases gifts have brought valuable publicity to the firms, as when the American Export Isbrandtsen Lines financed a new production of "Aida" at the Metropolitan Opera. Similarly, the Standard Oil Company of New

[5] See "Performing Arts Find an 'Angel' in Business," *Business Week,* March 13, 1965.

[6] Rockefeller Panel Report, p. 83, and *Corporate Contributions Report,* March 1965.

[7] Stoddard, pp. 34–35.

Jersey has financed a televised drama series utilizing several leading regional theater companies. And the Schlitz beer company
sponsored the New York Philharmonic's free open-air performances
in the summer of 1965, attracting as many as 70,000 people at
one concert — surely a successful advertising venture as well as a
source of revenue for the arts.

Other and somewhat more indirect arguments are advanced for
business support, all of which can be viewed either as Philistinism
or as manifestations of enlightened self-interest, depending on
one's point of view. For example, it is often asserted that the availability of performance in an area makes it easier for a company to
hire skilled employees and that, therefore, the arts can help attract
new firms. Robert Durland, president of Cain's Coffee Company
and president of the Oklahoma City Mummers Theatre, states:

> We're interested in attracting new business. Many of the firms
> we've brought in are more sophisticated industries, dealing, for
> instance, with space technology. . . . If you have a fine theater and
> a fine symphony it certainly is something a major industry will look
> at in choosing a new site.[8]

There is also evidence that other industries and services derive
some prosperity from the arts. Data obtained in our audience survey support this view. The respondents' reports on expenses other
than ticket purchases involved in attending a performance certainly indicate the economic significance of the arts for restaurants,
garages, and so on. Wunderlich tells of a company handling electric
advertising signs which estimated that if the legitimate theater
were to vanish from the New York scene, Times Square's advertising space would not be worth more than $0.25 on each dollar of its
present value. Wunderlich also cites figures on the economic effects
of the ten day Broadway blackout brought about by the Equity strike
at the beginning of the 1960–61 season. Restaurateurs estimated
that this blackout cost them $5 million. Eighty-nine ticket agencies
lost $250,000. More than $1 million was lost by garages. Cab driv-
ers lost $500,000. Hotel reservations declined 5 per cent.

Some business firms do, of course, also contribute in cases
where they have no other interest than participation in a worthy
undertaking. Perhaps the arts, following the proved and successful

[8] *Wall Street Journal*, March 19, 1964, p. 1.

precedent of education, could increase the number of firms which do so by forming an organization that would present their case more effectively. There is also evidence that the united campaign approach is attractive to business and this might well be used more frequently by established arts organizations in their appeals for business support. These approaches, together with a well-defined program, systematic budgeting procedures permitting reasonable estimates of need, and more extensive use of standard accounting and administrative procedures, might well increase the attractiveness of the performing arts to corporations.[9]

But some of these suggestions can only be implemented at a heavy cost. Aside from the administrative and other cash outlays which such a program would require, it might impose very real losses of freedom and effectiveness, especially on the younger and less established groups. Adherence to "sound business practices" has been known to exert a stultifying influence, ending the organizational informality that is sometimes inseparably associated with creativity and experimentation, a price which many groups might with good reason be unwilling to pay.

Labor Unions as Supporters of the Arts[10]

Though unions are often mentioned as potential supporters of the performing arts, the fact is that at present they rarely provide

[9] In determining which companies to approach, it is useful to recognize differences in giving propensities among different corporations. On the basis of figures provided by the National Industrial Conference Board, it would appear that smaller industrial corporations (those with less than $20 million in assets) which are locally owned and operated are relatively the most generous. Industrial companies gave 0.9 per cent of pre-tax income for all philanthropic purposes, while service industries gave only 0.5 per cent. Local companies gave more generously than national concerns.

Companies with over 10,000 employees devoted 4.5 per cent of their giving to "civic and cultural causes" (as defined in Appendix Table XIV–B), those with 5,000 to 9,999 employees gave 7.5 per cent and those with 500 to 999 employees gave 12 per cent for this purpose. Companies with foundations devote a larger proportion (5.7 per cent) of their giving to civic and cultural causes than do those without foundations (4.9 per cent), and so they too may be better candidates for solicitation by the arts. These figures are taken from John H. Watson, III, "Report on Company Contributions for 1962," *Business Management Record*, October 1963, pp. 24–33.

[10] Most of the materials in this section are taken from "Role of Labor in Support of the Performing Arts," an unpublished paper written by A. H. Raskin for the Rockefeller Brothers Panel.

any significant assistance. The main reason is easy enough to identify. The very low proportion of blue collar workers in the audiences that was revealed by our audience surveys shows why the unions have no mandate to make that sort of contribution. Their memberships, by and large, are just not interested. In fact, it has been alleged that the arts are sometimes considered by the union member to be the private domain of "high society," in which he has no interest and for which he may even have a positive aversion. The wide publicity given the ostentatious social activities associated with the openings of symphonic and operatic seasons are no help in this respect.

There have been a few noteworthy exceptions to the general lack of patronage by the labor unions. The AFL-CIO made sizable contributions to the National Cultural Center in response to direct pleas by President Kennedy, and unions in New York also bought quantities of Lincoln Center bonds. A number of union leaders took an active role in these undertakings. The International Ladies' Garment Workers Union, the Amalgamated Clothing Workers of America and other "needle trades" unions have a long history of interest in the arts, perhaps ascribable to the unusual ethnic composition of their membership.

The unions directly involved in the arts have been helpful, particularly in lobbying for governmental subsidies. Occasionally unions have supported performances through block ticket purchases and theater "benefits." But the prospects for large-scale union support for the performing arts are not very bright — certainly not as long as union members remain so small a proportion of the audience.

Universities as Patrons of the Arts

Universities are not patrons of the arts in the obvious sense. That is, rarely if ever do they make direct grants to performing organizations — they have trouble enough raising the money they need for themselves. Yet they are playing an increasingly important role, and that role is likely to expand in the future.[11] Universities have assisted the arts in various ways. They have helped to stimu-

[11] On the role of the universities, see W. McNeil Lowry and Rockefeller Brothers Panel Report, Chapter 9.

late interest in performance as part of the educational process. They provide a source of livelihood to composers, choreographers, writers and other creative and performing artists. They sometimes offer professional training for artists, they act as impressarios for visiting arts groups, and increasingly they are serving as homes for resident professional performing organizations.

For present purposes, two of these roles of the university are of prime importance: its functions as impressario and as home-base for resident companies. Almost all universities now bring professional music, dance and other performances to students, faculty members and local residents. This is often a no-profit, no-loss operation, with expenses covered in advance by the sale of subscriptions. Outside the major cities, the richest and most varied programs of performance and the best auditoriums are available in college and university communities. The college circuit has become a mainstay of all types of performing activity. Though university audiences generally are more conservative than is sometimes supposed, many chamber groups, performers of contemporary music and modern dance companies say they have survived only because of the interest of college and university audiences.

Universities are now increasingly sponsoring resident professional acting companies. Such groups perform at the University of California at Los Angeles, Princeton University and the University of Michigan. Several chamber groups, including some of the most noted, are in residence at college and university campuses.

Ideally, it is hoped that this sort of sponsorship will encourage higher standards of performance by allowing more rehearsal time and by reducing day-to-day financial pressures. A greater degree of experimentation is also looked for on the campuses for similar reasons. These hopes are often disappointed. Educational institutions cannot provide unlimited amounts of financing, and they too must resort to imposition of economies on the performing groups. They may also favor performances with sufficient box office appeal to keep operating deficits to a minimum. Thus, it is reported that contemporary and experimental plays are rarely performed by resident theatrical companies.[12]

Yet, in the long run, the solution to many of the financial prob-

[12] Levy, p. 75.

lems of the living arts may have to come through the colleges and universities. If the arts are unable to raise enough money on their own, as their financial gaps continue to increase they may have to turn even more to the colleges as fund raising agencies that can perhaps obtain for them the financing required for their survival. Lowry quotes Herman B Wells, former President of Indiana University, as having said that in our generation educational institutions have taken over the role of sponsorship for the arts that was once played by the German princeling. It is even possible that the university-sponsored performing group will be the pattern of the future.

The Foundations

The foundations, all told, gave in 1964 a total of approximately $850 million, or about 6 per cent of total private philanthropy. However, as in the case of the corporations, it is the trend in foundation giving rather than its current level which is most significant.

In the United States large-scale foundation activity dates from World War II or even from the mid-1950's.[13] Because the foundations are not taxed, figures on foundation giving cannot be as accurate or detailed as those for individual and corporate philanthropy. But we do have some estimates, which are summarized in Appendix Table XIV–C.[14]

In 1944 there were about 500 foundations in the United States having endowments of at least $50,000 each. Their assets totaled $1.8 billion, and their grants in that year amounted to $72 million.[15] Seventeen years later, a listing that included only foundations which either had assets exceeding $100,000 or made grants of no less than $10,000 reported 6,007 such foundations. Their total assets exceeded $14.5 billion and their grants amounted to $779 million.[16] All told, in 1964 some 24,000 organizations of the founda-

[13] For a brief history of foundation activity, see F. Emerson Andrews, *Philanthropic Giving*, Russell Sage Foundation, New York, 1950, p. 37 ff.

[14] From 1964 on, much better data will become available because of new Internal Revenue Service filing requirements. Foundations now must complete Forms 990–A and 1041–A, and the Foundation Library Center is tabulating the data provided.

[15] Andrews, *Philanthropic Giving*, pp. 91–93.

[16] Foundation Library Center, Annual Report, 1964, p. 10.

tion variety were known to exist, 16,000 of which were presumed to qualify as active United States foundations. The number of such institutions is currently increasing by about 1,500 a year, most of them small family ventures.[17]

Still another indication of the very rapid rate of growth of foundations is the estimate by the Foundation Library Center that two thirds of the assets of the 50 largest foundations are traceable to bequests received since 1939, and one third of this amount was obtained in the 1950's. These top 50 foundations hold title to more than half of all foundation assets.[18]

Foundations and the Arts

Foundations come in all sizes and varieties, ranging from the Ford Foundation with its annual grants of more than $200 million and assets of about $4 billion to small family foundations with assets of a few thousand dollars. The small foundations are, of course, the most numerous. In fact, it has been claimed that less than 1 per cent of the nation's foundations employ any full-time professional staff.[19] The range of activities of foundations varies from the entire sweep of philanthropy to the narrow interests of an individual donor. Hence, their giving patterns vary widely, and the picture one obtains of the distribution of their grants depends on the nature of the sample considered. One gets very different results if one examines only the records of the very large organizations or only the smaller family and company foundations.

Nevertheless, several clear patterns stand out. Education, which obtains between 25 and 50 per cent of the total, is the largest recipient of foundation giving (Appendix Table XIV–D). In fact, a distribution by broad categories considerably understates education's share of the foundation dollar since much of the money which apparently goes for other purposes (for example, the study of international affairs and the sciences) flows through educational institutions. Religion and the community chests (welfare activi-

[17] *Ibid.,* p. 7.

[18] *Ibid.,* p. 14.

[19] This is reported in "Foundation Support for the Performing Arts," an unpublished paper prepared for the Rockefeller Brothers Panel by Marilyn Shapiro.

ties) get small shares of foundation funds compared with their shares of other types of giving, though both seem recently to have been getting increasing amounts from this source. Foundations have given a far greater proportion of their grants to work in international affairs, science and the humanities (including the performing arts) than is the case with other types of private philanthropy. In recent years about 4 to 7 per cent of foundation grants have generally been devoted to the humanities. The only exception was in 1963, when nearly half ($20.2 million) of foundation grants to the humanities went to Lincoln Center. A drop in the Lincoln Center grants to $3.8 million in 1964 more than accounted for the apparent decline in outlays on the humanities between the two years.

Table XIV–1 shows in greater detail how the performing arts have fared in terms of foundation support.[20] As this table makes clear, in 1963 and 1964 the performing arts were the main beneficiary in the humanities category. Much of this support, however, is composed of what are essentially non-recurring grants, such as the Ford Foundation's $17.5 million grant to cultural centers in 1963 and its $8 million grant to the dance in 1964. The table does not include a grant of $85 million to orchestras announced by the Ford Foundation during 1965 but paid out later, and that is why the amount given to the performing arts in 1965 seems to have fallen below the 1963 and 1964 figures. It is also noteworthy that in 1963, a year for which we have data on the number of foundations making grants in each category, only 35 foundations gave grants of $10,000 or more to the performing arts (including music), and out of the roughly 6,000 foundations of substantial size at present in existence, only 65 made any grants of this amount to the humanities.[21]

Looked at the other way, foundations have played a crucial role

[20] Thanks to the careful work of the Foundation Library Center, our data on foundation support of the performing arts are probably more reliable than corresponding data for any other source of private support.

[21] Since many grants to the arts are under $10,000 or take the form of recurring support that is not included, this comparison probably overstates the disparity. Moreover, some grants were probably overlooked in the tabulation, as before 1964 no systematic method was available for the collection of these figures.

TABLE XIV-1

Grants of $10,000 and Over for the Humanities Reported to the Foundation Library Center in Recent Years[a]

Category	1962			1963				1964			1965[c]		
	No. of Grants	Amount (thousands)	Per Cent	No. of Fdns.	No. of Grants	Amount (thousands)	Per Cent	No. of Grants	Amount (thousands)	Per Cent	No. of Grants	Amount (thousands)	Per Cent
Performing Arts	12	$ 1,411	9	19	27	$33,606	70	63	$13,680	35	73	$ 6,490	17
Music	31	2,544	16	16	31	2,437	5	60	6,557	17	98	4,356	11
Total Live Arts	43	$ 3,955	25	35	58	$36,043	75	123	$20,237	52	171	$10,846	28
Art and Architecture	27	1,900	12	14	29	5,584	12	51	6,801	17	82	6,713	17
Museums	22	5,862	37	10	24	2,197	5	54	4,323	11	105	11,019	28
History	14	397	3	13	29	1,122	2	65	3,976	10	60	4,081	11
Language and Literature	13	2,905	19	8	17	2,107	5	23	1,139	3	15	1,836	5
Philosophy	1	10	0	2	2	57	0	3	60	0	5	380	1
General	3	623	4	2	5	642	1	13	2,876	7	64	3,944	10
Total	123	$15,652	100	65[b]	164	$47,752	100	332	$39,412	100	502	$38,819	100

SOURCE: Foundation Library Center Annual Reports, 1962, 1963, 1964, 1965. Grants were not always paid out in full in the year in which they were announced.

[a] Includes only foundation grants made directly to the humanities. The very substantial amounts indirectly supporting humanities are excluded — for example, the millions of dollars spent by the Ford Foundation under its "special university and special college programs" and under its program in "international training and research."

[b] Some foundations gave to more than one field; this is the non-duplicating total.

[c] Does not include the $85 million Ford Foundation grant to orchestras which was announced in 1965 but not distributed that year.

341

for a number of particular performing organizations. Indeed, without foundation support some groups would not have survived. A number of dance groups, including Martha Graham's, have relied heavily on foundation support, and so have many regional theaters. The performance of new operas in the United States might virtually have disappeared without foundation support. Yet the foundations provide only a relatively small proportion of the money that is given to the performing arts, and this situation is unlikely to change substantially in the foreseeable future.

The Ford Foundation with its huge assets has, of course, been the largest single supporter of the arts in recent years. A breakdown of grants to the performing arts between September 1960 and March 1963 showed that the Ford and the Rockefeller Foundations gave 35 per cent or $10 million out of a total of $28 million, and that over $7 million of this amount came from the Ford Foundation alone.[22] Four other foundations — the Avalon Foundation, the A. W. Mellon Educational and Charitable Trust, the E. and A. E. Mayer Foundation and the Old Dominion Foundation — together contributed another 10 per cent of the total. The bulk of the remaining 55 per cent that was contributed by other foundations went for construction of art centers, which were often associated with universities. Though several smaller foundations have done a great deal for particular organizations and art forms (for example, the B. de Rothschild Foundation and the Rebekah Harkness Foundation in the case of the dance), most of the foundation money going to particular organizations has come from these few very large institutions.

The Role of the Ford Foundation

Because the Ford Foundation has been the most important single contributor in recent years and is likely to continue in the lead, and because of the interesting characteristics of many of its arts support programs, its activities merit more detailed discussion. The Ford Foundation was established in 1936 as a family foundation to administer the philanthropic work of individual members of the

[22] See Shapiro.

Ford family. In 1950 its assets were multiplied by bequests from Henry and Edsel Ford. The Ford Foundation's program in the performing arts began in 1957, and since then it has devoted an average of about 4 per cent of its grants to this area.

The distribution of the Ford Foundation's grants between 1957 and 1964 is summarized in Appendix Table XIV–E and shown in detail in Appendix Table XIV–F. Over this period, $30 million was given to Lincoln Center and the National Cultural Center, and approximately $30 million more was allocated to other purposes, mainly to theater ($8.6 million, with a $6.1 million grant to nine resident theater groups in 1962), the dance ($8 million, with most of this going to the New York City Ballet and various other ballet groups in 1964), and opera ($6.2 million, of which about a million was given to the City Center Opera for the performance of contemporary works and $3.1 million to the Metropolitan Opera in 1963). The recently announced grant of $85 million to orchestras, which dwarfs all previous grants to the arts, certainly makes up for the limited support given to orchestras by the Foundation prior to 1965.

These grants have had several noteworthy characteristics. In many cases they have been made conditional upon the acquisition of matching sums from other donors by the beneficiary. Often they have been given to finance experimental ventures and types of performance which would otherwise not have been available. Examples are the contemporary opera performance program, designed to support the hiring of young singers, and a plan to encourage young playwrights and potential playwrights. As a corollary, the Ford grants have generally not undertaken to provide help to organizations in meeting their day-to-day financial needs, a fact which is often overlooked by other potential donors and by the general public. (The grant to orchestras is an important exception to this general characteristic.)

We conclude this chapter with a few somewhat general comments on the role of foundations in supporting the performing arts. It is plain that they have a special role to play. Because the large foundations can act with deliberation and can base their decisions about grants on an adequate program of preliminary research, they can undertake non-routine types of support which are nevertheless of critical importance.

As we have said, there are kinds of activities which are crucial for the future of the performing arts but which the individual organizations cannot afford to finance. One outstanding example is the contemporary and experimental work, whose performance may be financially disastrous for the individual organization and whose disappearance could drain the arts of their vitality. Another example is the special program designed to introduce young audiences to the performing arts in general. Viewed from the standpoint of immediate self-interest, funds devoted to this sort of future audience development are likely to be a poor investment for an individual performing organization. Yet this may be a most promising use of funds for a foundation whose activities are national in scope.

The foundations have undertaken a number of programs designed to meet just such needs, and criticism of them because of this emphasis seem to us to be unjustified. If there is a legitimate complaint about the handling of this type of grant, it is that inadequate publicity has sometimes been given to the restrictions placed upon their use. Recipients sometimes regard such a grant as a mixed blessing because it commits them to a new activity whose costs are not always fully covered, and former patrons of the organization, on hearing of it, sometimes reduce their own contributions in the mistaken belief that the organization's over-all financial needs are now less pressing.

The matching grant proviso has sometimes proved an effective countermeasure. In an interview, W. McNeil Lowry of the Ford Foundation emphasized that the Foundation has been very anxious to avoid use of its grants to supplant funds which would otherwise be given. In many cases, therefore, Ford grants have been made contingent upon the collection of matching funds by the group, and he could not recall a single case in which the potential recipient had failed to raise the money.

It is plausible that the amount of foundation money going to the arts will increase in the future. The example of Ford and the other large foundations can serve as a powerful motive force. And as federal funds increasingly become available to health and education, one may expect some "freeing" of foundation funds now devoted to these areas. Moreover, the increasing efforts devoted to publicizing the financial problems of the arts should also help to attract wider foundation interest, particularly among local foundations, which are perhaps best suited to support the activities of particular performing organizations.

Several reasons have been suggested to explain the limited interest shown in the performing arts up to this point by the bulk of the smaller foundations. Many of the arguments are the same as those discussed in the case of corporate contributions. For example, there is the view that one of the main handicaps of many performing organizations is their relatively unbusinesslike organization and administration, a shortcoming which is said to have made it difficult to direct foundation funds to the modern dance companies.

A special problem colors much of foundation giving to the arts. This arises out of the basic principle to which many foundations are committed — an emphasis on "seed money," on providing funds that will nurture an innovative activity through the period of its infancy, after which it can be left to fend for itself. Though the exceptions are growing, many a foundation grant is given for three to five years and then renewed only once. This procedure is said to have spawned promising activities in other fields and then let them die before they could accomplish anything significant. In the performing arts these reservations have particular force. If our basic analysis is correct, the financial problems of performing organizations never wither away — they cannot be expected to assume manageable proportions even over a long period. On the contrary, as an organization reaches a stage of administrative stability and becomes a mature and well-established enterprise, its income gap may well grow all the more rapidly. The very rapid rates of growth of the gaps of the Metropolitan Opera and the New York Philharmonic, which were described in Chapter XII, should leave no doubt on this point.

Support of the arts then requires long-term commitments, not stopgap attempts to provide temporary stimuli. Surely we have learned something since 1720, when that early foundation, the Royal Academy of Music, undertook to support opera in London "till Musick takes such Root, as to Subsist with less aid"; for as we saw, even then, "instead of less support, it constantly needed more."[23]

[23] Avery, p. lxi.

CHAPTER XV

Government Support in Practice

Having examined the financial support provided the arts by private sources, we come now to the subject of government assistance. We shall deal in this chapter with the facts of the matter, leaving to the next chapter a discussion of the principles involved.

Municipal Support

Unfortunately, there is no up-to-date, comprehensive set of figures on the amounts spent on the performing arts by the nation's municipalities. The most comprehensive source available is a Library of Congress survey of 46 cities for 1958–59.[1] This survey reports expenditures for performing arts purposes by 17 cities totaling $858,000. (See Appendix Table XV–A.) That amount is certainly negligible in comparison with the funds derived from the major sources of private support, and even in comparison with the same cities' outlay of $9 million on museums, which was also reported in the survey. Even so, it probably overstates the amount of direct municipal contributions since it includes grants for services and various other expenditures somewhat indirectly related to the performing arts.[2]

---

[1] House Hearings, I, pp. 316–21. An unpublished Rockefeller Brothers Fund survey of 47 municipalities in 1963 by John H. MacFadyen and Alan L. Campbell is also illuminating, but is not very helpful for our present purposes since it made no attempt to cover a representative sample.

[2] To a certain extent this is true also of corporation, foundation and even individual gifts, which are sometimes granted with a stipulation that arts organizations mount a new production or put on a certain number of free concerts.

Fairly complete information on city and county support in 1963–64 for major and metropolitan orchestras is available from the American Symphony Orchestra League's Annual Reports. In all, 17 major orchestras received more than a million dollars in that period, of which $966,000 came from city and county governments and $90,000 from Boards of Education. Eleven metropolitan orchestras reported grants totaling $215,000, including $201,000 from city and county governments and $14,000 from Boards of Education. Grants for which no services were required accounted for somewhat less than half of these amounts.

Spotty information can be obtained for other art forms, but no comprehensive picture.[3] However, on the basis of the list of recipients of municipal assistance in 1958–59, as reported to the Library of Congress, it seems plausible that orchestras received at least half of all municipal grants to performing arts organizations in that period. If, then, we double the orchestra figures just cited for 1963–64, we arrive at an over-all estimate of annual local government grants to the performing arts of about $2.5 million. This is a very rough estimate, of course, and it is, if anything, likely to be on the high side.[4] Unrestricted grants which do not require that services be performed amount almost certainly to less than $1 million a year.

Municipalities also assist arts groups in ways not involving direct grants — for example, by permitting them free, or virtually free, use of municipal auditoriums or by providing free lighting at concerts. In principle, a sum equivalent to the value of all these services should be added to the estimates of direct grants, but we have no way of making even a wild guess at the order of magnitude involved.

While some cities subsidize performing arts organizations, the same or other cities subject them to burdensome taxes. And while many performing arts groups are legally classed as non-profit or-

[3] For example, we know that at least 4 of the 23 repertory theaters surveyed by Sandra Schmidt received some local government support.

[4] It seems very unlikely that even the inclusion of county grants and updating to 1964 would raise the $858,000 Library of Congress figure of total municipal grants relating directly to performing arts activities to a figure in excess of $2 million.

ganizations, and so are exempt from most taxes, it must be remembered that the commercial theater audience accounts for a substantial proportion of the total audience of the arts. In New York City, theater operators pay license fees for their signs and their air conditioning, and a gross receipts tax of one half of one per cent is levied on all industry including the commercial theater. Though a 5 per cent city tax on theater tickets was eliminated in 1961, only a year later a 5 per cent occupancy tax was imposed. Theaters have recently been permitted to operate bars for very limited hours, but they are required to pay $1,700 annually for their liquor licenses although a tavern's license fee is only $1,500. In Minneapolis the Tyrone Guthrie Theater is still (1966) fighting through the courts an attempt by municipal authorities to impose a real estate tax of about $75,000 a year. And in New Hope, Pennsylvania, the producer of the Bucks County Playhouse told us that he paid a 4 per cent local tax on every ticket he sold.

The idea of municipal support for the performing arts is fairly new. While aid to museums has a long tradition and is now widely accepted, aid to performance seems to date back only to the 1920's when a few orchestras were provided assistance by their cities. Other art forms apparently received little if any such help until World War II. The principle that aid to the performing arts is a legitimate expenditure because the arts provide cultural and economic benefits to the communities which they serve now seems to be gaining rather wide acceptance among municipalities, and one has the impression that the magnitude of these expenditures has been increasing. Nevertheless, we suspect that the long-run outlook for municipal support is not bright, and that continued municipal taxation is a more likely prospect. The reason is that our cities are beset by exactly the same kinds of financial pressures which affect the performing arts. Municipal services such as education and police protection operate under productivity handicaps similar to those which cause costs in the arts to soar. At the same time, the municipalities are severely constrained in raising taxes generally, for tax increases are unpalatable politically, and, in any event, they may merely drive business and wealthier residents from the cities, thus ultimately reducing the tax base. Performing arts organizations, however, are rarely in a position to offer vigorous resistance to tax increases. In such circumstances it is hard to believe that urban governments will be able to resist the temptation to tax performing groups (particularly the commercial theaters), let alone add significantly to the funds they already provide to performing organizations.

This prognosis may turn out to be unduly gloomy if there should be a change in fiscal relationships among the federal, state and local governments. In recent years there have been a number of proposals aimed at sharing federally collected tax receipts with state and local governments to help them meet local needs more adequately. If some such scheme were adopted, the outlook for increased local government support of the performing arts would be much brighter. Counties, too, have been providing some support for the arts, and at least a few have taken over part of the financial burdens which cities formerly shouldered. Suburban growth may have provided sufficient tax revenues to enable counties to give increased assistance to the arts, while making such assistance harder for cities.

Support by the States

Data on state support for the performing arts are provided by the same source from which we obtained information on municipal aid. The Library of Congress surveyed all 50 states and received replies from 47 as to their assistance to the arts in 1958–59.[5] Of these, 34 gave no support, 10 offered clear-cut assistance and 3 were borderline cases (Appendix Table XV–B).

Aside from New York State with its half million dollar budget for the arts in 1963, most state budgets for this purpose are exceedingly small. In total the sums derived from state governments in 1959 amount to roughly $255,000, according to the Library of Congress survey. And, even making a substantial allowance for increases in support since 1959, it seems likely that direct state ex-

[5] The unpublished 1963 survey for the Rockefeller Brothers Fund mentioned in footnote 1 investigated activities in eight states in considerable detail, but there is no evidence that these eight states constitute a representative cross-section.

penditures on the performing arts still amount to considerably less than a million dollars.[6]

Aside from permitting taxpayers to deduct contributions to nonprofit organizations in computing state income taxes, support for the arts by the states takes two main forms: direct appropriations to specific projects, which is the most common approach, and appropriations through an arts council, New York State being the prime example of this latter approach.

Arts councils seem to be coming increasingly into fashion. The New York State Council on the Arts, organized in 1960, was the first state organization explicitly referred to as a "council," the first to concern itself with all the arts and the first to receive substantial public funds. According to Ralph Burgard, Executive Director of the Arts Councils of America, while only one state arts council existed in 1955, and only 2 in 1960, by 1965 a total of 38 such agencies had been created. Burgard suggests that within a few years each state will have either an arts council or an advisory body on the arts. A number of states which might not have considered forming a state arts council will now move in that direction in order to qualify for federal funds from the National Endowment for the Arts.

State arts councils can serve several purposes: they can coordinate arts activities in the state and in the region; they can serve as a united public voice for the arts; and they can work as an administrative agency supervising the expenditure of funds provided by the state. Some of the financial aspects of the work of the New York State Arts Council are described in Table XV–1. The most interesting point to be gleaned from these figures is the evidence that community support can be stimulated in this way: the amount the Arts Council has allocated to the support of tours declined from $330,000 in 1961–62 to $153,000 in 1964–65, yet in that time the number of touring performances has tripled.

---

[6] The climate of opinion in several states is suggested by the fact that as late as 1963 some of them had laws prohibiting direct support to the arts by municipalities and counties, at least without specific enabling legislation. (See MacFadyen and Campbell, "State and Local Government Support for the Performing Arts," p. 2.)

TABLE XV–1

New York State Council on the Arts: Support of the Performing Arts
Touring Program, 1962–1965

Year	Support of the Program	No. of Touring Perform- ances	Support Per Perform- ance	No. of Commu- nities Visited	No. of Touring Com- panies
1961–62	$330,000	92	$3,587	46	6
1962–63	264,500	107	2,472	53	9
1963–64	166,800	224	745	88	51
1964–65	153,300	277	553	92	71

SOURCE: Basic figures from the 1965 Annual Report of the New York State
Council on the Arts.

There have been a few complaints. Some of the smaller performing groups have objected to the paperwork required to obtain Arts
Council support, though our own examination of the forms utilized
by the New York Arts Council suggests that they are easy to fill
out and that the effort required of the applicant for funds could
hardly be reduced further. Another objection, which seems to have
more validity, involves problems that are probably beyond the
Council's control. Some experimental performing groups indicated
that, at least initially, the demand for their services had declined
as subsidies by the Council became available. It was suggested that
communities which had formerly sponsored their appearances felt
they could now afford the somewhat more expensive and more
conventional type of performance which they had undoubtedly preferred all along but which was previously beyond their means.
Nevertheless, reactions to the work of the New York State Council
seem to be strongly and predominantly enthusiastic, and suggest
that similar operations in other states would generally receive approbation.

To summarize, over-all support from most state governments is
still very small, undoubtedly smaller than the amount provided by
municipalities. But the principle of state support is rapidly gaining
acceptance, and one can predict with a fair degree of confidence
that funds from this source will increase in the future.

Federal Tax Exemptions

The main federal contribution to the performing arts comes indirectly, through various tax exemption provisions. The most obvious of these is the basic exemption of non-profit organizations from the corporate income tax. Since so many performing organizations operate at a deficit, savings as a result of this exemption probably do not amount to very much, but at least the arrangement simplifies their existence.

More important are the deduction provisions of the federal personal and corporate income tax laws mentioned in Chapter XIII. The question of deductible contributions first arose in 1913 when the initial income tax law was passed. It became an important issue in 1917 when taxes were raised because of the war. Many persons expressed the fear that higher taxes would make serious inroads into private philanthropy, and so a 15 per cent deduction for philanthropic contributions was permitted, a limit which was raised in 1952.[7] The issue arose again after the United States entered World War II, when a proposal to extend the standard deduction to tens of millions of taxpayers was viewed by many as a threat to the survival of non-profit activities. Obviously a person taking the standard deduction has no tax incentive to make charitable contributions. This time, however, Congress seemed to be of the opinion that giving is not heavily influenced by tax laws, and so no change in the deduction provisions was instituted.

In 1954 the limit on deductions was raised from the maximum of 20 per cent of adjusted gross income to a new ceiling of 30 per cent, which applied only if the additional 10 per cent went to churches, educational institutions or hospitals.[8] In 1964 the availability of the full 30 per cent was extended to many other non-profit groups including publicly supported arts organizations.[9]

---

[7] On the history of this legislation, see C. Harry Kahn, *Personal Deductions in the Federal Income Tax*, National Bureau of Economic Research, Princeton University Press, Princeton, N. J., 1960, pp. 13, 46–47.

[8] Kahn, p. 11.

[9] This 1964 amendment is not as significant for the arts as is sometimes suggested. It applies only to those donors who give more than 20 per cent of their adjusted gross income *to the arts alone*, and this must be a tiny group as most large givers probably contribute to many causes. The 1954 amendment

How much revenue does the government forego in permitting these tax exemptions? We estimate that the tax cost to the federal government of the deductions allowed for gifts to the performing arts in 1962 amounted to about $30 to $35 million.[10]

The uncollected-tax cost to the federal government is, however, a poor measure of the economic significance of tax deductions to performing organizations. The important question is to what extent private giving is stimulated by these provisions of the law. If individuals and corporations were to give the same amount in the absence of any deduction provisions, then the provisions could not be said to represent any government assistance to the arts, whatever the tax cost.

This is a very difficult problem to treat statistically since (a) the effectiveness of any set of deduction provisions can be expected to vary with the level of tax rates, and (b) in any event, our success in measuring the effect on private giving depends on our ability to estimate what private giving would have been in the absence of deduction allowances.

One way we can begin to look at the effectiveness of a deduction provision in stimulating gifts is to see how many persons took advantage of it. We find in examining the facts that only 1.1 per cent of the 25 million individual income tax returns submitted for the year 1962 reported contributions involving deductions of 20 per cent or more of adjusted gross income. But 9.5 per cent of the $7.5 billion in total deductions was accounted for by this small group of taxpayers.[11] This implies that a further increase in the permitted

already permitted anyone who gave 10 per cent of his adjusted gross income to education or any other of the accepted class of recipients to deduct another 20 per cent if he gave it to the arts.

[10] This is based on the assumption that corporations contributed roughly $20 million to the performing arts and that individuals gave roughly $75 million. The estimate for corporations is probably fairly accurate (see Chapter XIV). However, as was emphasized at the end of Chapter XIII, the figure on individual giving involves a considerable amount of guesswork. In any event, $75 million may be a bit on the high side in terms of the range of our estimate. In translating these estimates of giving into estimates of tax costs, we followed the general procedures designed by Kahn (pp. 56–58) and assumed that 50 per cent of each corporate gift dollar and 30 per cent of each individual gift dollar would otherwise have gone into taxes.

[11] U.S. Treasury Department, Internal Revenue Service, *Statistics of Income, Individual Income Tax Returns, 1962*, p. 8.

amount of deductible gifts is not likely to increase substantially the *number* of contributors, for obviously if only 1.1 per cent of all returns involve contributions greater than 20 per cent, very few persons are pressing anywhere near the current 30 per cent limit. However, the amounts involved might be considerably more substantial than the number of persons affected.

A more satisfactory approach, because it focuses on the incremental effects, is to examine contributions immediately before and after important changes in the deduction provisions. Kahn has done this,[12] and one of his important findings is that the institution of the standard deduction between 1940 and 1944 had no demonstrable effect on the share of income devoted to philanthropy. One might have thought that persons earning under $10,000 would have experienced a sharply reduced incentive for contributing, since taxpayers can take the standard deduction whether or not gifts are made. But Kahn's study, like an earlier one,[13] seems to suggest that, for lower and middle income groups at least, changes in tax rates and in deduction levels have little effect on the amount of giving.

Kahn also concludes that the increase in the limit on deductible income to 20 per cent in 1952 had little effect on over-all contributions. However, as we saw in Chapter XIII, a sharp increase in the contribution rates of the tiny fraction of taxpayers at the very top of the income scale was associated with the increases in the limits on contributions in 1952 and 1954. And the increases in contributions by this group may well have been significant for certain classes of beneficiaries, including the performing arts. Unfortunately, Kahn was unable to investigate this sub-area of philanthropy directly since the necessary data were unavailable. At any rate, his careful and workmanlike examination of the over-all effects does not suggest that further modification of the deduction provisions is likely to produce spectacular effects. There is certainly no positive evidence that much more can be accomplished for the arts in this way.

[12] Kahn, pp. 56–91.

[13] See Sydnor H. Walker, "Privately Supported Social Work," *Recent Social Trends in the United States* (Report of the President's Research Committee on Social Trends), Vol. II, New York, 1933, p. 1219.

It has been widely argued that the tax deduction is a questionable way for the government to encourage philanthropy because under these provisions a wealthy person is given a disproportionate degree of control over the disposition of government funds. If someone in the 20 per cent bracket makes a donation, the government, in effect, supports his gift by a rebate equal to 20 per cent of the total, while when a person in the 70 per cent bracket makes a donation, the government supplies 70 per cent of the total. Most specialists in public finance prefer a device usually referred to as the *tax credit*. Under this arrangement a person is permitted simply to reduce his tax payment by the same specified proportion of his contribution regardless of his income level. On grounds of equity, the tax credit is widely considered preferable to the deduction. However, it should be recognized that since the tax credit in effect increases the giving power of the less affluent at the expense of the wealthy, such a change might very well cause a decrease in the amount of support that is channeled to the arts.

Direct Support by the Federal Government

In 1965 a bill was passed authorizing the federal government to make a direct financial contribution to the performing arts. In order to appreciate the ground-breaking nature of this legislation, it is necessary to review briefly the government's earlier activities in this field.

Until 1962 federal responsibility to the arts was confined largely to the administration of private funds supporting some 40 chamber music concerts at the Library of Congress and some concerts at the National Gallery of Art, and the State Department program that sends American performing groups abroad as a cultural exchange with other countries. Earlier, during the great depression, the United States government itself underwrote performance costs on a substantial scale. Between 1935 and 1938 the WPA music project set up and subsidized 34 symphony orchestras employing some 2,500 musicians. It also supported opera and had a program to help composers. The Federal Theater Project of the WPA came into being in 1936; it was created by executive order, and was never explicitly authorized by Congress. When it was terminated by the

House of Representatives in 1939 it had provided over 60,000 performances, at a cost of slightly over $45 million. This program brought living theater to many places where it had never been seen before, and those of us who are old enough still recall the spirit of energy and creativity which it exuded. Its destruction in a ludicrous but tragic set of hearings before the House Committee on Un-American Activities is equally memorable.[14] But the Federal Theater Project cannot be construed as evidence of an inclination on the part of the government to inaugurate a program of support to the nation's arts, as it was a vehicle for the assistance of the unemployed rather than a program to help the arts as such.

In July 1954 the State Department inaugurated a cultural exchange program whose aims have broadened considerably from its initial use as a weapon of ideological warfare. In 1963–64 it sent 17 performing groups (of which perhaps 10 were professional companies) to Africa, Asia, Latin America and both Eastern and Western Europe. It has also subsidized concerts by American artists already abroad. The annual budget of this program has run at about $2½ million.[15] To more than one dance company and chamber group, the cultural exchange program has literally proved a lifesaver,[16] but several observers have commented on the irony of an arrangement which provides American funds to American groups only when they perform in other countries. Particularly curious are cases (reported to us by performing groups we interviewed) in which groups had been forced to disband, at least temporarily, because of economic pressures, and reconstituted with the aid of State Department funds so that they could be sent abroad to represent typical American cultural activity.

Since the end of World War II various pieces of legislation have been proposed in Congress to provide assistance to the arts *per se*, and in 1958 a bill was passed to permit the construction of a Na-

[14] For a fascinating history of the Federal Theater Project by its director and guiding spirit, see Hallie Flanagan's *Arena*.

[15] State Department fact sheet, Bureau of Educational and Cultural Affairs, September 1965. The figures on number of groups sent in 1963–64 were obtained from *Educational and Cultural Diplomacy — 1964*, Department of State Publication 7979, November 1965, pp. 121–22.

[16] See, for example, the testimony of Agnes De Mille in House Hearings, II, p. 187.

tional Cultural Center. However, according to Representative Frank Thompson of New Jersey, who has played an important role in efforts to bring the federal government to the aid of the arts, passage of the enabling legislation can be attributed largely to the fact that the Center was to be financed entirely by private funds.[17]

Both the Eisenhower and Kennedy administrations advocated support of the arts, and President Kennedy, not being optimistic about Congressional approval, created the President's Advisory Council on the Arts by executive order in June 1963. Because of the President's assassination this Council never functioned, never received any funds and, in fact, was never appointed. Earlier, in 1962, Kennedy had named August Heckscher to the newly created office of Special Consultant on the Arts, where he served as a temporary consultant whose primary task was the preparation of a report on the role of government in the arts. Mr. Heckscher called the task to which he was assigned "modest in scope and tentative in form," but nevertheless concluded that it marked "the beginning of a new phase in the history of art and government."[18]

During the Johnson administration the receptivity of Congress to arts legislation seems to have increased. In January 1964, legislation was passed transforming the National Cultural Center into a memorial for President Kennedy, and authorizing a $15 million federal grant for its construction. In August of 1964 Congress voted to establish the Advisory (now the National) Council on the Arts on a more permanent basis, authorizing an annual expenditure of $150,000, though only $50,000 was actually appropriated.

The federal government has also provided substantial funds to other cultural centers and other types of facility construction through its urban renewal program. The Lincoln Center, the Arena Stage in Washington, D.C. and the Charles Centre Project in Baltimore have all benefited from this activity. There has also been some indirect federal aid to the arts through educational legislation and assistance to educational television.

This is how matters stood when, in the fall of 1965, Congress

[17] Sabin, p. 16.

[18] Heckscher, p. 2.

approved a three year program providing an annual budget of $21 million for direct support of the arts and humanities. The official "Explanation of the Bill" describes as its purpose: "To develop and promote a broadly conceived national policy of support for the arts and humanities throughout the United States." It goes on to say:

> The bill establishes a National Foundation on the Arts and the Humanities, consisting of a National Endowment for the Arts, a National Endowment for the Humanities, and a Federal Council to insure coordination between the two endowments and with related Federal programs. . . .
>
> The National Endowment for the Arts provides matching grants to States, to nonprofit or public groups, and grants to individuals engaged in the creative and performing arts for the whole range of artistic activity. Where appropriate, renovation or construction of facilities are included. . . .
>
> Each Endowment is authorized $5 million for each of fiscal years, 1966, 1967, and 1968.
>
> A major objective of this legislation is to stimulate private philanthropy for cultural endeavors and State activities to benefit the arts. For these purposes an additional annual maximum of $5 million for the Humanities Endowment and $2.25 million for the Arts Endowment are authorized to match funds donated from private sources; and $2.75 million is authorized for the Arts Endowment, to enable each of the States (55 entities in all, including the District of Columbia and the territories) having a State arts agency to receive an annual grant of up to $50,000 on an even matching basis.
>
> For States without such an agency, a one-time grant of up to $25,000 (no matching requirements) would be made from these earmarked State funds. This would allow such States to conduct a survey leading to the establishment of a State agency for the arts and enable them to qualify for a $50,000 matching grant in subsequent years. State funding can begin July 1, 1966.
>
> Also for each fiscal year, 1966, 1967, and 1968, the Office of Education is authorized $500,000 for payments to State educational agencies for equipment and minor remodeling related to the arts and humanities; and for each of those fiscal years, $500,000 for training institutes to strengthen the teaching of the humanities and the arts in elementary and secondary schools.
>
> The term "the arts" includes, but is not limited to, music (instrumental and vocal), dance, drama, folk art, creative writing, architecture and allied fields, painting, sculpture, photography, graphic and craft arts, industrial design, costume and fashion design, motion pictures, television, radio, tape and sound recording, and the arts related to the presentation, performance, execution, and exhibition of such major art forms.

The 26 member National Council on the Arts, which administers the program under the chairmanship of Roger Stevens, by November 1965 had already approved projects totaling $2.7 million. Half a million dollars was set aside by the Council to found three professional theater companies to perform in cities where classical theater is currently unavailable. These companies will give free afternoon performances for students and moderately priced performances several evenings a week. One quarter of a million dollars has been allocated to help theaters outside New York produce new and experimental plays. The American Ballet Theatre received a $350,000 grant — the only established institution to receive funds in the initial allocation. Three quarters of a million dollars was set aside to support the work of individual creative artists — composers, choreographers, painters and sculptors. A $600,000 grant for a film institute, which would, among other things, train young people in the cinema arts, and $100,000 for studio facilities for painters make up most of the remainder of the initial allocation.

In view of the paucity and insignificance of federal support programs in the past, the act as written certainly represents a major break with tradition. However, the financial commitment involved — a maximum of $10 million per year for the arts — must be viewed in perspective. Ten million dollars is an annual expenditure of roughly 5 cents per capita. This is a very small sum in comparison with governmental outlays in other countries.

Support to the Arts in Other Countries

The fact that large-scale government support for the arts is common abroad has been widely publicized, but unfortunately, systematic data on this subject are unavailable.[19] Such data as do

---

[19] The most detailed set of quantitative estimates of government support abroad is provided by Munson. However, many of Munson's statistics seem to represent his own estimates rather than data taken from official sources. All of his figures seem to have been translated into dollars at the official rate of exchange. Booth and Dorian are excellent sources on the subject.

A really comprehensive set of figures is difficult to construct for a variety of reasons: one would need data on expenditures by *all* levels of government in each country; budgets often lump educational and cultural expenditures,

exist are not all very reliable, but at least they enable us to form some idea of the order of the magnitudes involved. In general the governments of all foreign countries for which we have data devote a much larger share of their expenditures to the arts than does the United States and have been providing such support for a considerable period of time.

Austria. Austrian patronage of the arts has a long history, going back at least to the construction of the opera house in Vienna by Joseph I in 1705.[20] This tradition has continued to the present and helps to account for the country's extraordinarily high level of support. Munson states that in 1961, $6.6 million was allocated to the arts by the Ministry of Education and, in addition, $5.5 million was given to the five national theaters. The nine provinces and states together contributed an additional $27.3 million, bringing the total to $39.4 million, or an average of more than $5.50 per person.

These figures undoubtedly include some outlays on museums and some expenditures by educational institutions in the arts area; even so, the amounts are very large, and though some observers have criticized the quality of the Austrian program, apparently Austria is ahead of all other countries in per capita expenditures. The support provided to the former court theaters, including the Vienna State Opera, illustrates the extent of the government's commitment to the arts: in the most recent year for which we have figures the federal government provided 70 per cent of the total cost of these theaters.[21]

Part of the Austrian government's expenditure is financed by a tax of about 5 per cent on movie tickets which brings in about $8 million a year, but a decline in movie attendance has led to proposals for a supplementary tax on television sets.[22] There already is such a tax on radio sets, with one schilling per month per set

including outlays on museums; as we have seen, government outlays on the arts often take forms such as the free use of facilities, which are difficult to quantify; and, in any event, it is not easy to find an acceptable way to translate expenditures in different currencies with different price levels into a single, readily comparable unit.

[20] On historical facts, see Dorian, pp. 9–23.

[21] Booth, p. 50.

[22] Booth, pp. 44–45.

being devoted to special cultural purposes. Of course, this sort of tax supports one art form at the expense of another.

Germany. As in Austria, government support of the arts in Germany has a very long history. Dorian tells us that by the eighteenth century over 300 courts in Germany were providing patronage to the arts.[23] Local governments provided about $112.5 million to West Germany's 135 theaters and operas in 1964, which amounts to a little less than $2.00 per person. Fifty-five of these theaters are privately owned.[24] It is reported that rising costs have caused a slight decrease in the number of private theaters despite the partial support they receive from public funds.

France. The French government also has long supported the arts, the Comédie Française having received royal recognition under Louis XIV in 1680. In 1963 the government provided $7.4 million to the five national theaters, which include the Opéra, the Opéra Comique and the Comédie Française. In addition, over $2.5 million was spent on regional theaters, ballet, orchestras, etc., making a total expenditure by the central government of about $10 million, or a little more than $.20 per inhabitant. Some funds are also contributed by municipal governments.[25]

Italy. According to Munson, about $8.5 million, an amount equal to about $.17 per capita, is assigned by the Italian national budget as a supplement to cultural expenditures made by the provinces and cities. These funds are derived from an entertainment tax of about 25 per cent on movie tickets, 10 to 15 per cent on theater tickets and a tax on radio sets.[26] A breakdown of the income of the La Scala Opera in Milan suggests that municipal support may be quite substantial. Of a total income of about $6.2 million in 1961, $1.3 million (about 21 per cent) came from box office receipts, $1.6 million (about 26 per cent) came from the national government, and the remainder, $3.3 million (about 53 per cent) was provided by the city of Milan.[27]

[23] Dorian, p. 224.

[24] See *Facts about Germany,* Press and Information Office of the Federal Government of Germany, 5th ed., 1964, and Munson, p. 22.

[25] Data supplied by the Cultural Division of the French Embassy.

[26] Munson, p. 35.

[27] Munson, p. 39.

The relatively large magnitude of continental government grants in comparison with ours is underscored by the fact that Austrian G.N.P. is less than 2 per cent of ours, and Italy, France, and West Germany have G.N.P.'s 6, 12 and 14 per cent of the American figure.[28]

Great Britain. Central government support for the performing arts is much more recent in Great Britain than in most continental countries, going back only to 1945 when the Arts Council was established, or at most to the beginning of World War II when a $50,000 grant was made to CEMA (Committee for the Encouragement of Music and Art), a private, volunteer group created in 1939 which later was transformed into the Arts Council.[29] Since 1945–46 Parliamentary grants to the Arts Council, which are shown in Table XV–2, increased markedly; between 1961 and 1965 they doubled. In 1964 the Arts Council grant amounted to a little more than $.17 per person. In 1961, when Italian national expenditures for this purpose are reported to have been at this level, Arts Council expenditures per capita were less than half this amount. It is true that in Great Britain, as in most other countries, local governments also provide support. However, while we do not know the extent of this support, we doubt very seriously that it is so great as to reverse the conclusion suggested by the size of the central government expenditures — namely, that British subsidies to the performing arts are rather low in comparison with those of a number of other European countries.[30]

Another perspective on the current magnitude of Arts Council support is provided by the right-hand side of Table XV–2, which shows annual outlays by the Ford Foundation translated into pounds sterling at the current rate of exchange. This comparison shows that in each of the past three years the Ford Founda-

[28] Calculated from *International Monetary Statistics,* September 1965, and *Statistical Abstract of the United States.* Official exchange rates were used in the comparison, though this is hardly an ideal procedure.

[29] Dorian, pp. 378–80.

[30] This is one reason why we chose Great Britain for our parallel study outside of the United States. In order to test our basic hypotheses we wanted to find a set of circumstancs which were fairly comparable with the situation in the United States; we wanted to study a country in which public subsidies were not so large as to obscure the underlying economic relationships.

TABLE XV–2

United Kingdom: Grants to the Arts Council, 1946–1965

Year	Grant (thousands)	Ford Foundation Arts Grants in U. S. (thousands)*
1945–46	£ 235	
1946–47	350	
1947–48	428	
1948–49	575	
1949–50	600	
1950–51	675ᵃ	
1951–52	875ᵇ	
1952–53	675	
1953–54	785	
1954–55	785	
1955–56	820	
1956–57	885	£ 111
1957–58	985	3,815
1958–59	1,100	156
1959–60	1,218	357
1960–61	1,500	304
1961–62	1,745	2,314
1962–63	2,190	9,429
1963–64	2,730	3,767
1964–65	3,205	

SOURCE: "Government and the Arts" (HMSO, London); 1946–1958 from 1958 issue, p. 24, and 1959–1965 from 1964 issue, p. 30.

ᵃ Includes £100,000 for Festival of Britain.

ᵇ Includes £300,000 for Festival of Britain.

* Converted to pounds sterling at the current rate of exchange.

tion has, by itself, spent more on the performing arts than has the Arts Council. Of course, in interpreting these figures one must not forget that our population is nearly four times as large as Great Britain's, and that our G.N.P. is roughly seven times as large.

The British experience with the Arts Council is quite instructive because it indicates the kinds of problems which arise when a country with no tradition of public support embarks on such a course. As might have been expected, there have been frequent complaints about the amount of support provided,[31] the lack of long-run commitments and the distribution of the available funds.

As has been the case in most other countries, the bulk of Arts Council support has usually gone to established organizations such as Covent Garden, Sadler's Wells and the National Theatre.[32] In this respect government support in most European countries has contrasted sharply with the work of some of the private foundations in the United States, which, as we have seen, have gone out of their way to help experimental efforts and have tended to avoid unrestricted grants to established organizations.

The major theme of this chapter has been the very small volume of direct government support for the arts in the United States. The relative magnitudes of direct contributions from each major source in 1964 are summarized in Table XV–3.

These figures involve a considerable element of guesswork, but the orders of magnitude are based on fairly firm information. The evidence suggests that, as of 1964, direct contributions from all levels of government amounted to no more than 4 per cent of the total support of $90 to $125 million given to the performing arts.

The grand total itself requires some explanation. It will be recalled that in Chapter VI the total income gap of the professional performing organizations was shown to be, very probably, under $25 million, and yet here we see that over $100 million seems to have been contributed to the arts in 1964. How does one account for the difference? The answer is that our income gap figure is,

[31] See, for example, Arts Council of Great Britain, 1959–60 Annual Report, p. 5, where it is pointed out that the government's grant had finally been increased to an amount equivalent to the cost of four miles of a new highway!

[32] See, for example, the Council's 1948–49 Annual Report, p. 7, which remarks, "It was agreed to concentrate on the needs of old-established companies rather than to allow. . . . limited funds to be dispersed in new directions." The concern that the old-established organizations, particularly the opera and the ballet, would swallow up all of the government's contribution to the arts is reflected in Lord Bridges' lecture: "I think it would be better to have two votes for the Arts Council . . . one vote for opera and ballet and another for all the other activities of the Council. The issue of how much money this country is prepared to spend on opera could then be squarely faced and settled without calling in question the extent and scope of the Council's other activities." (p. 20)

TABLE XV–3

Sources of Direct Contributions to the Performing Arts, 1964

Source	Approximate Amount (millions)	Per Cent of Total
Individuals[a]	$50–$75	55–61
Corporations[b]	20	21–16
Foundations[b]	20–25	21–20
Local Government[c]	2½	3– 2
State Government[d]	1	1– 1
Federal Government[e]	0	0– 0
Total	$93½–$123½	100 100

[a] See the conclusion of Chapter XIII.

[b] See Chapter XIV.

[c] See the first section of Chapter XV.

[d] See the second section of Chapter XV.

[e] Excludes over $2 million spent by the State Department to send American performing groups on overseas tours, because this is not a direct contribution and because the welfare of the performing arts is not its primary purpose.

in effect, only an operating deficit; it allows nothing for capital costs, such as the construction of new buildings. These can be very expensive. Lincoln Center alone cost some $150 million, and during 1964 funds were being collected for a number of other cultural centers. Thus, of the approximately $90 to $125 million contributed in 1964, we estimate on the basis of spotty data that between $50 million and $75 million probably went for such capital purposes. In addition, a considerable portion of what are listed as contributions cannot be classified as unrestricted gifts. Rather they consisted of payments for services rendered — special children's concerts, performances of new works and the like — and such funds did not directly help to close the income gap. Finally, some contributions went to college and university sponsored performance and some to amateur activity. Together these considerations explain why contributions were some four to six times larger than the total income gap and also show more clearly just how the gap is to be interpreted.

While at all levels — municipal, state and national — the volume of direct government assistance has been extremely small, aid from the municipalities has been the most generous so far. In the long run, however, there are reasons to doubt that a great deal more is to be expected from this source unless there is a major change in intergovernmental fiscal relations. The states are just beginning to move into the field of the performing arts in significant number. To date, with perhaps three or four exceptions, they have done little more than create an administrative or advisory framework, but there is some reason to expect increases in state contributions over the next decade. The federal government has given indirect support to the arts for nearly half a century by means of tax incentives, but there is evidence to suggest that further liberalization of deduction allowances would not lead to a significant increase in private contributions. The important development at the federal level was, of course, the passage in 1965 of the bill establishing the National Foundation on the Arts and the Humanities. Experience in other countries and experience in this country with the National Science Foundation and the National Institutes of Health suggest that the initial grant is likely to grow. However, the long-run future of government support to the arts in this country is by no means automatically assured. It will depend heavily on the effort devoted to convincing Congress and the general public of the need and appropriateness of this sort of program.

It is to the principles involved in government support for the arts that the next chapter is addressed. It discusses the questions which should be considered in deciding what the role of government ought to be.

CHAPTER **XVI**

On the Rationale
of Public Support

Evidence of growing financial gaps in the budgets of performing arts organizations and recurrent crises in their operations inevitably gives rise to the suggestion that more support should be provided to the arts by government. For some people, evidence that the typical income gap is likely to continue to grow is enough to settle the issue. Convinced that the performing arts make a contribution to our culture and are valuable as an end in themselves, they feel that the responsibility of society, as represented by its government, is perfectly clear. The argument is simple: if through no fault of their own the arts cannot survive without public support, the necessary support must be provided.

However, the conviction that government should do more for the arts is by no means universal. Even among members of symphony boards the case for government aid has hardly been considered obvious. As recently as 1953 a survey by the American Symphony Orchestra League showed that 99 per cent of the members of orchestra governing boards were strongly opposed to federal aid. Even though by 1962 a much larger proportion of this group took at least a middle ground and by 1965 "in a dramatic reversal of position . . . presidents and managers of nearly forty symphony orchestras endorsed federal support,"[1] doubts about the desirability of government support continue to be raised even by friends of the arts.

[1] American Symphony Orchestra League, *Newsletter*, March–April–May 1965, p. 1.

In this chapter we shall, therefore, examine some of the fundamental pros and cons of government support, paying particular attention to those issues which are amenable to economic analysis.[2]

Some Arguments for Government Support

"We are the only major nation on earth whose government still does so little about the nation's cultural treasure in the performing and visual arts, and it is high time that we caught up."[3] With these words a noted Senator stated clearly one of the most common arguments for government support — the argument by example. It is done elsewhere, why not here? The argument by precedent also takes another form: "Our government came to this conclusion [that federal assistance is warranted] about United States shipping in 1950, about agriculture in 1862, about education even before this."[4]

Though these analogies may be effective in forcing us to think about the issue, they suffer from two serious shortcomings. It does not necessarily follow that because support is appropriate for some social and economic activities it is equally desirable for others. Even more important, the argument by analogy provides no evidence that government assistance to the other activities cited was justified in the first place. To remedy this deficiency a variety of beneficial side effects reputed to flow from the arts are frequently brought to our attention, consequences ranging from those which serve the noblest purposes to those which cater to the most material ends, from the enrichment of the nation's expanding leisure time to the provision of employment opportunities.

Most often, however, the advocacy of public support is made to rest ultimately on what might be considered higher grounds, the "intrinsic value" of artistic activity. Lord Bridges put the matter most forcefully in his Romanes Lecture in 1958 when he stated, "The heart of this matter is surely that the arts can give to all of

[2] For a concise discussion of some of the subject matter of this chapter, see Robbins, Section II.

[3] Senator Jacob K. Javits, quoted in Stoddard.

[4] Stoddard, p. 3.

us, including those who lack expert knowledge of any of them, much of what is best in human life and enjoyment; and that a nation which does not put this at the disposal of those who have the liking and the capacity for it, is failing in a most important duty."[5]

Arguments Against Government Support

The one argument which most of us today would regard as an antediluvian manifestation is that poverty is good for the arts and stimulates creativity. "We want to develop a hungry theater," said one witness at the House Hearings on economic conditions in the performing arts, who went on to assert that only a hungry man feels compelled to say "what's in him."[6]

A more thoughtful objection to the use of government funds for the arts asserts that there are higher priorities, that poverty, disease, crime and ignorance have a stronger claim on government funds. Thus, Lord Bridges notes in his address a case where an expenditure related to the arts was attacked in the press on the basis that the money could have been used "to build six bungalows for old people" in the area. While this alternative use of funds may be appealing, it must be recognized that, as a practical matter, the money in question, if not used for the arts, may well not be employed to construct "six bungalows" or for any other similar purpose. In any event, even if one believes that more money should be spent on the poor, it does not follow that less should be spent on the arts. Perhaps economies should be effected instead in some other part of the government budget, or perhaps total outlays by the public sector should simply be increased. It is capricious and arbitrary to attack expenditures on the arts just because one believes some other projects have a higher priority. Such an argument is valid only if one can think of *no* better source of the requisite funds, and if one can be reasonably sure that the monies denied the arts would, in fact, be devoted to the six bungalows, or to whatever else is deemed worthier.

[5] 1958 Romanes Lecture, pp. 12–13.

[6] House Hearings, II, testimony of John D. Wentworth, managing director of the Washington Theater Club, Washington, D.C., p. 533.

An argument of a very different sort is that government support of the arts would serve mainly to displace private funds, which in turn implies that a great deal of government money would have to be spent to bring about a small increase in the total resources available to performing arts organizations.

Unfortunately, there is little evidence on the basic factual issue — the effect of government grants on private contributions.[7] We do know, at least on an impressionistic basis, that in Western European countries there is little private giving to the arts; and, as was noted in the last chapter, governments do provide considerable direct support in these countries. One possible inference is that government grants have discouraged private giving, but it is at least equally plausible that causation has flowed in the opposite direction — that it is because of a lack of private support that continental governments have felt obliged to spend considerable sums on the arts. To the best of our knowledge no strong tradition of private giving to the arts exists in any European country, and it may well be that private contributions would be small even in the absence of government grants.

Our audience survey shed some interesting sidelights on this question. If we compare by income class the proportion of persons who contribute to the performing arts regularly in Great Britain and the United States, we find that in the lower income brackets the proportion giving regularly is about the same in the two countries, but in the upper brackets there is a much lower rate of contribution in the United Kingdom. This distinction may be one result of the greater tax incentives provided in the United States, or it may mean that the wealthy are the first to reduce their contributions when the government begins to finance artistic activity. Of course, other explanations are also possible — for example, the effect of the higher over-all level of per capita income in the United States has to be considered — and it would be fatuous to pretend that the implications of these results are unambiguous.[8]

[7] Great Britain would seem to be an excellent locale for such a study, since a comparison of current patterns of giving with patterns before World War II and the inauguration of the Arts Council might be very enlightening, but no such investigation seems to have been conducted.

[8] The results of this comparison are summarized graphically in Appendix Figure XVI–A.

On the whole, we were somewhat surprised at the high proportion of contributions reported in our English audience surveys, as our examination of the financial records of leading performing organizations indicated that they obtained relatively little money from private contributions. We, therefore, studied the organizations to which English respondents said they contributed. Comparing a London orchestral audience with an orchestral audience in the United States, we found that in the American case two thirds of the organizations to which respondents reported donating were major professional groups, whereas in the London sample semiprofessional or amateur groups made up nearly half of the total. This finding suggests that where the state takes a major share of responsibility for the support of professional organizations, a higher proportion of private contributions will go to amateur activity.

An historical study of English philanthropy has emphasized that time and again private donors have directed attention to a need, and then, when society at large assumed responsibility for ministering to that need, moved on to new fields.[9] This does not mean that government grants to the performing arts would necessarily drive away private donors in the United States. Developments in the field of education provide evidence to the contrary. Here the government has been doing more and more, and yet private contributions have also been rising at a very substantial rate indeed.[10] It is also reassuring that the institution of private philanthropy seems so well established in the United States. For this reason, and perhaps because of our greater wealth, total charitable contributions are higher in this country than abroad. Moreover, no one has proposed government grants of a magnitude which would make private support redundant.

Another argument against public support is the danger of public control. Senator Barry Goldwater voiced the fears of many peo-

[9] See David Owen, *English Philanthropy, 1660–1960*, Belknap Press, Cambridge, Mass., 1964. Welfare activities and hospitals are obvious examples.

[10] See Council for Financial Aid to Education, *Guide Lines to Voluntary Support of America's Colleges and Universities*, Report on surveys conducted in 1954–55, 1956–57, 1958–59 and 1960–61, which shows that 728 institutions reported receiving somewhat less than $290 million in private support in 1954–55, while only eight years later, in 1962–63, 1,036 institutions reported receiving $911 million from private sources.

ple when he said that "the Federal Government eventually will do more harm in this field than good by overregulating it, by over-controlling it."[11] Americans are still haunted by the memory of the atmosphere of thought control which surrounded the demise of the Federal Theatre Project, and it is not easy to forget the moment when counsel for the House Unamerican Activities Committee asked Hallie Flannigan: "You are quoting from this Marlowe. Is he a Communist?"

This objection, that public support implies public control, though one of the most persuasive, has turned out to be one of the least valid in practice. There is ample evidence that government support in Western Europe has not meant public control. John E. Booth, reporting on the European experience, writes:

> The performing arts, under government support, are manifestly free from political pressure or interference. Broadly speaking, and exceptions exist, government does not impose its view. . . . Within the bounds of public acceptance, all are free to be exposed, experimentation is encouraged.
> The extent of the freedom is evidenced in the testimony of all concerned — government officials, producers, playwrights, and critics. . . . the freedom is implicit in the range of works produced year in and year out.[12]

And in our own country a review of experience suggests strongly that we must regard as unfortunate aberrations the WPA history and the more recent outburst of two Congressmen of considerable repute against "eroticism" in the dances of Martha Graham. In our researches we encountered no case of interference by state or local governments, even where the amount of assistance provided has been relatively large.[13] An official concerned with the Library of Congress concert series, one of the oldest government supervised arts programs in the country, told us that he could recall no instance where his decisions had been questioned or

[11] Senate Hearings, p. 180.

[12] Booth, p. vi.

[13] In an article in the *Newsletter* of the American Symphony Orchestra League (November–December 1963, pp. 13–14), the manager of the Milwaukee Symphony reported that his organization had been receiving funds from the city for four years and that not one city official had tried to interfere in any way. He suggested that his experience was applicable elsewhere.

where any attempt was made to influence his program, aside perhaps from an occasional call by a Congressman suggesting hesitantly that he would appreciate a hearing for a performer from his constituency.

Indeed, one can make a strong case to the effect that interference by private patrons is far more frequent and poses a far more imminent threat than does government control. It has been charged more than once that some performing organizations share the tribulations of the group "controlled by a handful of people who consider the operation as their own private domain. They dictate not only administrative policy, labor policy, fund raising policy, but public standards of taste . . ."[14] We know of at least one case where a leading patron of an orchestral group has virtually banned contemporary music; and where, in addition, the occasional performance of a pre-nineteenth century piece is suffered only as an obvious exercise in forbearance. Even the foundations have not escaped charges of undue influence — the Harkness Foundation's rift with the Joffrey Ballet is a notable case in point.[15] In such circumstances government support, instead of reducing the freedom of the arts, can serve to increase it. We conclude, then, that there is little factual basis for the fear that control would be an inevitable concomitant of government assistance.

There is, however, an associated danger which has much more substance. While government assistance may not circumscribe the freedom of the arts in any direct sense, it can effectively dampen their vitality. If support is channeled exclusively to old, established organizations, it can discourage experimentation and make for general stagnation. We have seen in the preceding chapter that this charge has been leveled against the Arts Council of Great Britain. However, the indictment is more telling in connection with arts programs in several other countries, where some of the famous old theaters and opera companies, recipients of heavy government support, are apparently suffering from an advanced

[14] House Hearings, II, statement of Mrs. Diane Fivey, San Francisco Executive Secretary of the American Guild of Musical Artists, p. 350. See also the letter by a member of the San Francisco Arts Commission, *New York Times*, Nov. 29, 1964, p. 49.

[15] *New York Times*, March 18, 1964, p. 48.

case of ossification. If, on the other hand, government support is spread thinly over a variety of enterprises of widely varying quality, in order to avoid the charge of "favoritism," the inevitable result is a diffusion of mediocrity. This is not an imagined danger. The state of stagnation of several European systems of higher education can be attributed at least in part to a misplaced egalitarianism in the distribution of government funds. When fifth-rate institutions and research projects are supported on a scale not far below the support given those of the highest quality, insufficient financing at the top level can lead to a "brains drain" if there is somewhere else to go.

But these perils, while potentially very serious, seem unlikely to apply in the case of the United States, at least in the imminent future. No one is suggesting support on a scale which would make government the exclusive source of funds for any activity, and a pluralistic arrangement in which private and public support both play a role automatically acquires checks and balances. Such a mixed system has been highly successful in maintaining the vitality of our system of higher education, and there is no obvious reason why it should not work just as well in the arts.[16]

The Market Test

There remains the fundamental objection to public support which arises out of the application of the market test to the performing arts. The Philistine is surely entitled to ask: If the arts do provide so much to their audiences, why are the audiences not willing to bear their cost? The most basic objection to government support of the performing arts is simply that those who want to see them ought to pay the price. "The small percentage of people who enjoy opera does not qualify it for public financial support," wrote one commentator, who went on to say: "If opera cannot pay for itself, the fault is with opera, . . . It has never been a principle

---

[16] There is, however, some danger that individual giving will follow patterns set by government grants. The psychological "seal of approval" conferred by government aid may supplement the effects of matching-funds requirements in diverting the flow of private funds toward the pattern adopted by public agencies. Apparently this has been the experience in Canada. (See Hendry, p. 64.)

of our society that the people as a whole should be forced to pay for the entertainment of a few — and it must not be so now."[17]

Though some may find it distasteful, this objection is not without merit. Insolvency *per se* does not constitute adequate grounds for public assistance. No doubt when the automobile first came into general use financial catastrophe threatened manufacturers of buggies, yet we hardly feel that public funds should have been poured into that industry. The reason is clear: if consumers did not value buggies sufficiently to purchase them in quantities and at prices high enough to permit their continued production, the manufacturers no longer had any reason for survival. They had failed the stern test of the market which says that goods and services should be produced only if they are worth their keep to the consumer. But then, one may ask, does not the same test apply just as harshly to the performing arts? If audiences do not want them sufficiently to cover their costs through admission charges, why should this fact be construed as a *prima facie* case for public support? Might it not argue the contrary — that live performance is an obsolete vestige of a handicraft economy which deserves no public assistance precisely because effective demand for it is inadequate?

This is a particularly telling argument in a discussion of government assistance, for government funds, unlike private gifts and contributions, are supplied *involuntarily* by many individual members of the public. If the arts are to receive help from government sources, it becomes important to explain why the performing arts should be among those privileged activities which are granted exemption from the market test.

The proper response, it may be felt, cannot be given on a materialistic level. Rather, it must be phrased in terms of finer and less tangible concepts: the inherent value of beauty and the ineffable contribution of aesthetic activity. To the man in the street, however, this may not be an acceptable answer. Indeed, it is likely to smack of things he rightly considers dangerous: paternalism, dictation of tastes and violation of consumer sovereignty. He may

[17] Letter from Mr. William Eugene Hudson of New York City, printed in the *New York Times Magazine,* November 12, 1961, and quoted in House Hearings, II, p. 236.

well ask whether we are to base the allocation of the nation's resources on the aesthetic standards of some group of individuals who consider the true standards of beauty to have been revealed only to them. If public funds are to be spent to provide "good performance" which the public does not seem to want, then might not the next step be the proscription of other types of performance which the public does desire — perhaps the prohibition of immoral drama, or the discouragement of jazz, or of modern art or of anything else which does not appeal to those who dictate the aesthetic standards. If we accept the sovereignty of the public — the fundamental principle that in a democracy choices are to be made by the citizens of the community — an appeal for the sanctity of the arts simply will not suffice.

But if, as we have shown, audiences are drawn from so limited a segment of the community, can one ever expect to demonstrate that government support of the arts accords with the desires of the public? The answer is to be sought in the nature of activities which, by general consent, are exempted from the market test. One does not expect the defense establishment to show a profit, the courts to pay for themselves or the elementary schools to cover their costs out of their revenues. There are good grounds for these exemptions — grounds fixed firmly in economic analysis and involving no departure from democratic ideals. Much of the remainder of this chapter will be devoted to a discussion of these grounds and an examination of their applicability to the performing arts.

It should be emphasized that our analysis is not intended to pre-judge the amount of government support that is desirable, or even, for that matter, to argue that government funds should necessarily be devoted to such purposes. Rather, it is our intention to describe the logic on which such a decision, one way or the other, should be based if it is to satisfy the criterion of rationality.

The Egalitarian Grounds

The economist recognizes three basic grounds which can legitimately be used to defend government subsidy of unprofitable activities. The first ground for government intervention in the economy is inequality of opportunity. We generally take it as an article of faith that it is undesirable for anyone to be kept from achieving as much as he can through the abilities with which he is endowed. It is, therefore, widely agreed that no market test need support the flow of public funds devoted to the opening of opportunities to the impecunious. This exemption is neither capricious nor merely a matter of tradition. The market test has been described as an election in which the consumer decides what commodities shall be produced and in what quantities. He decides this, not by casting votes, but by the way in which he spends his dollars. But it is very important to remember that under this system not all men have the same number of votes. The affluent consumer has a far greater influence on the course of events than does a purchaser whose finances are quite limited. Therefore, government funds intended to promote equality of opportunity directly or indirectly may be viewed as a means for improving the way in which the market election is conducted.

Now, one may well argue that the extremely narrow audience for the arts is a consequence, not of limited interest, but of the fact that a very large segment of the community has been denied the opportunity to learn to appreciate them. In part this may be so because many persons cannot easily afford the admission charges. However, the lack of facilities in many of the nation's communities also constitutes a denial of opportunity. How can people learn to enjoy the living arts if no plays, no concert performers and no dancers are available to them? People can be deprived of opportunities by phenomena other than poverty and ignorance, and if the government wishes to improve the situation as far as the arts are concerned, it may have to help in the provision of opportunities for attendance in many parts of the country where professional performance is now totally unavailable.

The Education of Minors

A second legitimate reason for government support can be dealt with briefly. It is maintained that while in a democracy most individuals can be left to decide for themselves how their incomes should be spent, some classes of people are not competent to make their own decisions. In particular this argument is applied to minors, with the result that the latter are not permitted to purchase alcoholic beverages, drive automobiles, or decide for themselves whether funds shall be devoted to their schooling. The application to the arts is immediate, and is not unrelated to our accepted policies on education. It is felt that if children and adolescents are not exposed to artistic performance during their minority, by the time they become adults it will be too late. The arts must be made available early, while tastes are still being formed and behavior patterns developed.

It should be made clear that while the logic of this argument is acceptable enough, it rests also on an allegation of fact which has yet to be tested: the hypothesis that taste for the arts is instilled by early experiences. No one seems to have any overpowering evidence that this is so. No one has tracked down the children who attended the New York Philharmonic's young people's concerts which were given continuously from 1898 (by the New York Symphony Society before it merged with the New York Philharmonic) until 1939, or the WPA performances, to see whether they subsequently showed greater interest in the arts than persons coming from otherwise similar backgrounds.

Public Goods and the Market Test

The third ground which can be used to justify government expenditures involves the class of commodities and services which the economist calls "public goods." Public goods are items which, when provided to one person, automatically and unavoidably become available to other members of the community as well. For example, if current efforts succeed in reducing air pollution in Los Angeles, pure air will have been supplied not just to one Angeleno and his family but to all the inhabitants of the city.

The provision of public goods cannot be entrusted to market forces alone. The profit motive and free enterprise, which work so effectively in bringing private goods to consumers when and as they want them, are subject to a fatal limitation as regulators of the supply of public goods. The reason is that commodities of the latter type lack the basic requisite of the market — saleability.

This is seen most easily in the case of an item such as national defense. To pose the relevant question — can the operation of our military forces be left in the hands of private enterprise? — is to answer it. The proposition is ridiculous on its face. Defense benefits everyone, but if an individual were sold "a piece" of it, just what would he have purchased? National security, which is vital to all citizens, cannot be sold to any one of them. When someone desires a good such as a shirt or a pound of potatoes he must pay its price or the seller will refuse to hand the item over to him. But if an individual cannot be excluded from the enjoyment of the benefits of a good, there is no way a private seller can enforce the payment of a fee which would cover his costs. One cannot hope to sell rights to unpolluted air in the city streets, and for this reason the idea of an air cleaning firm has never attracted private investors.

While public goods cannot pass the market test, it does not follow that such items are unwanted by the general public. Even though consumers cannot be made to pay for them, they may regard them as well worth their cost. In such a case it is the normal commercial mechanism and not consumer demand which has failed to function. A government's decision to supply a public good is, therefore, not necessarily a decision to flaunt the wishes of the consumer. On the contrary, government financing may be the only way in which the wishes of the body of consumers can be put into effect.

The Case of "Mixed Commodities"

The situation is slightly more complicated in the case of mixed commodities — goods and services whose characteristics are partly private, partly public. Education is a prime example. When a student attends a school or a university his own welfare (including his future earning ability) is thereby increased. In this sense education is a *private* good — it can be sold to an individual purchaser because it yields benefits specifically to him. But at the same time education is also a *public* service because it enriches society as a whole — it not only increases the productivity of the individual, it makes for a better life for everyone in the community. Without general education the democratic process as we know it could not function effectively.

Unlike pure public goods, mixed commodities can be expected to cover part of their cost by sale to the public. One can charge a price for the direct benefits which flow from the provision of facilities for higher education, for inoculations against contagious diseases, slum clearance projects, etc. This is possible because the consumer can be excluded from the enjoyment of direct benefits if he does not pay the fee. A student who refuses to pay tuition may not be permitted to attend the university, and a tenant who chooses not to pay his rent can be evicted.

The consumer cannot, however, be excluded from the indirect benefits associated with mixed commodities, since these are unavoidably made available to all members of the community. Therefore, the price tag which can be put on quasi-public goods may be insufficient to cover their cost of production. But, in this case, failure to pass the market test does not necessarily mean that the goods in question are unwanted; it merely reflects the fact that they are not amenable to ordinary commercial standards of valuation. In these conditions public support may be entirely justified as the only available means to make demand effective.

The Performing Arts as "Mixed" Services

The reader can readily see where all of this is leading. If the performing arts are mixed commodities which confer direct benefits on those who attend a performance but which also offer benefits to the community as a whole, government support of the arts might well be completely consistent with the desires of the entire community. To determine whether the arts do or do not fall into this category it is necessary to look closely at the advantages they offer to the public at large.

There are at least four types of general benefit which may flow from the arts. The first of these may perhaps be considered unworthy, but it is, nevertheless, very real — it is the prestige conferred on a nation by its performing arts. Many persons who themselves have no desire to attend an opera or a program of contemporary dance take pride in the international recognition conferred on our singers and the creativity of our choreographers. To them the availability of a number of fine orchestras is a measure of the achievement of America, and is therefore a prime source of satisfaction. They would be most unhappy if the United States became known abroad as a cultural wasteland, a nation in which mammon had put beauty and art to rout.

Lest this phenomenon — the prestige conferred by cultural activity — be considered insufficient justification for any substantial support, it need only be recalled that concern with our image is the prime justification behind many of the billions currently being expended on the space race. If the national feeling of achievement which would attend getting to the moon at an early date is worth the outlay of tens of billions on the propulsion of astronauts into space, then the expenditure of a small fraction of this amount to obtain the prestige offered by a viable performing arts establishment may also be justified. It is in this connection that the potential role of the arts in U.S. foreign policy has been stressed. George London testified before a House committee that "the arts were being used as a potent propaganda weapon of the cold war." He suggested that in many parts of the world the United States is considered "a purely materialistic country devoted to profits and consumers' goods, and bereft of spiritual or cultural values. This is a theme which particularly the Soviets pound upon and make political capital of."[18] The use of State Department funds to finance international tours of American companies can be regarded as a small first countermove.

A second equally materialistic set of indirect benefits which flows from the arts is the advantage that the availability of cultural activity confers on business in its vicinity — the fact that it brings customers to shops, hotels, restaurants and bars. On a national level, distinguished performing arts organizations may serve, analogously, as a significant tourist attraction.[19] A particularly good illustration was provided in an editorial in the *New York Times*

[18] House Hearings, II, p. 21.

[19] Booth (p. iii) points out that the encouragement of tourism is an important motivation behind some of the support provided in Western Europe.

Support whose form seems to recognize the relationship between performance and some types of business activity has been provided in San Francisco, where a tax is levied on hotel rooms and the proceeds are divided between convention bureaus and the arts.

which commented on competition among 117 communities in 46 states, each seeking to become the site of a $280 million facility for experimentation in nuclear physics. The editor reported:

> In setting up its criteria for a choice, the [Atomic Energy Commission] noted that the location should have adequate cultural and educational facilities for those who will work at the facility. The result has been much soul-searching in communities that would like to have the accelerator and realize that past neglect of local educational and cultural institutions casts a blight over their chances.
>
> Many local readers over the country are now becoming aware that a strong research-oriented university, a thriving symphony orchestra and a lively theater no longer can be ranked as frills. They are essentials for a community's economic expansion in an age when science and scientists play an unprecedentedly important role.[20]

A third and far more appealing type of social contribution credited to the performing arts involves future generations. One may well feel that ability to appreciate the arts cannot always be achieved without a suitable period of training and acquaintance.[21] We have all met people who admit they have never themselves learned to enjoy a particular art form, but feel it important that such an opportunity be available to other members of their families. This same phenomenon has a significant extension to the posterity of the community as a whole. We support programs for the conservation of natural resources and for improvement of architecture in part because few of us are willing to take the responsibility of passing on to future generations a country whose beauty has been destroyed.

But provision for the future requires support for the arts in the present. Though it is demonstrably false that the arts "when once destroyed can never be supplied," it is true that their rehabilitation is not likely to be quick or easy. There is the old saw about the

---

[20] *New York Times*, Aug. 15, 1965, p. 85. Note that all of the indirect benefits in such a case are usually derived locally, and so this is an argument which can serve as justification primarily for local support.

[21] We have already had occasion to note another type of indiscriminate benefit associated with training children to appreciate the arts. This is the fact that because of the great mobility of the American population, an organization providing children's concerts in one city is likely to be building future audiences for other cities. This clearly argues for federal rather than local support.

man who asked the secret of the lush lawns at Versailles and was told that the answer was simple: they need only be watered daily for three hundred years. The development of mature cultural activities, of exacting standards of performance, and of an understanding audience cannot be achieved overnight. Funds must be provided today if the arts are to be kept alive for tomorrow. A program to preserve the arts for the nation's posterity is a case of indiscriminate benefits *par excellence*. No one can say whose descendants will profit one hundred years hence from resources now devoted to that purpose. Neither can these benefits be priced and their cost covered by an admission charge. Though most Americans may be happy that future generations will have the arts available to them and are content to have funds spent for the purpose, there is no way in which the free market, unaided by public funds, can enable these desires to be realized.

Still another type of indirect benefit provided by the arts is their educational contribution.[22] If, as is generally conceded, a liberal education confers indirect and non-priceable benefits upon the community, the same must be true of the arts. If the teaching of the humanities makes for a finer civilization, for a richer community, for a better life for everyone, this is necessarily so with the arts as well; for without the arts a vital element is taken from the humanities. How can drama be taught if there is no drama available for the student to experience? What can the teaching of music mean if no one can hear performances of professional quality? If the arts are reduced to an atrophied relic of ancient history, a critical component of our educational system must concurrently be lost.

One main conclusion can be drawn from the analysis central to this chapter. If one agrees that the performing arts confer general benefits on the community as a whole, in the manner described above or in other ways, he must conclude that in part, and perhaps in large part, the arts are public goods whose benefits demonstra-

---

[22] The items mentioned are not the only indirect and indiscriminate benefits provided to the community by the performing arts. There are others; for example, the fact that the live performing arts serve as training grounds for the mass media.

bly exceed the receipts one can hope to collect at the box office. It is a long-standing tenet of economics that if the wishes and interests of the public are to be followed in the allocation of the nation's resources, this is the ultimate ground on which governmental expenditures must find their justification. Government must provide funds only where the market has no way to charge for all the benefits offered by an activity. When such a case arises, failure of the government to provide funds may constitute a very false economy — a misallocation of the community's resources, and a failure to implement the desires of the public. In such circumstances, government outlays are no manifestation of boondoggling bureaucracy, no evidence of creeping socialism, but a response to one of the needs of the society at large.

CHAPTER XVII

Prospects[*]

THE PAST bears within it the seeds of the future, and what we have learned about the performing arts and the nature of their financial problems may suggest the broad outlines of things to come. By juxtaposing the projected financial needs of live performance with the trends in contributions, one can see more clearly the magnitude of the financial task implicit in whatever aspirations one may hold for the future of the living arts.

The Income Gap

The Broadway theater is the only segment of the professional performing arts world, as defined by our study, which in recent years has come close to showing a profit. All the other groups of organizations have operated at a deficit, in that they have regularly earned less than they spent. This "income gap," which has had to be filled by contributions, has amounted to roughly 20 per cent of expenditures for the Metropolitan Opera, 45 per cent for 10 other operas, 30 per cent for the 5 largest major orchestras, 46 per cent for all 25 major orchestras and an average of 15 per cent for the regional theaters.

We estimate that in 1963–64 the total income gap for the nation's professional performing arts organizations, excluding the commercial theater, was between $20 and $23 million. This estimate does not include sums spent on the construction of cultural centers,

---

[*] Where in the course of this chapter it is necessary to include summary materials no source references are given. The reader can find the sources by consulting the appropriate earlier chapters.

auditoriums and so on; nor does it include semi-professional or amateur activity, or performances subsidized by colleges and universities.

Though small when compared with the Gross National Product, the income gap is increasing very rapidly. Even if expenditures and earned income were to grow at equal rates, the gap would grow along with them. If, for example, they increased by 5 per cent, the gap would also increase by 5 per cent. But expenditures have actually increased somewhat faster than earned income, and the gap has widened accordingly. Over the postwar period the income gap grew at an average annual rate of 6–7 per cent for a major orchestra in our basic set of eleven such orchestras, 8 per cent at the Metropolitan Opera and 9 per cent at Covent Garden in London.

One useful way of gauging the implications of these trends is by projecting them a decade or so into the future, say to 1975. A projection is not a forecast and certainly not an instrument of clairvoyance; it is a statistical device which tells us only what current trends presage for the future. Yet projections do indicate what is in prospect if things continue to change as they have in the past, and thus they present at least a minimal basis for planning and decision-making. In the present case, where the record of the past is not clear-cut, a single projected figure would give a specious impression of precision and reliability, and so we offer two basic sets of projections — a lower and a higher one — as an approximation to the limits of the range of possibility, if past trends continue.[1]

Our lower estimates indicate that the income gap for professional performing arts organizations currently in existence will grow at an annual rate of about 6 per cent. At that rate the gap will increase from $19.7 million in 1964 to $37.8 million in 1975 — nearly doubling over an eleven year period. Our higher, less conservative estimates foresee an 8.3 per cent annual growth rate in the income

[1] Both sets of projections are based on trends in costs and receipts of our basic eleven orchestras, our most consistent and reliable source of data; these trends have been fairly typical of the arts as a whole. The lower projections are based on growth rates from 1947 to 1964, and the higher projections on the more rapid growth rates which characterized the period 1961–1964. These projections are summarized in Table XVII–1; their derivation is explained in detail in Appendix XVII–1.

TABLE XVII–1

Income Gap Projections, 1975

	Base Year (1963–64) Values	Lower Projection (1975)	Higher Projection (1975)
DOLLAR AMOUNTS (millions):			
Existing Organizations	$19.7	$37.8	$47.4
"New" Organizations	—	10.6	13.3
Total	$19.7	$48.4	$60.7
IMPLICIT GROWTH RATES (per cent per year):			
Existing Organizations		6.1%	8.3%
"New" Organizations		—	—
Total		8.5%	10.8%

SOURCE: See Appendix XVII–1.

gap for existing organizations — an increase to $47.4 million by 1975.

On the basis of these estimated growth rates and of past trends in the rate of formation of new performing groups, we calculate that the total income gap of "new" organizations (founded between 1964 and 1975) might be somewhere between $10.6 and $13.3 million by 1975. Our assumptions as to the number of newcomers in the various art forms (Appendix XVII–1) are no more than educated guesses. In any event the figures are constructed in a manner which permits the reader who wishes to do so to try out any alternative surmise about the prospective rate of formation of new performing groups. He will see that most alternative assumptions produce no drastic change in the projected gap.

Combining the income gap projections for existing organizations with those for new organizations, we find that a total income gap for the performing arts of somewhere between $48 and $61 million can be expected by 1975. These projections imply an average annual growth rate in the total gap of 8.5 to 10.8 per cent.

The Outlook for Expenditures

Underlying these projections of the income gap is the assumption that over the next decade expenditures per organization will rise at a rate between 5 per cent and 7 per cent per year, as they did over the postwar period.[2] What reason is there, however, to think that outlays will continue to rise at so rapid a rate? It is true that trends in the number of performances need not continue as they have in the past, but there is something nearly inevitable about trends in cost per performance.

It is a thesis of this study that the root of the cost pressures which beset the arts is the nature of their technology. For the economy as a whole, productivity (output per man-hour) has risen at a remarkably steady rate of roughly 2½ per cent per year over the last half-century, and there is every reason to expect that the discovery of new knowledge and the invention of new techniques of production and capital accumulation will yield comparable increases in production per man per hour in the future. But the technology of *live* performance leaves little room for labor-saving innovations, since the end product is the labor of the performer. While increases in money wages in an industry such as auto manufacturing are offset, either partly or in full, by increases in productivity, the corresponding increases in salaries in the arts are directly translated into higher costs. The more successful such industries are in keeping up the rate of increase in their productive efficiency, the more will the cost of the living arts rise relative to costs in general.

Progress in general technology has had a considerable impact on the arts through new methods of presentation of performances to the public. The development of motion pictures, phonograph records, radio and television has caused a precipitous drop in the cost of providing an hour of entertainment to each member of the audience. But these innovations have not helped the live performing arts directly; in fact, the competition of the mass media for both audience and artistic personnel has sometimes had serious consequences for performing organizations. The effect of "talkies" on

[2] Again we are taking the experience of our sample of orchestras as representative of that of professional arts organizations in general.

theater attendance is well known, and, though it is hard to be certain, the evidence does suggest that the introduction and spread of television between 1947 and 1952 also had an adverse effect on attendance.

If the fundamental problem of the arts is, in fact, the nature of their technology, then one would expect costs per performance to rise more rapidly that the over-all price level. This has, in fact, been the case. Over the long period cost per performance rose faster than the price level in every case where we were able to obtain the relevant data:

— in the British theater between 1775 and 1964;
— for the New York Philharmonic between 1842 and 1964;
— for the Cincinnati Symphony Orchestra between 1920 and 1964;
— on Broadway, over various intervals from 1913 to 1961;
— for a wide variety of art forms and organizations over the postwar period.

This diagnosis is also supported by a comparison between the United States and Great Britain which reveals that, after adjustments are made for changes in the purchasing power of the dollar and the pound, real cost per performance has risen at about the same rate in both countries — a result that is certainly to be expected if the increase in real costs is attributable to a fundamental problem in the technology of the arts which knows no national boundaries.

The conclusion is clear: costs per performance should be expected to continue to rise more rapidly than the general price level. Whether the exact rate of increase will be more or less than the rate which has prevailed over the last decade is a more difficult question, the answer to which depends on: (1) the amount of price inflation; (2) the extent to which performers' salaries keep pace with wages and salaries in general; (3) the extent to which increases in the number of performances lead to savings in the average cost per performance.

Since the end of World War II performers' salaries have increased at about the same rate as wages in general, and our projections assume that this relationship will continue to hold. The salaries of artistic personnel are the largest single component in the budget of almost every performing organization; on the average, they constitute 30 per cent of total expenditures on Broadway, 40 per cent in opera and 64 per cent for the major orchestras. For this reason, even a small variation in the rate of change in performers' salaries would have a pronounced effect on cost per performance.[3]

Unemployment rates among performers — especially actors — are very high, and there is no evidence of any general shortage of performers at current salaries. But this has been true for some time, and has not prevented salaries from rising. The relative position of performers in the income distribution also suggests that pressures for increased performer incomes are likely to continue. The official census data for 1960 attest to the low economic status of performing artists: of 49 male, professional occupations ranked by income, actors stood thirty-fourth from the top, musicians and music teachers fortieth, and dancers and dancing teachers forty-eighth. While it is true that performers for top major orchestras such as the New York Philharmonic, the Metropolitan Opera and a few other organizations with full-year seasons average more than $10,000 per year, the salary levels of performers in many organizations are still scandalously low. Minimum weekly salaries in 1963–64 were as low as $60 off-Broadway, $50 at some regional theaters, $60 in some opera choruses and $40 in some dance groups. Even some of the major orchestras paid less than $100 per week to performers at the minimum scale.

Thus, equity considerations, combined with a growing unwillingness on the part of performers to accept genteel poverty as a way of life, suggest that performers' salary levels may be expected to

[3] Increases in performers' salaries, however, are not the sole explanation for the increases in cost per performance which have occurred over the past decade. Other costs have, if anything, risen faster. However, because these other costs have been smaller components of total costs, increases in them have had a smaller absolute impact. Looking ahead, there is no reason to expect these other costs to do anything but rise at much the same rate as they have risen in the recent past.

continue to rise at about the same rate as wages and salaries in general.

Cost per performance is also affected by the total number of performances given, and a statistical examination of the experience of a number of major orchestras indicates that cost per performance would have increased even faster during the postwar years had there not been a rather sharp increase in the total number of performances. While the number of performances given by some organizations can be expected to continue to increase, there is no reason to expect greater savings in cost per performance than were realized in the last decade (and hence are already reflected in our projections). On the contrary, as more companies operate on full-year schedules, opportunities to spread overhead costs over an increasing number of performances will diminish.[4]

The Outlook for Earned Income

In our projections we assumed that earned income would rise 3½ to 5½ per cent per year, continuing the trend during the postwar period. This refers largely to box office income, since, for most organizations, other sources of earned income are small.

The strength of public demand is, of course, a basic determinant of earned income prospects for any industry. Over the long run, the total audience for the performing arts can be expected to increase more rapidly than the population because of rising income, growing leisure time, and perhaps because of a stronger cultural inclination on the part of the American people. However, the oft-heard assertions that the United States is in the midst of an unprecedented "cultural boom" exaggerate the increases in performing arts activity which have occurred in recent years. Certainly, new cul-

[4] It is conceivable that cost per seat per performance could be reduced by building larger auditoriums, but this would require large capital outlays, an ability to sell more tickets and a willingness to accept whatever aesthetic loss might be involved by increasing the size of halls. The importance of theater size in determining cost per seat per performance is well illustrated by the situation off-Broadway, where the small houses transform an apparently inexpensive enterprise (average cost of $760 per performance in 1964 versus $6,600 for a major orchestra) into an expensive operation ($3.81 per seat per performance off-Broadway versus $1.91 for the major orchestra).

tural centers have been opening at an impressive rate — of 54 operating cultural centers which we surveyed in 1964, nearly one fourth had been opened since 1960 and more than half since 1950. Consumer expenditures for admissions to performing arts activities seem also to indicate a substantial cultural upsurge: these expenditures went up from $174 million in 1946 to $433 million in 1963. But this increase mainly represents growth in population, prices and real incomes, rather than a rise in interest in the arts at the expense of other activities. Of each $100 of disposable personal income, the identical share (11¢) was spent on admissions to live performances in 1963 and in 1946. By way of contrast, consumer expenditures on education and research per $100 of disposable income went up from 72¢ in 1946 to $1.41 in 1963.

The various art forms have experienced quite different rates of change in their level of activity since World War II. Even after allowance for increases in population, the regional theater and the dance have had substantial increases in attendance. Attendance at the major orchestras and the established opera companies has increased at about the same rate as the population. Off-Broadway activity exhibited a tremendous spurt during the 1950's, but its growth now seems to have stopped; in both number of new productions and number of performances the 1964–65 season fell well below the peaks reached in the 1961–62 through 1963–64 seasons, and at this writing there is no sign of a new resurgence. Though the extent of the decline in activity on Broadway has sometimes been exaggerated in the press, the evidence does show that in per capita terms Broadway has experienced drops in attendance and in number of performances, and an even sharper drop in number of new productions.

Looking at audience demand in 1963–64 in relation to the supply of performances, we find that a fair number of empty seats was the rule rather than the exception. In the usual case, about 20–30 per cent of the seats are unoccupied on a typical night, the exceptions being the Metropolitan Opera, Broadway hits, several repertory theater companies and some of the leading orchestras. But even when there is excess capacity, the gap between expenditures and earned income could typically not be closed even if all the seats were sold. Hence, important as it is for many groups to sell more tickets, increased sales alone cannot be expected to make deficits disappear.

What about increases in ticket prices? The cost of tickets has risen appreciably in recent years, but the extent of this rise has often been exaggerated. Between the 1930's and the 1950's most ticket prices (including tax) increased at almost exactly the same rate as the consumer price index — they were stationary in terms of purchasing power. In recent years prices on Broadway and at the Metropolitan Opera have risen somewhat more rapidly than this price index, but orchestra prices have still just about kept pace with the general price level. And ticket prices have not gone up as quickly as the associated costs of attendance, such as outlays on restaurants and transportation.

Ticket prices have also not risen as rapidly as cost per performance; this is true for almost all organizations over almost all periods for which data exist.

Ticket prices may have lagged behind costs in part because some managements feared that further price increases would lead to such significant reductions in the size of the audience that they would be economically self-defeating. We have no precise estimate of the average effect of a ticket price rise of a given amount on attendance. Ticket price increases seem generally to dampen audience demand to some extent, but the decrease in attendance is not nearly proportionate with the increase in prices. This view is supported by the fact that only 11 per cent of the respondents to our audience surveys said that they had tried to buy a less expensive ticket. Thus, such evidence as there is suggests that organizations could have increased their revenues by raising ticket prices more rapidly. It does not suggest, however, that in the future managements will raise prices more rapidly.

Another reason why ticket prices tend to lag behind costs is that many managements feel they have an obligation to serve the community, and would not want to risk limiting further either the number of people who attend or the composition of the audience. The Twentieth Century Fund audience survey evidence is directly relevant to this issue.

Classification of the American audience according to ticket price paid indicates that lower-priced seats are occupied by an audience which differs from the audience sitting in the higher-priced seats, though the differences are less than might have been expected. In general, the occupants of the lower-priced seats are younger, more apt to be students, more likely to be employed in the professions and less likely to be employed as managers, and have a lower family income.

The strongest test of the effect of ticket prices on audience composition is provided by a comparison of the characteristics of audiences at free open-air performances with other audiences. The differences here are greater than those between persons occupying various seats at the same performance, but they are still not overwhelming. The proportion of blue-collar workers increases from 3 per cent at regular performances to 7 per cent at free open-air performances, median family income falls from $12,300 to $9,400, and median educational attainment for males declines from some graduate work to four years of college.

If organizations were to use higher prices to prevent their income gaps from increasing further, how much would ticket prices have to increase? For earned income to continue to cover the same proportion of costs as it did in 1964 (actually the proportion has been declining), ticket income for a typical major orchestra would have to rise 5.5 per cent per year — doubling every 13 years — and ticket prices would have to rise by more than 70 per cent by 1975. This again is an extremely conservative figure, for, besides employing our lower estimate of the income gap, it assumes that increased ticket prices would have absolutely no adverse effects on attendance. Most organizations would have to increase their ticket prices at an appreciably higher rate in order to allow for some decline in audience.

What the higher-ticket-price alternative signifies can be shown more vividly by taking an extreme case, that of the Metropolitan Opera, whose income gap has been increasing at a rate of roughly 8 per cent per year. Suppose the Metropolitan were to try to stop this increase by raising ticket prices. Assuming that attendance did not decline in response to higher ticket prices, and that the Metropolitan offered the same number of performances per year, its 1974–75 price scale, even conservatively estimated, would compare as follows with its 1964–65 prices:

		1964–65	Hypothetical 1974–75
Orchestra	Front	$12.00	$21.96
	Rear	11.00	20.13
Parterre Boxes	Center	13.00	23.79
	Sides	11.00	20.13
Grand Tier		12.00	21.96
Dress Circle	Center	7.50	13.72
	Sides	6.50	11.90
Balcony	Center	5.50	10.06
	Sides	4.50	8.24
Family Circle	Center	3.50	6.40
	Sides	2.50	4.58
Standing	Orchestra	2.50	4.58
	Family Circle	1.50	2.74

Of course no one proposes this solution as a practical policy. The figures are intended only to dramatize the financial problem that looms before the Metropolitan Opera, and to a lesser degree, before other professional performing organizations.

Choice of repertoire is another determinant of audience size and composition, and the evidence leaves no room for doubt about the effects of "adventurous" productions. For example, when contemporary operas were presented, attendance fell, on the average, from 97 to 89 per cent of capacity at the Metropolitan Opera, from 65 to 39 per cent of capacity at the New York City Center, and from 83 to 67 per cent at Covent Garden. It follows that, at least in the short run, attendance can be increased by avoiding contemporary works. But such a policy would require a sacrifice of principle which some organizations are unwilling to accept — and the ultimate consequences for creativity in the arts are not hard to envision.

To sum up, the historical rates of increase in cost and income which underlie our projections are rooted in the technology of the arts, in patterns of demand and in attitudes toward the social role of the arts. There is no apparent reason to expect future costs to increase less rapidly or revenues more rapidly than they have in the recent past — if forced to choose between our high and low projections of the gap, we would certainly incline toward the former. By 1975, professional performing arts organizations may well have to raise $60 million in contributions if they are to cover the difference between their operating costs and revenues.

The Outlook for Contributions

Fortunately, contributions too have been growing. As a matter of historical record, organizations have either raised enough to cover the bulk of their operating deficits or they have tailored their expenditures to the available funds; otherwise they would simply not have survived. Add to this the recent upsurge in donations for the construction of cultural centers and the conclusion is inescapable — up to now, contributions to the arts have more than kept pace with the expanding income gap. But how long can contributions be expected to keep up with a total gap that may double in less than a decade? Is it reasonable to hope that the total flow of philanthropic funds from which the arts derive their share will be able to keep pace with the need?

Roughly 90 per cent of all private giving comes from individuals, and while individual gifts play a less dominant role in the finances of arts organizations than they do, for example, in the case of organized religion, they are still the most important single source of contributions. The willingness of individuals to contribute to the arts is shown by the fact that 40 per cent of the respondents in our audience survey indicated that they gave money to the performing arts either "regularly" or "occasionally." Among orchestra audiences, 48 per cent were in one or the other of these categories, while among Broadway audiences the proportion dropped to 25 per cent.

Individual philanthropic contributions as a percentage of adjusted gross income increased modestly but steadily from the 1920's to 1958. The contribution rate leveled off in 1958, but it is too early to know whether this is merely a temporary slowdown or the end of a long-term upward trend in the propensity to give.

More important for the arts than the course of total contributions is the trend in giving by the relatively well-to-do. Less than one fifth of all philanthropic giving comes from persons earning $25,000 or more, but education receives roughly three fourths of its support from this top income group, and it seems safe to assume that the performing arts are much like education in this respect. We know from our audience data that audiences are well-to-do and that the proportion of the audience who are regular contributors rises dramatically with income — from 4 per cent of audience members with incomes of $3,000 or less to 45 per cent of those in the $50,000-and-over category. Small contributors are very important to many organizations, both in terms of dollars given and in terms of interest and participation in the affairs of the organization, but it is the families with substantial incomes who are of primary importance from the standpoint of fund raising alone. Our estimates suggest that philanthropic contributions by families at the very top of the income distribution have been increasing at an average annual rate of about 5.8 per cent since 1954, compared with a growth rate of 5.6 per cent for individual contributions in general. Between 1958 and 1962, however, contributions of the top income groups increased only 3.8 per cent per year, compared with 5.3 per cent for total contributions.

Corporations provided roughly 5 per cent of all private philanthropy in 1964 and their share of the total has been growing. The performing arts have been receiving perhaps 3¢–4¢ of each corporate giving dollar, and they may well receive increased support from this source. In 1964 foundations provided about the same share of total philanthropy as corporations, and foundation giving has been increasing even more rapidly than corporate philanthropy. Contributions to the performing arts from this source have been dominated by the large foundations, especially the Ford Foundation, which has given more to the arts in the United States than the British Arts Council has given to the arts in Great Britain.

Weighting each source of private philanthropy by its share of total contributions to the performing arts (Appendix XVII–1), we are led to project the rate of growth of private contributions for all purposes at between 5.2 and 7.3 per cent per year, as shown in Table XVII–2. This, then, is the expected rate of expansion of the *total pool of resources* upon which the performing arts must draw,

TABLE XVII–2

Philanthropic Contributions, 1975 Projections

	Base Year (1963–64) Value	"Higher" Projection (1975)	"Lower" Projection (1975)
Dollar Amount (millions)	$19.7	$42.8	$34.4
Implicit Growth Rate (per cent per year)		7.3	5.2

in competition with all other claimants upon the country's philanthropic giving.[5]

Comparing these figures with our projections of the gap (Table XVII–3), we see that if giving to the arts were to grow at the same rate as the total pool of contributions, by 1975 the arts would experience an annual shortfall (net deficit after contributions from private sources) ranging somewhere between $5.6 and $26.3 million. The first and more optimistic of these figures is based on our lowest gap projection and highest contribution projection, while the higher net deficit figure is derived in the reverse fashion.

Of course the arts simply cannot, year after year, incur net deficits of this magnitude. Sooner or later, a serious decline of activity would be inevitable. These shortfall figures, therefore, reveal less about the future position of the performing arts than about the challenge they must begin to face. As measures of the sums of money which must somehow be obtained, beyond what the arts might expect to receive if their share of private philanthropy were to remain constant, these estimates are conservative. They imply merely that there will be no retrenchment in quality and availability of performance and that a relatively modest expansion in the number of performing organizations will occur. Some may feel

[5] Strictly speaking, the pool under discussion is not the total pool on which all recipients of private philanthropy depend. Trends in the giving of the lower income groups are weighted less heavily, and corporation and foundation giving more heavily, than would be proper if the objective were to estimate trends in total contributions to recipients of all types rather than to the performing arts alone. Though we have undertaken no calculations, we are confident that the contributions to which we are referring have been growing more rapidly than private philanthropy in general.

TABLE XVII–3

Combined Income Gap and Contributions Projections, 1975 (millions)

I.	Lower Income Gap Projection	$48.4
	Higher Contributions Projection	42.8
	Shortfall	$ 5.6
II.	Lower Income Gap Projection	$48.4
	Lower Contributions Projection	34.4
	Shortfall	$14.0
III.	Higher Income Gap Projection	$60.7
	Higher Contributions Projection	42.8
	Shortfall	$17.9
IV.	Higher Income Gap Projection	$60.7
	Lower Contributions Projection	34.4
	Shortfall	$26.3

SOURCE: Tables XVII–1 and XVII–2.

that an extrapolated status quo is an insufficiently demanding target. More ambitious goals would, of course, require more money.

In assessing in realistic terms the likelihood either of meeting the basic challenge or of attaining a still more ambitious goal, a key question is: How much of an increase, if any, can the arts achieve in their share of private philanthropy?

Increases in the share of the performing arts in the nation's pool of philanthropy will not come easily. After all, the arts are competing against many other worthy claimants whose technology is quite similar to their own, and whose financial needs may, therefore, be expected to grow correspondingly. Educational institutions, hospitals, churches and many other non-profit organizations can be expected to be under parallel pressures to increase their share of the total amount of support provided by private sources.

Yet the share of the arts is by no means fixed and immutable — or bound to decline. Indeed, in recent years their proportional share in total philanthropy has increased significantly. This conclusion cannot be demonstrated directly, because the required statistical information on the distribution of total contributions over time is not available. But it follows indirectly yet just as certainly from the facts that the income gaps of performing organizations have been increasing more rapidly than contributions in general, and that in any year contributions to the performing arts that have been used to defray operating costs have been approximately equal to the income gaps of the organizations. It is also very likely that contributions for non-operating purposes (new auditoriums, cultural centers, etc.) have increased even more rapidly, so that giving to the performing arts has surely been rising faster than contributions in general.[6]

While the recent record of giving to the arts is in and of itself encouraging, further encouragement can be derived from the possibilities of improvement in the methods used to raise contributions. The fund raising achievements of education are dramatic evidence of the kind of growth in contributed income which can occur. At least for a time, contributions to educational institutions were growing at a compound rate of 15 per cent per year.[7]

Thus, although the projected financial needs of the performing arts, even when based simply on extrapolations of recent trends, are considerably in excess of the projected rates of growth of the over-all pool of private contributions on which the arts depend, the situation is by no means hopeless. Viewed in the context of the total economy, the net deficits are small — even the largest of the shortfall figures given in Table XVII–3 is less than .005 per cent of a conservative estimate of disposable personal income in 1975.

[6] In analyzing the relationship between contributions and income gaps it must be recognized, however, that not all contributions used to defray operating expenses (let alone contributions earmarked for refurbishing auditoriums or building cultural centers) can be regarded as means to reduce the income gap. For example, a contribution made expressly for the purpose of financing a tour that would not otherwise have been undertaken may contribute nothing to reducing the organization's income gap, and may even increase the gap if it fails to cover the full amount of the increased deficit attributable to the tour. In short, increases in grants *for services* do not serve to fill the gap to the same extent as unrestricted gifts, and they may, in some circumstances, require increases in expenditure in excess of the grant itself. It is *unrestricted gifts* which must grow at the rates indicated in Table XVII–3 if the projected income gaps are to be covered.

[7] Council for Financial Aid to Education, *Guide Lines to Voluntary Support of America's Colleges and Universities*, New York (no date), p. 22.

The sums needed are by no means beyond the capabilities of a wealthy and expanding economy and energetic individuals dedicated to the welfare of the arts.

The Outlook for Government Support

Nor is the potential growth of private contributions the only way of meeting the needs of the performing organizations. The available data are much too flimsy to permit any estimate of the sums likely to be made available by municipal and state governments by 1975, but, at the state level at least, there is every reason to expect a considerable increase in support. Developments at the federal level, however, are apt to be particularly significant.

The outlook for government support depends to a considerable extent on the ability of advocates of such support to make an effective case for their position. But no matter what arguments are advanced, the amount of support provided will not be settled on the basis of abstract principles alone. The political realities are sure to play an important role.

One of the apparent disadvantages of the arts in this respect is the fact that they currently attract interest and support from only a small minority of the population. The data suggest that live professional performances are attended by less than 5 million different Americans in a year — that less than 3 per cent of our population goes even to a single performance. The Twentieth Century Fund audience survey showed that the audience at a typical performance is most unrepresentative of the general urban population in that it is:

— Relatively young
— Dominated by the white-collar occupations and especially by the professions
— Exceedingly well educated
— Very well off financially

Furthermore, while there has been some tendency toward wider regional distribution of professional performances, activity is still heavily concentrated along both coasts and especially in New York City. In 1963 New York City alone accounted for 39 per cent of the receipts collected by all classical music groups in the United

States and for 56 per cent of the receipts collected by theatrical establishments.

This socio-economic and geographic concentration of interest is not, however, necessarily a critical political disability if concern with the arts is indeed spreading along with the growth in the nation's educational level, its per capita income and the amount of available leisure time. Moreover, the minority of the public that is interested in the arts is endowed with a disproportionate share of the nation's social, economic and political power. The arts have already benefited greatly from the support of persons in influential positions. It is by stating clearly their belief in the value of the arts that labor leaders have been most useful to the arts, and the public support of many businessmen and political leaders, including several presidents of the United States, has exercised an extremely powerful influence, both in popularizing the role of the arts and in helping to "legitimize" them as subjects for support at the Congressional level.

Locally, too, the arts have benefited from the fact that many of their supporters, and particularly some of the members of the boards of the performing organizations, have traditionally been drawn from among civic leaders. We have already noted the great change among orchestral boards in their attitude toward government support. No doubt this has been a response partly to the increased economic problems besetting their organizations — difficulties which have reached a point where they can no longer be handled entirely by traditional methods. In part it may also be symptomatic of a shift in American political attitudes, which seem recently to have accommodated a much wider range of governmental responsibilities.

Given an influential and growing minority, one that strongly favors government support of the arts, the fact that not everyone attends live performance is not really critical. Indeed, it is hard to think of any type of government support, whether to the aviation industry or to agriculture, that goes directly to a majority of the nation's inhabitants. Moreover, few legislative programs have been developed and passed in response to a clarion call by an aroused and indignant public. After all, "leadership," that quality which is so strongly touted in political campaigns, if it means anything, must imply the ability to take the initiative, to undertake appropriate programs well before their necessity has become patent to everyone. The experience of the New York State Council on the Arts is but one indication that such efforts can meet with widespread approbation. One hears little criticism and certainly no general public outcry against programs of this kind. Thus, a system of support, once undertaken, may very well succeed in justifying itself politically and thereby assure its survival.

For several reasons, then, the long-run prospect for government support of the arts in this country seems favorable. What form such support will eventually take is still unpredictable. But the nature of the forces that have aligned themselves behind it, and the pressures that will manifest themselves as the financial circumstances of the performing organizations grow more difficult, portend an expansion of direct federal support for the performing arts.

The Future Dimly Glimpsed

This is as far as our empirical data will take us. But while our statistics are incapable of telling us more about the future, our analysis tempts us to probe a little further. As we have seen, it indicates that services, particularly services provided without the aid of complex technology, seem bound to grow more and more expensive, while, relatively speaking, manufactured goods become ever cheaper. Some service trades, like the vanishing domestic servant, will be all but priced out of the market by the remorseless pressures arising from their technological rigidity. Others, like fine restaurants, will be decimated in number, and may eventually become the exclusive province of the very wealthy. Still others, like the stately homes whose servicing grows ever more difficult, will survive only as museum pieces. Not all services face such a discouraging future, however. Some, such as education, will manage to expand their operations because society considers them sufficiently indispensable to pay the bill, whatever its magnitude.

Although professional performing organizations will find themselves in difficulty even over the next decade unless they obtain increased support, there are grounds for a reasonably optimistic assessment of their chances of meeting this challenge. Let us now consider for a moment what happens if we look ahead, not for a decade, but for a century — a period that is not unduly long in terms of the history of live performance. Let us take Gross National Product as a crude measure of the nation's capacity to give. If we assume, optimistically, that the nation's total output will grow at an annual rate of 4 per cent (the figure for the 1950–1960 decade was only 3.3 per cent), by the year 2065 it will have risen to 50.5 times its 1965 level. But if the income gap of the live professional performing arts rises at 8.5 per cent per year for a century, it will be multiplied by a factor of 3,800, to a total of $76 billion. What is relevant here is not the absolute amount of this astronomic figure but its relationship to the Gross National Product. Translating it back into 1964 terms, it is as though the arts' gap in 1964 had been not $20 million but $1.5 billion — which is a considerably larger proportion of the value of the nation's total output.

It is all too easy to toss about such large numbers, and they are not to be taken literally or even very seriously. They are offered only to illustrate a fundamental point — that the professional performing arts can be expected of necessity to make ever increasing demands on the public, not only absolutely but also relative to the real resources that are at its disposal.

However one feels about the long-run financial prospects for the non-profit performing groups, the outlook for the commercial organizations is clearly less promising. The commercial theater is subject to all the cost pressures which beset non-commercial live professional performance, for the technology of the two types of activity is essentially the same. But since the commercial theater receives no contributions, it cannot benefit from the growth in giving to the arts. Nor, in fact, can many small chamber groups and modern dance companies — those that subsist entirely without the aid of philanthropy. Perhaps as the Gross National Product continues to grow the public will become reconciled to ever increasing ticket prices, knowing that higher prices are required for the survival of these branches of live performance. Or perhaps we will devise some new procedure for the support of the commercial theater and these other groups, analogous to the evolving relationship between the private universities and the federal government.

Whatever happens, the long-run outlook for the commercial theater as it is currently organized seems grim.

But this future world, which is potentially so inhospitable to at least some types of professional performance, may be expected to provide a climate in which amateur activity can flourish. It is conducive to amateurism in two ways.

First, as productive efficiency increases, people can expect to have more leisure time in which to participate in performances and to develop reasonable levels of competence. Second, as the financial pressures besetting the professional groups increase, at least some of them may find it increasingly difficult to compete effectively, thus making it easier for amateurs to flourish. In fact, in some areas of activity amateur operation may be all that is financially feasible — the recent growth of the "off off-Broadway theater," in which actors, director and author may all be unpaid, can perhaps be ascribed in part to the financial problems of off-Broadway. In the non-profit sector of the performing arts there is hope that the necessary support will continue to come forth, so that professional and amateur activity may well be able to exist side by side and complement each other. But this area lives under the shadow of its own Gresham's law: without constant vigilance and willingness to bear the constantly rising costs of professional performance, amateur activity will tend to drive the trained performer from the field.

In this future world, then, professional performance may well survive and even prosper. But the cost of its preservation will be high and will rise inexorably. Fortunately, the very rise in productivity in other sectors of the economy which lies at the heart of the problem will also provide society with the wherewithal to pay the mounting bill if it is determined to do so. It is upon the strength of that determination that the future of the live performing arts depends.

LIST OF TABLES

List of Tables (continued)

LIST OF GRAPHS

List of Graphs (continued)

413

LIST OF APPENDICES

List of Appendices (continued)

APPENDIX III–1

Questionnaire Sent to 194 Municipalities, December 1964

CULTURAL CENTER STUDY
Economics of the Performing Arts
214 Western Way
Princeton, N. J. 08540

1. Name of facility _____

2. Address _____

3. Date opened to the public _____ or expected opening date _____

4. Is this facility considered to be a cultural center? _____

5. Cultural centers are often organized in order to satisfy rather specific community needs. Would you please check all of the following which apply to your center? Our center is

  a. _____ part of urban renewal project

  b. _____ part of expanded or redesigned civic center

  c. _____ part of university program in the arts

  d. _____ in conjunction with community program to attract new residents and business

  e. _____ not part of any other program

  f. other (please explain) _____

6. Cultural centers are financed in many ways. Please check which one of the following applies to your center:

  a. financed mainly by private funds _____

  b. financed mainly by foundation funds _____

  c. financed mainly by public funds _____

  d. financed by a combination of _____ and _____

  e. other (please explain) _____

7. It is well known that cultural center management is a challenging task. Please indicate which of the following general statements apply to your center:

---

a.

  1. center is administered by private organization _____

  2. center is administered by university group _____

  3. center is administered by municipal, state, or county government _____

b.

  1. center is administered by organization which has no other duties _____

  2. center is administered by organization which also has other responsibilities _____

  3. center is administered by group which is a combination of _____ and _____

c. other (please explain) _____

8. Cultural centers vary in the number and type of buildings they occupy. Please fill in the blanks which apply:

  a. our center consists of _____ building(s)

  b. our center's buildings are used only for cultural purposes, including museums, a library, classrooms, dramatic, operatic, orchestral, dance performances _____

  c. our center's buildings are also used for other purposes, such as _____

  d. when our buildings are used for cultural purposes, they are not used for other purposes at the same time _____

  e. when our buildings are used for cultural purposes, they may also be used at the same time for _____

9. Since our main concern in this study is the performing arts in cultural centers, we need to know where in your center live performances by orchestral, dramatic, operatic, or dance groups can take place.

  a. our center has _____ auditorium(s) in which such groups can perform

  b. our _____ (name of auditorium) can seat _____

  c. our _____ (name of auditorium) can seat _____

  d. our _____ (name of auditorium) can seat _____

  e. our _____ (name of auditorium) can seat _____

(Continued on following page)

421

APPENDIX III-1 (continued)

10. Please check all of the following which apply. For live performance we have

a. _____ an orchestra pit
b. _____ a proscenium stage
c. _____ a thrust stage
d. _____ an arena stage
e. _____ a stage workshop
f. _____ rehearsal rooms
g. _____ dressing rooms for _____ persons
h. _____ sq. ft. of scenery storage area
i. _____ a greenroom
j. _____ other equipment

11. Some centers prefer to be mainly a home base for resident dramatic, orchestral, dance, or operatic groups; some centers prefer their facilities to be used mainly by visiting groups; and some centers prefer a combined usage.
Please list representative groups which appeared in your center during the last year and which you expect to have appear during the coming year. (If your center is not yet operating, please list expectations for the first year.)

a. resident groups	prof., semi-prof., amateur	No. of performances

b. visiting groups	prof., semi-prof., amateur	No. of performances

12. Just as different kinds of groups perform at centers, so centers make varying kinds of financial arrangement with appearing groups. Please indicate which applies to your center:

resident groups

a. _____ fixed fee guarantee
b. _____ group rents hall and retains all box office receipts
c. _____ hall and group share receipts, hall getting _____%, group getting _____%
d. _____ other (please explain)

visiting groups

a. _____ fixed fee guarantee
b. _____ group rents hall and retains all box office receipts
c. _____ hall and group share receipts, hall getting _____%, group getting _____%
d. _____ other (please explain)

13. If you consider the next five years, which performing arts groups

a. are you committed to present?

b. are you negotiating to present?

c. would you like to present but have not yet approached?

14. About how far is your center from the nearest competing facility?

a. _____ under 2 miles
b. _____ 2 to 10 miles
c. _____ 11 to 50 miles
d. _____ over 50 miles
e. Please specify name and type of facility:

We very much appreciate your cooperation in filling out the questionnaire. If there is any further information you would like us to have, or if there are any comments you would like to make, please use the back of this sheet.

May we contact you for further questions in connection with the study?

Name _____ Position or Title _____

Address _____

Notes on the Major Orchestra Data

Financial and operating statistics for the major orchestras have been taken from annual reports compiled by the managers of the major orchestras.

Over the period 1936–37 through 1963–64, we were able to obtain major orchestra compiled reports for twenty of the seasons. No such reports could be located for the other eight seasons. The missing years consist of the war years (1940–41 through 1943–44), 1952–53, 1953–54, 1958–59, and 1959–60. (Partial reports do exist for 1940–41 through 1943–44.)

In all, 27 orchestras reported figures for the most recent season for which data are available (1963–64). Two of these were Canadian orchestras (Montreal and Toronto) and were excluded from the study for this reason. Of the remaining 25, two (Denver and Seattle) were such recent additions to the ranks of the majors that their figures could not be used in our analysis without producing distortions. The 23 other orchestras (Atlanta, Baltimore, Boston, Buffalo, Chicago, Cincinnati, Cleveland, Dallas, Detroit, Houston, Indianapolis, Kansas City, Los Angeles, Minneapolis, National (Washington), New Orleans, New York, Philadelphia, Pittsburgh, Rochester, St. Louis, San Antonio, and San Francisco) constitute what we term our "all major orchestras" set. Some of our results are reported for this set.

However, in analyzing the data, problems arise because not all of these 23 orchestras reported figures for each of the twenty seasons for which we have reports. The fact that some orchestras move in and out of the sample means that time series results are affected by the shifting composition of the group of orchestras reporting figures as well as by true time trends. To minimize this problem we selected a "basic" set of 11 orchestras which share the characteristic of having reported in at least nineteen of the twenty years for which we have major orchestra compiled reports. This "basic" set consists of Chicago, Cincinnati, Cleveland, Indianapolis, Kansas City, Minneapolis, National (Washington), Philadelphia, Pittsburgh, St. Louis, and San Francisco. Fortunately, the basic eleven turn out to be a rather good cross-section of major orchestras, viewed in terms of expenditure levels, geographic location, and operating characteristics.

APPENDIX TABLE III—A

APPENDIX TABLE III—A

Selected Categories of Expenditure, 1932–1963

	1929	1930	1931	1932	1933	1934	193
Aggregate Economic Indicators (in billions):							
Gross National Product	$104.4	$91.1	$76.3	$58.5	$56.0	$65.0	$72.
Disposable Personal Income	83.1	74.4	63.8	48.7	45.7	52.0	58.
Total Personal Consumption Expenditures	79.0	71.0	61.3	49.3	46.4	51.9	56.
Total Expenditures on Services	32.1	29.8	26.9	22.9	20.7	21.0	21.
"Performing Arts" Category (in millions):							
Admissions to Legitimate Theater and Opera and Entertainment of Non-profit Institutions (except athletics)	127	95	78	57	41	42	4
Other Selected Categories (in millions):							
Recreation (total)	4,331	3,990	3,302	2,442	2,202	2,441	2,63
Books and Maps	309	264	253	153	152	165	18
Magazines, Newspapers and Sheet Music	538	512	479	428	419	441	45
Radio and Television Receivers, Records and Musical Instruments	1,012	921	478	268	195	229	24
Admissions to Motion Picture Theaters	720	732	719	527	482	518	55
Admissions to Spectator Sports	66	65	57	47	50	65	7
Private Education and Research (total)	664	683	665	571	481	483	50

1936	1937	1938	1939	1940	1941	1942	1943	1944	1945	1946
82.7	$90.8	$85.2	$91.1	$100.6	$125.8	$159.1	$192.5	$211.4	$213.6	$210.7
66.2	71.0	65.7	70.4	76.1	93.0	117.5	133.5	146.8	150.4	160.6
62.6	67.3	64.6	67.6	71.9	81.9	89.7	100.5	109.8	121.7	147.1
23.5	25.1	25.0	25.8	26.9	29.0	31.5	34.7	37.7	40.4	46.4
50	53	58	64	71	79	92	118	142	148	174
,020	3,381	3,241	3,452	3,761	4,239	4,677	4,961	5,422	6,139	8,621
208	243	221	226	234	255	291	366	450	520	594
490	518	514	554	589	636	703	838	880	965	1,099
333	385	339	420	494	607	634	403	311	344	1,143
626	676	663	659	735	809	1,022	1,275	1,341	1,450	1,692
83	89	95	98	98	107	90	62	80	116	200
546	600	619	628	641	702	813	957	972	974	1,162

(*Continued on following page*)

	1947	1948	1949	1950	1951	1952	195
Aggregate Economic Indicators (in billions):							
Gross National Product	$234.3	$259.4	$258.1	$284.6	$329.0	$347.0	$36!
Disposable Personal Income	170.1	189.3	189.7	207.7	227.5	238.7	25:
Total Personal Consumption Expenditures	165.4	178.3	181.2	195.0	209.8	219.8	23:
Total Expenditures on Services	51.4	56.9	60.0	64.9	70.2	75.6	8]
"Performing Arts" Category (in millions):							
Admissions to Legitimate Theater and Opera and Entertainments of Non-profit Institutions (except athletics)	188	182	183	185	188	192	2
Other Selected Categories (in millions):							
Recreation (total)	9,352	9,808	10,122	11,278	11,704	12,257	12,8
Books and Maps	536	588	630	677	778	790	8
Magazines, Newspapers and Sheet Music	1,243	1,374	1,454	1,495	1,573	1,689	1,7
Radio and Television Receivers, Records and Musical Instruments	1,429	1,479	1,704	2,457	2,264	2,373	2,6
Admissions to Motion Picture Theaters	1,594	1,503	1,445	1,367	1,299	1,233	1,1
Admissions to Spectator Sports	222	233	240	223	221	221	2
Private Education and Research (total)	1,411	1,553	1,683	1,801	1,951	2,109	2,2

SOURCES: Aggregate Economic Indicators: *Economic Report of the President*, Janua 1964, p. 207, cols. 33–37, 42–46. All Personal Consumption Expenditures Figures: *S vey of Current Business*, 1954 National Income Supplement, pp. 206–9 (for 1929–19 data); 1959 Income and Output Supplement, p. 151 (for 1946–1955 data); July 196

1954	1955	1956	1957	1958	1959	1960	1961	1962	1963
363.1	$397.5	$419.2	$440.3	$444.5	$482.7	$502.6	$518.7	$556.2	$583.9
256.9	274.4	292.9	308.8	317.9	337.1	349.9	364.7	384.6	402.5
238.0	256.9	269.9	285.2	293.2	313.5	328.2	337.3	356.8	375.0
86.3	92.5	100.0	107.1	114.3	122.8	131.5	138.3	146.4	155.3
225	251	276	296	313	339	373	400	422	433
3,256	14,220	15,193	16,082	16,842	18,309	19,524	20,559	21,496	22,703
806	888	1,006	1,149	1,181	1,353	1,545	1,690	1,668	1,743
1,825	1,917	1,954	2,087	2,233	2,309	2,439	2,555	2,655	2,778
2,741	2,792	2,872	3,000	3,067	3,420	3,616	3,764	3,998	4,308
1,210	1,217	1,228	1,120	1,168	1,271	1,298	1,283	1,241	1,275
225	232	240	246	255	265	274	280	296	301
2,389	2,597	2,903	3,232	3,641	4,082	4,444	4,739	5,208	5,663

p. 14 (for 1956–1958 data); July 1964, p. 16 (for 1959–1963 data). As post-publication revisions sometimes occur, figures for the last few years should be considered subject to later possible revision.

427

Average Annual Percentage Increase in Expenditures in Selected Categories, 1932–1963, 1947–1963, 1961–1963[a]

	1932–1963	1947–1963	1961–1963
Aggregate Economic Indicators:			
Gross National Product	8.2	5.7	6.1
Disposable Personal Income	7.6	5.4	5.1
Total Personal Consumption	7.5	5.2	5.4
Total Expenditures on Services	7.4	7.2	6.0
"Performing Arts" Category:			
Admissions to Legitimate Theater and Opera and Entertainments of Non-profit Institutions (except athletics)	8.2	6.5	4.0
Other Selected Categories:			
Recreation (Total)	8.3	5.8	5.1
Books and Maps	8.7	7.9	1.6
Magazines, Newspapers and Sheet Music	7.0	4.9	4.3
Radio and Television Receivers, Records, Musical Instruments	11.4	6.4	7.0
Admissions to Motion Picture Theaters	3.0	1.1	0.3
Admissions to Spectator Sports	6.0	1.9	3.7
Private Education and Research (total)	8.8	9.1	9.3

SOURCE: *Survey of Current Business* data. For actual figures for the years 1929–1963 and detailed references, see Appendix Table III–A.

[a] Average annual growth rates were calculated by regressing the logarithms of the current dollar figures on time.

Consumer Expenditures on the Performing Arts, 1929–1963

	In Current Dollars (millions)	In Constant (1954) Dollars		Per $100 of Disposable Personal Income
		Total (millions)	Per Capita	
	(1)	(2)	(3)	(4)
1929	$127	$221	$2.51	$ .15
1930	95	171	1.91	.13
1931	78	156	1.72	.12
1932	57	127	1.38	.12
1933	41	83	.89	.09
1934	42	90	.96	.08
1935	44	93	.98	.08
1936	50	105	1.09	.08
1937	53	107	1.09	.07
1938	58	119	1.20	.09
1939	64	133	1.33	.09
1940	71	145	1.43	.09
1941	79	149	1.45	.08
1942	92	154	1.48	.08
1943	118	182	1.73	.09
1944	142	214	2.01	.10
1945	148	218	2.03	.10
1946	174	233	2.15	.11
1947	188	226	2.06	.11
1948	182	206	1.86	.10
1949	183	207	1.85	.10
1950	185	207	1.83	.09
1951	188	194	1.70	.08
1952	192	196	1.70	.08
1953	200	202	1.73	.08
1954	225	225	1.91	.09
1955	251	248	2.09	.09
1956	276	264	2.20	.09
1957	296	272	2.23	.10
1958	313	282	2.29	.10
1959	339	301	2.41	.10
1960	373	327	2.59	.11
1961	400	346	2.67	.11
1962	422	361	2.74	.11
1963	433	365	2.72	.11

(*Notes on following page*)

SOURCES:

Col. 1: Survey of Current Business data. See Appendix Table III–A.

Col. 2: Col. 1 divided by the G.N.P. implicit price deflator (1954 = 100), data for which are from the *Economic Report of the President,* January 1964, p. 214. Ideally, we would divide by an index of ticket prices for legitimate theater, opera, concerts, etc., but no such index, going back to 1929, is available. Thomas Moore has constructed an index of *top* prices to Broadway shows, and we considered using this measure here. However, Broadway prices may move differently from average prices, especially in a sharp depression such as occurred in the 1930's. To the extent that ticket prices have increased more rapidly than the G.N.P. implicit price deflator (see Chapter XI), the measure of "real" expenditures presented here *overstates* the true increase in the level of performing arts activity.

Col. 3: Col. 2 divided by the U. S. population 13 years of age and over. Population figures for 1929–1957 are from U. S. Bureau of the Census, *Historical Statistics of the United States: Colonial Times to 1957* (Washington, D. C., 1960), p. 8; more recent figures are from *Current Population Reports.*

Col. 4: Col. 1 divided by total disposable personal income. Disposable personal income data are from the *Economic Report of the President,* January 1964, p. 207.

APPENDIX TABLE III–D

Selected Consumer Expenditures Per $100 of Disposable Income, 1929–1963

	Adm. to Theater, etc.	Books, Maps	Mag., News-papers, Sheet Music	Radio & TV Receivers, Records, Musical Instruments	Adm. to Specta-tor Sports	Adm. to Movies	Private Education & Research
1929	$ .15	$ .37	$ .65	$1.22	$ .08	$ .87	$ .86
1930	.13	.35	.69	1.24	.09	.98	.92
1931	.12	.40	.75	.75	.09	1.13	1.04
1932	.12	.31	.88	.55	.10	1.08	1.17
1933	.09	.33	.92	.43	.11	1.05	1.05
1934	.08	.32	.85	.44	.13	1.00	.93
1935	.08	.31	.78	.43	.12	.95	.87
1936	.08	.31	.74	.50	.13	.95	.82
1937	.07	.34	.73	.54	.13	.95	.85
1938	.09	.34	.78	.52	.14	1.01	.94
1939	.09	.32	.79	.60	.14	.94	.89
1940	.09	.31	.77	.65	.13	.97	.84
1941	.08	.27	.68	.65	.12	.87	.75

(Continued on following page)

	Adm. to Theater, etc.	Books, Maps	Mag., News-papers, Sheet Music	Radio & TV Receiv-ers, Rec-ords, Musical Instru-ments	Adm. to Specta-tor Sports	Adm. to Movies	Private Educa-tion & Research
1942	.08	.25	.60	.54	.08	.87	.69
1943	.09	.27	.63	.30	.05	.96	.72
1944	.10	.31	.60	.21	.05	.91	.66
1945	.10	.35	.64	.23	.08	.96	.65
1946	.11	.37	.68	.71	.12	1.05	.72
1947	.11	.32	.73	.84	.13	.94	.83
1948	.10	.31	.73	.78	.12	.79	.82
1949	.10	.33	.77	.90	.13	.76	.89
1950	.09	.33	.72	1.18	.11	.66	.87
1951	.08	.34	.69	1.00	.10	.57	.86
1952	.08	.33	.71	.99	.09	.52	.88
1953	.08	.33	.70	1.03	.09	.46	.89
1954	.09	.31	.71	1.07	.09	.47	.93
1955	.09	.32	.70	1.02	.08	.44	.95
1956	.09	.34	.67	.98	.08	.42	.99
1957	.10	.37	.68	.97	.08	.36	1.05
1958	.10	.37	.70	.96	.08	.37	1.15
1959	.10	.40	.68	1.01	.08	.38	1.21
1960	.11	.44	.70	1.03	.08	.37	1.27
1961	.11	.46	.70	1.03	.08	.35	1.30
1962	.11	.43	.69	1.04	.08	.32	1.35
1963	.11	.43	.69	1.07	.07	.32	1.41

SOURCE: Calculated by dividing each of the respective categories by dispos-able personal income and multiplying the quotients by 100. Disposable per-sonal income data are from the *Economic Report of the President*, January 1964, p. 207. The other figures are from the *Survey of Current Business*.

Opera Activity, 1941–1964

Season	Total Number of Companies[a]	Total Number of Performances	Performances by Selected Major Companies		
			Metropolitan Opera	New York City Opera	Other Selected Companies[b]
1941–42	77	—			
1942–43	77	nearly 900			
1943–44	88	over 1,000			
1944–45	113	—			
1945–46	100+	—			
1946–47	100+	—			
1947–48	150+	—	216		
1948–49	219	—			
1949–50	214	2,500			
1950–51	316	—	205		
1951–52	312	—	213		
1952–53	386	2,704	212		
1953–54	444	2,500	207		
1954–55	543	3,217	217	101	
1955–56	600	3,581	214		
1956–57	703	3,644	233		
1957–58	728	3,953	233	90	81
1958–59	727	3,955	234		
1959–60	754	4,232	236		
1960–61	783	3,698	239		
1961–62	796	4,030	235	104	92
1962–63	795	4,606	237	87	100
1963–64	754	3,877	244		

SOURCES: The total numbers of companies and performances are from *Opera News*, December 18, 1961, December 10, 1962, December 16, 1963, December 14, 1964. The performance totals for the selected opera companies were determined on the basis of information supplied by the companies.

[a] Includes high school, college, other amateur, and professional companies.

[b] Chicago Lyric, Cincinnati Summer, Houston Grand, Kansas City Lyric, and Opera Society of Washington companies.

Dance Groups in the United States, 1959–1964[a]

	1959	1960	1961	1962	1963	1964[b]
Total Professional Groups	115	139	153	162	169	196
Foreign or Ethnic Groups[c]	37	44	56	63	70	80
American Groups	78	95	97	99	99	116
Regional or Civic, Semi-professional or Amateur Groups	—	—	—	70	88	97

SOURCE: *Dance Magazine*'s "Annual Directory of Dance Attractions," 1958–1964.

[a] Includes groups of more than two dancers which have an active repertoire of at least one full program, a company organization separate from a school group, and at least two performances before paying audiences.

[b] Part of the continuous growth in each category may be explained by the comparative novelty of the "Annual Directory." Dance companies which enter the listing in any year may have been in existence previously without having reported.

[c] The division into foreign or ethnic and American must be considered a rough estimate, as classification is difficult.

Professional Dance Activity in New York City, 1952–1965 (five months: October through February)

	1951 –52	1952 –53	1953 –54	1954 –55	1955 –56	1956 –57	1957 –58	1958 –59	1959 –60	1960 –61	1961 –62	1962 –63	1963 –64	1964 –65
Total Performances	110	186	169	197	233	164	273	168ᵃ	191	224	228	191	222	340
By Foreign or Ethnic Groups	23	57	87	101	90	21	129	55	78	62	57	69	65	135
By American Groups	87	129	82	96	143	143	144	113	113	162	171	122	157	205
Per Cent American	79	69	49	49	64	87	53	67	59	72	75	61	71	60

SOURCE: *Dance Magazine*, monthly "New York Calendar of Events" and occasional items from "Presstime" section.

ᵃ Does not include December performances.

Dance Tours in the United States, Month of October,[a] Selected Years, 1952–1964

	1952	1954	1956	1958	1959	1960	1961	1962	1963	1964
Total Towns and Cities Visited	28	41	106	124	109	142	196	110	251	117
Total Performances	46	88	115	151	131	192	220	156	277	191
At Colleges and Universities	—	—	—	18	4	5	21	17	39	32
By Foreign or Ethnic Groups	9	63	86	75	93	181	170	140	197	133
By American Groups	37	25	29	76	38	11	50	16	80	58
Per Cent American	80	28	25	50	29	6	23	10	29	30

SOURCE: *Dance Magazine.*

[a] Calendars generally list events from October 10 to November 10.

Broadway Activity, 1899–1964

| Season | Number of Shows | | Total Number of Perform- ances | Estimated Average Weekly Attendance in February (thousands) |
	Total Playing	New Productions (including revivals)		
	(1)	(2)	(3)	(4)
1899–1900		87		
1900–1901		96		
1901–2		90		
1902–3		98		
1903–4		118		
1904–5		127		
1905–6		111		
1906–7		129		
1907–8		110		
1908–9		118		
1909–10		144		
1910–11		131		
1911–12		140		
1912–13		162		
1913–14		128		
1914–15		133		
1915–16		115		
1916–17		126		
1917–18		156		
1918–19		149		
1919–20		144		
1920–21		152		
1921–22		194		
1922–23		174		
1923–24		186		
1924–25		228		
1925–26		255		
1926–27		263		270.2
1927–28	242	264	17,055	285.8
1928–29	231	225	17,529	253.7
1929–30	233	233	16,363	233.9
1930–31	188	187	12,639	151.0
1931–32	175	207	8,901	144.6
1932–33	124	174	8,257	127.7
1933–34	149	151	8,130	87.2
1934–35	155	149	9,141	103.5

Season	Number of Shows		Total Number of Performances	Estimated Average Weekly Attendance in February (thousands)
	Total Playing	New Productions (including revivals)		
	(1)	(2)	(3)	(4)
1935–36	119	135	8,649	120.3
1936–37	121	118	8,172	131.2
1937–38	111	111	8,128	140.0
1938–39	100	98	8,309	122.1
1939–40	96	91	7,916	103.7
1940–41	81	69	7,704	127.5
1941–42	86	83	7,240	110.9
1942–43	93	80	9,707	136.5
1943–44	96	97	8,889	201.3
1944–45	96	92	11,666	200.8
1945–46	99	76	11,328	187.4
1946–47	103	79	11,325	162.6
1947–48	89	76	10,254	138.9
1948–49	89	70	9,673	158.1
1949–50	69	57	8,983	165.3
1950–51	92	81	8,446	171.5
1951–52	89	72	8,614	176.3
1952–53	65	54	7,571	118.3
1953–54	66	59	8,485	170.3
1954–55	72	58	8,917	181.8
1955–56	70	56	9,390	185.8
1956–57	78	62	8,973	167.8
1957–58	85	56	8,247	167.5
1958–59	73	56	8,943	178.0
1959–60	76	58	9,214	183.6
1960–61	70	48	9,445	181.4
1961–62	73	53	9,055	175.1
1962–63	71	54	8,954	153.9
1963–64	82	63	7,975	

SOURCES:

Cols. 1 and 3: From a table compiled from *Best Plays* volumes and *Variety* by Thomas G. Moore.

Col. 2: Variety, July 22, 1964. For some inexplicable reason, probably having to do with slightly different coverage of the two series, the number of new productions exceeds the number of total shows playing in the early 1930's.

Col. 4: Estimated by Moore, by dividing dollar grosses by a ticket price index.

Off-Broadway Activity, 1953–1965

Season (June 1– May 31)	Productions					Performances		
			New					
	Total	Hold-overs	Non-reper-tory	Reper-tory	Totala	Total	Hold-overs	New Produc-tions
1953–54	23	0	17	6	23	971	0	971
1954–55	41	0	33	8	41	1,883	0	1,883
1955–56	46	0	38	8	46	2,072	0	2,072
1956–57	55	7	41	7	48	3,148	877	2,271
1957–58	79	11	63	5	68	4,491	1,705	2,786
1958–59	89	9	73	7	80	5,862	1,921	3,941
1959–60	114	14	82	18	100	6,803	2,510	4,293
1960–61	132	19	92	21	113	7,757	3,505	4,252
1961–62	145	20	103	22	125	8,049	3,329	4,720
1962–63	105	15	74	16	90	8,323	4,259	4,064
1963–64	131	24	86	21	107	9,296	4,153	5,143
1964–65	110	23	62	25	87	6,702	3,085	3,617

SOURCE: *New York Herald Tribune,* Drama Section, end of May or beginning of June, 1954–1965.

[a] Includes new musicals, new plays, revivals, special productions, the presentations of special companies such as the Savoyards, City Center and Phoenix, and those of visiting foreign troupes.

APPENDIX TABLE III–K

Trends in Activity for the "Average"[a] Major Orchestra, 1937–1964

	1936 -37	1937 -38	1938 -39	1939 -40	1940 -41	1941 -42	1942 -43	1943 -44	1944 -45	1945 -46	1946 -47	1947 -48	1948 -49	1949 -50
Season Length (weeks)	24.9	24.0	24.0	24.8	25.0	24.1	24.2	23.1	24.5	25.2	26.2	26.4	25.8	25.1
Number of Concerts														
Home Concerts (total)	60	52	54	58	62	64	67	62	61	62	64	64	62	65
Youth	7	7	7	11	Na	Na	Na	Na	12	13	14	12	12	12
Tour Concerts	14	19	20	25	26	30	22	18	27	34	41	36	34	28
Total Paid Concerts	74	71	74	83	88	94	89	80	88	96	105	100	96	93
Paid Attendance (in thousands)	152	163	169	194	0	0	0	0	222	254	248	249	225	221

(Continued on following page)

APPENDIX TABLE III–K (continued)

	1950 –51	1951 –52	1952 –53	1953 –54	1954 –55	1955 –56	1956 –57	1957 –58	1958 –59	1959 –60	1960 –61	1961 –62	1962 –63	1963 –64
Season Length (weeks)	25.4	25.4	0	25.6	25.6	26.3	26.5	26.2	0	0	27.6	27.7	28.7	29.6
Number of Concerts														
Home Concerts														
(total)	68	63	0	65	67	72	75	85	0	0	87	80	91	96
Youth	14	14	0	14	14	16	21	24	0	0	26	24	29	34
Tour Concerts	23	32	0	26	27	26	34	27	0	0	33	30	30	32
Total Paid Concerts	91	95	0	91	94	98	109	112	0	0	120	110	121	128
Paid Attendance (in thousands)	204	221	0	217	216	229	242	254	0	263	263	263	263	278

^a The "averages" given here are arithmetic means for our "basic" set of eleven major orchestras. These orchestras are Chicago, Cincinnati, Cleveland, Indianapolis, Kansas City, Minneapolis, National (Washington), Philadelphia, Pittsburgh, St. Louis, and San Francisco. They were selected because each reported in at least nineteen of the twenty years for which we have major orchestra compiled reports. This group also appears to be a good cross-section of all major orchestras. For the source of the data and a more detailed discussion of procedure, see Appendix III–2.

Trends in Activity for the "Average"[a] Major Orchestra, Annual Growth Rates

	Average Annual Percentage Increase		
	1937–1964	1947–1964	1961–1964
Season Length (weeks)	0.7	0.7	2.4
Number of Concerts Per Year			
All Home Concerts	1.9	2.6	4.0
Total Paid Concerts	1.9	1.7	2.5
Paid Attendance	1.7	1.1	3.6
Paid Attendance Per Capita	0.5	0.0	2.0

[a] Based on our "basic" set of eleven major orchestras. The growth rates used here are weighted by orchestra size because we are interested in industry trends. See Appendix III–2.

APPENDIX TABLE III–M

Percentage Distribution of Performing Arts Establishments,[a] by Region, 1958 and 1963

Region	Symphony Orchestras, Operas, Ballets		Other Classical Music Groups		Theatrical Presentations	
	1958	1963	1958	1963	1958	1963
New England	5.6	5.4	12.7	7.1	4.2	4.2
Middle Atlantic	27.1	22.4	37.3	29.7	45.9	45.2
East N. Central	10.3	14.3	20.6	20.0	13.8	13.3
West N. Central	7.5	6.1	5.9	6.5	4.2	4.9
South Atlantic	9.3	12.2	3.9	3.9	6.2	6.6
East S. Central	2.8	4.8	2.0	4.5	1.1	1.5
West S. Central	10.3	7.5	2.9	5.8	3.1	2.9
Mountain	2.8	4.8	2.0	3.9	1.6	2.6
Pacific	24.3	22.4	12.7	18.7	19.7	18.8
United States	100	100	100	100	100	100
(Number)	(107)	(147)	(102)	(155)	(1,762)	(1,843)

(*Notes on following page*)

SOURCE: *Census of Business, 1963, Selected Services,* U. S. Summary, BC 63–SA1, Table 2.

ᵃ "An 'establishment' is a single physical location at which business is conducted. An establishment is not necessarily identical with the 'company' or 'enterprise,' which may consist of one or more establishments." (*Census of Business, 1963,* p. 163 of volume cited above.) The Census reports number of establishments for both the "employer" universe — limited to those establishments with some employees and a payroll — and the "non-employer" universe, which includes individual entrepreneurs with no paid employees. The methods of data collection vary for the two universes; since the figures for the employer universe seem much more likely to be reliable, the "number of establishments with payroll" is used here.

APPENDIX TABLE III–N

Percentage Distribution of Performing Arts Establishments Per Capita, by Region, 1958 and 1963

Region	Symphony Orchestras, Operas, Ballets		Other Classical Music Groups		Theatrical Presentations	
	1958	1963	1958	1963	1958	1963
New England	10.9	10.6	26.1	14.6	9.8	9.8
Middle Atlantic	16.2	13.2	23.4	18.1	32.6	31.7
East N. Central	5.8	8.2	12.1	11.8	9.2	9.0
West N. Central	10.0	8.3	8.2	9.1	6.6	7.9
South Atlantic	7.4	9.3	3.3	3.0	5.9	6.0
East S. Central	4.7	8.2	3.6	7.9	2.2	3.0
West S. Central	12.6	8.8	3.7	7.0	4.5	4.1
Mountain	8.5	13.4	6.5	11.2	5.9	8.6
Pacific	24.0	20.2	13.1	17.4	23.2	20.1
United States	100	100	100	100	100	100

SOURCE: Same as Appendix Table III–M. "Raw" figures in that table were weighted by the reciprocals of each region's population expressed as a percentage of the total U. S. population, and each of the resulting figures was then divided by the sum of the weights to return to a base of U. S. = 100%.

Audience Survey Methods

Our audience information was obtained with the aid of printed questionnaires, one version for use in this country and a slight variant for England. (Copies are included at the end of this appendix.) The final form of the basic questionnaire was determined only after preliminary drafts had been pre-tested on sample audiences.

In designing our questionnaire we were careful to phrase the questions in such a way that the answers would be directly comparable with information provided by the United States Census. For example, in our question about the education of the individual, we asked him to indicate whether he had completed grade school, one to three years of college, four years of college, graduate or post-professional school. These are precisely the categories used by the Census. This procedure permitted a direct comparison of the figures we obtained for our audiences with the corresponding data for the population as a whole, both for the entire country and for the particular region in which a survey was conducted. Thus, one could tell directly how the education of the audience which attended a chamber concert compared both with that of the population of the United States and of the people living in the immediate area in which the performance took place.

Our questionnaires were given out to only a portion of the audience. As a rule they were tendered to half the patrons in the auditorium, but when audiences were extremely large they were given to one person in three or one person in four, depending upon the size of the group. In no case was a questionnaire given to every member of an audience. Whenever possible the questionnaires were inserted into the programs which ushers distribute to incoming patrons as they are being seated, thereby allowing the maximum amount of time for the respondents to complete them before leaving after the performance. In a covering letter, and where possible in a curtain speech, the audience was urged to complete the questionnaires and drop them into baskets that had been placed at the exits. It was stressed that respondents would remain completely anonymous, that there was no way to identify them.

Each survey was conducted and overseen by members of our own staff to insure that the same procedure was carried out each time, so that the surveys would be as comparable as possible. Our people would reach the auditorium before the doors were opened to the patrons and supervise the insertion of questionnaires into the programs in a given sequence. Usually one was inserted into every other program in the stacks to be handed out by the ushers, thus insuring a 50 per cent sample which would be distributed evenly throughout the theater. The primary purpose of this every-other-person sampling procedure was to minimize the possibility that both husband and wife would fill out questionnaires.

Once collected, the data were coded, that is, translated into standardized categories. After this they were transferred to punch cards and run through a computer on the basis of a specially constructed computer program. Printouts of the results pertaining to individual organizations were sent to the performing groups that had been surveyed.

The accompanying table summarizes the number of surveys conducted, the number of usable responses, and the response rates — all classified by art form. The organizations surveyed are listed in Appendix Table IV–B.

Twentieth Century Fund Audience Surveys: Kinds, Numbers, Response Rates

Kind of Organization	Number of Organizations Surveyed	Number of Performances Surveyed	Number of Responses	Median Response Rate (per cent)
Theater				
Broadway	8	17	2,252	25.0
Off-Broadway	6	24	1,786	53.0
Regional	21	47	6,023	60.0
Subtotal	35	88	10,061	54.0
Orchestras				
Major	12	28	9,479	
Other	2	2	486	
Subtotal	14	30	9,965	40.0
Opera	4	8	1,450	23.5
Dance	6	9	2,146	55.6
Ensembles	5	5	936	50.0
"Open Air"[a]	2	13	4,855	49.5
Total	66	153	29,413	49.3[b]

[a] Shakespeare-in-the-Park and Robin Hood Dell performances. These are both free.

[b] Weighted mean of the above median rates.

As explained in the text of Chapter IV, we ran a number of tests in an effort to determine the extent of bias in our survey findings. Appendix Table IV–C gives the results of several rank correlation tests.

Our basic "unit" of analysis consisted of a socio-economic profile for each art form. We then constructed an over-all profile of the U. S. audience, using a weighting scheme based on our estimates of attendance in 1963–64; the derivation of these weights is shown in Appendix Table IV–A. Appendix Table IV–J shows the effects on our over-all profile of using the attendance weights rather than (implicit) number-of-usable-questionnaires-collected weights. The differences are slight.

AUDIENCE QUESTIONNAIRE (United States)

PLEASE CHECK THE APPROPRIATE BOX OR FILL IN THE BLANK

First, some background information:

1. Male □ [1]
   Female □ [2]

2. Married □ [1]
   Not married □ [2]

3. Number of children _____

4. Your age:
   Under 20 □ [1]
   20 – 24 □ [2]
   25 – 34 □ [3]
   35 – 44 □ [4]
   45 – 59 □ [5]
   60 or over □ [6]

5. What is your occupation? _____

6. If you are not the head of your household, what is his or her occupation? _____

7. How much formal education have you completed? (Check highest level.)
   Grade school □ [1]
   1 – 3 years of high school □ [2]
   4 years of high school □ [3]
   1 – 3 years of college □ [4]
   4 years of college □ [5]
   Graduate or post-college professional school □ [6]

8. In which group did your total family income (before taxes) for last year fall?
   Under $3,000 □ [1]
   $3,000 – 4,999 □ [2]
   $5,000 – 6,999 □ [3]
   $7,000 – 9,999 □ [4]
   $10,000 – 14,999 □ [5]
   $15,000 – 24,999 □ [6]
   $25,000 – 49,999 □ [7]
   $50,000 or over □ [8]

Now, some questions about today's performance and the performing arts in general:

9. In what community do you live?
   _____ , _____
   (town)   (state)

10. How far is your home from this theater (or hall)?
    _____ (miles one way)

11. How did you hear about today's performance? (Check as many as applicable.)
    a) Mailing list announcement □ [1]
    b) Newspaper advertising □ [2]
    c) Newspaper story (including review) □ [3]
    d) Radio or television □ [4]
    e) Billboard advertising □ [5]
    f) Word of mouth □ [6]
    g) Other? (please specify) _____

12. Are you a season ticket holder?
    No □ [1]
    Yes □ [2]

13. Did you, or someone in your family, pay for your ticket to tonight's performance?
    No □ [1]
    Yes □ [2]

14. What price did you actually pay per ticket?
    $ _____

15. Before buying your ticket, did you try to buy a less expensive ticket?
    No □ [1]
    Yes □ [2]

16. A more expensive ticket?
    No □ [1]
    Yes □ [2]

17. In connection with your attendance at today's performance, how much was spent on:
    a) Public transportation (train, bus, taxi, etc.)? _____ $ _____
       –How many persons does this amount cover? _____
    b) Private passenger auto (please multiply 10¢ by no. of miles travelled, round-trip)? _____ $ _____
    c) Parking of private auto? _____ $ _____
       –Number of persons in car? _____
    d) Restaurant (including tips)? _____ $ _____
       –How many persons does this amount cover? _____
    e) Baby-sitter (please estimate cost)? $ _____

18. Have you, within the last five years, performed in:
    a) An amateur theatrical presentation?
       No □ [1]
       Yes □ [2]
    b) An amateur musical concert?
       No □ [1]
       Yes □ [2]
    c) An amateur ballet or modern dance presentation?
       No □ [1]
       Yes □ [2]

19. Excluding today, have you attended a theater performance within the last 12 months?
    No □ [1]
    Yes → How many times? _____

20. Excluding today, have you attended a symphony within the last 12 months?
    No □ [1]
    Yes → How many times? _____

21. Excluding today, have you attended an opera within the last 12 months?
    No □ [1]
    Yes → How many times? _____

22. Excluding today, have you attended a serious musical performance other than a symphony or opera (chamber, soloist, etc.) within the last 12 months?
    No □ [1]
    Yes → How many times? _____

23. Excluding today, have you attended a ballet or modern dance performance within the last 12 months?
    No □ [1]
    Yes → How many times? _____

24. Do you contribute money to performing arts organizations:
    Rarely, if ever? □ [1]
    Occasionally? □ [2]
    Regularly? □ [3]
    Please list arts organizations to which you have contributed within the last 12 months:
    _____
    _____
    _____

AUDIENCE QUESTIONNAIRE (Great Britain)

PLEASE MARK THE APPROPRIATE BOX OR FILL IN THE BLANK

First, some background information:

1. Male ☐ (1)
   Female ☐ (2)

2. Married ☐ (1)
   Not married ☐ (2)

3. Number of children ....

4. Your age:
   Under 20 ☐ (1)
   20 – 24 ☐ (2)
   25 – 34 ☐ (3)
   35 – 44 ☐ (4)
   45 – 59 ☐ (5)
   60 or over ☐ (6)

5. What is your occupation?
   ....

6. If you are not the head of your household, what is his or her occupation?
   ....

7. At what age did you complete your full-time education?
   14 or under ☐ (1)
   15 ☐ (2)
   16 ☐ (3)
   17, 18 or 19 ☐ (4)
   20 and over ☐ (5)

8. In which group did your total family income (before taxes) for last year fall?
   Under £500 ☐ (1)
   £500–£899 ☐ (2)
   £900–£1199 ☐ (3)
   £1200–£1749 ☐ (4)
   £1750–£2499 ☐ (5)
   £2500 or over ☐ (6)

Now, some questions about today's performance and the performing arts in general:

9. Where do you live? ....
   If in London, in what district? ....

10. How far is your home from this theatre (or hall)? .... (miles one way)

11. How did you hear about today's performance?
    (Mark as many as applicable.)
    (a) Mailing list announcement ☐ (1)
    (b) Newspaper advertising ☐ (2)
    (c) Newspaper story (including review) ☐ (3)
    (d) Radio or television ☐ (4)
    (e) Poster advertising ☐ (5)
    (f) Word of mouth ☐ (6)
    (g) Other? (please specify) ....

12. Did you, or someone in your family, pay for your ticket to tonight's performance?
    No ☐ (1)
    Yes ☐ (2)

13. What price did you pay per ticket? ....

14. Before buying your ticket, did you try to buy a less expensive ticket?
    No ☐ (1)
    Yes ☐ (2)

15. A more expensive ticket?
    No ☐ (1)
    Yes ☐ (2)

16. In connection with your attendance at today's performance, how much is being spent on:

    £ s. d.

    (a) Public transport (train, bus, taxi, etc.)? ....
        —How many persons does this amount cover? ....
    (b) Private car (please estimate roughly the cost in petrol, etc, here and return)
        —Number of persons in car? ....
    (c) Parking of car ....
    (d) Restaurant (including tips)? ....
        —How many persons does this amount cover? ....
    (e) Baby-sitter (please estimate cost)? ....

17. Have you, within the last five years, performed in:
    (a) An amateur dramatic show?
        No ☐ (0)
        Yes ☐ (1)
    (b) An amateur musical concert?
        No ☐ (0)
        Yes ☐ (1)
    (c) An amateur ballet presentation?
        No ☐ (0)
        Yes ☐ (1)

18. Excluding today, have you attended a theatre performance within the last 12 months?
    No ☐ (0)
    Yes — How many times? ....

19. Excluding today, have you attended a symphony concert within the last 12 months?
    No ☐ (0)
    Yes — How many times? ....

20. Excluding today, have you attended an opera within the last 12 months?
    No ☐ (0)
    Yes — How many times? ....

21. Excluding today, have you attended a serious musical performance other than a symphony or opera (chamber, soloist, etc.) within the last 12 months?
    No ☐ (0)
    Yes — How many times? ....

22. Excluding today, have you attended a ballet within the last 12 months?
    No ☐ (0)
    Yes — How many times? ....

23. Do you contribute money to performing arts organisations (other than by going to concerts, theatres, etc.)?
    Rarely, if ever? ☐ (1)
    Occasionally? ☐ (2)
    Regularly? ☐ (3)
    Please list arts organisations to which you have contributed within the last 12 months:
    ....

447

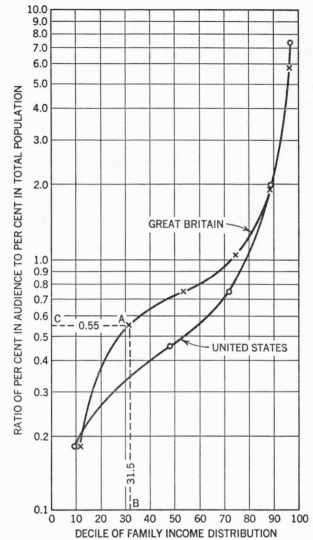

APPENDIX FIGURE IV–A

PER CENT OF AUDIENCE IN DIFFERENT INCOME CLASSES
RELATED TO INCOME DISTRIBUTION OF TOTAL POPULATION,
UNITED KINGDOM AND UNITED STATES

RATIO OF PER CENT IN AUDIENCE TO PER CENT IN TOTAL POPULATION

GREAT BRITAIN

UNITED STATES

C — 0.55 — A

31.5

B

DECILE OF FAMILY INCOME DISTRIBUTION

The horizontal axis shows the proportion of the population as a whole receiving no more than some given income, while the vertical axis gives the corresponding relative frequency figure for the audience. For example, the point labeled "A" corresponds to an income level which was not exceeded by 31.5 per cent of the general public (point B on the horizontal axis); but that income interval contained only about half as large (0.55 per cent) a proportion of the audience as the general population (point C on the vertical axis). The data used in preparing this graph are presented in Appendix Table IV–D.

Weighting of U. S. Performing Arts Profile

Art Form	Number of Usable Questionnaires	Estimated Annual Attendance in 1963–64[a]	Implicit Weights[b]	Explicit Weights[c]
Theater				
Broadway	2,252	6,600,000[d]	10	38
Off-Broadway	1,786	900,000	8	5
Regional	6,023	1,500,000	26	9
Subtotal	10,061	9,000,000	44	52
Orchestras (major only)	9,479	6,600,000	41	38
Opera	1,450	1,000,000[d]	6	6
Dance	2,146	750,000	9	4
Total	23,156	17,350,000	100	100

[a] For sources of attendance estimates and descriptions of the relevant populations, see Chapter III, pp. 50–69.

[b] Implicit weights are number of usable questionnaires for each art form divided by total usable questionnaires.

[c] Explicit weights are estimated attendance for each art form divided by estimated total attendance.

[d] These are preliminary estimates which we subsequently revised to 7 million and 1.7 million respectively. However, we did not revise our set of weights, since the differences in the over-all audience profiles would have been negligible.

Performances Covered by Twentieth Century Fund Audience Surveys, September 1963 through March 1965

Organization	Location	Number of Performances Surveyed
THEATERS		
"A Case of Libel" (Broadway)	New York, N.Y.	2
"A Funny Thing Happened on the Way to the Forum" (Broadway musical)	New York, N.Y.	2

(*Continued on following page*)

Organization	Location	Number of Performances Surveyed
Actor's Workshop	San Francisco, Calif.	
Encore Theater		1
Marines' Memorial Theater		2
Alley Theatre	Houston, Texas	2
American Shakespeare Festival	Stratford, Conn.	2
ANTA Theater (Lincoln Center Repertory Co.)	New York, N.Y.	4
"Any Wednesday" (Broadway)	New York, N.Y.	2
Arena Stage	Washington, D.C.	2
Barter Theater	Abingdon, Va.	2
Center Stage	Baltimore, Md.	1
Charles Playhouse	Boston, Mass.	4
Cherry Lane (off-Broadway)	New York, N.Y.	4
Circle in the Square (off-Broadway)	New York, N.Y.	4
Cleveland Play House	Cleveland, Ohio	
Brooks Theater		2
Drury Theater		2
Euclid–77th St. Theater		2
Dallas Theater Center	Dallas, Texas	2
Drury Lane	Chicago, Ill.	2
"Fiddler on the Roof" (Broadway musical)	New York, N.Y.	2
"Here's Love" (Broadway musical)	New York, N.Y.	2
Karamu Theatre	Cleveland, Ohio	
Arena Theatre		2
Proscenium Theatre		2
Martinique Theatre (off-Broadway)	New York, N.Y.	4
MacCarter Theatre	Princeton, N.J.	4
Mummers Theatre	Oklahoma City, Okla.	6
Nixon Theatre	Pittsburgh, Pa.	1

Organization	Location	Number of Performances Surveyed
Phoenix Theatre (off-Broadway)	New York, N.Y.	4
Seattle Repertory Theatre	Seattle, Wash.	4
"The Deputy" (Broadway)	New York, N.Y.	2
"The Physicists" (Broadway)	New York, N.Y.	2
"Theatre Four" (off-Broadway musical)	New York, N.Y.	4
UCLA Theater Group	Los Angeles, Calif.	2
"Who's Afraid of Virginia Woolf?" (Broadway)	New York, N.Y.	3
"Who's Afraid of Virginia Woolf?" (touring company)	San Francisco, Calif.	1
MAJOR ORCHESTRAS		
Atlanta Symphony Orchestra	Atlanta, Ga.	2
Baltimore Symphony Orchestra	Baltimore, Md.	2
Boston Symphony Orchestra	Boston, Mass.	7
Cincinnati Symphony Orchestra	Cincinnati, Ohio	2
Dallas Symphony Orchestra	Dallas, Texas	1
Los Angeles Philharmonic Orchestra	Los Angeles, Calif.	2
Minneapolis Symphony Orchestra	Minneapolis, Minn.	1
New York Philharmonic	New York, N.Y.	5
Pittsburgh Symphony Orchestra	Pittsburgh, Pa.	2
St. Louis Symphony Orchestra	St. Louis, Mo.	2
San Francisco Symphony Orchestra	San Francisco, Calif.	1
Seattle Symphony Orchestra	Seattle, Wash.	1
METROPOLITAN ORCHESTRAS		
Oklahoma City Symphony Orchestra	Oklahoma City, Okla.	1
Portland Symphony Orchestra	Portland, Oregon	1

(*Continued on following page*)

Organization	Location	Number of Performances Surveyed
OPERA		
Brooklyn Opera Company	Brooklyn, N.Y.	1
Houston Grand Opera Assn.	Houston, Texas	2
New York City Opera	New York, N.Y.	4
Opera Group of Boston	Boston, Mass.	1
DANCE		
Alvin Ailey Dance Theatre	Bronx, N.Y.	1
Merce Cunningham	Baltimore, Md.	1
Martha Graham and her Dance Company	New York, N.Y.	1
New York City Ballet	New York, N.Y.	3
Alwin Nikolais Dance Co.	New York, N.Y.	2
Paul Taylor Dance Co.	New York, N.Y.	1
SMALL MUSIC GROUPS		
American Brass Quintet	New York, N.Y.	1
Budapest String Quartet	New York, N.Y.	1
Columbia Group for Contemporary Music	New York, N.Y.	1
National Gallery Concerts	Washington, D.C.	1
New York Chamber Soloists	Ann Arbor, Mich.	1
OPEN-AIR PERFORMANCES		
New York Shakespeare Festival (free plays)	New York, N.Y.	4
Robin Hood Dell (free concerts)	Philadelphia, Pa.	2
BRITISH SURVEYS		
National Theatre	London	2
Ballet Rambert	London	1
New Philharmonia Orchestra	London	1
London Philharmonia Orchestra	London	1
London Symphony Orchestra	London	1
Sadler's Wells (opera)	London	1

Rank Correlations Between Response Rates and (1) Median Incomes, and (2) Per Cent of Males in "Professional" Occupations, by Art Form

	Spearman Rank Correlation Coefficient Between Response Rate and:	
	Median Income	Per Cent of Males in "Professional" Occupations
Broadway Shows (17)	−.28	+.35
Off-Broadway (24)	−.08	+.45*
Major Orchestra (28)	−.33*	+.16

SOURCE: Twentieth Century Fund audience survey.

* Significant at 5 per cent level but not at 1 per cent level. All other figures not significant at 5 per cent level.

APPENDIX TABLE IV–D

Summary of Relative Frequencies of Selected Audience Characteristics, U. S. and Great Britain

	Ratio of Per Cent in Audience to Per Cent in Total Urban Population	
	U. S.	Great Britain
AGE		
Under 20	0.19	.36
20–24	2.00	3.46
25–34	1.75	2.00
35–44	1.66	1.24
45–59	1.55	.93
60 and Over	0.69	.32
OCCUPATIONAL CATEGORY[a]		
Males:		
Professional–Technical	4.96	8.07
Managerial	1.70	1.75
Clerical and Sales	.76	1.25
Blue Collar	.05	.07

(Continued on following page)

	Ratio of Per Cent in Audience to Per Cent in Total Urban Population		
	U. S.	Great Britain	
Females:			
Professional–Technical	4.51	5.65	
Managerial	1.85	1.26	
Clerical	.73	1.35	
Sales	.33	.17	
Blue Collar	.05	.06	
EDUCATION[a]			
Males:			(Great Britain)
Grade School and Less			School-leaving Age:
Than 4 Yrs. High School	.04	.12	14 or Under
4 Yrs. High School	.29	.34	15
1–3 Yrs. College	1.31	1.45	16
4 Yrs. College	3.73	4.07	17, 18, 19
Graduate School	10.45	13.11	20 and Over
Females:			
Grade School and Less			
Than 4 Yrs. High School	.05	.06	14 or Under
4 Yrs. High School	.53	.31	15
1–3 Yrs. College	2.48	1.74	16
4 Yrs. College	5.93	4.71	17, 18, 19
Graduate School	15.80	15.67	20 and Over
FAMILY INCOME			
Less Than $3,000	.18	.18	Under £500
$3,000–$4,999	.30	.55	£500–£899
$5,000–$6,999	.45	.74	£900–£1,199
$7,000–$9,999	.74	1.02	£1,200–£1,749
$10,000–$14,999	1.96	1.91	£1,750–£2,499
(Over $15,000)	7.3	5.84	£2,500 and Over

SOURCE: Twentieth Century Fund audience survey.

[a] An arithmetic weighting phenomenon, which seems to have no particular economic significance, accounts for the fact that American relative frequencies are lower than British in all these categories.

Data on the Broadway Audience from *Playbill* Surveys, "Who's Who in the Theater," Selected Years, 1955–1964

	1955 –56	1958 –59	1959 –60	1960 –61	1963	1964
SEX						
Male	48.4%	48.8%	46.6%	52.1%	51.6%	50.2%
AGE						
Under 30	30.0%	21.0%	21.0%	29.5%	27.8%	28.4%
30–49	46.0	45.0	45.0	42.1	45.1	42.1
50–59	17.0	21.0	21.0	17.6	16.7	17.3
60 and Over	6.0	13.0	13.0	10.8	10.4	12.2
Median Age (yrs.)				40.3	39.5	40.5
OCCUPATIONAL CATEGORY (of head of household)						
Professional, Semi-professional, Managerial, Clerical, Sales		65.0%	69.1%	79.1%	79.0%	79.1%
Craftsman, Foreman, Operator		7.0	13.4	7.7	7.4	6.7
Services, Laborers		8.0	10.9	6.9	6.2	5.4
Other		10.0	6.6	6.3	7.4	8.8
INCOME						
0–$5,000	25%	15.2%	16.2%	9.5%	8.9%	5.4%
$5,001–$16,000	50	58.7	55.6	52.2	60.3	41.3
$16,000 and Over	25	26.1	28.2	38.3	30.8	53.3
Median Income			$9,650	$10,032	$11,011	$16,700
EDUCATION						
Males:						
Grade School				2.6%	2.1%	0.9%
High School				23.9	19.5	20.8
College				46.2	49.0	50.3
Graduate School				27.3	29.4	28.0
Females:						
Grade School				1.5%	1.6%	2.0%
High School				39.0	32.9	37.6
College				45.4	47.4	45.7
Graduate School				14.1	18.1	14.7

(*Continued on following page*)

	1955 –56	1958 –59	1959 –60	1960 –61	1963	1964
FREQUENCY OF ATTENDANCE	Average Number of Times Attended in Last 12 Months					
New Yorkers	8.5	8.6	8.2	7.8	7.9	7.8
Out-of-Towners	5.1	5.1	4.5	4.5	4.2	4.3
MEDIAN INCOME	Index (1959–60 = 100)					
Broadway			100	104	114	173
Population			100	104	109.5	115

APPENDIX TABLE IV–F

Profiles of U. S. Performing Arts Audiences, by Art Form

	Theater	Major Symphonies	Opera	Ballet	Ensembles
SEX					
Male	55.8%	47.4%	56.9%	48.8%	60.6%
AGE					
Under 20	9.0%	7.9%	6.1%	8.9%	9.3%
Over 60	6.0	14.0	8.7	6.8	6.8
Median Age	37 yrs.	39 yrs.	37 yrs.	35 yrs.	33 yrs.
OCCUPATIONAL CATEGORY					
Males:					
Employed Persons:[a]					
Professional	63.5%	68.5%	66.2%	64.3%	81.3%
Teachers	10.7	12.7	11.8	10.2	25.6
Managerial	21.6	19.1	19.6	16.6	11.5
Clerical and Sales	12.1	10.5	9.4	16.7	6.0
Blue Collar	2.8	1.9	3.8	2.4	1.2
Students[b]	16.2	19.0	12.8	9.4	23.8
Females:					
Employed Persons:[a]					
Professional	62.7%	68.2%	62.5%	63.4%	78.1%
Teachers	27.3	29.6	20.9	21.8	28.3
All Other	37.3	31.8	37.5	36.6	21.9
Students[a]	16.4	15.3	14.5	17.1	20.4
Housewives[b]	33.5	36.9	27.7	21.6	19.0

	Theater	Major Sym- phonies	Opera	Ballet	En- sembles
EDUCATION					
Males (age 25 and over):					
Grade School and Less Than 4 Yrs. High School	2.0%	1.8%	2.0%	1.6%	1.0%
4 Yrs. High School	6.2	4.2	5.5	5.9	1.4
1–3 Yrs. College	12.4	10.0	15.4	11.8	5.0
4 Yrs. College	23.2	23.1	21.4	26.6	16.8
Graduate School	56.3	61.0	55.6	54.2	75.9
Median Category	Grad. work	Grad. work	Grad. work	Grad. work	Grad. work
Females (age 25 and over):					
Grade School and Less Than 4 Yrs. High School	2.1%	2.5%	1.7%	1.9%	1.6%
4 Yrs. High School	15.6	11.7	13.1	16.0	6.4
1–3 Yrs. College	22.8	21.9	26.8	20.7	13.9
4 Yrs. College	27.2	30.7	26.6	24.1	26.3
Graduate School	32.3	33.2	31.9	37.2	51.8
Median Category	4 yrs. coll.	4 yrs. coll.	4 yrs. coll.	4 yrs. coll.	Grad. work
INCOME					
Over $5,000	92.5%	88.2%	89.7%	89.0%	86.0%
Over $15,000	41.0	35.4	31.2	31.2	30.5
Over $25,000	17.3	16.4	13.2	13.6	11.7
Median Income	$13,188	$11,870	$11,300	$11,016	$11,178
FREQUENCY OF ATTENDANCE	Average Number of Times Attended in Last 12 Months				
Theater	8.5	7.9	9.8	11.7	9.1
Symphony	2.2	9.7	4.2	3.6	5.7
Opera	1.0	1.7	5.4	2.9	1.7
Dance	0.9	0.9	2.1	5.8	1.6
Other Serious Music	1.8	3.2	3.1	2.6	8.7
NUMBER OF RESPONDENTS	9,976	9,936	1,442	2,136	934

SOURCE: Twentieth Century Fund audience survey.

[a] The number of employed persons is the base for the following percentages.

[b] The base for these percentages is the total number of respondents.

Profiles of U. S. Performing Arts Audiences, by Art Form, New York City Only

	All New York City	Broad-way	Off-Broad-way	Orches-tra	Opera	Ballet
SEX						
Male	53.4%	57.6%	54.7%	45.8%	57.6%	49.7%
AGE						
Under 20	7.7%	4.9%	7.8%	9.6%	6.6%	8.9%
Over 60	8.5	5.1	8.6	16.3	10.1	7.0
Median Age	38 yrs.	39 yrs.	39 yrs.	45 yrs.	37 yrs.	35 yrs.
OCCUPATIONAL CATEGORY						
Males:						
Employed Persons:[a]						
Professional	62.2%	55.7%	65.5%	64.1%	61.5%	63.8%
Teachers	9.5	7.1	12.0	7.4	11.6	9.6
Managerial	20.4	24.8	20.3	18.6	19.6	16.6
Clerical and Sales	14.8	16.5	11.8	15.7	13.6	17.2
Blue Collar	2.7	3.0	2.4	1.6	5.4	2.5
Students[b]	11.0	8.1	11.1	15.0	10.0	9.5
Females:						
Employed Persons:[a]						
Professional	61.1%	57.9%	62.8%	58.5%	58.1%	62.3%
Teachers	21.9	21.0	25.1	22.9	16.1	21.1
All Other	38.9	42.1	37.2	41.5	41.9	37.7
Students[a]	14.3	9.8	16.6	11.9	15.9	17.2
Housewives[b]	28.7	37.8	24.2	38.9	19.5	21.1
EDUCATION						
Males (age 25 and over):						
Grade School and Less Than 4 Yrs. High School	2.4%	2.9%	2.7%	2.4%	2.9%	1.6%
4 Yrs. High School	6.7	9.5	5.2	4.0	8.1	6.1
1–3 Yrs. College	13.0	16.0	11.6	9.6	18.0	11.9
4 Yrs. College	23.2	23.0	20.3	24.8	20.4	26.8
Graduate School	54.7	48.5	60.2	59.3	50.6	53.6
Median Category	Grad. work	4 yrs. coll.	Grad. work	Grad. work	Grad. work	Grad. work

	All New York City	Broad-way	Off-Broad-way	Orches-tra	Opera	Ballet
Females (age 25 and over):						
Grade School and Less Than 4 Yrs. High School	2.6%	3.6%	2.4%	3.0%	2.0%	2.0%
4 Yrs. High School	15.6	19.6	12.5	13.7	19.6	16.1
1–3 Yrs. College	22.9	26.0	19.7	23.6	29.2	20.7
4 Yrs. College	25.3	22.4	27.3	28.9	19.6	24.6
Graduate School	33.6	28.3	38.1	30.7	29.7	36.6
Median Category	4 yrs. coll.	4 yrs. coll.	4 yrs. coll.	4 yrs. coll.	3 yrs. coll.	4 yrs. coll.
INCOME						
Over $5,000	92.0%	94.7%	92.8%	94.2%	89.3%	88.8%
Over $15,000	40.7	45.5	42.4	50.7	30.8	30.7
Over $25,000	18.7	19.6	20.2	27.1	10.6	13.6
Median Income (dollars)	13,029	14,087	13,416	15,314	10,922	10,947
FREQUENCY OF ATTENDANCE	Average Number of Performances Attended in Last 12 Months					
Theater	9.8	8.1	11.0	10.2	11.6	11.8
Symphony	3.9	1.7	2.9	10.6	3.8	3.5
Opera	2.4	1.1	1.8	3.1	6.5	2.9
Dance	2.3	0.9	1.4	1.6	3.1	5.9
Other Serious Music	2.5	1.2	2.3	3.1	2.9	2.5
NUMBER OF RESPONDENTS	8,496	2,226	1,778	1,328	713	2,046

SOURCE: Twentieth Century Fund audience survey.

[a] The number of employed persons is the base for the following percentages.

[b] The base for these percentages is the total number of respondents.

Profiles of U. S. Performing Arts Audiences, by Art Form,
Outside of New York City

	Theater	Orchestra	Opera
SEX			
Male	55.5%	47.6%	56.2%
AGE			
Under 20	10.8%	7.6%	5.6%
Over 60	5.6	13.7	7.4
Median Age	36 yrs.	39 yrs.	37 yrs.
OCCUPATIONAL CATEGORY			
Males:			
Employed Persons:[a]			
Professional	66.4%	69.2%	71.3%
Teachers	11.9	13.5	11.9
Managerial	20.6	19.2	19.6
Clerical and Sales	10.1	9.7	7.0
Blue Collar	2.8	—	2.1
Students[b]	20.9	19.6	15.7
Females:			
Employed Persons:[a]			
Professional	69.6%	69.8%	67.7%
Teachers	30.6	30.7	26.6
All Other	35.4	30.2	32.3
Students[a]	18.7	15.9	13.2
Housewives[b]	34.8	36.6	35.4
EDUCATION			
Males (age 25 and over):			
Grade School and Less Than			
4 Yrs. High School	1.3%	1.6%	1.2%
4 Yrs. High School	5.1	4.2	2.9
1–3 Yrs. College	11.0	10.0	12.8
4 Yrs. College	24.2	22.9	22.5
Graduate School	58.5	61.3	60.6
Median Category	Grad. work	Grad. work	Grad. work

	Theater	Orchestra	Opera
Females (age 25 and over):			
Grade School and Less Than			
4 Yrs. High School	1.6%	2.5%	1.6%
4 Yrs. High School	14.9	11.3	7.8
1–3 Yrs. College	22.4	21.6	24.8
4 Yrs. College	29.1	31.0	32.2
Graduate School	32.1	33.6	33.7
Median Category	4 yrs. coll.	4 yrs. coll.	4 yrs. coll.
INCOME			
Over $5,000	91.5%	87.2%	90.2%
Over $15,000	38.8	33.0	31.5
Over $25,000	15.5	14.8	15.7
Median Income	$12,789	$11,379	$11,618
FREQUENCY OF ATTENDANCE	Average Number of Performances Attended in Last 12 Months		
Theater	7.9	7.6	8.1
Symphony	2.2	9.6	4.6
Opera	0.8	1.5	4.3
Dance	0.7	0.8	1.1
Other Serious Music	1.8	3.2	3.2
NUMBER OF RESPONDENTS	5,973	8,608	729

SOURCE: Twentieth Century Fund audience survey.

[a] The number of employed persons is the base for the following percentages.

[b] The base for these percentages is the total number of respondents.

Audience Profiles by Frequency of Attendance and Art Form

	Art Form and Frequency of Attendance			
	Broadway Theater			
	1	2–5	6–10	Over 1
SEX				
Male	67.9%	57.8%	57.3%	55.5%
AGE				
Under 20	12.1%	7.3%	2.3%	2.4%
Over 60	4.3	3.8	4.7	7.1
Median Age	35 yrs.	37 yrs.	40 yrs.	39 yrs.
OCCUPATIONAL CATEGORY				
Males:				
Employed Persons:[a]				
Professional	59.5%	54.8%	53.2%	59.6%
Teachers	6.8	6.7	5.5	10.4
Managerial	14.9	23.2	28.3	23.6
Clerical and Sales	17.6	17.8	16.7	15.5
Blue Collar	8.1	4.2	1.8	1.4
Students[b]	12.8	9.1	6.5	7.3
Females:				
Employed Persons:[a]				
Professional	36.4%	48.0%	61.9%	66.2%
Teachers	9.1	21.6	19.1	23.6
All Other	63.6	52.0	38.1	33.8
Students[a]	17.8	12.7	7.2	6.4
Housewives[b]	53.3	40.6	36.0	34.0
EDUCATION				
Males (age 25 and over):				
Grade School and Less Than 4 Yrs.				
High School	8.3%	3.6%	1.9%	1.0%
4 Yrs. High School	8.3	11.0	8.3	8.9
1–3 Yrs. College	22.2	17.4	16.4	10.9
4 Yrs. College	33.3	21.4	24.1	22.2
Graduate School	27.8	46.7	49.4	57.0
Median Category	4 coll.	4 coll.	4 coll.	Grad. Sch.

| | Art Form and Frequency of Attendance | | | | | | |
| Major Orchestras | | | | Regional Theater | | | |
1	2–5	6–10	Over 10	1	2–5	6–10	Over 10
8.5%	46.9%	49.2%	49.4%	57.3%	55.4%	55.5%	56.7%
2.8%	13.2%	7.9%	3.9%	15.9%	14.3%	9.7%	5.8%
9.6	7.0	11.3	17.9	5.9	4.1	4.9	7.0
3 yrs.	32 yrs.	38 yrs.	44 yrs.	33 yrs.	34 yrs.	36 yrs.	39 yrs.
8.9%	69.5%	70.8%	66.4%	58.8%	65.7%	69.1%	66.5%
1.2	13.6	13.5	11.2	8.8	11.6	11.2	14.2
7.0	17.4	18.7	20.4	14.9	21.2	20.1	21.4
1.2	10.6	9.2	11.4	18.2	9.8	9.6	9.0
2.9	2.5	1.3	1.8	8.1	3.2	1.2	3.0
7.5	25.9	18.2	14.6	28.2	25.3	18.6	16.1
0.3%	69.3%	72.0%	67.3%	39.4%	61.9%	66.9%	70.7%
4.5	27.9	28.5	31.9	14.1	33.0	31.2	31.8
9.7	30.7	28.0	32.7	60.6	38.1	33.1	29.3
8.2	23.7	17.1	10.6	15.7	23.6	20.2	11.2
6.0	31.7	35.7	38.8	38.6	34.9	34.2	34.2
3.2%	1.7%	1.1%	1.7%	3.4%	0.9%	1.0%	1.6%
6.5	2.5	3.2	3.7	20.7	6.0	2.9	2.7
1.4	9.9	8.5	10.8	17.2	12.9	10.5	7.3
4.0	25.2	22.6	22.8	19.3	29.0	22.1	22.1
4.9	60.7	64.5	61.0	39.3	51.2	63.5	66.3
Grad. Sch.	Grad. Sch.	Grad. Sch.	Grad. Sch.	4 coll.	Grad. Sch.	Grad. Sch.	Grad. Sch.

(*Continued on following page*)

| | Art Form and Frequency of Attendance | | | |
| | Broadway Theater | | | |
	1	2–5	6–10	Over 10
EDUCATION (*cont.*)				
Females (age 25 and over):				
Grade School and Less Than 4 Yrs.				
High School	12.5%	6.6%	0.5%	1.8%
4 Yrs. High School	53.1	28.7	14.4	9.4
1–3 Yrs. College	21.9	23.4	32.4	23.3
4 Yrs. College	6.2	21.3	20.8	26.9
Graduate School	6.2	20.1	31.9	38.6
Median Category	4 h.s.	1–3 coll.	4 coll.	4 coll.
INCOME				
Over $5,000	93.8%	93.8%	96.5%	95.0%
Over $15,000	25.0	35.7	50.8	57.4
Over $25,000	12.5	11.7	21.4	29.4
Median Income	$10,279	$12,545	$15,282	$17,638
	Average Number of Performances Attend			
FREQUENCY OF ATTENDANCE	in Last 12 Months			
Theater		2.6	6.2	15.7
Symphony	0.5	1.0	1.7	3.0
Opera	0.1	0.5	1.1	2.2
Dance	0.1	0.5	0.7	1.8
Other Serious Music	0.8	0.8	1.1	2.1
NUMBER OF RESPONDENTS	140	783	618	596

SOURCE: Twentieth Century Fund audience survey.

464

	Art Form and Frequency of Attendance						
Major Orchestras				Regional Theater			
1	2–5	6–10	Over 10	1	2–5	6–10	Over 10
5.8%	2.0%	1.9%	2.1%	5.1%	2.3%	0.8%	0.8%
20.8	10.8	10.2	11.1	35.0	18.5	12.9	8.4
23.7	22.7	20.2	20.7	26.5	23.6	20.8	19.6
27.0	32.3	32.7	30.0	17.1	29.3	30.9	30.5
22.8	32.2	35.0	36.2	16.2	26.3	34.6	40.7
1–3 coll.	4 coll.	4 coll.	4 coll.	1–3 coll.	4 coll.	4 coll.	4 coll.
81.3%	85.9%	89.3%	90.8%	87.2%	89.7%	93.1%	93.0%
22.7	27.6	38.6	40.6	23.6	30.8	43.1	47.7
9.1	11.8	16.7	20.0	8.5	10.7	16.2	21.8
$9,669	$10,494	$12,555	$12,928	$9,512	$11,341	$13,663	$14,511
Average Number of Performances Attended in Last 12 Months							
3.7	5.9	7.7	10.4		2.6	6.5	15.2
	2.6	6.5	16.1	0.8	1.3	2.1	4.0
0.6	1.0	1.4	2.7	0.2	0.4	0.7	1.6
0.3	0.5	0.8	1.4	0.2	0.4	0.7	1.4
1.2	1.8	2.6	4.7	0.8	1.1	1.8	3.1
717	2102	2461	3423	389	2010	1917	1444

The number of employed persons is the base for the following percentages.

The base for these percentages is the total number of respondents.

U. S. Performing Arts Profiles by Two Systems of Weighting[a]

	Profile with Implicit (Response) Weights	Profile with Explicit (Attendance) Weights
SEX		
Male	52.0%	52.8%
AGE		
Under 20	8.4%	6.9%
Over 60	9.5	9.0
Median Age	38 yrs.	38 yrs.
OCCUPATIONAL CATEGORY		
Males:		
Employed Persons:[a]		
Professional	66.3%	63.0%
Teachers	12.1	10.3
Managerial	19.7	21.4
Clerical and Sales	11.6	13.0
Blue Collar	2.5	2.6
Students[b]	16.8	13.9
Females:		
Employed Persons:[a]		
Professional	65.6%	64.2%
Teachers	27.2	25.4
All Other	34.4	36.3
Students[a]	16.0	15.1
Housewives[b]	33.1	35.2
EDUCATION		
Males (age 25 and over):		
Grade School and Less Than		
4 Yrs. High School	1.8%	2.2%
4 Yrs. High School	5.2	6.5
1–3 Yrs. College	11.3	12.8
4 Yrs. College	23.1	23.1
Graduate School	58.6	55.4
Median Category	Grad. work	Grad. work

	Profile with Implicit (Response) Weights	Profile with Explicit (Attendance) Weights
Females (age 25 and over):		
Grade School and Less Than		
4 Yrs. High School	1.3%	2.8%
4 Yrs. High School	13.4	15.3
1–3 Yrs. College	22.2	23.6
4 Yrs. College	28.5	26.7
Graduate School	33.7	31.6
Median Category	4 yrs. coll.	4 yrs. coll.
INCOME		
Over $5,000	90.0%	91.3%
Over $15,000	36.9	39.5
Over $25,000	16.1	17.4
Median Income	$12,286	$12,804
FREQUENCY OF ATTENDANCE	Average Number of Performances Attended in Last 12 Months	
Theater	8.2	8.4
Symphony	5.2	5.1
Opera	1.7	1.7
Dance	1.3	1.2
Other Serious Music	2.7	2.2
NUMBER OF RESPONDENTS	24,425	

SOURCE: Twentieth Century Fund audience survey.

[a] The two weighting systems are explained in Appendix Table IV–A.

[b] The number of employed persons is the base for the following percentages.

[c] The base for these percentages is the total number of respondents.

Questionnaire on Performers' Financial Circumstances

We realize that you will be unable to give exact replies to some of these questions, but would appreciate your making your estimates as realistic as possible.

1. How much income <u>from all sources</u> did you earn in 1964? $_____
   (If you filed a joint income tax return, please list your joint income)

2. Of this total, how much came from:

   a. Your own earnings from live performance $_____

   b. Your own earnings from TV (live or filmed), films and other appearances of this kind $_____

   c. Your own earnings in other capacities directly related to your profession as a performer, e.g., teaching or coaching $_____
   Please specify what jobs you held:

   d. Your own earnings in capacities <u>not</u> related to your profession as a performer $_____
   Please specify what jobs you held:

   e. Earnings of your spouse $_____
   Please specify job or jobs held:

   f. Other income (unemployment insurance, gifts, etc.) $_____

3. Are you in debt? [ ] No [ ] Yes If yes, how much $_____

4. List your necessary professional expenses last year (e.g., personal promotion, music, makeup, special classes, union dues, etc.)

   <u>Item</u>   <u>Amount</u>

5. Estimate how much has been spent on your professional training up to this point in your career (drama school, classes, etc.) $_____

6. How many children do you have under the age of 18? _____

7. Please use the back of this questionnaire to comment on your economic experiences and their implications for your profession.

DO NOT SIGN THIS QUESTIONNAIRE

Please return it to us in the attached self-addressed, stamped envelope. Thank you.

APPENDIX TABLE V–A   Income Distribution in 1959 of "Arts" Occupations[a]
(income from all sources; experienced civilian labor force)

	Number with Income (thousands)	Percentage Distribution					Median Income
		Under $3,000	$3,000–$5,999	$6,000–$9,999	$10,000–$14,999	$15,000 & Over	
MALES							
All Males 14 and Over	44,727	27	42	23	5	3	$4,720
All Males in Professional-Technical Occupations	4,486	11	29	38	13	9	6,778
Actors	8	23	30	25	11	10	5,640
Artists & Art Teachers	67	15	31	37	11	6	6,333
Authors	20	13	25	43	11	8	6,745
Dancers & Dancing Teachers	4	40	40	12	3	5	3,483
Musicians & Music Teachers	84	30	36	25	6	3	4,757
FEMALES							
All Females 14 and Over	20,445	63	33	4	0	0	2,333
All Females in Professional-Technical Occupations	2,623	37	48	13	1	0	3,711
Actresses	4	44	32	11	5	9	3,464
Artists & Art Teachers	35	40	41	16	1	1	3,743
Authors	7	48	32	10	4	6	3,189
Dancers & Dancing Teachers	15	70	22	6	1	0	1,680
Musicians & Music Teachers	105	71	22	6	1	0	1,566

SOURCE: U.S. Census of Population, 1960: Subject Reports, Occupational Characteristics, Final Report PC(2)–7A, Table 25. Detailed figures may not add to 100 per cent because of rounding.

[a] The figures presented here all pertain to the "income (from all sources) of the experienced civilian labor force." The Census also publishes figures for "earnings (does not include property income, etc.) of the experienced civilian labor force" and "wage and salary income of wage and salary workers in the experienced civilian labor force." (Tables 27 and 29 of the report cited.) In an effort to see if the relative positions of "arts" occupations varied appreciably depending on the income or earnings concept used, we made calculations analogous to those reported in the table for the other two concepts. For males, the results were nearly identical. For females, actresses were found to be appreciably worse off relative to all females engaged in professional-technical occupations when, instead of the total income concept, the "earnings" and "wage and salary income" concepts were used. Apparently, actresses have above-average non-salary incomes.

Income of Selected Groups of Performers During the 1964 Income Tax Year

Art Form (Number of Replies; Per Cent of Number Sent)	Median Total Income	Live Performances		TV & Related Sources			Teaching & Coaching		
		Median	Per Cent of Total Income	Per Cent Having Any	Range	Median	Per Cent Having Any	Range	Median
Actors:									
Hit Broadway Musical Cast (11; 22%)	$ 8,429	$ 6,900	82	55	$150–$4,000	$ 188	36	$50–$1,800	$ 620
Repertory Company A (8b; 27%)	7,400	5,000	68	86	960–3,800	1,124	0	—	—
Repertory Company B (17; 34%)	4,748	3,935	83	47	27–600	300	29	20–1,000	295
Members of Actors' Equity Unemployed at Time of Survey (9; 45%)	4,608	2,164	47	67	329–3,000	926	0	—	—
Musicians:									
Hit Broadway Musical Orchestras (15; 60%)	11,000	10,000c	91	42	200–1,000	1,000	50	100–4,000	1,000
Ballet Orchestra (7; 13%)	9,203	7,000	76	43	200–1,000	225	57	180–4,300	1,750
Opera Orchestra (9; 23%)	7,443	5,170	69	44	80–1,400	150	44	500–2,800	1,510
Chamber Orchestra (9; 43%)	13,000	5,000	38	67	123–3,000	225	78	500–2,500	1,500
Singers: Opera Chorus (11; 23%)	4,600	3,821	83	9	(162)	(162)	27	550–3,000	600
Dancers:									
Modern Dance Group (4; 13%)	5,535	797	14	25	(100)	(100)	(100)	40–5,000	1,035
Ballet Company (12; 30%)	4,075	3,781	93	58	34–100	34	0	—	—

a Parentheses indicate that the results are based on one figure.
b Questionnaire returned by non-income-receiving students omitted from rest of the calculation.
c Three replies omitted from the remaining calculations.

Earnings from Unrelated Sources			Earnings of Spouse			Other Income			
Per Cent Having Any	Range	Median	Per Cent Having Any	Range	Median	Per Cent Having Any	Range	Median	Art Form (Number of Replies; Per Cent of Number Sent)
									Actors:
9	($1,200)a	($1,200)	27	$344–$14,000	$4,500	27	$300–$1,200	$1,000	Hit Broadway Musical Cast (11; 22%)
14	(50)	(50)	29	697–1,500	1,099	71	191–4,000	532	Repertory Company A (8b; 27%)
24	200–8,000	539	29	200–20,567	3,932	24	75–7,890	114	Repertory Company B (17; 34%)
78	329–1,734	1,000	11	(8,262)	(8,262)	56	100–1,550	400	Members of Actors' Equity Unemployed at Time of Survey (9; 45%)
									Musicians:
25	1,000–2,000	1.800	17	1,500–10,000	5,750	0	—	—	Hit Broadway Musical Orchestras (15; 60%)
0	—	—	29	108–650	379	57	150–650	350	Ballet Orchestra (7; 13%)
0	—	—	11	(4,100)	(4,100)	22	400–500	450	Opera Orchestra (9; 23%)
22	100–300	200	56	2,000–10,500	6,384	44	250–1,585	300	Chamber Orchestra (9; 43%)
9	(500)	(500)	18	3,233–8,535	5,884	82	340–3,091	650	Singers: Opera Chorus (11; 23%)
									Dancers:
50	875–1,500	1,188	25	(8,900)	(8,900)	25	(500)	(500)	Modern Dance Group (4; 13%)
8	(300)	(300)	0	—	—	50	50–800	177	Ballet Company (12; 30%)

SOURCE: Questionnaire survey conducted by staff members of the Twentieth Century Fund study. The questionnaire is reproduced in Appendix V–1. There were 108 replies, a response rate of 23 per cent.

Weeks Worked in "Arts" Occupations, 1959, and Unemployment Rates as of April 1960

	Per Cent Who Worked:			Per Cent Unemployed, April 1960
	50–52 wks.	40–49 wks.	Less Than 40 Wks.	
MALES				
All Males 14 and Over	68.8	15.1	16.1	4.9
All Males in Professional-Technical Occupations	77.5	12.6	9.9	1.4
Actors	28.3	18.5	53.2	26.1
Artists, Art Teachers	71.6	16.3	12.1	2.3
Authors	74.6	12.9	12.5	2.7
Dancers, Dance Teachers	37.9	26.9	35.2	7.6
Musicians, Music Teachers	42.6	28.6	28.8	4.6
FEMALES				
All Females 14 and Over	51.1	16.9	32.0	5.1
All Females in Professional-Technical Occupations	38.4	22.5	39.1	1.4
Actresses	16.2	12.1	71.7	27.9
Artists, Art Teachers	37.5	23.7	38.8	3.5
Authors	54.7	15.2	30.1	2.8
Dancers, Dance Teachers	17.7	23.1	59.2	6.4
Musicians, Music Teachers	27.2	28.9	43.9	1.2

SOURCE: *U. S. Census of Population, 1960: Occupational Characteristics;* weeks worked from Table 14, unemployment rates calculated from Table 3.

"Real" Expenditures in the United States and in Great Britain,
Recent Years, by Art Form[a]

	Total Annual Expenditure Per Organization, in Man-Years of Labor	Expenditure Per Performance, in Man-Years of Labor
Orchestras:		
Five Largest (U. S.)	338	2.4
Symphony Orchestra A (G. B.)	362	2.4
All Twenty-five Majors (U. S.)	151	1.3
Regional Symphony Orchestra (G. B.)	188	.86
Opera Companies:		
Metropolitan Opera (U. S.)	1,387	5.7
Covent Garden[b] (G. B.)	2,051	3.8
Sadler's Wells Trust, Ltd. (G. B.)	796	1.6
Dance Companies:		
New York City Ballet (U. S.)	352	1.6
Ballet Company (G. B.)	72	.26
Theater:		
Off-Broadway Plays (U. S.)		.12
Regional Companies (U. S.)	49	.16
Regional Companies (27) (G. B.)	45	.15
Royal Shakespeare Company, Stratford and Aldwych (G. B.)	648	.72

Actual dollar and pound sterling expenditures are here divided by income per member of the labor force, as of 1962, in the respective countries — $6,307 and £951. (These figures were derived from data published in United Nations, *Statistical Yearbook, 1963*, New York, 1964.) The sources of the expenditure figures for U. S. organizations are given in Table VI–1. (Means are used here.) The British expenditure data were obtained directly from the financial statements of the organizations. Dividing dollar (or pound sterling) expenditures by income per member of the labor force provides a measure of the number of average man-years of labor which is equivalent to the expenditure figures.

Covent Garden puts on both opera and ballet.

Earned Income as Per Cent of Expenditures, Several British
Organizations, 1963–64

Organization	Expenditures	Income Gap	Income Gap as Per Cent of Expenditures
	(1)	(2)	(3)
Orchestras:			
London Orchestra A	£ 344,724	£ 61,641	17.7
London Orchestra B	213,014	26,510	12.5
Regional Orchestra	178,845	88,675	50.5
Opera Companies:			
Covent Garden	1,950,500	864,600	44.4
Sadler's Wells	756,951	498,586	65.9
Dance: A Ballet Company	68,038	29,925	44.2
Theaters:			
Stratford Royal Shakespeare	616,188	114,634	18.7
27 Regional Theaters:[a]			
Median	29,661	(6,492)	25
Interquartile Range	18,484–42,131	(10,136)–(3,528)	14–33

SOURCE: Financial statements of the respective organizations. Data for regional theaters
are for 1962–63.

[a] Barrow-in-Furness, Bromley, Canterbury, Carlisle, Century, Cheltenham, Colchester
Repertory, Coventry-Belgrade, Croydon New Penbroke, Derby Playhouse, English Stage
Co., Farnham Repertory, Guildford Theatre Club, Harrogate (White Rose), Horn-
church, Leatherhead Theatre Association, Lincoln Theatre Association, Loughborough
and District Theatre Association, Mermaid, Mobile, Northampton Repertory Players,
Oldham Repertory, Pioneer, Richmond Theatre Production, Salisbury Arts, Sheffield
Repertory, and Studio Theatres.

Average Annual Percentage Increase in Output Per Man-Hour,
Selected Industry Groups and Time Periods

	1909–1964	1929–1964	1947–1964	1961–1964	1929–1961	1947–1961
Private:						
1. Entire Private Sector	2.41	2.99	3.04	3.37		
2. Non-agricultural			2.48			
3. Manufacturing			2.49			
4. Non-manufacturing			2.50			
5. Cement Industry			4.70ᵃ			
6. Petroleum Refining			5.22ᵃ			
Private and Public:						
7. All Industries					2.3	2.6
Alternative 1:ᵇ						
8. Goods Sector					2.9	3.5
9. Service Sector					1.6	1.6
Alternative 2:ᶜ						
10. Goods Sector					2.5	3.1
11. Service Sector					1.6	1.7

SOURCE: For sectors 1–6 the rates were calculated by fitting a trend line through annual observations, i.e., regressing the logarithm of the value on time. The data for sectors 1–4 are from the 1965 *Manpower Report of the President,* p. 256, and the data for sectors 5–6 from U. S. Department of Labor, Bureau of Labor Statistics, *Indexes of Output Per Man-Hour, Selected Industries,* September 1964, pp. 23, 29. For sectors 7–11 the 1929–1961 rates are taken from Victor R. Fuchs, *Productivity Trends in the Goods and Service Sectors, 1929–1961,* Occasional Paper 89, National Bureau of Economic Research, New York, 1964, Table 2, p. 13, and Appendix A–2, pp. 47–48. We calculated the 1947–1961 rates in the same way, namely, by taking the differences between the rate of change of real output and the rate of change of man-hours, both calculated on a compound basis between terminal years.

ᵃ Based on years 1947, 1949–1962 only.

ᵇ These sectors are defined by Fuchs (p. 4) as follows:
   Goods = agriculture, mining, construction, manufacturing, transportation, communications and public utilities, and government enterprise
   Service = wholesale and retail trade, finance, insurance and real estate, services, and general government

ᶜ These sectors are defined by Fuchs (p. 4) as follows:
   Goods = goods excluding agriculture and government enterprise
   Service = services excluding real estate, households and institutions, and general government

Size of Broadway Casts, 1895 to 1964

Season	Average Size of Cast	Per Cent of Total Productions with Casts of:			
		1–9	10–19	20–29	30 and over
1894–95	17.2	7.9	67.0	18.1	7.1
1898–99	20.7	0.9	68.5	17.6	13.0
1903–04	24.2	8.8	36.9	30.8	23.6
1908–09	21.2	16.5	47.7	12.9	22.9
1913–14	15.8	18.9	51.5	24.2	5.3
1918–19	15.4	17.6	61.5	16.2	4.7
1923–24	14.6	21.3	57.9	16.4	4.4
1928–29	18.5	18.7	47.2	20.5	13.5
1933–34	17.7	26.2	44.3	15.4	14.1
1938–39	23.9	18.6	36.3	22.6	22.6
1943–44	18.1	18.4	48.4	22.5	10.8
1948–49	17.7	18.3	45.0	21.7	15.0
1953–54[a]	21.9	24.6	39.4	14.8	21.3
1958–59[a]	23.1	27.9	32.8	9.8	29.5
1963–64	25.8	25.7	24.4	16.2	33.8
Off-Broadway: 1963–64	10.8	60.2	24.6	9.1	1.1

SOURCE: Compiled from *The Best Plays of 1894–95* and subsequent issues, Dodd, Mead and Company, New York.

[a] May include a few off-Broadway shows.

Choice of Price Index and Some Sources of Bias

Throughout Chapter VIII we utilized the wholesale price index as our measure of price change, rather than the consumer price index. The basic reason for this is that we were trying to compare the cost of supplying a particular product (live performance) against the cost of supplying commodities in general, and the wholesale price index seems in principle to fit this concept more closely. Moreover, the consumer price index seems inappropriate because it is based on the "market basket" of a lower middle class family, which is of no particular relevance to our discussion. In addition, this index gives substantial weight to the retail price of food. But, since the days of the New Deal, food prices have depended at least in part on government decisions as well as market conditions, and must therefore be considered somewhat arbitrary prices from the point of view of our analysis.

Nevertheless, our qualitative results were unaffected by this decision, as a number of sample calculations showed. Between 1947 and 1964 the consumer price index rose at 2 per cent per year as compared with 1.4 per cent for the wholesale price index, but all of our cost growth figures for that period, as shown in Table VIII–3, exceed 2 per cent. This is also true for the other periods dealt with in that table.

One other possible source of distortion was usually easy to deal with. In calculating growth rates we preferred to take the results of regression calculations rather than computations based on two more or less arbitrarily chosen terminal years. The dangers of the latter approach are clearly illustrated by the Cincinnati data. That orchestra's cost per performance (Table VIII–1) rose at an average rate of 2.2 per cent per year between 1920 and 1964, as compared with a 0.4 per cent rate of growth of wholesale prices. Had we chosen 1921 instead of 1920 as our base year, because of the rapid fall in the price level between these two years, our calculation would report that cost per concert for the Cincinnati Orchestra had risen more slowly than the price level.

As we have noted, quality changes are another possible distorting influence, one for which adjustments are not easily made. In general, the quality of orchestra concerts has no doubt tended to improve over time, but the same is true of the quality of many of the commodities represented in the wholesale price index. Whether these two biases are fully offsetting is a moot point.

Another bias may enter our comparisons when the composition of the "basket" of commodities whose prices are combined to obtain this index is revised periodically to take account of changes in the relative importance of different commodities. As such a revision often reflects a switch in demand from comparatively expensive goods to relatively inexpensive goods, the wholesale price index is likely to rise less rapidly than an index of the prices of a fixed set of commodities. This "substitution effect" is likely to bias the wholesale price index downward in comparison with our measures of the costs of live performances, which take no account of any tendency for consumers to substitute less expensive activities, such as movies, for live performances.

The Cost Curve Regressions

To determine the cost relationships for our basic eleven orchestras we ran a number of regression analyses, each of which may be described very briefly.

First, to find whether unit costs do decline with number of concerts, we ran a linear regression between the number of concerts per season, C, and real expenditure per concert, E/C. Thus, our equation had the form $E/C = a + bC$. For ten of our eleven orchestras the b turned out to be negative, indicating that economies are in fact present. The regression coefficient was significant at the 95 per cent level in nine of the eleven cases, and at the 99 per cent level in eight of the eleven cases. Thus, it is hard to escape the conclusion that at least up to a point economies of scale are available to the orchestras.

Second, to see whether our result was a misleading trend phenomenon we ran a three variable linear regression $E/C = a + bC + wT$ where T represents calendar time. Instead of eliminating the effect of number of concerts, this caused an improvement in the behavior of the b coefficients. Now all eleven of them became negative and nine of them achieved significance at the 99 per cent level (with the other two still significant at the 95 per cent level). The w's (the coefficient of the T's) were positive in eight of the eleven cases, implying that there is a secular upward drift in real cost greater than that which is explained by increases in the minimum salary level (our price deflator). But only five of the w coefficients were significant at the 99 per cent level and only six at the 95 per cent level. Hence "time" does not seem to be as powerful a determinant of cost per concert as is the number of concerts per season.

Third, we tried a quadratic relationship to see whether the U-shaped cost curve of economic analysis was applicable. Here our regression equation was $E/C = a + bC + vC^2$.

The results gave us the expected negative value of b and the expected positive value of v in eight of our eleven cases. For these eight cases the median value of R^2 was about .8. Both these coefficients were significant at the 99 per cent level in six cases, and not significant in the others.

Though we never reran this regression with time added in as a variable, we are confident, on the basis of a parallel calculation, that it would have made little difference.

The following table sums up our results for five orchestras[1] in which the quadratic calculation yielded significant results (orchestra D is the one whose data are shown in Figure VIII–5).

Orchestra	R^2	Value of b	"t"	Value of v	"t"	Unit-Cost-Minimizing Number of Concerts	Number of Concerts Performed, 1964	Current Elasticity of Unit Cost with Respect to Number of Concerts
A	.87	−2.29	9.5	.001	8.6	127	152	1.35
B	.91	−2.58	5.6	.014	4.1	91	90	−0.05
C	.74	−3.55	4.1	.02	3.4	89	94	0.51
D	.89	−2.12	5.5	.0083	3.9	129	109	−0.67
E	.86	−1.39	5.2	.0047	3.6	147	155	0.26

Note that according to the table three of the five orchestras are currently operating slightly beyond their minimum cost level. Naturally, the corresponding elasticities of real average cost with respect to number of performances are positive. Among these three are the two orchestras currently offering the largest number of performances per season in our group of five. Moreover, both of those with negative elasticities have elasticities less than unity in absolute value — further increases in number of concerts would yield less than proportionate reductions in unit costs. This is precisely what one should expect, for otherwise the marginal costs of a concert could be zero or negative.[2]

We also undertook a parallel set of regressions, using expenditures on artistic personnel alone instead of total unit costs. There was then a marked improvement in results. The same six orchestras as before yielded results significant at the 99 per cent level, and for five of these orchestras the R^2 ranged between .90 and .99. The general shapes of the average cost curves remained much the same even though, perhaps a bit surprisingly, the minima now generally called for a somewhat larger number of concerts per season.

[1] We omit the sixth because there were some ambiguities in the last year's data when, apparently, the orchestra was sometimes split into three subgroups, all of which seem to have performed simultaneously. This makes the results more difficult to interpret.

[2] Note that orchestra A exhibits an elasticity of 1.35, a figure that is hardly plausible. Perhaps the inclusion of a trend variable would have eliminated this anomaly.

This implies that unit administrative costs typically begin to increase at a number of concerts smaller than the turning point in expenditures on performers' salaries. Probably the improved statistical fit is explained simply by the elimination from the data in our last set of regressions of erratic expense items such as tours, repairs and maintenance.

APPENDIX TABLE VIII–A

New York Philharmonic Financial Statement, for the Year 1850

Receipts		Expenditures	
By cash on hand	$ 128.57	To 64 dividends, including fractions	$1,752.00[a]
" 67 subscribers	670.00	" Rent of Apollo Rooms	221.50
" Assoc. members	1,126.25	" Advertising	90.56
" Extra tickets	303.50	" Professional aid, viz: Lasar, $5; Scherpf, $5; Hoch, $5; Engelmann, $5; Diescher, $5; Schmid, $5; Groschel, $5; Halma, $5; Hegelund, $5; Dodworth, $3.	48.00
" Fines of actual members	73.25	" Music	85.32
" Taxes of actual members	242.25	" Printing	103.25
" Initiation fees	100.00	" The following appropriation, viz: secretary, $100; Fecher, $108.12; Mrs. S, $75.	283.12
" Diplomas	3.00	" Sundries — collecting, crape, carpenters, stationery, etc.	127.29
" A. Dodworth, $1; Mendelssohn, $5; and Schierwagen, $5.	11.00	" Members, over their dividends	92.12
" Balances of outstanding accounts of last year	49.99	" Cash on hand	4.65
" Amount drawn from savings bank	100.00		
	$2,807.81		$2,807.81

Additional Information

Number of Players	64	Number of Concerts	4	Number of Subscribers	67
Average Salary (share)	$32	Subscription Price	$10	Number of Associate members	226

SOURCE: Copied from the historical files of the Philharmonic Society of New York.

[a] This large expenditure is the sum distributed to the musicians, the word "dividends" connoting the fact that the orchestra was organized as a cooperative.

Broadway Theater: Changes in Pay Scales for Different Job
Categories, 1953–1965

Job Category	Weekly Scale (minimum) in 1964–1965	Average Annual Percentage Change				Total Percentage Change, 1953–1965
		1953– 1957	1957– 1960	1960– 1965	1953– 1965	
Actors	$125.00	4.1	3.6	2.4	3.3	47.1
Stage Managers:						
Dramatic	208.70	3.9	2.8	1.9	2.8	39.1
Musical	259.30	3.0	2.2	1.6	2.2	29.7
Assistant Managers:						
Dramatic	147.95	10.1	2.6	1.9	4.7	74.1
Musical	178.35	10.7	2.2	2.2	4.9	78.4
Musicians:						
Drama:						
Contract Houses	135.00	2.7	3.0	2.5	2.7	37.5
Non-contract Houses	175.00	—	2.9	1.8	—	—
Musicals:						
Contract Houses	180.00	2.8	3.0	1.2	2.1	29.0
Non-contract Houses	223.20	—	3.0	1.0	—	—
Engineers	147.00	6.0	1.3	2.3	3.3	47.0
Stagehands:						
Department Heads	181.00	3.4	0.9	2.5	2.4	33.0
Assistants	160.00	3.4	1.0	8.5	4.8	76.4
Wardrobe Attendants:						
Supervisor	125.00	5.6	0.9	1.7	2.8	38.9
Dressers	74.48	9.3	5.5	1.1	4.9	77.3
Ushers	39.00	7.5	0.0	3.4	3.9	57.6
Ticket Takers	66.50	8.6	0.0	2.8	4.0	59.1
Stage Door Attendants	73.50	9.2	0.0	2.8	4.2	63.0
Treasurers	180.00	3.1	0.0	6.7	3.8	56.5
Porters	78.00	1.5	2.5	2.9	2.3	31.6
Cleaners	51.50	3.7	2.5	2.0	2.7	37.3

SOURCE: Information for years 1953, 1957, 1960 from Wunderlich; information for the 1964–65 season supplied by the League of New York Theatres.

APPENDIX TABLE IX–B

Theater Advertising, 1947–1964

	1947	1957	1962	1964	Average Annual Percentage Change 1947–1964	Average Annual Percentage Change 1957–1962
Price Per Agate Line: [a]						
Broadway	$1.39	$1.85	$2.15	$2.20	2.7	3.0
Off-Broadway	.91	.99	1.28	1.32	2.2	5.3
Estimated Annual Lineage: [b]						
Broadway	—	375,695	462,688	—	—	4.3
Off-Broadway	—	87,938	175,206	—	—	14.8
Lineage Per Performance: [c]						
Broadway	—	43.6	51.4	—	—	3.7
Off-Broadway	—	23.0	21.4	—	—	-1.4

[a] Weekday rate, supplied by the *New York Times,* without allowance for volume discount. Broadway productions pay the "Amusements" rates and off-Broadway productions pay the "Neighborhood Theaters" rates. The figures for 1962 are averages of the rates effective prior to June 5 and the rates effective from June 5 to the end of the year.

[b] Based on a count of the number of agate lines of advertising in the *New York Times* for 12 Thursdays and 12 Sundays in the respective years (the 2nd Thursday and 2nd Sunday of each month). These figures were then inflated by factors reflecting the relationship between Thursday and Sunday advertising volume and total weekly advertising by Broadway and off-Broadway shows. The adjustment factors were obtained through an intensive analysis of five sample weeks.

[c] The figures for number of performances were taken from Appendix Tables III–I and III–J.

Minimum Weekly Salaries
of Broadway and Off-Broadway Actors, 1954–1968

Year	Broadway		Off-Broadway		Off-Broadway as Per Cent of Broadway	
	Rehearsal Pay	Regular Pay	Rehearsal Pay	Regular Pay	Rehearsal Pay	Regular Pay
1954	$ 55.00	$ 85.00	$ 5.00	$30.00	9	35
1955	55.00	85.00	5.00	30.00	9	35
1956	55.00	85.00	10.00	40.00	18	47
1957	65.00	100.00	15.00	40.00	23	40
1958	70.00	103.50	15.00	40.00	21	39
1959	75.00	103.50	20.00	45.00	27	44
1960	82.50	111.00	20.00	45.00	24	41
1961	87.50	112.50	45.00	45.00	51	40
1962	92.50	115.00	45.00	45.00	49	39
1963	97.50	117.50	50.00	50.00	51	43
1964	97.50	125.00	60.00	60.00	62	48
1965	107.50	125.00	65.00	65.00	60	52
1966[a]	115.00	127.50	65.00	65.00	57	51
1967[a]	122.50	130.00	—	—	—	—
1968[a]	130.00	—	—	—	—	—

SOURCE: Compiled from agreements in the files of Actors' Equity.

[a] According to agreement negotiated in 1965.

Trends in Performer Salaries and in Earnings of
Operatives and of Salaried Employees, Great Britain, 1946–1963

	Average Annual Percentage Change		
	1946–1963	1950–1963	1957–1963
Performers:			
Regional Orchestral Musicians[a]	4.2	5.2	6.8
Covent Garden:[b]			
Opera Chorus	4.2	5.5	6.5
Corps de Ballet	4.2	5.5	4.8
Opera Orchestra	—	4.4	5.7
Others:			
Operatives, All Industries[c]	6.1	6.2	4.7
Salaried Employees[d]	—	—	5.2
Salaried Employees of National and Local Government[e]	—	—	5.7
Retail Price Index		3.9	2.4

[a] Rank-and-file members. Compiled from data supplied by the Secretary of the British Musicians' Union.

[b] Data supplied by Covent Garden.

[c] From 1960 on, the figures are based on the average weekly earnings of manual workers; despite the somewhat lower average pay of such workers, it is likely that, during the short period covered, the rate of change was similar to that for "operatives." The "operatives" series is from United Kingdom, *Annual Abstract of Statistics*, various years. The "manual worker" series is from United Kingdom, *Statistics on Incomes, Prices, Employment, and Production*, No. 13, June 1965, p. 8.

[d] Covers administrative and technical grades and clerical and analogous grades. Data from United Kingdom, *Statistics on Incomes, Prices, Employment, and Production*, p. 48.

[e] Includes teachers and national health service employees. Data from United Kingdom, *Statistics on Incomes, Prices, Employment, and Production*, p. 49.

APPENDIX X–1

Number of Performances and Audience Size

While the typical length of season is currently increasing, primarily in response to the demands of the performers, it is by no means obvious that the increased number of performances will bring with it a corresponding increase in the size of the total audience. There is some reason to expect that when more performances are provided, more tickets will be sold. If most of the orchestras that are lengthening their seasons are also developing new types of concerts, new series and different types of orchestral service, these may attract new persons to attend or they may lead others to attend more often. The new performances will probably take place on nights of the week or at times of the year which are convenient for some persons who would otherwise not have been able to come. But, other things being equal, we may well suspect that more frequent performance will serve, in part, just to spread the concert audience more thinly.

Since, as we saw in Chapter VIII, cost per concert does decrease up to a point as the number of concerts goes up, it is important to see whether the added concerts can be expected to bring an additional audience of average size along with them. Obviously, if attendance per concert declines sufficiently as the number of concerts grows, economies of scale will not help finances.

We compared average attendance per concert with the number of concerts per season for two of the major orchestras for which we had obtained statistically significant cost functions (see the appendix to Chapter VIII). Appendix Figure X–A shows what we found for the same orchestra whose unit cost curve is depicted in Figure VIII–4. It is evident from the diagram that average attendance does fall somewhat with the number of concerts.[1] Furthermore, the decline shown in the diagram is probably a considerable understatement of the rate of decrease involved in the underlying relationship. Many of the historical increases in number of con-

---

[1] Actually the decline is small in terms of the historical relationship shown in Appendix Figure X–A. An increase of 1 per cent in number of concerts yields at 1964 attendance levels a decrease of about 0.3 per cent in attendance per concert, a loss of about 8 persons per concert. With an average of slightly more than 100 concerts per season, this would reduce attendance by a total of about 800 admissions. Since, however, the new concert would on the average be attended by about 2,500 persons, it would bring in a net gain of some 1,700 paid admissions.

RELATION BETWEEN ATTENDANCE PER CONCERT AND NUMBER OF CONCERTS, FOR A MAJOR ORCHESTRA

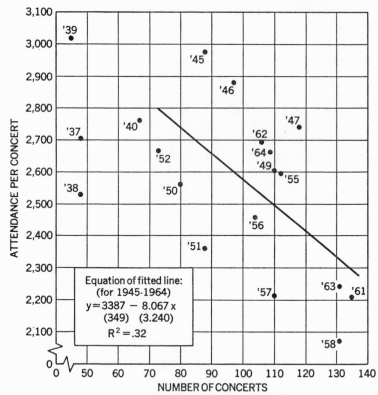

certs occurred only in response to popular demand when the potential audience was already available. If the increased number of performances had been undertaken haphazardly, without regard for autonomous demand changes, and if the new concert had been required, as it were, to hunt up its own audience, one may surmise that the resulting decrease in attendance per concert would have been far more marked. But as more orchestras strive for year-round operation, the number of concerts per season is bound to increase, whether or not they are accompanied by a considerable decline in attendance per concert.

While a larger supply of performances does increase the *total* audience, it undoubtedly yields diminishing returns in terms of audience per concert, and so it is not always an unmixed financial blessing.

How Audiences Hear about Performances, by Art Form

Heard About Performance by:	Per Cent of Those Surveyed While Attending:[a]					
	All Paid Perform-ances	Theater	Major Orches-tras	Opera	Dance	Chamber Music, etc.
Mail	25.2	23.8	22.8	40.3	24.6	42.4
Newspaper Ad	34.0	40.0	23.7	44.4	47.5	27.4
Newspaper Story	22.3	32.0	15.6	17.5	16.1	7.6
Radio or TV	5.9	7.2	5.7	4.2	3.2	1.7
Billboard	3.4	3.9	1.9	5.7	4.3	7.5
Word of Mouth	34.5	43.2	27.2	30.4	31.9	27.0
Other Means	29.4	17.9	47.6	16.7	16.3	18.9

SOURCE: Twentieth Century Fund audience survey.

[a] The base for these percentages is the number in the audience who answered the indicated item in the questionnaire. The percentages sum to more than 100 because many people hear about a performance from more than one source.

How Audiences Hear about Performances in New York City, by Art Form

Heard about Performance by:	Per Cent of Those Surveyed While Attending:[a]						
	All Paid Perform-ances	Broad-way Theater	Off-Broad-way Theater	Major Orches-tras	Opera	Ballet	Chamber Music, etc.
Mail	16.8	3.0	15.2	17.4	38.7	22.9	27.4
Newspaper Ad	42.0	44.4	47.9	19.3	44.1	49.0	31.6
Newspaper Story	28.9	54.0	37.4	10.2	10.2	16.2	7.0
Radio or TV	5.9	14.1	5.1	1.2	0.6	3.3	0.0
Billboard	4.2	6.6	1.5	1.7	7.2	4.4	4.7
Word of Mouth	35.6	52.1	38.9	16.5	22.7	32.0	30.1
Other Means	21.9	15.0	15.3	59.2	13.5	16.3	19.9

See notes to Appendix Table X–A.

Audience Overlap, by Art Form

Art Form and Number of Times Attended	Per Cent of Those Surveyed While Attending:[a]					
	All Paid Perform- ances	Thea- ter	Major Orches- tras	Opera	Dance	Chamber Music, etc.
Theater:						
No Times	7.1	6.0	9.0	6.1	4.1	7.9
1–4 Times	32.0	33.2	32.8	29.6	24.0	30.6
5–9 Times	28.8	32.2	26.1	25.9	28.4	26.1
10 or More Times	32.1	28.6	32.1	38.4	43.5	35.4
Average Number of Times	8.2	7.5	7.9	9.8	11.7	9.1
Symphony:						
No Times	28.8	48.2	8.2	30.9	34.5	16.7
1–4 Times	32.5	36.9	24.3	38.6	40.9	40.5
5–9 Times	17.6	8.6	28.1	14.5	12.6	21.6
10 or More Times	21.2	6.3	39.5	16.1	12.0	21.2
Average Number of Times	5.2	2.2	8.7	4.2	3.6	5.7
Opera:						
No Times	53.6	66.3	48.1	21.6	45.8	44.5
1–4 Times	36.4	28.0	41.3	52.6	36.9	47.1
5–9 Times	6.5	3.8	7.6	15.0	8.5	5.8
10 or More Times	3.5	1.9	3.0	10.9	8.8	2.6
Average Number of Times	1.7	1.0	1.7	4.4	2.9	1.7
Ballet and Modern Dance:						
No Times	55.0	61.4	57.4	45.7	25.2	44.6
1–4 Times	38.8	35.3	39.3	41.8	46.4	47.0
5–9 Times	4.0	2.3	2.6	8.0	14.5	6.6
10 or More Times	2.3	1.0	0.7	4.6	13.9	1.8
Average Number of Times	1.3	0.9	0.9	2.1	4.8	1.6

Art Form and Number of Times Attended	Per Cent of Those Surveyed While Attending:[a]					
	All Paid Perform- ances	Thea- ter	Major Orches- tras	Opera	Dance	Chamber Music, etc.
Other Serious Music (chamber, etc.):						
No Times	42.7	52.3	36.6	41.3	40.8	12.7
1–4 Times	39.0	36.8	41.3	37.4	42.0	33.1
5–9 Times	10.8	7.1	13.1	11.9	10.1	24.5
10 or More Times	7.5	3.8	9.0	9.5	7.1	29.7
Average Number of Times	2.7	1.8	3.2	3.1	2.6	7.7

SOURCE: Twentieth Century Fund audience survey. See Chapter IV for details.

[a] The tabulation represents responses to the question: *"Excluding today, have you attended a theater [or "symphony" or other, depending on the audience group being surveyed] performance within the last 12 months? If so, how many times?"* This wording explains how there can be a "no times" answer for "Theater" on the part of persons attending a theater performance the night of the survey; and similarly for the other art forms.

APPENDIX TABLE X–D

Audience Overlap in New York City, by Art Form

Art Form and Number of Times Attended	Per Cent of Those Surveyed While Attending:						
	All Paid Perform-ances	Broadway Theater	Off-Broadway	Major Orches-tras	Opera	Ballet	Chamber Music, etc.
Theater:							
No Times	4.4	6.6	2.6	2.9	4.7	4.0	6.3
1–4 Times	27.9	36.6	23.0	24.1	28.0	24.1	32.8
5–9 Times	29.1	28.9	32.8	29.1	25.0	28.2	25.2
10 or More Times	38.6	27.9	41.5	44.0	42.4	43.7	35.7
Average Number of Times	9.8	7.1	10.0	10.2	11.6	11.8	9.4
Symphony:							
No Times	37.0	56.7	38.4	8.5	38.3	34.8	20.1
1–4 Times	35.0	32.1	41.1	19.8	33.4	40.9	44.1
5–9 Times	12.7	6.4	11.0	25.6	12.9	12.5	15.9
10 or More Times	15.3	4.8	9.5	46.1	15.5	11.8	19.8
Average Number of Times	3.0	1.7	2.0	0.6	2.8	2.5	5.2

No Times	49.3	67.5	52.7	37.8	23.5	45.1	40.3
1–4 Times	35.5	26.1	35.4	41.1	43.1	37.1	46.8
5–9 Times	8.2	4.2	7.3	11.7	15.2	8.7	8.1
10 or More Times	7.0	2.2	4.6	9.3	18.1	9.1	4.8
Average Number of Times	2.4	1.1	1.8	3.1	5.5	2.9	2.1
Ballet and Modern Dance:							
No Times	44.4	61.9	47.6	45.5	36.3	24.6	45.7
1–4 Times	42.7	34.7	45.7	46.0	41.7	46.4	45.2
5–9 Times	7.6	2.1	4.4	6.3	14.2	14.8	6.9
10 or More Times	5.4	1.2	2.4	2.3	7.8	14.2	2.3
Average Number of Times	2.3	0.9	1.4	1.6	3.1	4.9	1.8
Other Serious Music (chamber, etc.):							
No Times	45.5	61.5	43.1	39.7	42.9	41.3	12.8
1–4 Times	38.0	31.5	41.8	39.3	36.7	41.7	35.6
5–9 Times	9.3	4.4	9.0	12.8	10.6	9.8	22.3
10 or More Times	7.2	2.6	6.1	8.2	9.8	7.2	29.3
Average Number of Times	2.5	1.2	2.3	3.1	2.9	2.5	7.9

Profile of Customers at Macy-Shubert Box Offices
and of the Broadway Audience[a]

	Macy's	Broadway
SEX		
Male	38.6%	57.6%
AGE		
Under 20	8.2	4.9
Over 60	11.0	5.1
Median Age	40 yrs.	39 yrs.
EDUCATION		
Males:		
Grade School and Less Than		
4 Yrs. High School	3.3%	2.9%
4 Yrs. High School	13.3	9.5
1–3 Yrs. College	16.7	16.0
4 Yrs. College	33.3	23.0
Graduate School	33.3	48.5
Median Category	4 yrs. coll.	4 yrs. coll.
Females:		
Grade School and Less Than		
4 yrs. High School	10.8%	3.6%
4 Yrs. High School	5.4	19.6
1–3 Yrs. College	32.4	26.0
4 Yrs. College	24.3	22.4
Graduate School	27.0	23.8
Median Category	4 yrs. coll.	4 yrs. coll.
INCOME		
Over $5,000	94.7%	94.7%
Over $15,000	40.8	45.5
Over $25,000	19.7	19.6
FREQUENCY OF ATTENDANCE AT THEATER	Average Number of Times Attended in Preceding 12 Months	
No Times	16.9%	6.6%
1–4 Times	37.4	36.6
5–9 Times	28.9	28.9
Over 9 Times	16.9	27.9

(Notes on following page)

SOURCE: Based on 83 responses to our Macy's box office questionnaire and 2,226 responses to our Broadway audience survey.

ᵃ In our Macy's box-office study patrons were surveyed on one Wednesday and one Friday in the spring of 1964. The ticket sellers at the main R. H. Macy's store on Herald Square and three of the branches in White Plains and Long Island were instructed to hand a questionnaire to each person who purchased tickets, and ask him to fill it out and drop it into a box with a slot on top. We used the following questionnaire:

1. Male .... ☐ (1)
   Female .... ☐ (2)

2. Married .... ☐ (1)
   Not married .... ☐ (2)

3. Number of children _____

4. Your age:
   Under 20 .... ☐ (1)
   20 — 24 .... ☐ (2)
   25 — 34 .... ☐ (3)
   35 — 44 .... ☐ (4)
   45 — 59 .... ☐ (5)
   60 or over .... ☐ (6)

5. What is the occupation of the head of your household?

   _____

6. How much formal education have you completed?
   (Check highest level.)
   Grade school .... ☐ (1)
   1 — 3 years of high school ☐ (2)
   4 years of high school ...... ☐ (3)
   1 — 3 years of college ...... ☐ (4)
   4 years of college .... ☐ (5)
   Graduate or post-college professional school .... ☐ (6)

7. In which group did your family income (before taxes) for last year fall?

   Under $3,000 .... ☐ (1)
   $3,000 — 4,999 .... ☐ (2)
   $5,000 — 6,999 .... ☐ (3)
   $7,000 — 9,999 .... ☐ (4)
   $10,000 — 14,999 .... ☐ (5)
   $15,000 — 24,999 .... ☐ (6)
   $25,000 — 49,999 .... ☐ (7)
   $50,000 or over .... ☐ (8)

8. In what community do you live?

   _____   _____
      (town)   (state)

9. To what show did you purchase a ticket (tickets)?

   _____

10. What price did you pay per ticket?_____

11. Is at least one of the tickets you have just purchased for your own use?
    No .... ☐ (1)
    Yes .... ☐ (2)

12. How many theatre performances have you attended within the last 12 months?_____

13. Are you satisfied with the service provided by this Macy-Shubert ticket booth?
    No .... ☐ (1)
    Yes .... ☐ (2)

Audience Response to Contemporary Operas[a]

	Number of Performances		Per Cent of Capacity[b]	
	"Contemporary"	"Other"	"Contemporary"	"Other"
Metropolitan Opera				
(1962–63)	13	179	88.9[c]	96.9[c]
New York City Opera (City Center):				
1961–62	20	22	41.4	66.4
Fall 1962	7	27	30.6	64.4
Average	14	24	38.6	65.4
Lyric Opera of Chicago				
(1961)	4	24	54.7[c]	90.0[c]
Covent Garden:				
1957–58	14	120	66.5	76.6
1958–59	5	119	46.5	81.9
1959–60	4	144	35.9	82.7
1960–61	14	142	89.9	86.3
1961–62	13	107	73.0	84.3
1963–64	23	110	58.5	85.6
Average	12	122	66.6	82.9

SOURCE: Calculated from data for each performance of each opera provided by the respective opera companies.

[a] A "contemporary opera" is defined as one written after World War I.

[b] Actual attendance as per cent of capacity attendance unless otherwise indicated.

[c] Receipts as per cent of capacity gross.

Audience Response to "Adventurous" Programs,
Royal Festival Hall, 1962–1964[a]

	Number of Performances		Average Attendance as Per Cent of Capacity	
	"Adventurous"	"Popular"	"Adventurous"	"Popular"
Season:				
1961–62	101	125	58.9	80.4
1962–63	82	134	59.4	77.3
1963–64	91	96	56.0	78.8
Orchestra:				
London Symphony	54	31	60.8	74.9
London Philharmonic	42	43	48.9	70.4
New Philharmonic	31	48	70.5	90.1
BBC	33	5	48.4	80.6
Royal Philharmonic	3	5	43.0	77.3
Other[b]	111	223	64.1	83.4
Ticket Price Category:[c]				
Top Price			49	66
Middle Price			54	75
Low Price			75	92

SOURCE: Appendix to the Goodman Report.

[a] "Popular" programs are defined as "those devoted *exclusively* to the performance of familiar or frequently played works in the standard orchestral repertoire (e.g., the symphonies, concertos, overtures, etc. of Haydn, Mozart, Beethoven, Schubert, Brahms, Tchaikovsky, Dvorak . . .)." "Adventurous programs" are defined as "those which contain one or more works which do not fall naturally into the popular category (such as the symphonies of Schumann, Mahler, Bruckner . . .)." Also, most of the music by twentieth century composers is considered "adventurous."

[b] "Other" includes visiting orchestras, programs sponsored by musical societies, self-promoted concerts and charity concerts.

[c] Top ticket price is over 15s.; middle is between 7s. 6d. and 15s.; low price is 7s. 6d. or less.

Ticket Expense and Associated Costs of Attendance at Live
Performances, in New York City, London, and Among Persons
Attending Free Outdoor Performances in the United States,
1963–64

| | | Average Spent Per Person | | |
Expense Category	Per Cent Incurring Each Expense	By Persons Incurring Each Expense	By All Who Paid for Own Tickets	Per Cent of Total Expense
NEW YORK CITY (paying members of the audience)				
Public Transportation	54	$1.33	$0.71	8.2
Auto Transportation	37	2.29	0.87	10.0
Total Transportation	(87)	(1.82)	(1.58)	(18.2)
Restaurant	42	5.20	2.20	25.3
Baby Sitter	12	2.89	0.34	3.9
Total Non-ticket Expense	92	4.40	$4.10	47.3
Ticket Expense	100	4.58	4.58	52.8
Total Expense			$8.68	100
LONDON (paying members of the audience)		£ s. d.	£ s. d.	
Public Transportation	57	4 11	2 10	13.0
Auto Transportation	34	3 4	1 2	5.3
Total Transportation	(88)	(4 6)	(3 11)	(18.3)
Restaurant	40	10 6	4 2	19.1
Baby Sitter	5	1 10 5	1 5	6.5
Total Non-ticket Expense	91	10 8	9 6	43.9
Ticket Expense	100	12 7	12 7	56.1
Total Expense	100		1 1 13	100

Expense Category	Per Cent Incurring Each Expense	Average Spent Per Person	
		By Persons Incurring Each Expense	By All Members of the Audience
FREE OUTDOOR PER-FORMANCES IN NEW YORK AND PHILADEL-PHIA (all members of the audience)			
Public Transportation	46	$0.76	$0.35
Auto Transportation	50	1.04	0.52
Total Transportation	(94)	(0.92)	(0.86)
Restaurant	25	2.18	0.55
Baby Sitter	6	1.99	0.12
Total Non-ticket Expense	98	1.56	$1.53
Ticket Expense	0	0	0
Total Expense			$1.53

SOURCE: Twentieth Century Fund audience survey.

NOTE: Auto transportation is figured at $.10 per mile. The ticket expense item excludes persons who reported ticket expenses in excess of $10 per seat; the number who did so is small, and most of them apparently named the amount they paid for an entire season's subscription.

Ticket Expense and Non-ticket Expense, Averages by Art Form, United States, New York City and London, 1963–1965

	Average Ticket Expense	Average Non-ticket Expense	Average Total Expense	Ticket Price as Per Cent of Total Expense
All United States:				
Theater	$4.18	$4.20	$8.38	49.9
Major Orchestras	3.18[a]	2.16	5.34	59.6
Opera	4.07[b]	2.98	7.05	57.7
Ballet	3.54	3.04	6.59	53.7
All Art Forms	3.66	3.16	6.82	53.7
New York City:				
Broadway	6.26	5.94	12.20	51.3
Off-Broadway	4.40	4.16	8.56	51.4
Major Orchestra	4.42[a]	3.37	7.79	56.7
Opera	3.91[b]	3.15	7.06	55.4
Ballet	3.59	3.12	6.71	53.5
All Art Forms	4.58	4.10	8.68	52.8
All British				
(London)	12s. 3d.	9s. 6d.	£1 1s. 9d.	56.3

SOURCE: Twentieth Century Fund audience survey. The number of respondents varies according to art form and region. See Chapter IV.

[a] Includes non-subscription tickets (which are more expensive than subscription tickets), and is therefore not comparable with data reported elsewhere.

[b] Because no surveys were conducted at the Metropolitan Opera, this figure is relatively low.

See Note to Appendix Table XI–A.

Changes in Ticket Prices and in the Retail Price Index: Some Long-Period Comparisons for Great Britain

Organization and Time Period	Average Annual Percentage Increase (Compound Rate)[a]	
	Ticket Price	Retail Price Index
Covent Garden Theatre (1760) and Royal Shakespeare Theatre:[b]		
1760 to 1964	0.8	1.0
1760 to 1961	0.6	1.0
Royal Shakespeare Theatre:[c]		
1880 to 1964	2.1	1.5
1880 to 1961	1.6	1.5
1880 to 1955	1.4	1.4
A Major London Orchestra, 1895 to 1939[d]	1.1	1.3
Covent Garden Opera, 1901 to 1938[e]	1.4	1.4
A Provincial Orchestra, 1911 to 1964[f]	2.3	2.8

SOURCE: Ticket prices were obtained directly from the individual organizations except as noted below. The retail price index numbers for the years from 1915 to 1964 are based on the Ministry of Labour's Index of Retail Prices and were compiled from the following sources: 1915 to 1938 from *Abstract of British Statistics*, ed. R. R. Mitchell, Cambridge, 1962, p. 478; 1939 to 1947 from *Ministry of Labour Gazette*, January 1947, p. 7; 1948 to 1950 from the same publication, January 1956, p. 6; 1951–1964 from Ministry of Labour, *Statistics on Incomes, Prices, Employment and Production*, No. 13, June 1965. These various publications use different years as base periods, and we employed overlapping years to put the entire series on a 1950 = 100 base. There are no strictly comparable figures for the years prior to 1915. For this period we used the Phelps Brown–Hopkins index (see Chapter VIII, p. 183), and connected it to the retail price index by taking the ratio of the two indexes in 1915 as a conversion factor.

[a] Calculated on the basis of terminal years only. More than one set of dates is shown for the Royal Shakespeare Theatre because of the sharp rise in its ticket prices since 1955.

[b] The average ticket price at the Covent Garden Theatre in 1760 was 2.9s. This average was calculated in the usual way (by dividing capacity gross by number of seats); the raw data are from Stone (p. li). The ticket price figures for 1961 and 1964 are the median ticket prices charged at the Stratford-on-Avon spring and summer Shakespeare Festivals.

(*Notes continued on following page*)

ᵉ Ticket price growth rates are averages of the growth rates for both minimum and maximum ticket prices.

ᵈ The ticket price growth rate is the average of the growth rates for the minimum priced reserved seat and the maximum priced reserved seat. The comparison ends in 1939 because after the war the London orchestra performed in a much larger hall; comparisons of prewar and postwar ticket prices are, therefore, hazardous.

ᵉ Growth rate for the stall price.

ᶠ Growth rate for the top ticket price.

APPENDIX TABLE XI–D

Indexes of Top Broadway Ticket Prices (including tax) and of Consumer Prices, 1927–1965 (1927 = 100)

Year	Straight Shows	Musicals	Price Index Consumer
1927	100	100	100
1928	101	117	99
1929	95	117	99
1930	97	129	96
1931	99	113	88
1932	87	94	79
1933	85	79	75
1934	91	71	77
1935	96	83	79
1936	90	89	80
1937	92	91	83
1938	86	89	81
1939	90	89	80
1940	83	95	81
1941	90	89	85
1942	93	95	94
1943	93	89	100
1944	94	99	101
1945	108	110	104
1946	118	115	112
1947	130	117	129
1948	128	119	139
1949	135	136	137
1950	141	130	139
1951	131	128	150
1952	151	155	153
1953	146	149	154

Year	Straight Shows	Musicals	Consumer Price Index
1954	162	156	155
1955	165	148	154
1956	165	149	157
1957	185	170	162
1958	194	176	166
1959	197	183	168
1960	203	193	170
1961	198	197	172
1962	211	201	174
1963	212	200	176
1964	211	205	179
1965	211	208	182[a]

SOURCE: Average top prices for 1927–1962 were taken from Moore; they are averages for February which he calculated from *Variety*. We calculated similar averages from *Variety* for subsequent years (issues of Feb. 27, 1963, Feb. 26, 1964, Feb. 17, 1965), and put all of the dollar figures on a 1927 = 100 base.

[a] Estimated by finding the ratio between the Jan.–June values of the consumer price index in 1965 and its Jan.–June values in 1964, then multiplying the 1964 price index by this ratio.

Indexes of Major Orchestra Ticket Prices (average subscription series price, including tax), 1928–1964 (1937 = 97)

Season	Basic 11 Major Orchestras[a]	3 Major Orchestras[b]
1927–28	—	100
1928–29	—	115
1929–30	—	115
1930–31	—	115
1931–32	—	115
1932–33	—	115
1933–34	—	99
1934–35	—	99
1935–36	—	99
1936–37	97	97
1937–38	97	94
1938–39	93	96
1939–40	95	96
1940–41	—	96
1941–42	—	96
1942–43	—	110
1943–44	—	110
1944–45	125	120
1945–46	126	124
1946–47	139	134
1947–48	139	134
1948–49	148	142
1949–50	140	142
1950–51	143	146
1951–52	168	146
1952–53	—	145
1953–54	—	150
1954–55	143	150
1955–56	149	150
1956–57	162	150
1957–58	145	159
1958–59	—	160
1959–60	—	169
1960–61	165	173
1961–62	192	173
1962–63	188	179
1963–64	205	179

(*Notes on opposite page*)

ᵃ This series was constructed by dividing actual receipts from subscription concerts by the number of tickets sold, and is erratic because of variations in the relative demand for more expensive and cheaper seats. The series was put on an index basis with 1936–37 = 97, which is the value of the 3-major-orchestras index in that year, in order to facilitate comparisons of the two indexes.

ᵇ This series is based on figures for the New York Philharmonic, Cincinnati Orchestra and Pittsburgh Orchestra. It reflects ticket prices of only the New York Philharmonic up to 1937 (i.e., the season 1936–37), of both the New York Philharmonic and the Cincinnati Orchestra from 1937 to 1940 and of all three orchestras from 1941 on.

For the New York Philharmonic we obtained the subscription price per performance of a parquet seat from 1928 through 1964; for the Cincinnati Orchestra, the subscription price per performance of a front orchestra seat from 1937 through 1964; for the Pittsburgh Orchestra, the average subscription price of a seat at a regular series concert (capacity gross divided by number of seats) from 1941 to 1964. All of these prices include tax. A composite index for the three orchestras was constructed as follows: we put the New York Philharmonic prices on an index basis with 1928 = 100; we then put the Cincinnati Orchestra prices on the same index basis by setting the Cincinnati price for 1937 at 97, which was the value of the New York Philharmonic index in that year; next we put the Pittsburgh Orchestra prices on the same index basis by setting the Pittsburgh price equal to the average of the New York and Cincinnati index values for 1937; finally, we took a simple average of the indexes for the three orchestras.

Attendance as Percentage of Capacity: Postwar Trends for Basic Eleven Major Orchestras and the Metropolitan Opera

Season	Basic 11 Major Orchestras[a]	Metropolitan Opera[b]
1947–48	82	
1948–49	75	
1949–50	80	
1950–51	74	
1951–52	74	
1952–53		
1953–54	72	91
1954–55	71	91
1955–56	77	94
1956–57	74	94
1957–58	78	95
1958–59		97
1959–60		97
1960–61	82	96
1961–62	82	97
1962–63	79	96
1963–64	78	97
1964–65		95

SOURCE: Calculated from data supplied by individual arts organizations.

[a] Regular series subscription concerts only; arithmetic mean of percentage-of-capacity figures.

[b] Box office receipts as a percentage of capacity gross.

Percentages of the Audience Who Tried to Buy More and
Less Expensive Seats, by Art Form

	Tried to Buy a Less Expensive Seat	Tried to Buy a More Expensive Seat
All United States:		
Theater	11.6	4.2
Major Orchestra	5.7	4.5
Opera	4.5	5.3
Ballet	5.8	12.4
All Art Forms	11.1	6.9
New York City:		
Broadway	15.5	6.5
Off-Broadway	17.0	3.8
Major Orchestra	8.5	4.7
Opera	3.6	4.6
Ballet	5.9	12.9
All Art Forms	16.2	5.3
All British (London)	11.6	5.0

SOURCE: Twentieth Century Fund audience survey. The number of respondents varies according to art form and region. See Chapter IV.

APPENDIX TABLE XI–H

Effects of Ticket Price on Audience Composition

Age, Occupation, Art Form	Ticket Price Paid							
	$1.00–$1.99	$2.00–$2.99	$3.00–$3.99	$4.00–$4.99	$5.00–$5.99	$6.00–$6.99	$7.00[a]–$7.99	$8.00[a]–$9.99
AGE								
Median Age (in years):								
All Paid Performances (U. S.)	30	36	38	41	41	42		
Major Orchestras	33	38	42	44	45	47		
Broadway	*	*	33	36	37	43	40	41
Off-Broadway	*	35	35	40	45	40		
London[b]	29	29	34	34	39	*	41	
OCCUPATION (of males)								
Students:								
All Paid Performances (U. S.)	36.0%	17.4%	16.6%	10.2%	9.7%	5.4%		
Major Orchestras	34.6	14.8	13.3	10.4	9.0	6.0		
Broadway	*	*	16.3	13.5	8.5	3.2	5.3%	4.7%
Off-Broadway	*	*	20.3	11.4	4.2	*		
London[b]	21.3	23.0	11.8	13.3	7.1	*	7.4	
Teachers:								
All Paid Performances (U. S.)	18.5%	16.4%	13.7%	10.7%	9.7%	5.8%		
Major Orchestras	18.3	16.5	11.8	11.2	9.5	3.7		
Broadway	*	*	10.7	16.1	12.8	4.7	3.8%	3.2%
Off-Broadway	*	*	20.3	11.4	4.2	*		
London[b]	11.5	18.1	17.1	6.7	5.9	*	8.3	

Professional:

All Paid Performances (U.S.)	72.8%	71.8%	71.7%	66.1%	64.7%	56.0%		43.2%
Major Orchestras	73.7	72.4	71.8	68.5	68.4	57.0		
Broadway	*	*	73.3	64.4	67.5	58.4	52.8%	
Off-Broadway	*	*	68.6	72.0	59.0	*	*	
London^b	66.7	67.9	58.1	48.7	61.2	*	60.0	
Managers:								
All Paid Performances (U.S.)	13.0%	15.6%	16.2%	20.4%	24.0%	27.7%		31.5%
Major Orchestras	12.6	15.5	17.3	20.7	21.7	21.5		
Broadway	*	*	12.0	17.8	19.7	23.5	26.4%	
Off-Broadway	*	*	17.0	16.6	29.2	*	*	
London^b	15.5	8.0	22.5	25.2	28.2	*	30.0	
Blue Collar:								
All Paid Performances (U.S.)	3.9%	2.2%	2.6%	1.9%	1.4%	1.7%		3.5%
Major Orchestra	8.8	1.5	2.1	1.7	1.3	2.8		
Broadway	*	*	4.0	1.7	0.9	2.7	3.1%	
Off-Broadway	*	*	2.5	1.9	0.7	*	*	
London^b	4.6	4.6	3.9	5.9	2.4	*	3.3	

EDUCATION (of males)
Some Graduate Work:

All Paid Performances (U.S.)	62.2%	62.5%	62.0%	59.9%	57.8%	59.9%		46.1%
Major Orchestras	62.5	63.6	63.7	64.1	66.0	60.2		
Broadway	*	*	43.1	51.3	55.3	57.1	51.0%	
Off-Broadway	*	*	56.1	68.1	53.2	*		

FAMILY INCOME (median)

All Paid Performances (U.S.)	$ 8,861	$10,924	$12,291	$14,114	$15,779	$19,461		$19,752
Major Orchestras	8,809	11,010	12,682	15,444	19,098	26,157		
Broadway	*	*	10,000	12,173	12,829	15,903	$18,454	
Off-Broadway	*	9,318	11,203	14,203	17,292	19,063		
London^b	4,634	4,130	5,313	4,643	6,255	*	7,000	

(Continued on following page)

APPENDIX TABLE XI-H (continued)

Age, Occupation, Art Form	Ticket Price Paid							
	$1.00–$1.99	$2.00–$2.99	$3.00–$3.99	$4.00–$4.99	$5.00–$5.99	$6.00–$6.99	$7.00–$7.99	$8.00[a]–$9.99
	Average Number of Times Attended							
FREQUENCY OF ATTENDANCE								
Own Art Form (U. S.):								
Major Orchestras	10.7	9.7	9.3	8.9	9.2	9.4		
Broadway	*	*	6.5	6.8	7.5	7.1	8.1	6.6
Off-Broadway	*	10.0	10.6	9.1	10.4	11.1		
All Art Forms:								
All Paid Performances (U. S.)	20.9	18.8	19.1	21.4	19.4	18.1		
Major Orchestras	23.7	22.7	23.8	23.3	25.3	26.6		
Broadway	*	*	11.4	11.7	12.2	12.4	13.6	
Off-Broadway	*	17.6	19.9	17.7	19.4	18.3		
London[b]	33.5	25.5	27.8	25.5	24.4	*	26.7	9.7

SOURCE: Twentieth Century Fund audience survey.   * Less than 50 observations; hence, no summary figure is given.

[a] In all cases except Broadway the number of persons reporting a ticket price over $6.99 was very small, and there is reason to question the accuracy of at least some of the questionnaires which did indicate abnormally high ticket prices. Hence, except on Broadway, no figures are given for these ticket price intervals.

[b] The ticket price intervals used here are half the U. S. intervals; i.e., the $1.00 to $1.99 U. S. interval is $.50 to $.99 for the British data; $2.00 to $2.99 is $1.00 to $1.49, etc. The British prices were converted to dollars on the basis of £1 = $2.80.

Audience Composition at Free Performances and at
Paid Performances

	All Paid Performances	Free Open-Air Performances
SEX		
Male	52.0%	47.6%
AGE		
Under 20	8.4%	15.9%
Over 60	9.5	6.3
Median Age	38 yrs.	28 yrs.
OCCUPATIONAL CATEGORY		
Males:		
Employed Persons:[a]		
Professional	66.3%	63.6%
Teachers	12.1	10.4
Managerial	19.7	13.9
Clerical and Sales	11.6	15.6
Blue Collar	2.5	7.0
Students	16.8	31.8
Females:		
Employed Persons:[a]		
Professional	65.6%	60.7%
Teachers	27.2	22.5
All Other	34.4	39.3
Students	16.0	26.2
Housewives	33.1	16.1
EDUCATION		
Males (age 25 and over):		
Grade School and Less Than		
4 Yrs. High School	1.8%	4.2%
4 Yrs. High School	5.2	8.4
1–3 Yrs. College	11.3	13.6
4 Yrs. College	23.1	24.1
Graduate School	58.6	49.7
Median Category	Grad. work	4 yrs. coll.

(*Continued on following page*)

	All Paid Performances	Free Open-Air Performances
Females (age 25 and over):		
Grade School and Less		
Than 4 Yrs. High School	2.3%	4.5%
4 Yrs. High School	13.4	21.5
1–3 Yrs. College	22.2	20.3
4 Yrs. College	28.5	24.5
Graduate School	33.7	29.2
Median Category	4 yrs. coll.	4 yrs. coll.
INCOME		
Over $5,000	90.0%	84.1%
Over $15,000	36.9	22.9
Over $25,000	16.1	10.0
Median Income	$12,286	$9,409
FREQUENCY OF ATTENDANCE	Average Number of Performances Attended in Last 12 Months	
Theater	8.2	7.5
Symphony	5.2	4.5
Opera	1.7	1.4
Dance	1.3	1.1
Other Serious Music	2.7	2.3

SOURCE: Twentieth Century Fund audience survey.

ᵃ The number of employed persons is the base for the following percentages. The percentage of teachers is a component of the "Professional" category.

The Income Gap: Recent Growth Rates

Organization	Period	Average Annual Percentage Increase[a]	(R^2)
New York Philharmonic	1948–1964	5.2	(.28)[b]
Cincinnati Symphony Orchestra	1947–1964	4.7	(.90)
Basic 11 Major Orchestras	1947–1964	6.9[c, d]	(.96)
Metropolitan Opera	1951–1964	8.2	(.56)
Covent Garden	1951–1964	9.3[e]	(.84)

SOURCE: Data supplied by individual organizations and by the American Symphony Orchestra League.

[a] Calculated by fitting a trend line to the logarithms of the annual observations.

[b] The low R^2 can be ascribed to the sharp fluctuations in expenditures and earned income associated with major tours. If we exclude years when gross tour expenditures exceeded $50,000, the average annual percentage increase is 5.0 ($R^2 = .58$).

[c] "Grants for services" are not included in earned income. In 1963–64 about half of the major orchestras received some income from this source, generally from a city government in exchange for a commitment on the part of the orchestra to put on a certain number of free concerts. In recent years such grants have been counted as a part of earned income by the major orchestras, but this was not the practice in earlier years. We did try to adjust the earlier figures to conform with current practice, and a calculation for the income gap including grants for services in earned income yields a growth rate of 6.5 per cent per year.

[d] Weighted average of the growth rates for the individual orchestras, mean orchestra expenditures serving as weights. The R^2 is for yearly totals of orchestra expenditures and is included here to indicate the steadiness of the over-all rate of increase. We also made calculations for two other sets of orchestras, our "Postwar 15" and "All 23," and found rates of increase in the average income gap of 6.9 per cent and 7.4 per cent, respectively, excluding grants for services. The closeness of these rates to the 6.9 per cent rate for our basic set of 11 major orchestras is encouraging.

[e] As in the case of the New York Philharmonic, the finances of Covent Garden were affected significantly in some years by major tours. The growth rate given here excludes such years (1951, 1954, 1956, 1958, 1961). An alternative calculation including these years resulted in a larger annual growth rate: 12.5 per cent ($R^2 = .82$).

Number of Performances and Length of Run, London and Broadway Theater, 1949–50 to 1963–64

Season	London				New York (Broadway)	
			Total Performances			
	Pro-duc-tions Play-ing[a]	Average Number of Perform-ances	All Produc-tions (col. 1 x col. 2)	Of Plays That Opened & Closed in Same Season	Produc-tions Playing	Total Perform-ances
	(1)	(2)	(3)	(4)	(5)	(6)
1949–50	69	190	13,110		69	8,983
1950–51	65[b]	245	15,925		92	8,446
1951–52	72[b]	181	13,032		89	8,614
1952–53	62[b]	198	12,276	90	65	7,571
1953–54	68	215	14,620	84	66	8,485
1954–55	68	247	16,796	90	72	8,917
1955–56	71	182	12,922	104	70	9,390
1956–57	66[b]	199	13,134	83	78	8,973
1957–58	69[b]	201	13,869	79	85	8,247
1958–59	63	190	11,970	100	73	8,943
1959–60	84	155	13,020	72	76	9,214
1960–61	85	127[c]	10,795	76	70	9,445
1961–62	74	151[c]	11,174	75	73	9,055
1962–63	83[b]	111[c]	9,213	68	71	8,954
1963–64	101			57	82	7,975

SOURCE: *Theater World Annual,* Vols. 1–15, and Table III–8 above.

[a] Excludes repertory and other productions given for a limited period.

[b] Includes several plays with no number of performances reported. All such plays were assumed to have the average number of performances.

[c] To obtain figures for these years, we calculated the average number of per-formances in the years 1956–57, 1957–58 and 1959–60 for all plays which did not close in the same year they opened, and used this figure (373) as the average for those still running.

Method of Estimating the Trend in Contributions
by the Top Income Group

Our objective is to estimate the trend in contributions by some arbitrarily chosen top percentage of the population ranked according to income — say the top 1 per cent. The tax data are not tabulated in such a way as to make it possible to obtain the desired figures directly. The only relevant set of figures available shows the amount of contributions reported on individual returns falling into various income classes. By aggregating the classes down to the $50,000 level of adjusted gross income we obtained the contributions series for 1954, 1958 and 1962 shown in column 1 of the following table.

	Unadjusted Total of Contributions (in millions) Reported on Returns with $50,000 or More of Adjusted Gross Income	Estimates of Contributions (in millions) by a Constant Percentage of Top Income Recipients
	(1)	(2)
1954 (base year)	$438.3	$438
1958	639.2	594
1962	799.1	690

SOURCE: Derived from *Statistics of Income, Individual Income Tax Returns.*

However, in any period when incomes in general are rising, the total amount of contributions reported on returns with adjusted gross incomes in excess of any fixed dollar figure will increase simply because a larger and larger percentage of returns will have incomes greater than the boundary amount. For example, between 1954 and 1962 the number of returns in the $50,000-and-up category increased by 67 per cent while the total number of returns increased only 15 per cent.

In calculating the adjusted figures shown in column 2 we corrected for this distorting influence. We are indebted to Dr. Joseph Pechman of the Brookings Institution for suggesting the method of adjustment we used, which is explained most easily by reference

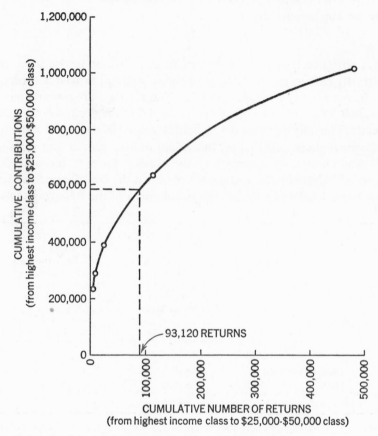

Basic data for this graph were obtained from *Statistics of Income*.

to the graph above. In this graph we have plotted the cumulative amount of contributions (from the highest income class through the $25,000–$49,999 class) against the cumulative number of returns (again, from the highest income class through the $25,000–$49,999 class) for 1958. We then connected the points to form a smooth curve, which shows the relationship between cumulative contributions and cumulative number of returns.

Now, if there had been no population increase between 1954 and 1958, we could have obtained our adjusted estimate of the contributions of our top income group simply by taking the number of returns in the $50,000-and-up income class in 1954 (89,110) and

516

finding from our curve the amount of contribution corresponding to this number of returns in 1958. However, as population expands, contributions also increase and all our contributions growth rate figures reflect this influence. To allow for population growth in estimating contributions by our top income group, we increased the 1954 number of returns in proportion to the increase in the number of people 25 and over in the population between 1954 and 1958, and thus obtained a figure of 93,120 returns as our cut-off. (Use of the increase in this age category as our index of population growth is admittedly arbitrary, but any other reasonable measure would have yielded much the same results. The reason for using some measure of population growth rather than simply the increase in number of returns is that, as was noted earlier, the number of returns increases relative to the population simply because as incomes rise more people meet the filing requirement. But the newcomers to the tax rolls are, by assumption, concentrated at the bottom of the income distribution and their inclusion in our index of growth would have had a distorting effect.)

The final step was to take the figure of 93,120 returns in 1958 and find the corresponding amount of contribution from the curve — which was roughly $594,000, the figure recorded in the table.

We estimated the contribution figure for 1962 in an analogous fashion.

Individual Philanthropic Contributions, 1917–1962

	Itemized Income Tax Returns[a]				All Income Tax Returns		
		Itemized Contributions				Estimated Total Contributions[e]	
Year	Per Cent of All Returns[f]	Adjusted Gross Income (millions)	Amount (millions)	Per Cent of Income (col. 3 ÷ col. 2)	Adjusted Gross Income[b] (millions)	Amount (millions)	Per Cent of Income (col. 6 ÷ col. 5)
	(1)	(2)	(3)	(4)	(5)	(6)	(7)
1917[d]		$11,664	$245	2.10			
1920[e]		25,571	387	1.51			
1922		23,577	425	1.80			
1923		27,481	535	1.95			
1924		28,468	533	1.87	$62,049	$973	1.57
1925		24,356	442	1.81	67,137	954	1.42
1926		24,606	484	1.97	69,431	1,031	1.48
1927		25,368	508	2.00	70,130	1,114	1.59
1928		28,473	541	1.90	73,545	1,110	1.51
1929		28,225	540	1.91	75,597	1,084	1.43
1930		21,116	434	2.06	62,233	969	1.56
1931		16,067	354	2.20	48,969	805	1.64
1932		13,830	317	2.29	36,978	751	2.03
1933		12,964	282	2.18	36,445	700	1.92
1934		14,524	280	1.93	44,127	790	1.79
1935		16,683	310	1.86	48,447	828	1.71
1936		21,241	390	1.84	57,676	985	1.71
1937		23,478	445	1.90	61,559	1,057	1.72
1938		21,026	414	1.97	55,561	1,001	1.80
1939		25,518	499	1.96	64,674	1,177	1.82
1940		39,921	740	1.85	70,152	1,254	1.79
1941	60.4[f]	45,501	1,002	2.20	85,101	1,520	1.79
1942	56.0	59,594	1,450	2.43	107,172	1,944	1.81
1943	53.5	75,062	1,836	2.45	129,035	2,449	1.90
1944	17.9	32,694	1,258	3.85	137,495	2,567	1.87
1945	17.0	34,955	1,450	4.15	140,185	2,762	1.97
1946	16.6	39,569	1,639	4.14	156,065	3,088	1.98
1947	18.9	45,862	1,974	4.30	171,563	3,559	2.07
1948	17.0	44,890	1,881	4.19	184,795	3,898	2.11
1949	18.7	46,825	2,032	4.34	184,292	3,966	2.15
1950	19.5	55,116	2,260	4.10	201,446	4,359	2.16

Year	Itemized Income Tax Returns[a]				All Income Tax Returns		
			Itemized Contributions			Estimated Total Contributions[e]	
	Per Cent of All Returns[f]	Adjusted Gross Income (millions)	Amount (millions)	Per Cent of Income (col. 3 ÷ col. 2)	Adjusted Gross Income[b] (millions)	Amount (millions)	Per Cent of Income (col. 6 ÷ col. 5)
	(1)	(2)	(3)	(4)	(5)	(6)	(7)
1951	20.9	65,261	—	—	226,603	—	—
1952	22.7	73,643	3,116	4.23	240,645	5,521	2.29
1953	24.9	82,871	3,556	4.29	254,450	6,036	2.37
1954	26.7	92,334	3,893	4.22	252,987	6,216	2.46
1955	29.0	108,528	—	—	—	—	—
1956	31.2	123,719	4,878	3.94	295,320	7,318	2.48
1957	33.7	—	—	—	—	—	—
1958	35.2	145,359	5,694	3.92	319,550	7,998	2.50
1959	37.3	—	—	—	—	—	—
1960	39.5	181,131	6,750	3.73	355,931	9,030	2.54
1961	—	—	—	—	—	—	—
1962	42.2	212,754	7,516	3.64	392,166	9,842	2.51

SOURCE: The data for 1917–1956 (1954 in the case of columns 5–7) are from C. Harry Kahn, *Personal Deductions in the Federal Income Tax*, National Bureau of Economic Research, Princeton University Press, 1960, Tables 13, 17 and 57. Figures for more recent years have been calculated from U. S. Treasury, Internal Revenue Service, *Statistics of Income, Individual Income Tax Returns*, which is also the original source from which Kahn derived his figures.

[a] Includes both taxable and non-taxable returns. Taxable returns, of course, account for the bulk of contributions and adjusted gross income. Figures include returns of fiduciaries up to 1944 only.

[b] These figures include not only the adjusted gross income reported on tax returns but also estimates of unreported adjusted gross income and estimates of the adjusted gross income of non-filers. For the derivation of these figures through 1954, see Kahn, Appendix A. Our estimates for years since 1954 are based on a derived relation between Kahn's concept of adjusted gross income and the Commerce Department's personal income figures. Between 1948 and 1954 (excluding 1952, which apparently was affected in strange ways by the Korean War) Kahn's figures for adjusted gross income ranged between .880 and .895 of personal income, the average ratio being .887. Given the stability of this relation, we multiplied personal income by .887 in order to obtain estimates of adjusted gross income from 1954. Alternative calculations using available components of the difference between total adjusted gross income and adjusted gross income reported on tax returns yielded results nearly identical with those reported in the table.

(Notes continued on following page)

e Kahn estimated total contributions by scaling reported contributions to an estimate for people who did not file income tax returns and for those who chose the standard deduction (see his Appendix F). Our figures for years after 1954 were obtained the same way, except that we arbitrarily set the estimated contributions of non-filers at $50 million each year.

d For tax returns showing net incomes above $2,000 only.

e For tax returns showing net incomes above $1,000 only.

f Prior to 1941, taxpayers did not have the option of taking a "standard deduction" in lieu of itemizing their deductions; the percentage itemizing is in effect 100 for the early years.

APPENDIX TABLE XIII–B

Individual Philanthropic Contributions, by Income Class, 1962

Adjusted Income Class	Itemized Income Tax Returns			All Income Tax Returns: Estimated Total Contributionsª	
	Per Cent of All Returns	Itemized Contributions		Contributionsª	
		Amount (millions)	Per Cent of Total	Amount (millions)	Per Cent of Total
	(1)	(2)	(3)	(4)	(5)
Under $3,000	15.2	$ 355.9	4.7	$ 770	7.8
$3,000–$4,999	24.4	845.8	11.3	1,365	13.8
$5,000–$9,999ᵇ	19.9	2,990.0	39.8	4,009	40.7
$10,000–$24,999	14.8	1,968.9	26.2	2,321	23.6
$25,000–$49,999	18.2	556.4	7.4	578	5.9
$50,000–$99,999	4.7	330.8	4.4	331	3.4
$100,000–$499,999	1.5	320.9	4.3	321	3.3
$500,000–$999,999	0.8	56.4	0.8	56	0.6
$1,000,000 and Over	0.5	91.0	1.2	91	0.9
Total, All Income Classes	100	$7,516.1	100	$9,842	100

SOURCE: U. S. Treasury Department, Internal Revenue Service, *Statistics of Income, Individual Income Tax Returns, 1962.*

ª The difference of $2,326 million between itemized contributions ($7,516 million) and our earlier estimate (Appendix Table XIII–A) of total contributions ($9,842 million) was allocated among the income classes below $50,000 (which include almost all of the non-itemized returns) in proportion to the share of total adjusted gross income in all non-itemized returns in each income class. This amounts to assuming that persons who did not itemize in each of these income classes had the same contributions rates — a reasonable assumption, given the results in Appendix Table XIII–C.

ᵇ All of the deductions for contributions and all of the adjusted gross income reported on non-taxable itemized returns from $5,000 up are included here even though unknown (but undoubtedly very small) proportions belong to higher income categories.

Individual Philanthropic Contributions as Per Cent of Adjusted Gross Income, by Income Class, 1943 and 1962, and Average Amount Contributed, 1962

Adusted Gross Income Class	Contributions as Per Cent of Adjusted Gross Income			Average Amount Contributed in 1962, by Persons Itemizing Contributions
	On All Returns, 1943	On Itemized Returns, 1962[a]	Estimate for All Returns, 1962[b]	
	(1)	(2)	(3)	(4)
Under $3,000	2.4	6.3	2.5	$ 131
$3,000–$4,999	2.2	4.4	2.6	178
$5,000–$9,999[c]	2.1	3.4	2.6	241
$10,000–$24,999[d]	1.9	3.1	2.7	421
$25,000–$49,999[d]	2.0	3.4	3.2	1,138
$50,000–$99,999	2.4	4.3	4.1	2,845
$100,000–$499,999	3.1	7.9	7.6	12,733
$500,000–$999,999	4.7	10.8	10.3	71,632
$1,000,000 and Over	5.1	13.7	12.7	268,392
Average, All Income Classes	2.3	3.6	2.8	$ 299

SOURCE: All figures for 1962 calculated from *Statistics of Income, Individual Income Tax Returns, 1962*, Table E, p. 6. The figures for 1943 in column 1 were calculated from data in F. Emerson Andrews, *Philanthropic Giving*, Russell Sage Foundation, New York, 1950, p. 53.

[a] Contributions on itemized returns as a percentage of adjusted gross income on itemized returns.

[b] See column 4 of Appendix Table XIII–B for total contributions estimates; these are divided by total adjusted gross income for each class.

[c] All of the deductions for contributions and all of the adjusted gross income reported on non-taxable itemized returns from $5,000 up are included here even though unknown (but undoubtedly very small) proportions belong to higher income categories.

[d] $20,000 is the cut-off in the 1943 column.

APPENDIX TABLE XIII–D

Individual Philanthropic Contributions, by Income Class and by Type of Recipient, 1962 (itemized income tax returns)

Adjusted Gross Income Class	Religious Organizations	Community Chest, Red Cross, etc.[a]	Hospitals	Educational Institutions	"Other," including Performing Arts[b]	All Organizations
		Per Cent of Those Reporting Any Contributions Who Contributed to Each Type of Recipient				
Under $3,000	76	51	2	2	35	
$3,000–$4,999	76	61	2	3	37	
$5,000–$9,999[c]	80	71	3	4	38	
$10,000–$24,999	82	77	8	13	54	
$25,000–$49,999	81	80	28	37	79	
$50,000–$99,999	81	83	41	51	86	
$100,000–$499,999	79	85	54	62	92	
$500,000–$999,999	73	79	54	64	94	
$1,000,000 and Over	74	82	60	72	96	
Average, All Income Classes	79	69	4	6	42	

Average Contribution by Those Who Contributed to
Each Type of Recipient

Under $3,000	$ 125	$ 26	$ 27	$ 47	$ 61	$ 79
$3,000–$4,999	164	35	42	37	80	99
$5,000–$9,999°	205	47	43	76	102	123
$10,000–$24,999	329	85	58	83	129	180
$25,000–$49,999	674	238	171	241	337	374
$50,000–$99,999	1,111	593	405	738	1,055	831
$100,000–$499,999	2,342	1,960	625	4,020	6,396	3,483
$500,000–$999,999	6,073	10,223	10,263	23,067	41,541	19,731
$1,000,000 and Over	10,528	18,223	25,792	66,782	189,724	70,043
Average, All Income Classes	$ 229	$ 62	$ 112	$ 176	$ 141	$ 149

(Continued on following page)

APPENDIX TABLE XIII–D (continued)

Adjusted Gross Income Class	Religious Organizations	Community Chest, Red Cross, etc.[a]	Hospitals	Educational Institutions	"Other," including Performing Arts[b]	All Organizations
		Total Contributions Reported (millions)				
Under $3,000	$ 256.8	$ 37.0	$ 1.3	$ 3.0	$ 57.8	$ 355.9
$3,000–$4,999	593.4	101.9	3.2	5.1	142.2	845.8
$5,000–$9,999[c]	2,038.3	417.6	13.8	38.2	482.1	2,990.0
$10,000–$24,999	1,264.7	305.6	21.3	50.3	326.1	1,968.9
$25,000–$49,999	267.8	92.6	23.0	43.3	129.8	556.4
$50,000–$99,999	104.4	57.5	19.4	43.6	106.0	330.8
$100,000–$499,999	46.3	41.9	21.6	62.7	148.4	320.9
$500,000–$999,999	3.5	6.3	4.3	11.7	30.6	56.4
$1,000,000 and Over	2.6	5.1	5.2	16.2	61.9	91.0
Total, All Income Classes	$4,577.8	$1,065.6	$113.1	$274.1	$1,484.9	$7,516.1

SOURCE: Calculated from *Statistics of Income, Individual Income Tax Returns, 1962,* Table E, p. 6. Includes taxable and non-taxable returns.

[a] This is what is known officially as the "other charitable organizations" category, and it also includes such organizations as the American Heart Association and the American Cancer Society.

[b] The official definition of this category is: "organizations not elsewhere classified or not specifically stated . . . including literary, educational and scientific foundations, libraries, museums and zoos." (*Statistics of Income,* p. 8.)

[c] As explained in note b to Appendix Table XIII–B, all deductions reported on non-taxable returns from $5,000 up are attributed to this income class.

Individual Philanthropic Contributions: Percentage Distribution of
Contributions of Each Income Class by Type of Recipient, 1962

Adjusted Gross Income Class	Percentage of Itemized Contributions Going to:					
	Religious Organi- zations	Comm. Chest, Red Cross, etc.ᵃ	Hospi- tals	Educa- tional Insti- tutions	"Other," including Perform- ing Artsᵇ	All Organi- zations
	(1)	(2)	(3)	(4)	(5)	(6)
Under $3,000	72.1	10.4	0.4	0.8	16.3	100
$3,000–$4,999	70.2	12.0	0.4	0.6	16.8	100
$5,000–$9,999ᶜ	68.2	14.0	0.5	1.3	16.1	100
$10,000–$24,999	64.3	15.5	1.1	2.6	16.6	100
$25,000–$49,999	48.1	16.6	4.1	7.8	23.3	100
$50,000–$99,999	31.6	17.4	5.9	13.2	32.0	100
$100,000–$499,999	14.4	13.1	6.7	19.5	46.2	100
$500,000–$999,999	6.2	11.2	7.7	20.7	54.2	100
$1,000,000 and Over	2.9	5.6	5.7	17.8	68.0*	100
Average, All Income Classes	60.9	14.2	1.5	3.6	19.8	100

For source and notes see Appendix Table XIII–D.

* This undoubtedly consists largely of gifts to family foundations.

Individual Federal Income Tax Returns Reporting Income of a
Million Dollars or More, 1914–1962

Year	Number of Returns	Total Adjusted Gross Income on These Returns (millions)	Average Income Tax Rate (per cent)	Income after Tax	
				Amount (millions)	As Per Cent of Disposable Personal Income
	(1)	(2)	(3)	(4)	(5)
1914	60				
1915	120				
1916	206	$464	11	$413	
1917	141	307	36	198	
1918	67	137	65	48	
1919	65	153	65	54	
1920	33	77	64	28	
1921	21	49	63	18	
1922	67	141	35	91	
1923	74	152	24	116	
1924	75	156	30	109	
1925	207	422	16	355	
1926	231	494	17	412	
1927	290	601	16	502	
1928	511	1,109	17	924	
1929	513	1,212	16	1,021	1.23
1930	150	360	17	299	0.40
1931	77	166	16	139	0.22
1932	20	35	46	19	0.04
1933	50	87	32	59	0.13
1934	33	58	55	26	0.05
1935	41	74	55	33	0.06
1936	61	108	71	31	0.05
1937	49	85	72	24	0.03
1938	57	110	44	62	0.09
1939	45	81	65	28	0.04
1940	52	96	70	29	0.04
1941	57	106	62	40	0.04
1942	40	87	75	22	0.02
1943	55	99	88	12	0.01
1944	62	110	69	34	0.02
1945	71	123	65	43	0.03
1946	94	184	60	74	0.05

Year	Number of Returns	Total Adjusted Gross Income on These Returns (millions)	Average Income Tax Rate (per cent)	Income after Tax	
				Amount (millions)	As Per Cent of Disposable Personal Income
	(1)	(2)	(3)	(4)	(5)
1947	114	215	61	84	0.05
1948	149	258	59	106	0.06
1949	120	256	57	110	0.06
1950	219	433	60	172	0.08
1951	171	345	62	131	0.06
1952	148	289	62	109	0.05
1953	145	275	61	106	0.04
1954	201	407	55	185	0.07
1955	263	551	53	260	0.09
1956	268	550	52	262	0.09
1957	217	427	54	195	0.06
1958	236	483	48	250	0.08
1959	265	540	49	278	0.08
1960	295	584	48	303	0.09
1961	381	727	47	385	0.11
1962	342	670	46	359	0.09

SOURCE: U. S. Treasury Department, Internal Revenue Service, *Statistics of Income, Individual Income Tax Returns.*

Share of Top Income Recipients in Total Family Personal Income (before tax), 1929–1962

| Year | Share (per cent) Received By: | |
	Top 5%	Top 20%
1929	30.0	54.4
1935–36	26.5	51.7
1941	24.0	48.8
1944	20.7	45.8
1946	21.3	46.1
1947	20.9	46.0
1950	21.4	46.1
1951	20.7	44.9
1952	20.5	44.7
1953	19.9	44.7
1954	20.3	45.2
1955	20.3	45.2
1956	20.2	45.3
1957	20.2	45.5
1958	—	—
1959	20.0	45.6
1960	19.6	45.4
1961	19.6	45.5
1962	19.6	45.5

SOURCE: U. S. Bureau of the Census, *Statistical Abstract of the United States*, 1963 and 1964 editions; and U. S. Bureau of the Census, *Historical Statistics of the United States, Colonial Times to 1957*, Series 6104, 6105, p. 166.

Individual Philanthropic Contributions as Per Cent of Income, in Income Classes Over $25,000, Selected Years, 1922–1962 (itemized taxable returns[a])

	Income Class[b]			
Year	$25,000–$49,999	$50,000–$99,999	$100,000–$499,999	$500,000 and Over
1922	2.2	2.6	3.5	6.7
1924	2.2	2.8	3.4	5.7
1925–29[c]	2.0	2.3	2.6	3.4
1932–34[c]	2.7	3.6	5.0	5.5
1937	2.1	2.8	4.0	6.4
1939	1.7	2.3	4.3	6.1
1941	2.1	2.5	3.4	5.4
1943	2.0	2.4	3.0	4.5
1945	3.0	3.5	4.8	6.7
1947	3.1	3.6	4.8	6.7
1949	3.1	3.3	4.6	6.6
1954	3.3[d]	3.9	6.7	11.7
1956	3.3	4.1	6.9	11.9
1958	3.4	4.4	7.7	14.9
1960	3.5	4.2	7.8	12.4
1962	3.4	4.3	7.8	12.3

SOURCE: Figures for 1922–1956 from C. Harry Kahn, *Personal Deductions in the Federal Income Tax,* National Bureau of Economic Research, Princeton University Press, 1960, Table 19, pp. 74–75. We derived the figures for 1958–1962 from *Statistics of Income, Individual Income Tax Returns,* the same annual publication from which Kahn derived figures for the earlier years.

[a] Fiduciary returns are included in years up to and including 1949.

[b] Net income classes until 1943; adjusted gross income classes thereafter.

[c] Average.

[d] $20,000–$49,999.

Charitable Bequests, 1924–1961

Year	Total Number of Federal Estate Tax Returns[a] (1)	Gross Estates (millions) (2)	Charitable Bequests (millions) (3)	Bequests as Per Cent of Gross Estates (col. 3 ÷ col. 2) (4)
1924	13,011	$2,541	$ 76	2.99
1925	14,013	2,958	116	3.92
1926	13,142	3,386	227	6.70
1927	9,353	3,146	131	4.16
1928	8,079	3,503	216	6.17
1929	8,582	3,844	154	4.01
1930	8,798	4,109	223	5.43
1931	8,333	4,042	220	5.44
1932	7,113	2,796	191	6.83
1933	8,727	2,027	96	4.74
1934	10,353	2,244	146	6.51
1935	11,110	2,435	106	4.35
1936	11,605	2,296	128	5.57
1937	15,037	2,768	127	4.59
1938	15,932	3,047	200	6.56
1939	15,221	2,746	179	6.52
1940	15,435	2,633	143	5.43
1941	15,977	2,778	175	6.30
1942	16,215	2,725	155	5.69
1943	15,187	2,627	186	7.08
1944	14,303	2,908	202	6.95
1945	15,898	3,437	192	5.59
1946	—	—	—	—
1947	20,899	4,224	186	4.40
1948	23,356	4,775	223	4.67
1949	24,552	4,933	296	6.00
1950	25,858	4,918	206	4.19
1951	27,958	5,505	274	4.98
1952	—	—	—	—
1953	—	—	—	—
1954	36,699	7,412	355	4.79
1955	36,595	7,467	398	5.33
1956	—	—	—	—
1957	—	—	—	—
1958	—	—	—	—

Year	Total Number of Federal Estate Tax Returns[a]	Gross Estates (millions)	Charitable Bequests (millions)	Bequests as Per Cent of Gross Estates (col. 3 ÷ col. 2)
	(1)	(2)	(3)	
1959	55,685	11,648	699	6.00
1960	—	—	—	—
1961	64,538	14,622	951	6.50

SOURCE: U. S. Treasury Department, Internal Revenue Service, *Statistics of Income, Estate Tax Returns,* various years.

[a] These are returns for citizens and resident aliens. The number of returns is affected by the filing requirement. In 1924 reports had to be filed for all estates of $50,000 and up; the amount was raised to $100,000 in 1926, reduced to $50,000 in 1932, and to $40,000 in 1935; in 1942 it was raised to $60,000, the present amount.

APPENDIX TABLE XIII–J

Audience Profiles According to Frequency of Contributions to Performing Arts Organizations

Audience Characteristics	All Major Orchestras Persons Contributing:			All Off-Broadway Theaters Persons Contributing:		
	Regularly (1)	Occasionally (2)	Rarely (3)	Regularly (4)	Occasionally (5)	Rarely (6)
SEX						
Male	44.2%	46.5%	50.9%	53.7%	53.4%	56.5%
AGE						
Under 20	1.0%	3.0%	11.9%	2.9%	4.5%	9.0%
Over 60	27.6	15.9	6.6	15.1	12.1	5.2
Median Age	52 yrs.	45 yrs.	31 yrs.	48 yrs.	45 yrs.	35 yrs.
OCCUPATIONAL CATEGORY						
Males:						
Employed Persons:[a]						
Professional	57.7%	66.4%	74.6%	64.8%	61.5%	67.1%
Teachers	9.0	11.4	14.8	8.6	11.8	12.8
Managerial	30.1	19.3	13.7	24.8	26.2	17.9
Clerical and Sales	10.7	13.0	9.3	9.5	11.8	12.5
Blue Collar	1.5	1.3	2.4	1.0	1.5	2.4
Students	2.3	8.3	29.2	0.0	6.1	13.7

Females:

Employed Persons:[a]						
Professional	73.4%	66.6%	67.9%	52.3%	62.4%	63.7%
Teachers	32.4	29.5	27.5	20.5	26.5	27.0
All Other	26.6	33.4	32.1	47.7	37.6	36.3
Students	2.4	6.0	25.8	6.3	6.0	22.5
Housewives	58.1	39.4	25.7	43.2	23.8	20.7

EDUCATION

Males (age 25 and over):

Grade School and Less Than Four Yrs. High School	1.3%	1.9%	1.7%	3.8%	3.1%	2.5%
4 Yrs. High School	5.0	3.6	3.4	1.9	4.6	5.8
1–3 Yrs. College	10.7	10.1	9.6	9.4	13.3	11.5
4 Yrs. College	25.1	23.8	22.2	21.7	16.8	21.8
Graduate School	57.9	60.6	63.2	63.2	62.2	58.4
Median Category	Grad. sch.	Grad. sch.	Grad. sch.	Grad. sch.	Grad. sch.	Grad. sch.

Females (age 25 and over):

Grade School and Less Than 4 Yrs. High School	2.3%	3.1%	2.0%	2.4%	1.3%	2.2%
4 Yrs. High School	11.4	11.7	11.7	11.9	6.9	14.3
1–3 Yrs. College	23.1	22.0	20.3	25.0	23.9	15.6
4 Yrs. College	32.3	28.4	31.2	31.0	25.8	26.6
Graduate School	30.9	34.8	34.9	29.8	42.1	41.2
Median Category	4 yrs. coll.	4 yrs. coll.	4 yrs. coll.	4 yrs. coll.	4 yrs. coll.	4 yrs. coll.

INCOME

Over $25,000	35.6%	16.8%	8.5%	40.4%	22.4%	15.2%
Over $15,000	59.5	39.3	24.2	65.2	47.9	36.9
Over $5,000	96.8	92.9	83.0	97.5	95.8	91.6
Median Income	$18,981	$12,850	$9,718	$21,122	$14,604	$12,348

(Continued on following page)

Audience Characteristics	All Major Orchestras Persons Contributing:			All Off-Broadway Theaters Persons Contributing:		
	Regularly (1)	Occasionally (2)	Rarely (3)	Regularly (4)	Occasionally (5)	Rarely (6)
TICKET PURCHASES						
Per Cent Purchasing Season Tickets	85.1%	73.6%	55.1%	41.9%	40.0%	25.1%
Average Ticket Price Paid	$3.72	$3.55	$3.12	$4.81	$4.44	$4.57
Total Non-ticket Cost (average)	$2.44	$2.37	$2.05	$4.46	$4.12	$4.15
FREQUENCY OF ATTENDANCE		Average Number of Times Attended in Last 12 Months				
Theater	9.9	8.6	6.9	13.5	11.4	8.7
Symphony	12.6	9.5	7.0	5.2	4.2	2.0
Opera	2.6	2.1	1.3	4.0	2.7	1.1
Other Serious Music	4.1	3.6	2.6	3.5	3.0	1.9
Dance	1.2	1.1	0.7	2.1	1.9	1.1
NUMBER OF RESPONDENTS	2,031	2,235	4,612	205	397	1,044

SOURCE: Twentieth Century Fund audience survey.

[a] The number of employed persons is the base for the following percentages. The percentage of teachers is a component of the "Professional" category.

APPENDIX TABLE XIII-K

Per Cent of Major Orchestra Respondents Contributing Regularly to Performing Organizations, by Income Class and by Occupation, Education and Frequency of Attendance

Selected Audience Characteristics	Income Class							All Income Classes
	Under $2,000	$3,000–$4,999	$5,000–$6,999	$7,000–$9,999	$10,000–$14,999	$15,000–$24,999	$25,000 or Over	
Occupation (males):								
Teachers	0.0	4.7	12.8	17.9	16.7	29.4	43.6	18.0
All Professional	5.4	6.7	10.8	11.5	16.7	25.8	47.5	21.2
Managerial	—	0.0	5.0	23.1	34.5	40.1	53.6	38.5
Education (males):								
Up to 4 Yrs. High School	41.2	30.0	12.4	24.8	33.3	36.6	33.8	28.4
1–3 Yrs. College	0.0	0.0	6.0	19.3	16.0	36.0	62.2	26.4
4 Yrs. College	0.0	6.8	11.6	13.5	25.4	29.1	48.2	26.7
Graduate School	3.9	6.5	11.8	13.4	17.2	27.2	47.8	23.4
Frequency of Attendance at Symphony:[a]								
None	2.0	0.0	2.4	0.8	6.6	10.1	12.3	5.0
1–4 Times	3.0	3.0	2.0	7.2	8.7	15.2	26.4	9.0
5–9 Times	5.1	5.8	12.2	11.1	17.3	22.8	41.3	16.8
10+ Times	8.2	12.7	15.7	24.6	30.7	39.2	62.0	30.6

SOURCE: Twentieth Century Fund audience survey. a Number of times attended in last 12 months.

Philanthropic Contributions of Corporations, 1936–1962

Year[a]	Net Profit Before Deductions for Contributions (millions)	Contributions Deducted (millions)	Contributions as Per Cent of Net Profit (col. 2 ÷ col. 1)
	(1)	(2)	(3)
1936–37	$ 7,771	$ 30	0.39
1937–38	7,830	33	0.42
1938–39	4,131	27	0.65
1939–40	7,178	31	0.43
1940–41	9,348	38	0.41
1941–42	16,675	58	0.35
1942–43	23,389	98	0.42
1943–44	28,126	159	0.57
1944–45	26,454	234	0.88
1945–46	21,345	266	1.25
1946–47	25,399	214	0.84
1947–48	31,615	241	0.76
1948–49	34,588	239	0.69
1949–50	28,387	223	0.79
1950–51	42,831	252	0.59
1951–52	43,800	343	0.78
1952–53	38,735	399	1.03
1953–54	39,801	495	1.24
1954–55	36,721	314	0.86
1955–56	47,949	415	0.87
1956–57	47,412	418	0.88
1957–58	45,073	417	0.93
1958–59	39,224	395	1.01
1959–60	47,655	482	1.01
1960–61	44,499	482	1.08
1961–62	47,034	512	1.09

SOURCE: U. S. Treasury Department, Internal Revenue Service, *Statistics of Income, Corporate Tax Returns,* various years.

[a] The figures given here for, say, 1936–37 are for accounting periods which ended *between* July 1, 1936 and June 30, 1937. That is, corporate returns are partly on a fiscal year basis and partly on a calendar year basis.

Corporate Philanthropy, by Recipient, 1962

	465 Companies		276 Companies without Foundations		189 Companies with Foundations	
	Amount (thousands)	Per Cent of Total	Amount (thousands)	Per Cent of Total	Amount (thousands)	Per Cent of Total
	(1)	(2)	(3)	(4)	(5)	(6)
Health and Welfare:						
Federated Drives: United Funds, Community Chests, and the like	$39,280	25.5	$18,402	27.3	$20,878	24.1
Health, Welfare, Hospitals	16,682	10.8	8,076	12.0	8,606	9.9
Other Local and Miscellaneous	7,142	4.6	3,222	4.8	3,920	4.5
Total Health and Welfare	$63,104	40.9	$29,700	44.0	$33,404	38.5
Education:						
Higher Education:						
Scholarships and Fellowships	$12,103	7.9	$ 5,651	8.4	$ 6,453	7.4
Research Grants (not treated as a business expense)	4,040	2.6	1,692	2.5	2,348	2.7
Capital Funds for Buildings	9,419	6.1	3,658	5.4	5,761	6.6
Capital Funds for Endowment	276	.2	97	.2	180	.2
Funds for Extra Compensation for Faculty	1,151	.7	609	.9	542	.6
Direct Unrestricted Grants	17,662	11.5	7,555	11.2	10,107	11.7
Unrestricted Grants — Other	16,324	10.6	8,045	11.9	8,278	9.6
Secondary Education	3,556	2.3	1,070	1.6	2,485	2.9
Total Education	$64,531	41.9	$28,377	42.0	$36,154	41.7

(Continued on following page)

APPENDIX TABLE XIV–B (continued)

	465 Companies		276 Companies without Foundations		189 Companies with Foundations	
	Amount (thousands) (1)	Per Cent of Total (2)	Amount (thousands) (3)	Per Cent of Total (4)	Amount (thousands) (5)	Per Cent of Total (6)
Civic and Cultural (symphonies, little theaters, libraries, museums, and the like)	$ 8,239	5.3	$ 3,333	4.9	$ 4,907	5.7
Other						
Religious Causes	$ 589	.4	$ 179	.3	$ 410	.5
Groups Devoted Solely to Economic Education	1,756	1.1	804	1.2	952	1.1
Causes Whose Principal Objective Is Aid to Other Countries	2,726	1.8	897	1.3	1,829	2.1
Causes Other Than Above	10,856	7.1	4,105	6.1	6,751	7.8
Total "Other"	$15,927	10.3	$ 5,985	8.9	$ 9,942	11.5
Dollars Not Identifiable Because Donee Is Unknown	$ 2,341	1.5	$ 97	.2	$ 2,244	2.6
Grand Total	$154,142	100.0	$67,491	100.0	$86,651	100.0

SOURCE: John H. Watson, III, "Report on Company Contributions for 1962," *Business Management Record*, October 1963.

538

Foundation Grants, 1944–1965, Various Estimates
(millions of dollars)

	Foundation Library Center, and Andrews, Over-All Estimates[a]	Giving — USA, Over-All Estimates[b]	Foundation Library Center, Grants of $10,000 or More[c]
	(1)	(2)	(3)
1944	$ 72		
1949	133		
1957	626	$500	
1958		505	
1959		700	
1960		710	
1961	779	625	$351
1962		700	315
1963		819	324
1964			556[d]
1965			649[d]

[a] Estimates for 1944 and 1949 from F. Emerson Andrews, *Philanthropic Giving,* Russell Sage Foundation, New York, 1950, p. 93. Estimate for 1957 from the *Foundation Directory,* Edition 1, edited by Ann D. Walton and F. Emerson Andrews, published for the Foundation Library Center by Russell Sage Foundation, New York, 1960, Table 21. The individual foundation reports aggregated to obtain the over-all estimate are for "the latest year" for the particular foundation, which in the case of the 1961 Directory was generally 1956, 1957 or 1958. Estimate for 1961 from the *Foundation Directory,* Edition 2, 1964, Table 20. Again the individual foundation data are for various years, generally 1960, 1961 and 1962.

[b] *Giving — USA,* Annual Reports of the American Association of Fund-Raising Counsel. The exact sources of the estimates are not named; however, they appear to have been based in large measure on rough estimates from the Foundation Library Center.

[c] Annual Reports of the Foundation Library Center, 1963, 1964 and 1965. Some of the figures may involve grants for earlier years which were reported in the year shown.

[d] Not comparable with figures for earlier years. Internal Revenue Service requirements led to a considerable increase in the number of foundation grants reported for 1964. Thus, an unknown but appreciable part of the increase between 1963 and 1964 is attributable to an increase in information, rather than to an increase in foundation spending.

Grants of $10,000 or More Reported to the Foundation Library
Center in Recent Years, by Major Field

Field	1957–58[a]	1960[b]	1961	1962	1963	1964[c]	1965[c]
	Amount (millions)						
Education	$178	$210	$107	$145	$ 83	$186	$164
Health	} 91	66 {	68	32	35	129	103
Welfare			43	20	24	44	104
International Activities	—	—	62	52	82	74	128
Sciences	45	78	37	45	47	58	60
Humanities (including performing arts)	14	16	25	16	48	39	39[d]
Religion	—	—	9	5	5	26	51
Other	21	19	—	—	—	—	—
Total	$349	$389	$351	$315	$324	$556	$649[d]
	Percentage Distribution						
Education	51	54	31	46	26	33	25
Health	} 26	17 {	19	10	11	23	16
Welfare			12	6	7	8	16
International Activities	—	—	17	17	25	13	20
Sciences	13	20	11	14	14	11	9
Humanities (including performing arts)	4	4	7	5	15	7	6[d]
Religion	—	—	3	2	2	5	8
Other	6	5	—	—	—	—	—
Total	100	100	100	100	100	100	100

SOURCE: Foundation Library Center, Annual Reports, 1961, 1963, 1964, 1965.
Grants were not always paid out in full in the year in which they were announced.

[a] The grants of 129 large foundations (assets of $10 million or more).

[b] The grants of 154 large foundations.

[c] Both the total amount of grants reported and the distribution of grants are affected
by a sharp increase in the number of foundations reporting information, due
mainly to new Internal Revenue Service filing requirements.

[d] Does not include the $85 million Ford Foundation grant to orchestras which was
announced, but not distributed, in 1965.

APPENDIX TABLE XIV–E

Ford Foundation Grants to the Performing Arts, 1957–1964 (thousands of dollars)

Fiscal Year (ending Sept. 30)	Performing Arts Grants								Total Grants	Arts as Per Cent of Total
	Orchestras (1)	Opera (2)	Other Music (3)	Dance (4)	Theater (5)	Grants in Aid (6)	Cultural Centers (7)	Total Arts Grants (8)	(9)	(10)
1957	$ 210	$ 270	—	—	$ 130	—	$ 2,500	$ 3,110	$ 153,394	2.0
1958	—	350	$ 75	—	259	—	10,000	10,684	79,034	13.5
1959	30	—	5	$ 150	56.5	$ 195	—	437	109,354	0.4
1960	—	2.5	205	—	559	233	—	1,000	160,753	0.6
1961	—	110	317.5	12.5	244	88.5	—	852.5	144,551	0.6
1962	—	224	155	—	6,100	—	—	6,479	223,258	2.9
1963	1,365	4,998	2,105	60	60	312	17,500	26,400	212,286	12.4
1964	—	250	687	7,807	1,217	587.5	—	10,548	225,136	4.7
1965	85,003	1,703[a]	2,542.5	1,833[a]	20	—	—	6,102[b]	281,559[b]	2.2[b]
Total	$86,608	$7,908	$6,092	$9,862	$8,645	$1,416	$30,000	$65,611[b]	$1,589,324[b]	4.1

SOURCE: Compiled from Ford Foundation Annual Reports and press releases. Grants were not always paid out in full in the year in which they were announced.

[a] Arbitrarily includes half of $3.2 million grant to the New York City Center of Music and Drama.

[b] Does not include the $85 million grant to orchestras which was announced, but not distributed, in 1965.

Résumé of Ford Foundation Grants to the Performing Arts, 1957–1964

1957

1. Orchestras: American Music Center, Inc.

$210,000 for a three year experiment in multiple regional performances of new symphonic works.

2. Opera:
   a. City Center of Music and Drama

$105,000 for a performance by the New York City Opera Company of a modern American repertoire in 1958.

   b. New Orleans Opera House Association

$165,000 for a three year program by the Experimental Opera Theater of America to enable talented young singers to make their debuts.

3. Theater: (Cleveland) Play House

$130,000 for an experiment in the development of talented actors and in extending professional theater to small towns of the Middle West.

4. Cultural Centers: Lincoln Center for the Performing Arts

$2,500,000 — a non-program grant.

1958

1. Opera: City Center of Music and Drama

$310,000 for a continuation of the program begun in 1957.

2. Music *per se:* Tulane University

$75,000 for the Archive of New Orleans Jazz.

3. Theater:
   a. New Dramatists Committee

$45,000 for a three year project designed to give added experience in production to outstanding directors. $213,600 to aid in administration of grant-in-aid program for playwrights.

   b. New England Opera Theater

$40,000 for experiment in new types of theatrical scenery.

4. Cultural Centers: Lincoln Center

$10,000,000 — a non-program grant.

1959

1. Orchestras

$30,000 to ten orchestras for the performance of newly commissioned works written by concert artists receiving grants-in-aid.

2. Music *per se:*

   a. Music Educators National Conference $5,000.

   b. Young Composers Program   **$71,100.**

3. Theater:

   a. (Cleveland) Play House $30,500 for a continuation of the program begun in 1957.

   b. Program for Creative Development of Theater Directors (part of theater directors grants-in-aid program listed in 4 below) $26,000 for engagement of additional professional actors (Alley Theater, Houston, $6,000; Art Inst. of Chicago, Goodman Memorial Theater, $10,000; Company of the Golden Hand, Berkeley, $2,500; Oregon Shakespeare Festival Association, $7,500).

4. Grants-in-Aid:

   a. Theater Directors and Concert Artists $164,000.

   b. Dance $150,000 for training and performances of young dancers (administered by Ballet Society, Inc.).

1960

1. Opera:

   a. City Center $2,500 for continuation of the program begun in 1957.

   b. American Operatic Repertoire Program $110,000 for payments to participating opera companies for commissioning new American operas.

2. Music *per se:*

   a. Young Audiences, Inc. $180,000.

   b. Tulane University $25,000 for continuation of the Jazz Archive program begun in 1958.

   c. Program for Concert Artists $77,600.

3. Theater: Resident Actors Program $559,000 for the Actors' Workshop, Alley Theater, Arena Stage and Phoenix Theater.

4. Grants-in-Aid $155,680 for directors and poets and fiction writers with theater and opera houses.

1961

1. Opera:

   a. City Center $70,000 for the production of new American operas.

(Continued on following page)

b. San Francisco Opera
Association

$40,000 for the production of a new American opera.

2. Music *per se:*
   a. Peabody Conservatory of
      Music

$397,500 for a development and demonstration program to aid promising American conductors over a three year period.

   b. Young Composers Project

$88,500.

3. Theater Communications Group

$244,000 to improve cooperation among professional, community and university theaters in the United States.

4. Dance: Ballet Society, Inc.

$12,500 for training and performances of talented young dancers.

1962

1. Opera: City Center of Music
   and Drama, Lyric Opera of
   Chicago, San Francisco Opera
   Association

$224,000 for the production of new American operas.

2. Music *per se:*
   a. Opera Association of New
      Mexico

$22,800 for a symposium for young composers to be held in connection with a Stravinsky Festival in Santa Fé during August 1962.

   b. The National Music Camp

$9,500.

   c. Peabody Conservatory of
      Music

$50,000 for a continuation of the conductors' program begun in 1961.

   d. Young Composers Program

$94,000.

   e. Tulane University

$56,000 for a continuation of the program begun in 1958.

3. Theater: Resident Theater
   Program

$6,100,000 to Actors Studio, Actor's Workshop, Alley Theater, American Shakespeare Festival Theatre and Academy, Arena Stage, Tyrone Guthrie Theatre, Fred Miller Theater, Mummers Theatre, and the UCLA Theater Group, to help these professional groups "reach and maintain new levels of artistic achievement and financial stability."

4. Grants-in-Aid	$452,100 for choral directors, concert soloists, opera singers and other talented individuals. $122,550 for administrative interns, in professionally staffed orchestras, theaters and dance companies.

1963

1. Orchestras: New York Philharmonic	$1,365,000 — a non-program grant.
2. Opera:	
a. Metropolitan Opera Association	$3,100,000 — a non-program grant — and $25,000 for studio readings.
b. Civic Opera	$1,727,625 to thirteen civic opera companies "to help them increase the number of productions and volume of their support from local patronage."
c. City Center	$147,000 for the production of new American operas.
d. American Operatic Repertoire Program	$59,000 for payments to opera companies for commissioning new American operas (increase).
3. Music *per se:*	
a. Music Educators National Conference	$1,380,000 — six years continuation of the Young Composers Program and additional activities in the public schools, such as pilot projects to identify creative pupils, school seminars and workshops on contemporary music.
b. Julliard School of Music	$252,000 — a non-program grant.
c. New York Pro Musica Antiqua	$465,000 to enable the organization to reach a position of self-support within the next ten years, and for the staging of four medieval music dramas.
d. Louisville Free Public Library	$7,800 for a composer in residence.
e. Young Composers Program	$15,200.
4. Dance: School of American Ballet	$60,000 assistance in planning nationwide foundation program to strengthen ballet.
5. Theater: Stratford Shakespearean Festival of Canada	$60,000 under resident theater program.

(*Continued on following page*)

6. Grants-in-Aid

$471,500 to opera singers, poets and writers associated with theater and opera and other talented individuals. $160,650 for administrative interns, in professionally staffed orchestras, theaters and dance companies.

7. Cultural Centers:
   a. Lincoln Center

$12,500,000 — a non-program grant.

   b. National Cultural Center

$5,000,000 — a non-program grant — conditional upon the National Cultural Center's obtaining $25,000,000 from other private sources.

1964

1. Opera: City Center

$250,000 for the production of contemporary opera.

2. Music *per se:*
   a. Young Audiences

$582,000.

   b. Eight Independent Schools of Music

$580,000 for scholarships to talented students.

3. Dance: Eight Ballet Companies

$7,806,750 to improve instruction and performances in local communities.

4. Theater:
   a. American Place Theater

$225,000.

   b. Theater Communications Group

$795,000 under cooperative program among non-profit theater companies.

   c. American Shakespeare Festival Theatre and Academy

$196,800 increase under resident theater program.

5. Grants-in-Aid

$556,000 for film makers, playwrights, professional instrumentalists and other talented individuals in the arts. $142,675 for administrative interns, in professionally staffed orchestras, theaters and dance companies.

1965

1. Orchestras: Symphony Orchestra Program

$85,000,000 appropriation to assist in the development and consolidation of American symphony orchestras.

546

2. Opera and Dance:
   a. Connecticut Opera Association — $103,000 to increase number of performances and size of repertory.

   b. Symphony Society of San Antonio — $3,000 under Civic Opera Program.

   c. City Center of Music and Drama — $3,200,000 to assist the transfer of N. Y. C. Opera and N. Y. C. Ballet to Lincoln Center and for expansion of their operations.

   d. Foundation for American Dance — $155,000 to enable the Robert Joffrey Ballet to go into active production and inaugurate a program of special training for dancers.

   e. Martha Graham School of Contemporary Dance — $6,000.

   f. New York Public Library — $72,000 for use of computer techniques to catalog dance collection.

3. Other Music:
   a. George Peabody College for Teachers — $42,500 for conferences of choral directors in southwestern universities.

   b. Manhattan School of Music — $2,000,000 for school's expansion program.

   c. Peabody Institute of Baltimore — $500,000 for faculty salaries and scholarships.

4. Theater: University of Minnesota — $20,000 for post-doctoral research on psychology of the theater.

5. Grants-in-Aid — $84,505 for administrative interns, in professionally staffed orchestras, theaters and dance companies.

SOURCE: Ford Foundation Annual Reports and press releases. The grants recorded in this table were not always paid out entirely in the years in which they were announced. The figures used do not reflect (1) unpaid grants on which the terms and conditions of grant could not be met or (2) unexpended balances returned to the Foundation upon completion of a grant.

City Expenditures Directly Related to the Performing Arts, 1958–59

City	Recipient	Amount
Atlanta	Symphony Guild; Pops Concerts; Theatre Under the Stars	$ 18,500
Baltimore	Bureau of Music	119,994
Buffalo	Philharmonic Orchestra Society; Kleinhaus Music Hall	57,300
Houston	Civic Theatre, Symphony	28,000
Kansas City	Philharmonic Orchestra; Starlight Theater	52,755
Los Angeles	Bureau of Music	196,998
New Orleans	Philharmonic; Opera House; Crescent City Concerts	8,375
New York	Brooklyn Institute of Brooklyn Academy of Music	165,376
Norfolk	Symphony	2,000
Philadelphia	Robin Hood Dell; Philadelphia Grand Opera	100,000
Pittsburgh	Symphony	35,000
Rochester	Civic Music Association; Opera	30,000
Sacramento	Philharmonic	4,500
St. Paul	Civic Opera	10,000
San Antonio	San Pedio Playhouse	1,500
San Diego	Symphony	10,000
Seattle	Art Commission, Public Music	18,234
Total, 17 Cities		**$858,532**

SOURCE: House Hearings, I, pp. 318–20. This table is based on a survey conducted by the Legislative Reference Service of the Library of Congress in 1959 at the request of several members of Congress. Forty-six cities, selected on the basis of their population or because they were known to give municipal support to the arts, were sent questionnaires; 38 replied. This table includes only cities that reported expenditures apparently related to the performing arts. However, some of these figures may include art forms other than live performance.

State Expenditures Directly Related to the Performing Arts, circa 1958–59

State	Recipient	Amount
Connecticut	Preservation of the Goodspeed Opera House	$10,000
Kentucky	Louisville Symphony Orchestra (primarily for childrens' concerts)	$106,000
Maryland	Baltimore Symphony Orchestra	$25,000
Massachusetts	Summer Theater at Metropolitan Boston Art Center	N.A.
New York	New York State Council on the Arts	$50,000
	Jones Beach Stadium loaned for summer musical shows. Saratoga Springs Reservation Theater loaned to a professional summer stock company. Free concerts and chamber music provided at the Reservation's Hall of Springs. Parks and other facilities made available for such performing arts activities as the Watkins Glen dance festival, the Arena Theater at Albany and free Shakespearian drama in Central Park.	Financial value of this support not available.
North Carolina	North Carolina Symphony (performs many free concerts)	State makes up the operating deficit.
Rhode Island	Newport Music Festival	$5,000
	Free Concerts for Public Schools	$7,000
	Free Public Concerts	$7,000
	Free Public Opera	$7,000
	Providence Philharmonic Orchestra	$2,500
	Irish Music Festival	$2,500

(*Continued on following page*)

State	Recipient	Amount
Utah	Utah Symphony Orchestra	$13,000
	Music Contest	$325
Vermont	Vermont Symphony Orchestra	$5,000
Virginia	Barter Theater	$15,000

SOURCE: House Hearings, I, pp. 126–42. This table is based on a survey conducted by the Legislative Reference Service of the Library of Congress in February 1960 at the request of several members of Congress. Questionnaires were sent to the 50 state governors and 47 replies were received. The table encompasses only those states which reported expenditures directly related to the performing arts as defined in this study. Thus, although Florida indicated expenditures on behalf of the Stephen Foster Memorial Commission, which supports folk dancers and music, Kansas reported an expenditure of $200,000 for pageants of history and Wisconsin reported an outlay of $225,843 on a state radio broadcasting system, these states are not listed. Similarly, support flowing through educational institutions is not included in this table.

APPENDIX FIGURE XVI-A

PROPORTION OF AUDIENCE CONTRIBUTING REGULARLY
TO THE PERFORMING ARTS, BY INCOME CLASS,
UNITED STATES AND UNITED KINGDOM

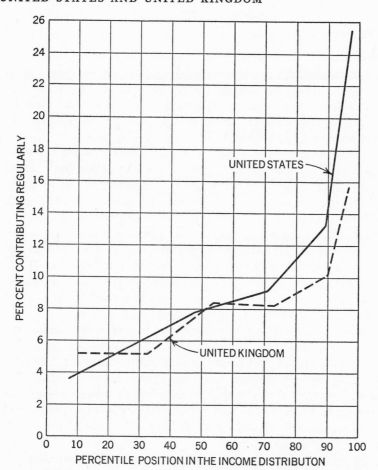

This graph enables us to estimate the percentage of the audience in
each percentile of each country's income distribution who contribute
regularly. Thus, the line for the United States suggests that among persons in the 30th percentile (29 per cent of the population have lower
incomes than they do), 6 per cent contribute regularly.

Derivation of Projections of the Income Gap and Private Contributions

The Income Gap

Our income gap projections to 1975 consist of two components: a projection of the combined income gap of the existing (as of 1963–64) performing arts organizations of the types included in our study; and a projection of the income gap associated with the new organizations which can reasonably be expected to come into being between 1963–64 and 1975.

(1) We projected the combined gap of all the existing organizations on the basis of the financial experiences of our basic set of eleven major orchestras, which, as we demonstrated in Chapters VIII–XII, have been sufficiently typical of professional arts organizations in general to make this a reasonable procedure.

In projecting the income gap for the typical member of our major orchestra set the simplest procedure would have been to take the growth rate for the income gap itself directly from Chapter XII and apply this rate to our base year gap. It seemed preferable, however, to use the growth rates for expenditures and earned income (from Chapters VIII and X); to project these amounts; to obtain the change in the income gap by subtraction; and then to calculate the implicit growth rate for the income gap. Our reason for preferring this approach is that the trends in expenditure and earned income have been more stable than the trend in the gap itself, which, because of its residual character, is more subject to sharp year-to-year fluctuations. In statistical terms, the R^2's for the expenditure and earned income regressions are much higher than the R^2 for the income gap regression.

The detailed derivation of our higher and lower projections is shown in the accompanying table. The higher projection is based on the use of growth rates for the 1961–1964 period, when orchestral activity spurted, while the lower projection is based on growth rates for the 1947–1964 period.

Applying the lower implicit growth rate of 6.1 per cent per year to our lower estimate of the combined income gap for 1964 of $19.7 million, we obtain a 1975 projection of $37.8 million; applying the higher implicit growth rate of 8.3 per cent per year, we obtain a 1975 projection of $47.4 million.

	Base Year (1963–64) Amount (thousands)	Growth Rate	Projected 1975 Amount (thousands)	Implicit Growth Rate for Income Gap
HIGHER PROJECTION				
Expenditures	$1,006	6.9%	$2,095	
Earned Income	563	5.6	1,025	
Income Gap	$ 443		$1,070	8.3%
LOWER PROJECTION				
Expenditures	$1,006	4.8%	$1,685	
Earned Income	563	3.6	831	
Income Gap	$ 443		$ 854	6.1%

Had we used the directly calculated growth rates for the income gap rather than the implicit growth rates obtained from expenditure and income projections, we would have obtained still higher projections. The directly calculated gap growth rates are 9.4 per cent for the 1961–64 period and 6.9 per cent for the 1947–1964 period.

(2) To the preceding projected gaps for existing organizations we added projections of gaps for "new" organizations. These latter projections were obtained by making certain admittedly arbitrary assumptions about the likely increase in the number of organizations in each category by 1975 (that there will be 3 more major orchestras, for example), and then projecting the average gap for each type of organization in 1963–64 (from Chapter VI) forward to 1975 at the same implicit growth rates used above (6.1 per cent for our lower projection and 8.3 per cent for our higher projection). Thus we obtained:

Assumed Increase in Organizations	Projected Gap in 1975 (millions)	
	Lower Projection	Higher Projection
3 major orchestras	$ 2.20	$ 2.70
A net addition of 5 metropolitan orchestras	0.85	1.10
2 more "smaller" (i.e., not Metropolitan Opera size) opera companies	0.21	0.26
A doubling in the number of regional repertory theaters (from 30 to 60)	6.80	8.60
A 25 per cent increase in dance activity	0.53	0.66
Total	$10.59	$13.32

In making assumptions about the number of new organizations in each category we were guided by the general discussion of trends in activity in Chapter III. There is, of course, nothing immutable about these assumptions, and we have presented the calculations in such a way as to permit the reader who thinks, for example, that there will be 5 more major orchestras rather than 3 to adjust the projections accordingly. (He would merely have to multiply the $2.2 million figure by 5/3 and then substitute the resulting figure [$3.7 million] for the $2.2 million.)

(3) Finally, we added together our projected increases in the gap for the old and new organizations to obtain our total projections of $48.4 million (lower) and $60.7 million (higher). The implicit growth rates are 8.5 per cent per year and 10.8 per cent, respectively.

Private Contributions

To obtain our projected values of private contributions in 1975, we estimated over-all growth rates for private contributions (a higher and a lower growth rate) and applied these to the estimated income gap in 1963–64 of $19.7 million. Use of the 1963–64 income gap estimate as the base for our contributions projection amounts to assuming that contributions exactly equaled the income gap in the base year. For reasons explained in the text, this seems a reasonable assumption.

Our estimates of over-all growth rates (7.30 per cent per year as a higher estimate and 5.24 per cent as a lower estimate) are weighted averages of estimates of growth rates for the various private sources of support, the relative amounts of contributions received by the performing arts from each source serving as weights, as shown in the table below.

Source of Contributions	Higher Estimate			Lower Estimate		
	Growth Rate (1)	Weight (2)	Col. 1 x Col. 2 (3)	Growth Rate (4)	Weight (5)	Col. 4 x Col. 5 (6)
Living Donors	5.8%	49%	2.84%	3.8%	55%	2.09%
Bequests	12.0	9	1.08	8.0	6	0.48
Corporations	5.7	19	1.08	5.7	19.5	1.11
Foundations	10.0	23	2.30	8.0	19.5	1.56
Over-all Growth Rate			7.30			5.24

The growth rates for each source were obtained as follows:

Living Donors. See Chapter XIII, especially Appendix XIII–1. The 5.8 rate is an estimate of the average annual growth rate in the contributions of the top income group between 1954 and 1962, while the 3.8 rate is our estimate for the 1958–1962 interval. For reasons explained in detail in Chapter XIII we think that trends in contributions by the higher income groups are more significant for the arts than trends in total contributions of living donors. In fact, however, the two sets of trends are quite similar.

Bequests. See Chapter XIII. The higher growth rate was obtained by fitting a regression line to the logarithms of the figures in col. 3 of Appendix Table XIII–J for the years 1947–1961. Those figures are for bequests on estates of $60,000 or more, and the use of this constant-dollar cut-off produces an upward bias in our higher growth rate. (For a detailed explanation, see Appendix XIII–1, where we discuss an analogous problem in estimating contributions by living donors.) The lower growth rate for bequests is based on a rough guess as to the order of magnitude of this bias.

Corporations. See Chapter XIV. The growth rate was obtained by fitting a regression line to the figures in col. 2 of Appendix Table XIV–A for the years 1948–1962.

Foundations. See Chapter XIV. The higher and the lower rates here are both "guesstimates," based primarily on inspection of Appendix Table XIV–C. Since an unknown share of the increase in foundation grants suggested by the figures in this table must be attributed to changes in reporting habits, no formal regression lines were calculated.

The weights used to construct the over-all growth rates are based on the estimates presented in the last section of Chapter XIV, with one modification: we had to apportion our estimate of individual contributions between contributions of living donors and bequests. The weights used to obtain our higher over-all growth rate are based on the assumptions that total individual contributions in 1962 equaled $62 million (the mid-point of the $50-to-$75-million range given in Chapter XIV) and that bequests equaled 20 per cent of the contributions of living donors. The weights used to obtain the lower growth rate are based on the same total contribution assumption but on a different assumption about the relative importance of bequests: here it is assumed that bequests equaled 10 per cent of the contributions of living donors. Figures on the relative importance of bequests and contributions of living donors are given in Table XIII–1.

S E L E C T E D

B I B L I O G R A P H Y

Actors' Equity Association. "Equity Rules Governing Employment." New York, various years.

American Federation of Musicians. "The Symphony Musician Speaks Out." Mimeographed release, New York, April 15, 1961.

American Symphony Orchestra League. Compiled Annual Reports. Vienna, Virginia.

———. *Newsletter.*

———. *Report on a Study of Governing Boards of Orchestras,* 1958. Arts Council of Great Britain. Annual Reports (since 1952).

———. *Report of the Committee on the London Orchestra* (Arnold Goodman, Chairman). April 30, 1965.

Avery, Emmett L. *The London Stage 1660–1800. Part 2: 1700–1729.* Southern Illinois University Press, Carbondale, Illinois, 1960.

Baltimore Symphony Subscribers Analysis. Sidney Hollander Associates, Baltimore, February 1963, mimeographed.

Bernheim, Alfred L. *The Business of the Theater,* Benjamin Bloom, Inc., New York, 1932 (reissued 1964).

Birkenhead, Thomas Bruce. "The Economics of the Broadway Theaters, 1962–63." Dissertation, New School for Social Research, New York, uncompleted.

Booth, John E. "Government Support to the Performing Arts in Western Europe." Paper prepared for the Rockefeller Brothers Panel, unpublished.

Bridges (Lord). *The State and the Arts,* Romanes Lecture, Oxford, June 3, 1958. Clarendon Press, Oxford, 1958.

Broadcasting Magazine survey of the national FM radio audience, June 4, 1962.

Carnegie Hall surveys. Two surveys by Spencer Claire Associates, Inc., Warwick, Rhode Island; done under the auspices of *High Fidelity/ Musical America* Magazine, Great Barrington, Massachusetts, 1963, 1964.

Charles Playhouse Survey by Professor Thomas Raymond of the Harvard Business School.

Dorian, Frederick. *Commitment to Culture.* University of Pittsburgh Press, Pittsburgh, Pennsylvania, 1964.

Erskine, John. *The Philharmonic-Symphony Society of New York: Its First Hundred Years.* Macmillan Company, New York, 1943.

Flanagan, Hallie. *Arena.* Duell, Sloan & Pearce, New York, 1940.

Ford Foundation. Annual Reports.

Foundation Library Center. Annual Reports, 1962 to date.

Selected Bibliography (continued)

Goodman Report. *See under* Arts Council of Great Britain.
Graf, Herbert. *Producing Opera for America*. Atlantis Books, New York, 1961.
Great Britain. H. M. Treasury. "Government and the Arts." H. M. Stationery Office, London, various years.
Guthrie (Tyrone) Theater survey. "Analysis of the Guthrie Theater Audience," December 1963, Twin Cities Marketing and Research Department of Batten, Barton, Durstine & Osborn, Inc.
Harding, Alfred. *The Revolt of the Actors*. William Morrow & Co., New York, 1929.
Heckscher, August. "The Arts and National Government," Report to the President, May 28, 1963.
Hendry, Thomas B. "Trends in Canadian Theater," *Tulane Drama Review*, Vol. 10, Fall 1965, p. 64.
Hering, Doris, ed. "Twenty Five Years of American Dance," *Dance Magazine*, New York, 1954.
Krehbiel, Henry Edward. *The Philharmonic Society of New York*. Novello, Ewer & Co., New York and London, 1892.
Lefkowitz Hearings. Inquiry into Financing and Ticket Distribution Practices in the New York Legitimate Theatre before Louis J. Lefkowitz, Attorney General of the State of New York and Samuel A. Hirshowitz, First Assistant Attorney General. Vol. I, December 10, 1963. Vol. II, December 11, 1963.
Leiter, Robert D. *The Musicians and Petrillo*. Bookman Associates Inc., New York, 1953.
Levy, Richard. "University Theatre: Embarrassing Riches," *Tulane Drama Review*, Vol. 10, Fall 1965.
Lloyd, Margaret. *The Borzoi Book of Modern Dance*. Alfred A. Knopf, New York, 1949.
Lord, William J., Jr. *How Authors Make a Living*. The Scarecrow Press, New York, 1962.
Lowry, W. McNeil. "The University and the Creative Arts." Address before the Association of Graduate Schools, October 24, 1961, reprinted by the Ford Foundation.
MacFadyen, John H., and Campbell, Alan I. "State and Local Government Support for the Performing Arts." Paper prepared for the Rockefeller Brothers Panel, unpublished.
————. Survey of 47 municipalities in eight states on national support of the performing arts, made in 1963 for the Rockefeller Brothers Fund.
Minneapolis Star Metro poll report, August 1965.
Mitchell, Arnold. *Marketing the Arts*. Address delivered November 8, 1962 and published by the Stanford Research Institute. This address is a summary of Arnold Mitchell and MaryLou Anderson, *The Arts and Business*, Long Range Planning Report No. 140, Stanford Research Institute, Menlo Park, California, 1962.
Moore, Thomas G. "The American Theater: Past, Present, and Future." Carnegie Institute of Technology, Pittsburgh, Pennsylvania, 1965, unpublished.

Selected Bibliography (continued)

Mueller, John H. *The American Symphony Orchestra*. Indiana University Press, Bloomington, Indiana, 1951.

Munson, Henry Lee. "Money for the Arts, The What, How and Why of Government Aid to the Arts in Seven Free Countries of Europe." Harold L. Oram, Inc., New York, mimeographed, no date.

Murdock, Lawrence C., Jr. "S.R.O. and S.O.S.: The Performing Arts Paradox," *Business Review*, Federal Reserve Bank of Philadelphia, March 1962.

New York State Council on the Arts. Annual Report, 1965.

Pedicord, Harry W. *The Theatrical Public in the Time of Garrick*. Kings Crown Press, New York, 1954.

Playbill survey. "Who's Who in the Audience," compiled and issued annually since 1955 by Playbill, Inc., New York.

Poggi, Emil J. "The American Theater: An Economic Study, 1870–1931." Dissertation, Columbia University, New York, 1964, unpublished.

Raskin, A. H. "Labor as Performer and Practitioner in the Arts." April 9, 1964, mimeographed.

———. "Role of Labor in Support of the Performing Arts." Paper prepared for the Rockefeller Brothers Panel, unpublished.

Robbins, Lionel C. R. (Lord). "Art and the State," in *Politics and Economics*. St. Martin's Press, New York, 1963.

Rockefeller Panel Report. *The Performing Arts: Problems and Prospects*. McGraw-Hill Book Company, New York, 1965.

Sabin, Frances. "Government and the Arts," *Musical America*, January 1962.

Sadler's Wells Theatre Audience Survey in London. Martech Consultants Ltd., London, January 1965, mimeographed.

Schmidt, Sandra. "Regional Theaters: Some Statistics," *Tulane Drama Review*, Fall 1965; originally published in Vol. 10, No. 1, September 1965.

Schonberg, Harold C. "The National 'Culture Explosion' Is Phony," *Saturday Evening Post*, July 13–20, 1963.

Shapiro, Marilyn L. "Foundation Support for the Performing Arts." Paper prepared for the Rockefeller Brothers Panel, unpublished.

Stoddard, Hope. *Subsidy Makes Sense*. International Press, Newark, no date; articles reprinted from *International Musician*, the publication of the American Federation of Musicians.

Stone, George Winchester, Jr. *The London Stage 1660–1800. Part 4: 1747–1776*. Southern Illinois University Press, Carbondale, Illinois, 1962.

Survey of Current Business. U. S. Department of Commerce, monthly.

Theater World Annual, Vols. 1–15.

Toffler, Alvin. *The Culture Consumers*. St. Martin's Press, New York, 1964.

UCLA Theater Subscribers' Analysis, Winter 1964, carried out by UCLA Theater, University of California, Los Angeles, unpublished.

United States. Department of Labor, Bureau of Labor Statistics. "Employment Outlook in the Performing Arts," Bulletin No. 1300–65, 1965.

———. House of Representatives. *Hearings on Aid to Fine Arts* before the

559

Selected Bibliography (continued)

Select Subcommittee on Education of the Committee on Education and Labor, 87th Congress, 1st Session, on HR 4172 and HR 4174. Hearing held in Washington, D. C., May 15, 1961. Government Printing Office, Washington, D. C., 1961. (Cited as House Hearings, I.)

——. ——. *Hearings on Economic Conditions in the Performing Arts* before the Select Subcommittee on Education of the Committee on Education and Labor, 87th Congress, 1st and 2nd Sessions. Hearings held in New York, N. Y., November 15, 16 and 17, 1961; San Francisco, California, December 7 and 8, 1961; and Washington, D. C., February 5 and 6, 1962. Government Printing Office, Washington, D. C., 1962. (Cited as House Hearings, II.)

——. Senate, *Government and the Arts*. Hearings before a special Subcommittee on Labor and Public Welfare, 87th Congress, 2nd Session, on S.741, S.785 and S.1250, August 29, 30 and 31, 1962.

Watts, John H. "Economics of the New York Legitimate Theater, 1948–1958." Dissertation, Columbia University, New York, uncompleted.

Wharton, John F. *A Fresh Look at Theatre Tickets*. Report to the Legitimate Theatre Industry Exploratory Commission, 1965.

Wiley, John M. *Records: Facts and Figures — 1964*. Columbia Records Market Research (annual publication).

Wunderlich, Bert. "The Broadway Legitimate Theater: An Economic Study." Senior thesis, Princeton University, Princeton, New Jersey, 1962, unpublished.

Bridges, Lord, 365n, 370, 371
Broadcast Music Inc., 143
Broadcasting magazine, 72
Broadway theater: *see* Theater
(Broadway, and theater in
general)
Brooklyn Academy of Music, 548T
Brooklyn Opera Company, 85, 452T
Bucks County Playhouse, 197, 205,
255, 349
Budapest String Quartet, 452T
Budgets: *see* Expenditures of or-
ganizations
Buffalo, 548T
Burgard, Ralph, 325, 327, 351
Business corporations
contributions to all causes, 329–33,
335n, 536T, 537T
financial support of arts, 333–4,
366T, 399
stimulation of, 333–5
income tax deduction allowance,
330, 332, 353–4

C

California, University of (Los An-
geles), 337
Canada, contributions to the arts,
376n
Capital accumulation, scope for, 165
Capital costs, support for, 366, 402
Carnegie, Andrew, 16
Carnegie Hall surveys, 72
"Case of Libel, A," 449T
Cast size, 29–30, 476T
Census of Business, 63, 65
Center Stage (Baltimore), 450T
Central City Summer Opera, 29
Chamber music: *see* Orchestras,
chamber
Charles Centre Project (Baltimore),
federal aid, 358
Charles Playhouse (Boston), 72,
450T
Chase, Lucia, 31
Cherry Lane Theatre (New York
City), 450T
Chicago Lyric Opera, 29, 250, 254,
496T, 544T
Chicago Symphony, 16, 155
Choreographers
administrative and teaching role,
31
financial circumstances, 113
income sources, 126

Cincinnati, theater, 27
Cincinnati Symphony Orchestra, 16,
184, 189n
audience survey coverage, 451T
expenditures, trend, 294F
expenditures per concert, 187–94,
188T, 189n, 190T, 391, 477
financial contributions to, 319
income (earned), trend, 294F
income gap, trends, 294F, 298,
513T
ticket price rise, 271–2
Circle in the Square, 27, 450T
Cities and counties
support by, 347–50, 366T, 374,
513n, 548T
legal restrictions, 351n
and public control, 374
total, estimate, 348
taxation and license fees, 348–50
City Center: *see* New York City
Center
Civic Repertory Theater (New York
City), 156
Clark, W. A., 16
Claudel, Paul, 26
Cleveland Orchestra, 17
Colleges and universities
as audience for arts, 31, 53, 337,
435T
federal funds received, 153
financial support of arts, 336–8
resident groups, 337
excluded from income gap
figures, 151
Columbia Broadcasting System, 285
Columbia Group for Contemporary
Music (New York City),
452T
Columbus (Ohio), orchestra, 17
Comédie Française, 362
Community orchestras: *see* Orches-
tras, community
Company of the Golden Hand, 543T
Composers
difficulty in getting works performed, 108–9
expenses, types of, 108–9
financial circumstances, 107–9
income sources, 108
Concentration, geographic: *see* Geographic distribution
Conductors, authority, 18
Congressional hearings, 100
professional training, 130
unemployment compensation, 128
Connecticut, 549T

Connecticut Opera Association, 547T
Consumer price index, long-term
    trends, 216F
"Contract" theater, 9n
Contributions (private) to all
    causes, 305ff.
  by corporations, 306T, 329–33,
      335n, 536T
    type of recipient, 537T
  by foundations, 306T, 338–40,
      539T, 540T
    humanities, 341T
  by individuals, 306–7, 518T
    bequests, 322–3, 530T
    high-income recipients, trends,
        321–2, 328
    vs. income, 312–17, 314F, 316F,
        317F, 520T, 521T, 522T, 525T,
        529T
    and income tax deductions limi-
        tation, 311–12
    type of recipient, 315–17, 522T,
        525T
    measurement of, 309, 311, 515–
        17
  trends, 309–12, 310F, 398
  by source, 306T, 306–7
  projections, 399, 400T
Corporations: see Business corpora-
    tions
Cost curve regressions, 479–81
Cost-cutting measures, 175–6
Costs of performance: see Expendi-
    tures of organizations
Costumes
  as cost item, 214T
  responsibility for, 21, 23
Counties: see Cities and counties
Covent Garden, 28n, 200
  attendance 238T, 254, 496T
    at contemporary operas, 254,
        397, 496T
  expenditures of, 142, 200–201,
      473T, 474T
  government support, 365
  income gap, 150, 297F, 298, 299F,
      388, 474T, 513T
  salaries, 121, 145, 212, 486T
  ticket prices, 265, 270T, 501T
  see also Royal Ballet
Covent Garden Theatre, ticket prices,
    182–3, 501T
"Cultural boom," 8, 35–9, 68–9
  activity trends in various art
      forms, 50–63, 68
  admissions expenditures as evi-
      dence of, 42–9, 68

"Cultural boom" (cont.)
  attendance, total, by art form, 67T,
      67–8
  cultural centers as evidence of,
      39–41
  geographic patterns of activity,
      63–7
  literature of, 36–9
  theater activity as evidence of, 88
Cultural centers
  construction dates, 40
  facilities, 41
  federal support, 358
  Ford Foundation support, 340,
      343, 541T, 542
  number, 40, 41
  questionnaire, 421–2
  see also Lincoln Center; National
      Cultural (Kennedy) Center
Culture, money spent or donated for,
    36
Culture Consumers, The, 36
Cunningham, Merce, 30, 452T

D

Dallas Symphony Orchestra, 451T
Dallas Theater Center, 450T
Dance
  activity trends, 51F, 52–3
  advertising, effectiveness of, 489T
  attendance, 52, 67T
    frequency of, 77T, 457T, 459T,
        461T, 464T, 466T, 490T,
        492T, 512T
    at visiting troupes' performances,
        32
  attendance costs
    ticket vs. non-ticket, 500T
  audience composition, 84–6,
      456T, 458T
  audience survey coverage, 444T,
      449T
  colleges and universities as au-
      dience source, 53
  expenditures of companies, 138T
    deficits, net, 155T
    in man-years of labor, 473T
    per company, 473T
    per performance, 138T, 473T;
        trends, 198, 199T
    per seat, 138T
    trends, 198, 199T
  financial contributions to, 155T
    by foundations, 30–31, 342;
        Ford grants, 343, 541T, 542T

New York City Center of Music and
Drama
Ford Foundation grants, 542–7T
ticket prices, controversy with
Lincoln Center, 281
New York City Opera
attendance, 254, 496T
blue collar workers, 85
contemporary operas, 254, 397,
496T
audience survey coverage, 452T
expenditures of, 145n
per performance, 198, 199T
Ford Foundation grant, 343
number of performances, 432
New York Philharmonic Orchestra,
17
audience survey coverage, 451T
early history, 16, 187, 292, 482
expenditures of, 184–6, 185T,
291ff.
per performance, 186–94, 188T,
189n, 190T, 192n, 194n, 391
Ford Foundation grant, 545
free concerts in Central Park, 276,
334
income (earned), trends, 291ff.,
293F
income gap, trends, 291ff.
annual increase, 298, 513T
salaries, 115T, 219n, 392
ticket prices, 271, 275
young people's concerts, 380
New York Pro Musica Antiqua, 545T
New York Public Library, 547T
New York Shakespeare Festival, 101,
452T
New York State
support by, 350, 351, 549T
Council on the Arts, 113, 351,
352, 405
New York State Theater, 24
New York Symphony, 16
New York Times
on "cultural boom," 37
on economic role of arts, 383–4
on off-Broadway, 58
on plight of drama, 57
theater advertising in, 215–16,
484T
New York World's Fair, 52, 55
Newman, Danny, 250–51
Newport Music Festival, 549T
Nikolais (Alwin) Dance Co., 452T
Nixon Theatre (Pittsburgh), 450T
Norfolk, 548T

North Carolina, 549T
North Carolina Symphony, 549T

O

Oakland, orchestra, 17
Occupation of audience, 75T, 79–80,
81F, 84–8 *passim*, 94, 282
Great Britain, 90T, 92, 93
see also the Audience profiles
"Oklahoma!", 113
Oklahoma City, theater, 27
Oklahoma City Symphony Orchestra,
451T
Old Dominion Foundation, 342
Old Vic: *see* National Theatre
O'Neill, Eugene, 26, 244
Open air performances: *see* Free
outdoor performances
Opera
activity trends, 50–52
administration and organization,
29–30
advertising, effectiveness of, 489T
amateur activity, 50, 52, 432n
attendance, 50, 67T
vs. capacity, 238T, 506T
contemporary works and, 254,
496T
frequency of, 77T, 457T, 459T,
461T, 464T, 466T, 490T, 492T
attendance costs, ticket vs. non-
ticket, 500T
audience composition, 84–6, 456T,
458T, 460T
audience survey coverage, 444T,
449T
cast size, 29–30
contemporary works, economic
effects of, 254–5, 496T
early history, 28–9
expenditures of companies, 29–30,
138T, 139–40; trends, 197,
198, 198F, 199T
components, 142–5, 144F, 213T
deficits, net, 155T
in man-years of labor, 473T
per company, 473T
per performance, 138T, 140–42,
473T; trends, 197, 198, 198F,
199T
per seat, 138T, 140–42
financial contributions to, 155T,
307
by foundations, 342; Ford
Foundation, 343, 541T, 542T

Orchestras (major, and orchestras in general) (*cont.*)
income (earned) (*cont.*)
"grants for services" treated as, 513n
median, 149T
trends, 241–3, 242F, 291ff., 293F, 294F, 295F
income gap, 152T
average, 240n
vs. expenditures, 148, 149T
median, 148, 149T
per cent of income, 240
trends, 291ff., 293F, 294F, 295F, 299F
location of, 33(map)
number, 17, 32, 39
number of concerts, by type, 62, 439T, 441T
rehearsal costs, 109, 129, 203–4
salaries, 17, 107, 114T, 120–22, 148
vs. other costs, 144F; trends, 210ff., 210F, 211F
season length, 17, 122–3, 439T, 441T
staff size, 18
subscription series, 250–51, 256
ticket prices, 260F
vs. cost per concert, 271, 272T
trends, 266, 268F, 504T; annual increase, 270T, 272T
tours, 62, 439T
women, hiring of, 228–9
see also categories below; and see individual orchestras; Music; Composers; Musicians
Orchestras, chamber
advertising, effectiveness of, 489T
attendance at concerts, 88
frequency of, 490T, 492T
audience composition, 84–6, 456T
government support, 357
income gap, 150n
Orchestras, community, 17
Orchestras, metropolitan
attendance at concerts, 61, 67T
share in total, 60
defined, 17
expenditures of, 138T
deficits, net, 154, 155T
expenditures per concert and per seat, 138T, 140–42
financial contributions to, 155T
by government, 348
income gap, 149T, 152T
location of, 33(map)

Orchestras, metropolitan (*cont.*)
number, 17
salaries, 116T, 122
Oregon Shakespeare Festival Association, 543T
Output per man-hour, as measure of productivity, 162n; *see also* Productivity

P

Pacific states, 63–4, 441T, 442T
Palace Theater (New York City), 24
Papp, Joseph, 101
Peabody (George) College for Teachers, 547T
Peabody Conservatory of Music, 544T
Peabody Institute of Baltimore, 547T
Pedicord, Harry W., 265
Pensions: *see* Fringe benefits
Performers
demand for, effect of mass media, 229–30
earnings from live performances, 114T, 133T
per cent of total income, 132, 134
and season length, 122–3
financial circumstances, 100–101, 169
survey methods, 124; questionnaire, 468
fringe benefits, 130–32
income from all sources, 132–4, 133T, 221–5, 222T
non-monetary rewards, 169
number, trends, 222T, 226–30
number per company, range, 32, 34
output per hour, as arts productivity factor, 164
professional expenses, 130
rehearsal time, 128–9
salaries, 113–21, 124–6
annual increase, 217, 218T, 220; Great Britain, 225
economic conditions and, 220–21
Great Britain, 486T
vs. other costs: *see* Artistic personnel
vs. other occupations, trends, 225
outlook, 391–2
unemployment, 127–8, 226, 228–30
Census criteria of, 227

575

Performers (*cont.*)
unemployment compensation, 128, 132
weeks worked in year, 128
working conditions, 128–30, 134
see also specific types of performers
Phelps Brown–Hopkins price index, 183n
Philadelphia, 548T
Philadelphia Grand Opera, 548T
Philadelphia Orchestra, 16, 17
Philanthropy, defined, 305
Philanthropy, private: *see* Contributions (private) to all causes; *for arts see* Financial support (contributed)
Phoenix Theater, 3, 27, 451T, 543T
"Physicists, The," 451T
Pianists, 38
Pittsburgh, 548T
Pittsburgh Symphony Orchestra, 451T, 502–5
Play House (Cleveland), 450T, 542T, 543T
Playbill surveys, 79, 83n, 87–8, 455T
Playwrights
contract arrangements, 22
difficulty in getting works produced, 112–13
financial circumstances, 109–13
income, 110, 111–12, 147
royalties and fees, vs. other Broadway costs, 143, 144F, 214T
Poggi, Emil J.
on little theater, 25–26
on playwrights, 246n
on theater activity, 55
Population, profile of urban, 75T
Population increase, and admissions expenditures, 44–5
Portland (Oregon) Symphony Orchestra, 17, 451T
President's Advisory Council on the Arts, 358
President's Council of Economic Advisers, 170n
Press agents, 23
Price indexes
consumer, 216F, 477
G.N.P. implicit price deflator, 180, 430n
Great Britain, 183
Phelps Brown–Hopkins, 183n
service, 180
Warren-Pearson, 190n
wholesale, 188F, 190T, 196T, 477

Price-level changes
admissions expenditures and, 44
expenditures of organizations and, 8, 189ff.
Great Britain, 183
wage-productivity relationship and, 170
Princeton University, 337
Private support: *see* Financial support
Producers, theatrical
duties and responsibilities, 21–23
fund-raising by, 22
impermanence of operations, 20–21
income sources, 23, 147
subsidy of off-Broadway theater, 26
Productivity (output per man-hour) in arts, 162ff.
benefits from general technological advance, 163–5
capital accumulation and, 165
mass media, 163, 390
performers' labors as end product, 164
stagnation
costs per performance and, 169
factors in, 163–5
implications for costs, 167–72, 179–80
wage rates and, 168–72
see also Technology of live performance
Productivity (output per man-hour) in economy as a whole
annual increase, 162, 390
goods sector, 166–7, 475T
selected industries, 475T
service sector, 166–7, 171, 475T
implications of differential rates of increase, 167–72, 179–80
measurement of, 162n, 166
on semi-log graph vs. ordinary scale, 176–9, 178F
and wage trends in manufacturing, 221
Professional performance, defined, 6, 67n
Professional-technical occupations, incomes, trends, 222T
Professions, members of
frequency of contribution, 532T, 535T
per cent of audience: *see the* Audience profiles
Providence Philharmonic, 549T

581

Tulane University, 542T, 543T
Tulsa, orchestra, 17
Twentieth Century Fund audience
    surveys: *see* Audience
    surveys
"Twofer," 261

U

UCLA Theater Group, 72, 83n, 451T,
    544T
Unemployment: *see* Employment
    and unemployment
Unions, 230–34
    "contract" vs. "non-contract"
      house, 9n
    featherbedding, 9, 232–4
    financial support of arts, 335–6
    restrictions on filming choreogra-
      pher's works, 113n
    restrictions on recordings, 109
    rules on working conditions, 128–9
    and season length, 121–3
    and wage levels, 232, 233, 234
United Fine Arts Fund of Cincinnati,
    327
    corporate gifts to, 333
Universities: *see* Colleges and uni-
    versities
University of Minnesota, 547T
Ushers
    salaries, Broadway theater, 483T
    supplied by theater owner, 21
Utah, 550T
Utah Symphony Orchestra, 550T

V

Variety, 54, 239n
Vermont, 550T
Vermont Symphony Orchestra, 550T

Vienna State Opera, government
    support, 361
Violins, how to be efficient with
    fewer, 165n
Virginia, 550T

W

Wardrobe attendants, salaries, 215,
    483T
Warren-Pearson price index, 190n
Washington (D.C.), theater, 27, 28
Washington Square Players, 26
Waste, as cause of financial pres-
    sures, 10
Watts, John H., 148n, 226n
Wells, Herman B, 338
Wentworth, John D., 371
West End (London), 302
West North, West South, Central
    region, 441T, 442T
"Who's Afraid of Virginia Woolf?",
    451T
Wholesale price index
    annual increases, selected periods,
      190T, 196T
    long-term trends, 188F
Winston-Salem Community Arts
    Council, 326
WPA
    Federal Theater Project, 28, 356–7,
      374
    music project, 356
Wunderlich, Bert, 334

X-Y-Z

"Ye Bare and Ye Cubb," 18
Young Audiences, Inc., 543, 546
Zolotow, Sam, 57